THE MEXICAN ECONOMY

A Publication of the Economic Growth Center, Yale University

THE MEXICAN ECONOMY

Twentieth-Century

Structure and Growth

BY CLARK W. REYNOLDS

New Haven and London, Yale University Press, 1970

Copyright © 1970 by Yale University.
All rights reserved. This book may not be
reproduced, in whole or in part, in any form
(except by reviewers for the public press),
without written permission from the publishers.
Library of Congress catalog card number: 74–115378
International standard book number: 0–300–01344–2

Designed by Sally Sullivan,
set in Times Roman type,
and printed in the United States of America by
The Colonial Press Inc., Clinton, Mass.

Distributed in Great Britain, Europe, and Africa by
Yale University Press, Ltd., London; in Canada by
McGill-Queen's University Press, Montreal; in Mexico
by Centro Interamericano de Libros Académicos,
Mexico City; in Australasia by Australia and New
Zealand Book Co., Pty., Ltd., Artarmon, New South
Wales; in India by UBS Publishers' Distributors Pvt.,
Ltd., Delhi; in Japan by John Weatherhill, Inc.,
Tokyo.

To Dorothy

Contents

TABLES

FIGURES

Foreword

This volume is one in a series of studies supported by the Economic Growth Center, an activity of the Yale Department of Economics since 1961. The Center is a research organization with worldwide activities and interests. Its research interests are defined in terms of both method of approach and subject matter. In terms of method, the Center sponsors studies which are designed to test significant general hypotheses concerning the problem of economic growth and which draw on quantitative information from national economic accounts and other sources. In terms of subject matter, the Center's research interests include theoretical analysis of economic structure and growth, quantitative analysis of a national economy as an integral whole, comparative cross-sectional studies using data from a number of countries, and efforts to improve the techniques of national economic measurement. The research program includes field investigation of recent economic growth in twenty-five developing countries of Asia, Africa, and Latin America.

The Center administers, jointly with the Department of Economics, the Yale training program in International and Foreign Economic Administration. It presents a regular series of seminar and workshop meetings and includes among its publications both book-length studies and journal reprints by staff members, the latter circulated as Center Papers.

Gustav Ranis, Director

Preface

Only a non-Mexican might be expected to attempt a task such as this—to review in one volume the history of twentieth-century economic development in Mexico. And only a non-Mexican economist would have the temerity to confine the analysis primarily to quantifiable aspects of this history. For as many have insisted, and as some of the subsequent analysis will suggest, the ultimate explanation of Mexico's vast renaissance may well be found in psychological rather than material dimensions. Yet, like the bullet holes that pockmark the walls of so many Mexican villages, economic statistics are the graceless reminders of significant historical events. In a country which is steadily rising from a level of subsistence, the forces of life and death meet in the marketplace, and many trade at the margin of survival. That is why a measurement of the process of exchange of goods and services is an important first step in the examination of social welfare achieved, opportunities foregone, and prospects for the future.[1]

1. The author follows in the path of numerous visitors who have sought to describe and explain aspects of twentieth-century Mexican economic change. Some of the most notable of these, as of the mid-1960s, were Eyler Simpson, *The Ejido, Mexico's Way Out*; Nathan Whetten, *Rural Mexico*; Frank Tannenbaum, *Mexico, The Struggle for Peace and Bread*; Sanford A. Mosk, *Industrial Revolution in Mexico*; Howard Cline, *The United States and Mexico*, and *Mexico*; Raymond Vernon, *The Dilemma of Mexico's Development*; and Frank Brandenburg, *The Making of Modern Mexico*. A now classic work commissioned by the World Bank, *The Economic Development of Mexico* (Johns Hopkins Press, 1953) provides a detailed statistical record of Mexican development from 1939 to 1950. Considering the difficulty of the problem, the pitfalls besetting previous writers, and the good sense of most Mexican economists who have steered clear of sweeping interpretations of the long process of growth, particularly from a statistical viewpoint, it might seem presumptuous to add another work at this time. Yet no one of the authors mentioned above was in the position to benefit from the wealth of data on the Mexican economy that is now becoming available, nor was the theory of economic growth and development sufficiently advanced to permit even

During the past half-century, Mexico was broken apart by revolution and reconstructed through political and social reform. The entire structure of the economy was changed, partly through direct economic forces and partly through political and social events which were themselves influenced by economic factors. In the process the national market has been unified, a third of the population has moved to the cities, the level of living has quadrupled and the economy has recovered from earlier setbacks so as to achieve one of the most rapid rates of growth in the hemisphere.

In this volume an attempt is made to reproduce and in some cases to construct statistical time series and benchmark data which illustrate the process of secular change in the national and regional economy. In order to reveal the most important structural changes, a number of years have been selected for cross-sectional treatment with particular attention to the structure of production and employment. Regional breakdowns are provided both for agriculture and manufacturing. The data are normally presented by decades. While some of the statistical series and benchmark data have previously appeared in print or in the monographic literature, the majority have been assembled by staff economists of the Department of Economic Studies of the Bank of Mexico, the author, his students, and research assistants during the past four years. During the process of collection the data have been revised many times and should not be regarded as the last word, much less as official estimates.

Out of long exposure to these statistics and through several years of fruitful discussion with Mexican colleagues, I have developed a set of hypotheses which represent preliminary attempts to provide a general explanation of Mexico's economic transformation. In this volume it is assumed that the reader has some familiarity with the general history of twentieth-century Mexico and is able to superimpose on the economic record the major political and social events of the last sixty years. An attempt is made to free the analysis as much as possible from aprioristic historical periodization, so that the economic events themselves may be used to interpret political and social change rather than vice versa.

---

a tenuous integration of this material until very recently. It may still be premature to offer a set of hypotheses to explain the development of the entire economy. One hopes that the effort, far from providing a last word on the subject, will provoke a lively debate and stimulate more detailed research on individual topics than time or the ability of the author permit.

While a nation's growth may be thought of as a simultaneous set of interactions of economic, political, and social phenomena, it is convenient to treat certain interactions as though they occurred in isolation. If the parameters that relate economic variables show marked changes from one period to the next, we may then use economic facts to shed light on simultaneous political and/or social events such as the collapse of the banking system, unrest and uncertainty in rural areas, the passing of revolutionary legislation, the impact of foreign wars, and the like. It is hoped that the analysis presented here and the statistics which underlie it will be useful to other social scientists engaged in the study of contemporary Mexico as well as to the general public. It is also hoped that Mexico's baptism by fire during the Revolution and its aftermath may be investigated with greater scholarly detachment now that the opportunity to estimate the cost of violent social change and its potential benefits, sector by sector and region by region, begins to become possible.

The central theme of the work is the interaction between agriculture and industry. An examination of the data from Mexican agriculture reveals its dual character. Small, primitively cultivated plots exist alongside medium and large-scale farms which use the most modern techniques to produce cash crops for urban and foreign markets. The old form of subsistence cultivation is gradually being displaced, at least in relative terms, by commercial agriculture. This has permitted a rising share of the work force to move toward the cities in response to better economic opportunities in industry and commerce. The process of agricultural transition and urban migration was interrupted by Mexico's historic agrarian reform which began during the Revolution, was greatly accelerated during the 1930s, and continues into the 1960s. Much hitherto underutilized land was expropriated and redistributed in small plots to the peasants. Commercial cultivation tended to shift to newly opened regions in the north and northwest where major works of investment in rural economic infrastructure were carried out by the federal government during the 1940s and early 1950s.

There is considerable evidence that Mexican policy makers, by providing peasants with land while at the same time expanding the land area in modern cultivation, accomplished the joint objectives of greater social justice and rising economic productivity. In any event, commercial agricultural production has continued to expand along with that of industry, reflecting the balanced growth of the rural and urban sectors of the economy. This in turn has meant a widening of national markets, greater foreign exchange available for capital goods and intermediate goods imports, and a broader geographical and sectorial distribution of income than would have been true without one or the other aspect of agricultural policy. By avoiding excess urbanization, the agrarian reform has made it possible for the government to invest a rising share of its revenues in capital expenditures since the 1930s. Private investors have tended to respond favorably to the external economies created by public infrastructure investments. Thus the rate of capital formation in Mexico is now one of the highest in the hemisphere.

Our analysis strongly suggests that the performance of the Mexican economy since 1940 may be traced in large part to institutions and attitudes that arose during the preceding decades of revolution and reform. Agriculture, foreign investment, and the banking system were subjected to much stronger central control than heretofore. It therefore became possible for the government to engage in a large amount of indicative investment planning in the private sector, calling for a greater balance in the growth of both industry and agriculture than would otherwise have occurred. While policies arising from the period of revolution and reform contributed to subsequent rates of growth in agriculture and industry, they had a net retarding effect on mining and petroleum production and resulted in more capital intensity of production than was perhaps optimal. Still, the overall rate of investment was almost certainly much higher under the actual system of indicative planning and direct public investment that prevailed since 1940 than would have existed under laissez-faire. This effect probably offset the loss of efficiency attributable to public investment subsidies. An assessment of the full impact of public expenditure on the growth of agriculture and industry requires an examination of indirect effects which the data do not permit. Nevertheless, the record indicates that, despite scanty information and rudimentary technical ability, the federal government performed a remarkably farsighted and successful job in steering the economy out of social and economic chaos toward sustained growth with a minimum of waste and distortion.

This study is the product of four years of research from 1963 through 1967 sponsored by the Economic Growth Center at Yale University. I spent a total of twenty-three months in field work in Mexico, traveling over 18,000 miles, mostly by car, visiting almost every major center. In addition to this research I taught courses in economics at El Colegio de México, the Centro de Estudios Monetarios Latinoamericanos, and the School of Agriculture of the National Autonomous University at Chapingo. The Department of Economic Studies of the Bank of Mexico generously provided me an office, this facility being only the smallest part of the many courtesies and kindnesses extended by that institution and its staff.

I owe a debt of gratitude to my Mexican friends for making so freely available the products of their research, many of which represented years of patient labor. These statistics, analyses, and intuitive hypotheses, which were shared so unselfishly, have done much to build a foundation for this study and to cement together its various elements. Mexico possesses a "new group" of economists who are academic in the best sense of the word, engaged in lively and stimulating discussion, unafraid of either professional or political criticism. I consider myself fortunate to have been able to join this debate. My sentiments are those which must have been felt by the anthropologist Stephens and his artist Catherwood, who went to Yucatán over a hundred years ago and carried away plaster casts and sketches of the magnificent Mayan sculpture. They did not participate in that civilization; they did little to explain it; and they could not have located the ruins without the help of able guides. But by drawing general attention to previously hidden treasures they added to our knowledge and appreciation of Mexican history and stimulated new areas of inquiry. Although the present volume is on a different aesthetic plane, it will call attention, I hope, to the many material accomplishments that Mexico has achieved during this century.

The guides on whom I depended during my research are too numerous to mention in detail. Certain individuals, however, stand out as having spent long hours as warm friends and firm critics going over details of the manuscript. These include, most importantly, Leopoldo Solís and James Wilkie, Mexican economist and American historian, who, while bearing no responsibility for the outcome, provided valuable encouragement and commentary each step of the way. The friendships of Fernando Rosenzweig and Jesus Silva-Herzog F. also must be mentioned as helping to provide the cordial atmosphere so conducive to research during my sojourn in Mexico. In addition, R. Albert Berry, Christopher Clague, Raymond Goldsmith, Shane Hunt, Bruce Johnston, Donald Keesing, Simon Kuznets, Gustav Ranis, Victor Urquidi, and Pan Yotopoulos have read and criticized the manuscript in detail. Their comments were invaluable in the preparation of the final draft for publication. Special credit goes to secretary Lynn Brooks who has tirelessly worked to decipher my handwriting, and has served as copy editor, research assistant, and bibliographer, in addition to her normal duties. Research assistance in preparation of the statistical appendix was provided by Rosamond Peirce and Margery Coen. Mrs. Coen also did much to improve style and correct errors in the earlier drafts of the manuscript and prepared valuable new material both in the text and appendixes. Final credit and inestimable gratitude go to my wife Dorothy. She has been a continual source of encouragement and strength during the long hours of work which the study entailed. Her comments and suggestions are reflected throughout the book. In many respects it may be regarded as the work of a team rather than of an individual.

C. W. R.

Redwood City, California
December 1969

Introduction

The remains of many civilizations bear witness to the fact that for thousands of years Mexico has been shaped by the forces of nature as well as by the transforming power of ideas. In the building of pyramids and temples, dams and superhighways, there has been an interaction of mind and matter for which it is difficult, if not impossible, to assign the direction of causality. Viewing this process of interaction in historical perspective, the development economist is forced to raise questions that he is ill equipped to answer with his rudimentary tools of analysis.

What was the source of leadership, technology, and organizational ability which enabled the Mayans to assemble thousands of laborers and skilled craftsmen to build the great priestly city of Palenque in the jungles of Chiapas over a millennium ago? What innovations in maize culture or changes in climate permitted the cultivators to raise crops capable of sustaining this huge labor force over scores of years, despite enervating heat, swarms of insects, and debilitating disease? Why did that civilization eventually fall, the temples return to jungle, and the citizens to an ignoble subsistence—music, religion, astronomy all but forgotten? The still unsolved mystery of the rise and fall of Palenque is only one among many untold stories of cultures which have bloomed and died in the course of Mexican history. Each had its peculiar set of institutions to provide an economic surplus capable of supporting great works of economic and social infrastructure, permitting the society to move to ever higher levels of civilization. Each was subjected to external and internal shocks which eventually brought about its decline.

In the same manner the widely heralded "Mexican miracle" of today has behind it a priesthood, ornaments, ethos, and goals that are

1

as peculiar and as interesting as those that characterized the Mayan civilization at the time of Palenque. What is the structure of this system? How has it changed? What are its implications for the welfare of society? How important have been its ties with other cultures, including the overshadowing one to the north? What difference does it make that Mexico began to develop long after the Industrial Revolution, during an era of accelerated technological change, at a time when social expectations were rapidly rising? What were the positive and negative effects of revolution on the history of Mexican economic development? These are the questions which underlie the analysis in this and the following chapters.

THE "MEXICAN MIRACLE": A RECENT PHENOMENON?

Mexican output has increased more than ten times since 1900 while per capita product has virtually quadrupled (see Table 1.1). The country today accommodates over 40 million inhabitants, or two and one-half times as many as at the turn of the century. For the majority of these citizens contemporary economic growth has brought with it higher levels of real income and welfare along with the promise of a continually improving way of life. Yet the growth trends of the past sixty-five years have been very uneven, as the economy has responded to the vicissitudes of international trade cycles and internal political and social change. In some sectors the economy seems to have behaved better before than after the 1910 Revolution (see Table 1.4). During the first decade of the twentieth century, total and per capita gross domestic product (GDP) grew at impressive rates. Indeed, the 3.3 percent annual growth rate of GDP during those years rivaled the performance of the postrevolutionary period. The 2.2 percent rise in per capita product during the last days of the administration of President Porfirio Díaz was higher than that of the period from 1925 to 1965.

In the twenty-five years since 1940, the economy has registered an almost fivefold increase in production while population has doubled. Per capita product has risen from 1,075 pesos in 1940 (measured in 1950 prices) to 2,335 pesos in 1965. Depending upon the conversion factor used, the level of national income in 1965 represented a purchasing power of from 300 to 400 U.S. dollars per person, or four times what it was in 1900. What makes the post-1940 growth performance so impressive to outside observers is that it occurred in a country which, in the immediately preceding period, had by government decree redistributed more than half of its cultivated land, expropriated its railroads and petroleum industry, and secularized as well as socialized education.

Much recent research on Mexican economic growth has been confined either to the prerevolutionary or post-1940 years. Such an approach has been more than justified by the shortage of statistical source material for the intervening decades which, if it exists at all, is incomplete and relatively inaccessible. But the result has been that the conclusions reached by those relying on existing economic research have often suggested that the period of revolution and reform from 1910 to 1940 was a time of economic disruption and that the institutional changes which took place during those three decades were of relatively little importance during the subsequent period of rapid growth. It might be easy for the person unfamiliar with Mexican history to infer from the data that only when the disturbing influences of revolution, world depression, and agrarian reform were removed was it possible for Mexico to get "back on the track" and resume the rapid growth which had been "interrupted" thirty years before. The present study takes a very different approach. Insofar as possible, it attempts to bring together evidence from numerous independent sources to estimate some of the positive and negative influences of the process of revolution and reform on the sectoral performance of the regional and national economy. This approach stresses the social evolutionary character of economic development in evaluating the extent to which the "Mexican miracle" of recent decades is in fact a miracle, the relative influence of earlier economic activity, and the role of previous institutional change on post-1940 patterns of growth.

PROBLEMS IN THE ANALYSIS OF ECONOMIC GROWTH WITH STRUCTURAL CHANGE

Economic development in the Mexican case has brought with it entirely new combinations of natural and human resources. As a result, its analysis is beset by major problems of definition, measurement, and interpretation. It is not sufficient merely to measure the process of exchange, since the marketplace at any point in time is the creature of those who comprise it and have command over its resources at that moment. Its values are the values of its participants;

and when an economy changes as Mexico has changed, the values of its participants are reshaped as well. The weight of individual values in the social welfare of a nation is also subject to change over time. As an economic system moves from a series of self-sufficient enclaves into a unified national market and as that market joins the commerce of nations, the division of labor increases, the fortunes of some are made and others broken, some regions and industries thrive and others languish. The distributions of income, product, and final demand vary with the process of economic growth and, in many cases, incomes become less equal and the gap between rich and poor more extreme. All of this is of fundamental importance to the social historian though it may be difficult to uncover from the statistical evidence available. The forces that bring down individuals, governments, and nations may not always be subject to precise measurement. Though facts may be silent and though they seldom speak for themselves, the development historian is best equipped to deal with quantifiable evidence. It is not sufficient for him simply to say "the data are unreliable" and pass on to other matters. Instead it is necessary to pick and choose among the relevant statistical indicators, to select the best measures available, and to qualify them with other kinds of evidence from written and oral tradition. In so doing, the present author has confronted a number of problems of measurement and interpretation which are detailed in the following section.

The statistical problem

Data on the Mexican economy vary widely in quality for different periods and between activities at any point in time. Reasonably reliable estimates of gross production in manufacturing, mining, agriculture, and transportation, as well as total federal government expenditure are available back to 1900 with the exception of the period between 1910 and 1925. The economic statistics collected during the last decade of the dictatorship of Porfirio Díaz (1900–10) are generally of a higher quality than those of the succeeding three decades, although they are distinctly inferior to the post-1940 statistics. Annual series for such important sectors as commerce and services (which constitute over a third of GDP) are extremely uneven and unreliable before 1940. Mexican gross domestic product is estimated on the basis of aggregate output indexes weighted by cross-sectional estimates of the distribution of GDP for selected years. An input-output table for 1950 provides a basis for value-added weighting of gross production indexes from 1939 to 1965. The indexes of GDP for earlier years are calculated on the basis of 1930 and 1940 value weights. Information on the distribution of income among households or by final expenditure is available only for selected years since 1940.

Regional breakdowns of statistics are most readily obtainable for agricultural production. Data are available on mining, commerce, and transportation for selected years based upon censuses of varying reliability that have been conducted since 1930. Data on regional price relatives are aviailable only for selected years. Most price indexes are based on Mexico City sources and do not necessarily reflect regional trends or disparities. Wage series are of doubtful quality and consist primarily of legal minimum wage figures rather than actual wage levels, especially for earlier years. All of these factors suggest that the margin of error of the statistical indicators is a function of the time period and activity under consideration.

Where strong discrepancies exist among alternative estimators of the same activity, two or more alternative series are presented in the text with footnotes which provide an explanation for the author's preference. While absolute levels of alternative indicators may show wide differences at any point in time, their real rates of growth (with the exception of gross investment data) tend to be comparable, especially for periods of a decade or longer. Errors in the estimators therefore appear for the most part to be serially correlated, minimizing disturbances in the analysis of growth. Moreover, the structural changes focused upon in the study have been so sharp that the conclusions based upon them are not seriously altered by the application of a 5 percent margin of error to the estimators.

While these caveats suggest that the figures presented in this study may at times be shaky, it is nonetheless felt that they provide a far more substantial foundation for the analysis of contemporary economic development than would be possible on the basis of subjective evaluation or casual empiricism alone. In every case where it has been possible to do so, the author has qualified the statistical material with independent value judgments drawn from the literature and oral tradition and has sought to improve the reliability of the estimators by working from original source material. Moreover, internal consistency checks have been continually applied to the series, and where discrepancies exist these are pointed out in the footnotes to the chapters or in the Statistical Appendixes.

The aggregation problem

The fact that Mexico is a geographically and socially diverse nation with a highly uneven regional distribution of natural and human resources greatly complicates the analysis of its economic structure and growth. Once referred to as "many Mexicos," the country consists of thousands of relatively isolated communities—many with their own dialects—engaging in primitive forms of economic activity of a subsistence nature. It is highly probable that interregional trade and internal commerce in Mexico were more highly developed at the time of the Aztecs than they were in the mid-nineteenth century. Since then, a network of railroads, roads, airways, and corresponding communication and power grids have increasingly unified regional markets. Nevertheless, regional differentials in output and productivity are still enormous, particularly in agriculture and manufacturing. Even in the same area, primitive forms of cultivation are applied across the road from modern commercial farms. Medieval artisanry is being carried on in the shadow of modern factories. The difficulties that these disparities present for aggregative economic analysis are sobering. Not just dual but multiple techniques have survived in the same sector of economic activity for decades, and although the proportion of traditional to modern technology in the total output of these sectors has fallen sharply over time, the transition has been very uneven from sector to sector and region to region. Hence the process of development in Mexico must be analyzed not as a simple set of relationships between two major production sectors (agriculture and industry), but as a complex series of internal structural changes within each, which in turn affect the other. Even in the most simple presentation of agricultural and industrial development, the number of production relationships that should be estimated tends to surpass the limitations of data.

Insofar as possible, the present study attempts to separate the data on agricultural and industrial production into five major regions and to analyze it by decades since 1930. Regional disaggregation ideally should be based upon relatively common geophysical and socioeconomic characteristics. Earlier attempts to do so were made by Paul Yates who provided data on certain aspects of income and growth for selected states during the 1950s.[1] Fernando Zamora attempted a regional analysis of the whole economy for one year by dividing census data for 1957 into seven major zones that, in his judgment, represented relatively similar economic regions. These zones were not restricted to state boundaries, so that the analysis required a detailed decomposition of census data by *municipio*. As a result, it was necessary to omit several important sectors of tertiary industry, as well as data on the public sector, and interregional and international trade.[2] As several attempts at more disaggregative analysis proved impractical, the present study confines itself to a treatment of the five census regions of the country: the North, North Pacific, Center, South Pacific, and Gulf.[3] While these regions are by no means homogeneous topographical or economic units, due to their relatively large size and the fact that they have by necessity been circumscribed by state lines, they represent relatively common internal economic characteristics. Still, the regions of the northeast are far more prosperous than those of the north central area (both in the North Zone in the present study). The regions around Mexico City, Guadalajara, and Puebla are far more developed than those in Hidalgo, Tlaxcala, or Michoacán; yet all are grouped in our Central Zone. There is no great geophysical or economic similarity among

1. Paul Lamartine Yates, *El Desarrollo Regional de México.*
2. Fernando Zamora, *Diagnóstico Económico Regional, 1958.* Zamora divides Mexico into seven zones—Noroeste, Altiplano, Nororiental, Central, Pacífico Sur, Golfo Istmico, and Sureste. The zones correspond neither to state boundaries nor to the five regional groupings used in government censuses of population, agriculture, industry, commerce, and transportation. The study is designed to give a broad cross-sectional view of the status of the Mexican economy in the 1950s to guide government investment policy, particularly for soil nutrients, inoculation of cattle, regional development centers, and in the development of other aspects of regional economic infrastructure. It presents partial figures on intrasectoral output, intersectoral income distribution (relying heavily upon the application of national coefficients to regional output and population figures), and projections of the "normal" development of the regions through 1965, based upon past trends. The study is based upon the assumption that natural economic zones are created by topography owing to the importance of transport costs in Mexico, and that the nature of Mexican production tends to be associated with altitude and climatic factors rather more than by the concentration of population. Indeed, Zamora supposes that population concentration (particularly in the center of the country) in the past has been due to natural topographical and climatic conditions, since the North was traditionally an arid region, while the South was subjected to heavy periodic rainfall, pestilence, and other disadvantages traditionally associated with the subtropics.
3. The composition of these regions is described in Chapter 3.

Veracruz, Chiapas, and Yucatan; yet these are all included in the Gulf region. The limitations of time and data have dictated the present level of disaggregation. Its usefulness is demonstrated in the following chapters as a first step in the direction of a more detailed analysis of Mexican growth. Nevertheless, with the exception of those on agriculture and manufacturing, the majority of the indicators used are national rather than regional, and the analysis is accordingly subject to the limitations which this imposes.

The periodization problem

Many analyses of Mexican economic development begin with the year 1940, ignoring the preceding history except for purposes of comparison with prerevolutionary years. This follows the time-honored convention in economic historical analysis of avoiding periods during which major exogenous disturbances to economic relationships have occurred, because of their complex and untypical character. Hence times of war, revolution, pestilence, and famine are often removed from time series analysis to justify the *ceteris paribus* assumptions which customarily underlie the estimation of economic behavioral parameters. This convention is somewhat less meaningful, however, when the subject at hand is analysis of the process of economic *development* rather than stability or growth along a smooth expansion path.

The classic Schumpeterian definition of development takes it to be "a distinct phenomenon, entirely foreign to what may be observed in the circular flow or in the tendency toward equilibrium. It is spontaneous and discontinuous change in the channels of the flow, disturbance of equilibrium, which forever alters and displaces the equilibrium state previously existing." [4] While Schumpeter focused on the transformation of the structure of production particularly through the application of entrepreneurship to innovation, the present analysis includes changes in the structure of distribution and final demand by which the "new combinations" that Schumpeter stressed are affected. This is predicated on the conviction that economic development analysis must attempt to consider all major changes in the structure of distribution and final demand as well as changes in the structure of production, whether they have resulted from economic, social, political, or other historical factors.

4. Joseph A. Schumpeter, *The Theory of Economic Development,* Chapter 2.

By tracing the process of structural change in Mexico through the period of most severe institutional upheaval (1910–40), it is beginning to be possible to determine in what way economic and non-economic social variables interacted so as to bring about eventual sustained growth. It has been mentioned already that the statistical material pertaining to the years of revolution and reform is at best of a limited and unreliable nature. The time series and benchmark statistics for these intervening years must therefore be used with considerably more qualifications than those before 1910 and after 1940. It is nevertheless felt that the advantages obtained from including this data in the analysis far outweigh the disadvantages.

The periodization employed, therefore, embraces three major episodes: the last years of the dictatorship of Porfirio Díaz (1900–10); the years of revolution, recovery, and institutional reform (1910–40); and the ensuing years during which development was considerably influenced by the rise and fall of foreign demand associated with World War II and the Korean War as well as urbanization, public expenditure, and government import substitution policy (1940–65). These three major epochs are defined not only by the policies of their respective political administrations but also by the behavior of the aggregate economic indicators themselves. Annual indexes of agricultural and industrial production, government taxation and expenditure, and trade, as well as population estimates interpolated from decennial censuses, suggest that the process of rapid economic expansion under Porfirio Díaz was cut short (except in the mining and petroleum sectors) after 1910. Although most of the major production sectors of the economy had recovered from the Revolution by 1925, the onset of world depression in the late 1920s triggered a decline in the economy by sharply reducing the demand for Mexican export staples. By the early 1930s this recession was beginning to have widespread political repercussions. The decline in output which took place in the late 1920s and early 1930s as a result of the world depression was followed by pressures on the government to speed up economic reforms promised in the Constitution of 1917. Subsequent reforms in rail transport, agriculture, mining, and the nationalization of the petroleum industry added uncertainty and institutional upheaval to the already depressed conditions of trade. Hence the economy did not achieve a rate of growth equivalent to that of the last years of the Porfiriato until the early 1940s. This was accomplished in part by the recovery of world demand for Mexican

exports and in part by the adjustment of the forces of supply and
demand to changing institutions and attitudes brought about by the
period of revolution and reform. Since 1940, population and output
trends have been steadily upward although at varying rates. Hence
the inflection points in the major economic indicators are such as to
dictate periods of relative turning points in the economy around
1910 to 1914, 1925 to 1928, and 1938 to 1941. The present study
has used these turning points to divide time series and construct
benchmark estimates in terms of the three major epochs of Mexican
economic growth since 1900.

While major growth phases in this study are identified by inflection
points in the aggregate economic indicators, this is not true of the
subperiods chosen. The latter have been selected, not because of
trends or cycles in the statistics themselves, but primarily because of
the availability of benchmark estimates of output and employment
taken from the corresponding decennial economic and demographic
censuses. Although the subperiods 1930/40, 1940/50, 1950/60, and
1960/65 have been chosen because of the relative availability of
statistics at the beginning and end of each period, the period around
1950 represents a functional dividing line between the war and postwar economy characterized by strong excess demand and inflation and
the post-1950 years of growth with relative price stability. An alternative approach would have been to group the data around minor
economic cycles, such as those associated with World War II and
the Korean War, the cycle during the late 1950s, and the subsequent
growth phase beginning in the early 1960s. By breaking the short
periods into arbitrary intervals rather than attempting to follow
minor cycles, the following study is better suited to the analysis of
secular change than to short-term instability. This emphasis makes
sense in view of the difficulty of estimating changes in the level of
employment on an annual basis. Temporary imbalances between observed and capacity levels of output must therefore be inferred from
price level behavior. Since most Mexican price indexes refer only to
the capital city, considerations such as the degree of underemployment of labor and the capital stock are ambiguous at best.

One alternative approach would be to group the data by six-year
presidential administrations. Since the process of Mexican development has depended increasingly upon the vicissitudes of public policy,
and since each presidential administration is characterized by its
unique set of fiscal priorities as well as abilities to implement policy,

a "presidential cycle" approach to the data has some merit. The present periodization is, however, based on the alternative assumption that degrees of freedom in monetary and fiscal policy are determined by underlying structural changes in the pattern of production, income distribution, and final demand. Hence the public sector in a mixed economy such as Mexico, which depends to a large extent on private decision making, is constrained by past economic performance and future expectations of the private sector, making it inappropriate to analyze the underlying growth process in terms of time periods which are derived from explicitly political considerations.

The political-economic identification problem

Since the present study deals primarily with economic relationships against a sketchy background of political, social, and psychological change, it may be regarded at best as partial analysis. Although the three major time periods selected coincide with major epochs of social and political change, the precise interaction between economic and noneconomic variables is not spelled out. This makes it difficult to determine causal relationships among the economic variables themselves, a problem that is endemic to the analysis of developing economies in which broad aspects of social change are involved. By providing historical benchmarks by which to view the structure of production, distribution, and final demand as it has changed over time, the present study makes it possible to infer some changes in economic parameters that might be derived from other aspects of social change such as population growth, urbanization, changes in social values, expectations about future economic growth, the distribution of political power, and the like. But merely to record changes in the economic structure is not sufficient to derive causal links between previous patterns of economic activity and subsequent processes of economic growth. For example, the thirty years prior to 1910 represented a period of rapid and sustained growth in both output and population. Per capita product was rising steadily. Yet there is considerable evidence that the process of rapid economic growth brought about growing social unrest and political instability. This was due not to growth per se but to the way in which growth was taking place and to the distribution of income, wealth, and political power associated with it. The years from 1910 to 1940 represent planned and unplanned changes in social, political, and economic institutional parameters caused by the failure of the previous expansion phase to produce stable equilibrium among the social and political dimensions of the system. It would have been impossible to have predicted the consequences of the Revolution and subsequent restructuring of society on the economy after 1910 on the basis of previously observed economic relationships alone, even though these relationships did play a role in changing the economic structure. If a growth model were applied to the long process of Mexican economic development that included only economic variables, it would be subject to serious identification problems in that a number of crucial simultaneously interacting social and political corollaries of the economic performance would be omitted from its specification. These missing variables would themselves be responsible for fundamental changes in economic relationships. In short, economic yields and propensities are in part explained by the distribution of income, wealth, political power, and social prestige, which themselves have been determined by previous economic behavior. Thus what economists tend to call economic parameters, that are supposedly institutionally determined in the short run, are over the long run social variables responding to a more general dynamic system of social interaction in which economic relationships are but a subset of equations.

The implications of ignoring this identification problem are less serious in short period analysis of economic stability or in considerations of growth of relatively homogeneous, highly industrialized economies. The implications are far more serious if the economy begins as a disequilibrium system with sharp regional and sectoral disparities in income and product. One would expect this type of system, once it begins to grow, to register notable changes in underlying institutional and behavioral parameters that subsequently would alter the process of economic transformation. Unfortunately, social scientific analysis is not yet sufficiently well developed to provide a static social equilibrium system analogous to the Walrasian economic general equilibrium system, much less dynamic models capable of accommodating all relevant social variables. This means that a partial analytical approach must be adopted for the time being in analyzing the economic development of such a system. One alternative is to set up ad hoc hypotheses of social change that assume historically deterministic processes of social, political, and economic interaction. Empirical evidence is then assembled to provide associational confirmation or rejection of the ad hoc model. An alternative approach is to deal strictly with economic changes, analyzing them as though no other social variables were operative in the process of economic change. Either model tends to produce a historical analysis characterized by serious identification problems.

The development historian must find some intermediate path that avoids a simple recording of significant historical events devoid of analytical content. The present study is an attempt to follow the middle road by looking at the economic record, insofar as possible examining economic explanations of economic change, and arriving at an unexplained residual in performance data which can be related to other dimensions of social behavior. For example, much of the growth of the Mexican economy can be explained by drawing into production hitherto underutilized natural and human resources through high and rising rates of savings and investment. While this suggests that economic growth has been economically determined, increases in the rates of savings and investment as well as improved efficiency in resource allocation might well be explained by shifts in behavioral parameters that are socially and politically determined. On the basis of past experience, economists using economic models alone have tended to underestimate the growth potential of the Mexican economy. The literature is full of forebodings of those who have failed to introduce into their analysis attitudinal or organizational considerations which, although not readily accommodated by existing theoretical models, appear to have been important in explaining success or failure at crucial points in the growth process. Mexican economic development analysis is accordingly a scholarly exercise in planned obsolescence. The primary objective of a study such as this is to stimulate further research that will clarify and expand the facts available, and increase the explanatory power of the theoretical models applied to them. Despite the problems enumerated above, enough material is now available on Mexico's recent history to more than justify the present research. It will, we hope, be expanded and improved upon in the years to come, particularly in terms of the role of revolution and social reform in the process of economic growth.

FRAMEWORK OF THE PRESENT STUDY

With the above qualifications in mind, the present study introduces a secular analysis of the process of growth and structural change of the Mexican economy in terms of the best statistical indicators currently available. Rates of growth of inputs and output are accepted as reasonably accurate, although the absolute levels of many of the statistics are considered to be subject to significant margins of error.

The data are disaggregated on a regional and sectoral base whenever possible. The following chapter provides an introduction to the long-run growth performance of the Mexican economy by briefly surveying major trends in output, population, and selected inputs. Chapter 2 goes on to examine the changes in the structure of production, income, final demand, and the rural/urban income and population shares associated with these trends. Changes in the anatomy of the economy and society over the past sixty years are used to introduce hypotheses relating to the relationship between growth and structural change that are examined in detail in the following chapters.

The two major production sectors, agriculture and manufacturing, are first set apart for detailed treatment in Chapters 3 to 5. An estimate is made of the relationship between the growth of inputs and output in each of these sectors, and residuals are derived by decade and region (for agriculture) to arrive at an estimate of relative productivity increases. The linkages between agriculture and manufacturing of importance to overall economic growth are then analyzed in terms of both real output and financial flows. Changes in regional productivity and employment levels are used to evaluate the impact of expanded internal and external trade on growth of the economy as a whole.

After analyzing the relationship between agricultural and industrial growth since 1930, the book goes on, in Chapter 6, to analyze the relationship between structural change and growth as it has influenced the pattern of foreign trade over time. Shifts in comparative advantage resulting from both the market-induced process of economic evolution and public policy decisions are inferred from the changing pattern of trade, particularly in terms of import substitution in manufacturing during the postwar period. Brief attention is given to the growth and stability implications of Mexico's proximity to American markets. Chapter 7 examines the historical pattern of public taxation and expenditure in order to estimate the overall contribution of fiscal policy to growth. While stabilization policy is also considered, it is subordinated to questions concerning the long-run impact of public and private decision making on the process of economic growth. The final chapter summarizes the findings in terms of the central theme, which relates shifts in the distribution of population (rural/urban), income, and final demand to the relatively balanced growth of agriculture, industry, and services.

1

Three Epochs of Mexican Economic Growth: 1900–1965

One does not explain Mexico. One believes in Mexico, with fury, with passion, and in alienation.

Carlos Fuentes, *Where the Air Is Clear* (1960)

The following is a historical synopsis of the major aspects of change in the Mexican economy since 1900. These highlights and their statistical corollaries divide themselves, as explained in the Introduction, into three principal epochs: the last decade of the dictatorship of Porfirio Díaz (1900–10), the period of revolution and reform (1910–40), and the period of sustained growth since 1940 which is separated into two intervals (1940–50 and 1950–65).

THE LAST DECADE OF THE PORFIRIATO: 1900–10

The foundations of the modern Mexican economy are customarily regarded as having been laid following the restoration of the Republic in 1867. Earlier attempts to apply the technological developments of the Industrial Revolution to Mexico's rich natural resources, in mining in the 1820s and in manufacturing in the 1840s, were repeatedly frustrated by internal political disorder and foreign intervention during the first fifty years after Independence in 1821. This is reflected in a comparison of per capita product at the beginning and end of the nineteenth century. Although reliable statistical time series on gross domestic product in Mexico extend back only to 1900, two contemporary estimates were made of the economic product of New Spain at the end of the Viceroyalty. By slightly adjusting these measures and relating them to our own estimates of GDP in 1900, a rough comparison can be made between the levels

15

Table 1.1
Income Levels in the Mexican Economy, 1900–65

	GDP (*million 1950 pesos*)	*Per Capita GDP* (*1950 pesos*)
Porfiriato		
1900	8,540	628
1910	11,825	780
Revolution and Reform		
1925	17,081	1,102
1930	14,946	903
1935	17,820	990
Development		
1940	21,658	1,075
1945	30,520	1,323
1950	41,060	1,553
1955	55,312	1,793
1960	74,317	2,064
1965	99,700	2,335

Sources and Methods: A description of the method of estimating GDP to 1940 and alternative procedures is presented in Appendix C, "A Brief History of National Income Estimation in Mexico." Estimates for 1939–65 appear in Appendix D, "Mexican National Economic Accounts."

The population figures used in computing per capita GDP through 1960 can be found in Appendix Table E.1. The population figure of 42,698,000 persons for 1965 is from United Nations, *Monthly Bulletin of Statistics*, 22 (June 1968): 3. Alternative methods of establishing a U.S. dollar equivalent for values expressed in constant (1950) pesos are described in Chapter 3, footnote 8, pages 98-99.

of total and per capita economic product in real terms in the period around 1803 and 1900.[1]

These estimates indicate that per capita product at the end of the Viceroyalty was between 600 and 1,000 pesos of 1950 value. Since per capita product in 1900 was a mere 628 pesos (Table 1.1) it

1. These calculations are described in detail in Appendix A, *The Per Capita Income of New Spain Before Independence and After the Revolution*. A recent alternative estimate, using the U.S. wholesale price index rather than the fine gold equivalent of the silver peso as a deflator and assuming the peso/dollar exchange rate in 1803 was 1/1, arrived at a much lower figure for per capita product in that year (45 U.S. 1950 dollars). William Paul McGreevey, "Recent Research on the Economic History of Latin America," pp. 97–100. By comparison, our estimate of 1803 per capita product reflated to 1950 pesos and converted at the 1950 exchange rate of 8.643 pesos/U.S. dollar gives an estimated figure of 70 to 114 1950 dollars in 1803. Even if the low estimate is used, per capita product grew at less than 1 percent per annum during the period 1803–1900.

would appear that net economic growth over the nineteenth century did not surpass population growth significantly. The much higher Mexican per capita product of today may therefore be attributed to recent historical developments rather than to the years between Independence and the Restoration of the Republic in 1867 (when per capita product may well have declined) or to the early years of the Porfiriato when rapid growth in output, accompanied by an accelerated rate of population growth, barely permitted pre-Independence levels of per capita output to be recovered as of 1900.

Since the Conquest, Mexico has operated well within the limitations on output imposed by its stock of natural resources. The population in 1521 was as large as it was in 1850, and some say even larger, although by the mid-sixteenth century it had fallen well below pre-Conquest levels. Disease, forced labor, the use of rich farmland to graze European cattle, Spanish monopolies of production and commerce, as well as internal and external restraints on trade, all combined to reduce both population and output.[2] Undiminished, however, was the rich resource base that had caused New Spain to be called "the Jewel in the Crown of Castile." The abrupt decline of population in the sixteenth century and its failure to recover earlier levels for several centuries means that much of Mexico's economic growth between 1821 and 1900 may well be explained by a more nearly complete use of existing resources which were previously in excess supply. Preliminary to this process was the political and economic unification of the country that occurred along with major foreign investments in railroads, electric power, and other forms of economic infrastructure.

An earlier increase in the rate of population growth took place at the end of the eighteenth century, due in part to new vaccines against typhus and in part to increased mining production and the income it provided as a result of technological innovation and expanded trade encouraged by the Bourbon dynasty in Spain. Nevertheless, the population in 1803 (estimated by Humboldt at 5.8 million) remained considerably below the immediate post-Conquest figure of 7 to 9 million. Thus the effect of the Bourbon reforms, and perhaps those of the early Porfiriato as well, was rather to permit the restoration of former

2. Woodrow W. Borah, "*New Spain's Century of Depression*"; George Kubler, "Population Movements in Mexico 1520–1600"; Shelburne F. Cook and Lesley Byrd Simpson, "The Population of Central Mexico in the Sixteenth Century."

Table 1.2
Population of Mexico, 1803–1960

	1	*2* Active population as percent of total population (*percents*)	*3* Agricultural labor force as percent of active population (*percents*)	*4* Crude birth rate (*per 1,000*)	*5* Crude mortality rate (*per 1,000*)	*6* Rate of natural increase of population (*per 1,000*)
	Population (*thousands*)					
1803	5,837	—a	–	–	–	–
1856	8,283	–	–	–	–	–
Porfiriato						
1877	9,384	–	–	–	–	–
1900	13,607	35	62 (66)	–	–	–
1910	15,160	35	67	46.0	32.9	13.1
Revolution and reform						
1921	14,800	34	71	45.3	28.4	16.9
1930	16,553	31	70 (68)	44.3	26.7	17.6
Development						
1940	20,143	30	65	43.5	23.5	20.0
1950	26,433	32	58	44.5	17.8	26.7
1960	36,003	32	54	45.8	12.5	33.3

a Dash indicates data not available.

Sources: Column 1: Appendix Table E.1.

Column 2: The percentages for 1910 and 1921 are from *Anuario Estadístico, 1930*, "principal occupation," excluding categories 33 (domestic labor, including housewives), 35 (*improductivos*, "those unable to work"), and 36 (occupation unknown), which accounted for 33 percent, 30 percent, and 3 percent of the population, respectively, in 1921. The percentage for the years 1930 to 1960 are from *Censo General* of each year.

Column 3: Appendix Table E.2. According to Keesing, "Structural Change Early in Development," the estimates of active population are too high for the years before 1930 and too low in 1930. Keesing's estimate of the percentage of overestimation of active to total population in 1895 was applied to the figure for 1900. This adjustment would raise the share of the agricultural labor force to total active population from 62 to 66 percent. His higher estimate of total active population in 1930 would cause the agricultural share of the labor force to fall from 70 to 68 percent (see figures in parentheses and also Table 2.3).

Columns 4 and 5: The birth and mortality rates are from Collver, *Birth Rates in Latin America*, p. 145. The rates for 1910 average the years 1905–09; for 1921, 1920–24; for 1930, 1925–29; for 1940, 1935–39; for 1950, 1945–49; and for 1960, 1955–59.

Column 6: Column 4 minus Column 5.

levels of real income and population than to cause any net increase in the number of mouths which the country could feed.

During the first half of the nineteenth century, population growth showed a cumulative annual rate of increase of only 0.7 percent (Table 1.3). The years after the Juarez Reform of 1857 involved ex-

Table 1.3
Annual Rates of Growth of Population, 1803–1960
(compound annual growth rates)

1803/1856	0.7
1856/1877	0.6
Porfiriato	
1877/1900	1.6
1900/1910	1.1
Revolution and reform	
1910/1930	0.4
1930/1940	2.0
Development	
1940/1950	2.8
1950/1960	3.1

Source: Table 1.2.

propriation of church lands, foreign occupation, guerrilla warfare, and finally expulsion of the French, before the stabilizing influence of the Díaz regime was felt in the late 1870s. During this period the population growth rate fell to 0.6 percent (Table 1.3).[3] Political order was reimposed and peace and stability gradually returned to Mexico under Díaz. The government actively promoted foreign investment in agriculture, mining, power and communications industries —all of which resulted in rapid rates of growth for the monetized sector of the economy. During this time, population growth first accelerated and then decelerated (Table 1.3). The reduction in banditry, removal of local customs duties (*alcabalas*) that had hampered internal trade, gradual commercialization of agriculture, expansion of raw material and primary product exports, and the creation of economic infrastructure, while somewhat increasing the productive base of the economy, also permitted a more efficient allocation of resources that brought about gains in income through internal and

3. The reader should be cautioned that population estimates between the colonial enumeration of 1793 and the first official census of 1895 are extremely speculative.

external trade. Historical enclaves began to be replaced by a market economy, particularly in regions where mining and commercial agriculture flourished.

By 1900 there were 13.6 million people in Mexico, double the number of a hundred years before, with more than half of the growth occurring during the last quarter of the century. These statistics suggest that population growth in Mexico responded rapidly to the first "push" of modern economic development after having long been constrained by under-capacity output, particularly in agriculture. As late as 1910 agriculture supported 70 percent of the population. In the later years of the Porfiriato, and especially after 1900, the rate of population growth declined to 1.1 percent (Table 1.3). This deceleration has been associated with evidence of falling real wages and lagging growth in agriculture that allegedly occurred despite increases in per capita output between 1900 and 1910.[4] Since there was little net immigration at any time in the past 150 years, and since improvement in health conditions tended to reduce the mortality rate and increase the birth rate, one would not have expected the rate of population growth, once it had begun to accelerate, to fall after 1900 unless economic conditions had actually deteriorated for important segments of the population. For example, during the period 1900–10 the region showing the slowest rate of population growth was the Center, which lagged far behind all other parts of the country. Since this zone was most characterized by peasant cultivation rather than the production of cash crops for export, and since subsistence cultivation lagged behind commercial agriculture (Chapter 3), the regional imbalance in population growth lends support to the contention that slowing population growth was a function of levels of living of the rural population. Increased net emigration of Mexicans to the United States after 1900 also provides evidence that economic growth during

4. The rate of growth of GDP in the laste decade of the Porfiriato (3.3 percent per year in Table 1.4) was 1.3 percent greater than that of the period 1877 to 1900, according to El Colegio de México, *Estadísticas Económicas del Porfiriato*. These estimates are based upon the gross output of agriculture, manufacturing, mining and metallurgy, and government expenditures expressed in constant prices (pp. 61, 105, 106, and 323). It is noteworthy that most of the growth was in the export sectors, since total agricultural production between 1877 and 1907 grew at a cumulative annual rate of 0.6 percent while production of the four sectors grew at a rate of 2.6 percent for the whole period, population growing at 1.4 percent. The same source shows real wages in agriculture rising by 24 percent between 1885 and 1895, and then falling by 17 percent from 1895 to 1910 (pp. 147–51).

the latter Porfiriato became less and less capable of absorbing increases in the labor force brought about by previous high rates of population growth.[5] This may be explained in part by a look at the major economic indicators of the period.

The Mexican economy at the beginning of the Porfiriato was characterized by relatively abundant and underutilized arable land and mineral resources and a plentiful supply of unskilled labor. Foreign markets for its agricultural and mineral exports were large and growing, so that the principal factors limiting growth were investable funds, administrators, and technicians. Foreign investment increased rapidly between 1877 and 1910, bringing with it the organizational skills necessary to mobilize Mexican labor and natural resources. As a result, growth was rapid and sustained for over three decades. While data are available only for selected sectors of the economy (principally agriculture, cattle, and forestry; some manufacturing, mining and petroleum production; and government services), detailed commodity trade statistics exist for the entire period and data on occupational structure may be obtained from the population censuses of 1895, 1900, and 1910. This material is sufficient to give a reasonably good picture of economic performance between 1877 and 1910. The evidence suggests that growth was led by extractive industries, export crops, and manufacturing. Between 1877–78 and 1900–01 the mineral and metallurgical industries grew at a compound annual rate of 7.3 percent, manufacturing industries at 2.8 percent, and combined agricultural, cattle, and forestry exports at 6.1 percent, although total combined production in agriculture and related activities grew at only 0.5 percent per year.[6]

The growth process from 1900 to 1910 is summarized in Table 1.4, the figures of which indicate a continuation and even accelera-

5. Moisés González Navarro, *La Colonización en México, 1877–1910* especially pp. 123 f; also, Secretaría de Economía, Dirección General de Estadística, *Estadísticas Sociales del Porfiriato, 1877–1910.*

6. These growth rates are derived from quantum indexes of total value of production expressed in pesos of 1900–01 value, as published in El Colegio de México, *Fuerza de Trabajo,* pp. 61, 105, 106, and 323. The combined sectors of economic activity covered in that volume account for approximately 64 percent of value added in 1910 and grew at a compound rate of 2.1 percent between 1877–78 and 1900–01. Since little is known about the behavior of the rest of the economy during the Porfiriato, it would be inappropriate to assume that GDP also increased at 2.1 percent per year. Indeed, it is likely that transportation, commerce, construction, and nongovernment services surpassed the growth of mining, manufacturing, and agriculture, causing GDP to rise at a higher rate than 2.1 percent per annum before 1900.

Table 1.4
Growth Rates of the Mexican Economy, 1900–65
(compound annual rates of growth)

	Porfiriato 1900/10	Revolution and Reform		Development			1925/65
		1910/25	1925/40	1940/50	1950/60	1960/65	
1. Gross domestic product	3.3	2.5	1.6	6.7	6.1	6.1	4.5
2. Population	1.1	0.1	1.6	2.8	3.1	3.4	2.6
3. Per capita product	2.2	2.4	0.0	3.9	3.0	2.7	1.9
4. Agricultural production[a]	1.0	0.1	2.7	5.8	4.3	4.3	4.2
5. Manufacturing production	3.6	1.7	4.3	8.1	7.3	8.1	6.4
6. Mining and petroleum production	7.2	5.6	−1.9	2.5	5.3	4.2	1.7

[a] "Agricultural Production" in this table includes crop production, animal husbandry, forestry, and fishing.

Sources and Methods: The data on which these growth rates are based can be found in Tables 1.1, 2.1, and Appendixes C and D. The data before 1940 are based on indexes of gross value of production in constant (1950) prices and after 1940 on value-added data in 1950 prices. The assumption is made that the share of value added to gross value of production did not vary before 1940 in any individual sector.

tion of earlier trends. The combined growth of representative sectors of the economy, which for convenience we have assumed increased at the same rate as GDP after 1900, rose from 2.1 percent in the earlier period to 3.3 percent between 1900 and 1910. The growth again was led by mining and petroleum production (7.2 percent), agricultural production for export (5.6 percent), and manufacturing production (3.6 percent), while the performance of total agricultural production lagged far behind (1.0 percent per annum).[7]

The economic policies of the Porfiriato have since been subjected to scathing criticism for their unbridled economic liberalism. Yet this

7. The relatively slow growth of overall agricultural production (which includes crops, animal husbandry, and forestry) between 1900 and 1910 reflects an absolute decline in output between 1907–08 and 1910–11 due to unfavorable weather conditions. The annual rate of growth between 1900 and 1907 was somewhat higher, or 2.6 percent. This compares with the author's calculation of crop production by region, which gives a compound rate of growth of 2.8 percent for the same period (Chapter 3, Table 3.3). Between 1877 and 1907 the combined growth of production of these rural activities was only 1.0 percent per annum. Nevertheless, the production of export crops grew by 6.0 percent over the same period.

is not because they failed to accomplish their principal objective of rapid and sustained economic growth. Owing partly to a slower rate of population growth after 1900, the growth of per capita product accelerated from a rate of 0.5 percent per annum before 1900 to 2.2 percent between 1900 and 1910 (Table 1.4). Indeed, the high rate of expansion of GDP observed during the last decade of the Porfiriato was not experienced again until after 1940, except for a brief period of recovery from the Revolution in the early 1920s. Over the whole Porfiriato, the economic growth rate was perhaps 2.6 percent per annum, compared with a rate of population growth of 1.4 percent. While there is doubtless an upward bias in the figures owing to improving coverage of the data, this is offset by the disproportional growth of new sectors not included in our representative index, so that the general trend indicates rising production and productivity through most of the thirty-five-year period.

What these figures do not reveal and what, in retrospect, has brought forth much criticism of Díaz's policies, is the special character of economic growth during the Porfiriato. Mexico was following the pattern of a typical export economy, which depends upon increasing exploitation of natural resources with cheap labor and foreign capital and technology to expand production for overseas markets. As in many other Latin American countries of the time, this type of export-led growth brought prosperity to some portions of society but almost entirely excluded much of the population from the development process.[8] Its effect on the pattern of output and employment is analyzed in somewhat more detail in Chapter 2. Suffice it to say that the proportion of gross domestic product generated by the principal export industries increased much more rapidly than their share of employment.

As a result, output per employed worker was extremely high in mining, more than average in manufacturing, and considerably below average in agriculture both before and after 1900. In 1895, al-

---

8. A comparable example of export-led growth in Chile is presented in my "Development Problems of an Export Economy," in Markos Mamalakis and C. W. Reynolds, *Essays on the Chilean Economy,* Part 2. For a Peruvian example, see Jonathan V. Levin, *The Export Economies.* A general resumé of the "staple" theory of export-led growth in the context of the Canadian experience is found in Richard E. Caves and Richard H. Holton, *The Canadian Economy*, Chapter 2. See also M. H. Watkins, "A Staple Theory of Economic Growth"; and Richard E. Caves, " 'Vent for Surplus' Models of Trade and Growth," and "The Export-led Growth Model as a Research Tool in Economic History" (unpublished).

though mining and other extractive industries accounted for only 2 percent of employment in the three sectors, they produced 18 percent of the combined output. As of 1910, the employment share in mining remained constant but its output share had increased by one-half to 30 percent. On the other hand, agriculture accounted for 81 percent of employment and only 59 percent of output in 1895, and, although its employment share remained approximately the same in 1910, its output share had dropped by one-fifth, to 47 percent.

These figures suggest that the increased income associated with rapid growth of the economy, attributable particularly to extractive industries, cash crops, and manufacturing, did not transmit itself to the labor force in terms of proportional increases in wages and salaries. Instead, income growth in the leading sectors was being captured by the owners of capital, land, and subsoil resources. Such a redistribution of income in the direction of profits, interest, and rent permitted a rising rate of savings out of gross domestic product, but these savings accrued increasingly to foreigners as the distribution of ownership of capital and natural resources shifted to non-Mexicans.[9]

9. Rosenzweig estimates the sectoral breakdown of foreign investment in 1911 to have been as follows: (1) the largest extractive industries were almost exclusively in foreign control since owners of older mines that operated with primitive metallurgy and mule power were usually unable or unwilling to invest in modern mining techniques; (2) electric power facilities and other public utilities were almost wholly foreign-owned since capital was provided jointly with imported technology; (3) railroads were mostly foreign-owned, although the Mexican government provided subsidies of from 15 to 18 percent of the cost of construction to the Mexican-owned lines (the most important being the Ferrocarril de Hidalgo, with less than 200 kilometers); (4) banking was virtually controlled by foreigners (94 percent) but much of the capital represented savings earned within Mexico by foreign merchants and manufacturers, reflecting the fact that European and American merchandising houses generally reinvested in other sectors of the economy; (5) in manufacturing, the textile industry counted on 20 percent Mexican capital and involved heavy French ownership, although half of the "foreign" funds were reinvestments of profits earned in Mexico (thus, in reality, 60 percent of the financing was Mexican in origin), combined Mexican and foreign funds participated in the development of the steel industry, while basically Mexican-owned industries included food and beverage processing, sugar mills (usually located on the haciendas), flour mills, and the wine industry; (6) the entire traditional and artisan sector of the economy was primarily Mexican-owned, as was most of (7) agriculture. Foreign investment in agriculture was concentrated in the cattle ranches of the North, cotton, rubber, sugarcane, and coffee plantations, and especially those developed during the last decade of the Porfiriato. Fernando Rosenzweig, "El desarrollo económico de México de 1877 a 1911," pp. 405–54. (See next footnote.)

The export industries were incapable of employing the large and rising number of unskilled workers who were becoming available as a result of land consolidation and natural increase in the population. Meanwhile the growth of manufacturing production had two opposing effects on the demand for labor: employment in artisanry declined and employment in machine manufacturing production increased. From 1895 to 1900 the negative effect was outweighed by the positive, and real wages increased in manufacturing along with the share of employment. But from 1900 to 1910 real wages in manufacturing declined along with its labor share while the share of labor in services and agriculture increased. The growth of machine manufacturing from 1900 to 1910 therefore tended to displace artisans at a greater rate than workers were absorbed into the new plants and mills.[10] In one case, for example, the number of textile workers in Mexico fell by 8,000 from 1895 to 1900 and by 12,000 more from 1900 to 1910[11] even though real output in that industry rose by 37 percent and 31 percent respectively during the two periods.[12]

In addition to an increasing concentration of real and financial assets and income in the hands of a small group of local and foreign investors, the increasingly external orientation of the economy after the restoration of the Republic tended to render it more sensitive to international trade cycles. The gradual unification of national markets increased the sensitivity of income recipients in individual localities to disturbing influences from abroad. Hence, fluctuations in the terms of trade for Mexico's principal exports began to be reflected in the level of real wages and the purchasing power of the peso throughout the economy. A general decline in terms of trade after 1905 produced severe repercussions on real income in all monetized sectors of the economy—effects from which it had not recovered by the time of the Revolution. So we see that, by 1910, the export-led growth that was superficially so successful had within it the seeds of internal economic, social, and political instability. Although it brought about the first

10. Much of the analysis is based upon Rosenzweig, "El Desarrollo Económico." This monograph represents the most complete analytical summary of the economic history of the Porfiriato to date, relying as it does upon statistics prepared for the *Historia Moderna de México* series. Some of the statistical material appears in Rosenzweig, "La Industria," in Daniel Cosío Villegas, ed., *Historia Moderna de México,* vol. 7 ("El Porfiriato: La Vida Economica"), Tome I, pp. 311–481.

11. Rosenzweig, "El Desarrollo Económico," p. 444.

12. El Colegio de México, *Fuerza de Trabajo,* p. 106.

major integration of national markets along with vastly improved internal transport and communication, domestic demand was inadequate to provide a major market for industry capable of employing the rising labor force, nor were profits in industry sufficient to prevent a gradual draining off of earnings from the export sector in the form of interest and principal remitted abroad.

THE PERIOD OF REVOLUTION AND REFORM: 1910–40

From 1911 to the late 1920s Mexico was the scene of political and social unrest. The most serious military clashes occurred during the two years 1914 and 1915, when most of the country was involved in the conflict at one time or another.[13] Class was pitted against class, army against army, region against region, and Mexicans against foreigners. Except in a few enclaves that were protected by private armies (particularly the foreign-owned mining and petroleum industries and some plantations), fear and uncertainty were the normal state of affairs. This was not without its economic repercussions, particularly in agriculture, on which the welfare of the majority of the population depended. Population growth, which had slowed during the last years of the Porfiriato, halted after 1910. Even taking into consideration undercounting in the 1921 census (Table 1.2), the net decline in population between 1910 and 1921 was 360,000 people. Given the natural rate of increase that would have been expected during those years in the absence of revolution, the total death toll due to civil war, malnutrition, and disease was probably closer to one million. If population had grown at the same rate between 1910 and 1930 as during the last decade of the Porfiriato, the economy would have been supporting 18.8 million persons in 1930 rather than 16.5 million, as recorded in the census of that year.[14] The active share of

13. Robert E. Quirk, *The Mexican Revolution 1914–1915*.
14. The lowest regional growth rates between 1910 and 1930 were for the Center (not including the Federal District) and the North. These were the areas most affected by armed conflict. Population grew most rapidly in the North Pacific, Gulf, and Federal District. Veracruz, in the Gulf region, was subject to U.S. military occupation. Mexico City, although occupied alternately by opposing forces, was not besieged at any time and suffered little violence. The North Pacific was the site of occasional clashes between constitutionalists and conventionists between 1914 and 1915, but on a more moderate scale than the major battles in the North Central and Central regions of the country between the armies of Villa and Obregón.

population fell sharply between 1910 (35 percent) and 1930 (31 percent).[15] Despite its death toll, the Revolution did not notably affect the composition of the labor force, since the percentage of men in the sixteen-to-thirty age group was 27.2 percent in 1910 and 26.9 percent in 1921.

The rate of growth over the first half of the period is indicated in Table 1.4. Gross domestic product between 1910 and 1925 shows a net increase of 2.5 percent per annum, owing in particular to the successful performance of the large mining and petroleum enclaves which, by insulating themselves from the most serious effects of the military phase of the Revolution, grew at a rate of 5.6 percent per year. More dependent on internal markets, manufacturing lagged seriously behind (growing only 1.7 percent), while agricultural production, which most reflected the disturbed state of affairs in the domestic market in terms of both supply and demand conditions, grew at only 0.1 percent per year (Table 1.4). Except for mining and petroleum, most sectors of the economy appear to have experienced declines in output from 1914 to 1916, barely recovering earlier levels by 1920. Thus the net growth in GDP between 1910 and 1925 actually represents first decline and then rapid recovery, with net growth taking place only after 1920, when peace and relative political stability had been reestablished under the presidencies of General Obregón (1921–24) and Calles (1925–28).

The adverse effect of the Revolution on the economy, while difficult to measure statistically, has been described as follows:

The revolutionary years, and 1913–16 in particular, were marked by great destruction and disorganization affecting in different degrees all phases of economic life and all parts of Mexico. Security, confidence, and public credit vanished. The currency was destroyed and the banking system almost completely wiped out. Railway facilities were destroyed and communications demoralized. The livestock population was seriously depleted and agricultural output gravely declined. Mining output was heavily reduced until war prices led to increased production in the face of great difficulties. Public expenses mounted and public revenues were replenished only by the accidental concurrence of oil

15. Since this figure probably does not include all of those seeking employment in either year, it understates the potential work force, particularly in 1930 when the economy was severely depressed.

development and mining recovery under the stimulus of the
European war.[16]

Recovery was fairly steady after the economy reached a low point
in 1915, as is shown by a number of statistical indicators of the
time, including the production and export of metals, railroad traffic,
the sale of electric light and power,[17] output of textiles, iron and steel
and other manufactures, and agricultural exports. The economy

16. Joseph E. Sterrett and Joseph S. Davis, *The Fiscal and Economic Condition of Mexico,* pp. 227 ff.
17. Ibid. Sterrett and Davis provide data on light and power generated
in three principal districts by the Mexico Light and Power Company between
1907 and 1927. The total figures for El Oro, Pachuca, and the Mexico District are presented in column 1; column 2 gives the Mexico District subtotal;
and column 3 represents the share of column 2 used for commercial light
and power in the Mexico District. (The remainder was used for the tramway,
pumping system, and public lighting.) This series provides a rough index of
power consumed in Central Mexico and reflects the disturbing influences of
the Revolution (1914–16) as well as the water shortage of 1921.

Power Generated and Sold by Mexico Light & Power Company 1907–27
(000,000 kw hours)

	Total of El Oro, Pachuca, Mexico Districts	Mexico District	
		Subtotal	Commercial Light and Power
	1	2	3
1907	120	65	46
1908	158	78	44
1909	164	81	47
1910	216	97	57
1911	282	102	59
1912	316	115	68
1913	329	113	62
1914	272	114	56
1915	200	79	39
1916	235	92	43
1917	294	118	67
1918	330	127	73
1919	380	144	82
1920	428	160	91
1921	370	149	88
1922	442	173	103
1923	477	191	114
1924	523	208	125
1925	561	232	144
1926	593	262	166
1927	606	283	178

Source: Data furnished by the company as cited in Sterrett and Davis,
Fiscal and Economic Condition of Mexico, p. 213.

shifted once again from a net importing to a net exporting basis for cattle and rice, and increased its imports of agricultural machinery and implements, automobiles, iron and steel products, etc. After 1921 oil production did decline sharply, though this was a conspicuous exception to the general upward trend. The process of recovery was disrupted by a number of factors between 1918 and 1928, including an influenza epidemic (1918–19), overthrow of the Carranza government (1920), the world business depression and a domestic drought (1921), the De la Huerta Revolt (1923–24), conflicts between the church and state and between oil companies and the government (1926–28), and a threatened military revolt in the autumn of 1927.

The climate for investment remained uncertain throughout the 1920s, particularly in agriculture. As Sterrett and Davis report:

> In certain respects the agrarian policy and the limitations upon foreigners have restricted the recovery of agriculture and the livestock industry. Internal dissensions and strained international relations have repeatedly shaken confidence in such a way as to cause exports of capital and discourage investment in Mexico. But evidence of many kinds shows convincingly that progress, rather than instability or stagnation, has been characteristic of Mexico in the past twelve years.[18]

Much of the uncertainty among private investors stemmed from the fact that the Mexican economy turned inward upon itself after the Revolution, as the government attempted to redress the imbalances in asset ownership, income distribution, and political power that had intensified during the previous phase of growth. The goal of social equity was now added to that of economic development in the minds of policy makers, although it was widely recognized that to finance the expenditures that these new policies required necessitated high tax revenues from the traditional economic sectors that could be sustained only if the latter were permitted to grow as well.

The first phase of the Revolution had been violent and costly in terms of both manpower and materials. Much of the cost resulted from efforts to reform a rigid system of privilege that had grown up around a social and economic structure which now was being forced to change its character radically. Paradoxically, the Revolution itself was financed out of revenues from mining, petroleum, and other ex-

18. Ibid., p. 228.

ports throughout the most violent years of armed conflict. In the same manner, subsequent reforms also depended on revenues from these sources. In order to alter the structure of the economy and the path of growth, it was now necessary to squeeze the excess profits and economic rents from these activities while at the same time attempting to bring about their expansion. Neither income nor asset ownership is relinquished without a fight, any more than is political power or military control. Restructuring an economy and society customarily entails the redistribution of income, real wealth, and political power, whether or not these policies are pursued directly. During the first stage of the Mexican Revolution the explicit transfer of asset ownership was minimal relative to the forced transfer of political power through military measures. Nevertheless, those clashes often took on aspects of economic class struggle between landless peasants and wealthy *hacendados,* such as in the Zapata movement in South Central Mexico, and between workers and management, as in the textile strikes of Rio Blanco, Veracruz, and in the copper strikes of Cananea, Sonora. There was widespread popular pressure to Mexicanize asset ownership and redistribute to the whole population the benefits from natural resource exploitation. It was recognized by revolutionary leaders that commercial agriculture and mining depended upon government-sponsored works of economic infrastructure; yet the income from these activities benefited only a small number of local and foreign investors and a tiny fraction of the working class.

Under the circumstances it is not surprising that little evidence can be found for much new private investment, at least until well into the 1920s. Foreign loans were virtually impossible to obtain, since the postrevolutionary administrations refused to acknowledge the external debts of their predecessors and threatened to increase taxes and even expropriate existing foreign enterprises. By 1920 the banking system had completely collapsed; paper money was not generally accepted; specie and foreign exchange went into hoards; and, in the absence of accredited banks of issue, a major liquidity crisis ensued. As a result, the inflation of the peso that had taken place during the war years was followed by deflation throughout the 1920s. Local sources of investable funds accordingly dried up, and without new investment there was little increase in productive capacity.

By the late 1920s, Mexico was well ahead of 1910 in mining and petroleum production, electric power generation, and telephone installations, and somewhat ahead of 1910 in manufacturing.[19] The cattle industry had not yet fully replaced the herds that had been decimated by the Revolution, and crops of corn, wheat, and beans remained below 1910 levels, although agricultural output in general was somewhat larger (see Chapter 3). Sterrett and Davis, writing in 1928, noted that:

> Educational facilities have been increased, sanitary conditions somewhat improved, and the standard of living on the whole somewhat raised. It is true that the present position—political, agricultural, industrial, commercial, financial, and social—is very far below the ideal, and much below the standard that is reasonably within the power of Mexico eventually to reach. The task will require years to accomplish in full, but the recent tendencies have been clearly upward.[20]

These writers felt that future growth potential was good for oil, mining, and exports of cattle and vegetable products. Planned public investments in hydroelectric power installations and highways were considered to be "of basic importance to social and economic intercourse, and distinctly helpful to improvement in agriculture, industry, and domestic and foreign trade." The government's emphasis on education, better labor conditions, and social organization was expected potentially to provide a great stimulus to production as well as to widened domestic markets.[21]

The rapid recovery of the economy during the 1920s is noteworthy, but the institutional basis for sustained growth was by no means established during the period. The new goals of the public sector were not sufficient in themselves to accomplish their objectives without costly changes in the structure of the economy and society to make Mexican institutions consistent with those goals. Commenting on these new social policies and the changes they would require for fulfillment, Sterrett and Davis admit, at the end of their report:

> A desire for a better economic and social life was one of the basic causes of the revolution and no Government could long survive that neglected it. There is, of course, a general recognition of the fact that it will require a number of years to meet the

19. Ibid., p. 229.
20. Ibid.
21. Ibid., pp. 229 ff.

requirements of the people, but that they must be met within a reasonable period can be accepted as settled.[22]

Recovery was no sooner under way than the economy was struck by world depression in 1929. Overnight, the markets for Mexico's principal exports broke, bringing income and internal demand down with them. Gross domestic product declined, until by 1930 it was 12.5 percent below 1925, and it did not recover earlier levels until after 1940 (Table 1.1). It became difficult for the political élite, which revolved around ex-President Calles, to maintain its gradualistic program of implementation of the reform articles of the Constitution. Calles's hopes that the normal process of economic growth would bring about improved social equality and income distribution through the market mechanism without the need for radical legislation, became hollow once the capitalistic markets of the world were in a state of collapse. In the state of Michoacán, Governor Cárdenas was already beginning to implement major land reforms in response to growing demands from his constituents. His activities as governor, although they passed relatively unnoticed outside of the state, were a foretaste of things to come once he assumed the presidency in 1934. The export-induced decline in mining, petroleum, and commercial agriculture was followed by gradual recovery in the early 1930s, particularly in manufacturing and other sectors serving the domestic economy. This recovery was influenced by a number of structural reforms. The railroads were nationalized, the pace of land reform was accelerated, land was expropriated, beginning in the temporary administration of President Portes Gil (1929–30) and increasing after 1934 under Cárdenas. The petroleum industry was expropriated in 1938. While agriculture recovered fairly rapidly from the effects of the depression and agrarian reform, mining and petroleum production in 1940 were much below 1925 levels. The net growth between the two years was 4.3 percent per annum for manufacturing, 2.7 percent for agriculture, and −1.9 percent for mining and petroleum production (Table 1.2). Overall growth of gross domestic product was no more rapid than that of population (1.6 percent), resulting in approximately the same per capita product in 1940 as in 1925.

The years of reform from 1930 to 1940 evidenced a new trend in population growth. Mortality rates, which had fallen by six per thousand between 1910 and 1930, fell by an additional three per

22. Ibid., p. 241.

thousand during the 1930s. The (live) birth rate, which had been fairly steady from 1910 to 1930, suddenly increased by ten per thousand in the 1930s (Table 1.2). The cause was in part apparently better health conditions associated with a higher rate of urbanization after the Revolution, and in part an improvement in the economic welfare of the masses as more rural workers received their own land and agricultural production recovered and then surpassed 1925 levels.

The performance of output in agriculture deserves careful examination in this respect, since we have noted that after 1934 there was a vast acceleration in land expropriation and redistribution. This subject is treated in Chapters 3 and 4. Industrial production and urban employment also rose despite world depression and the flight of foreign capital, as the nation began to seek out domestic markets and sources of growth.[23] The 1930s marked the beginning of a vast migration away from Mexico's impoverished and isolated rural hamlets toward the expectation of a better life in the cities and in the growing commercial agricultural centers of the north and coastal regions. The North led the country in population growth, while the Center and South Pacific regions lagged behind. Reflecting this steady movement from the center to the periphery of the country and from rural to urban centers, the share of the Center (less the Federal District) in total population fell from 41 percent in 1930 to 35 percent in 1960, while the agricultural labor force as a share of active population, after rising between 1910 and 1930, fell by six percentage points in the 1930s, seven in the 1940s, and four more in the 1950s (Table 1.3).

The period of reform represented much more than a reallocation of resources in response to changing relative prices among export, import competing, and domestic activities. Rather it involved a fundamental change in asset ownership in agriculture and the petroleum industry, and the promise of high and uncertain rates of taxation in mining, which essentially altered the distribution of wealth and expected income streams for private and particularly foreign investors in these activities. As there was little incentive to invest in these activities, their capacity failed to expand between 1925 and 1940, and many firms permitted net depreciation to take place. Meanwhile

23. Note that the regions with the greatest percentage of subsistence agriculture, least likely to benefit from health measures and most affected by agrarian reform, showed the slowest rate of demographic change—the Center (less the Federal District) and South Pacific.

the government gave preferred tax treatment to those branches of economic activity that would be more likely to serve domestic than foreign markets.

What might the growth of output have been between 1910 and 1940 under the extreme hypothesis that the Revolution and reform had not occurred? Too many fundamental changes took place in the structure of the economy over the three decades between 1910 and 1940 to permit anything but the roughest calculation of what might have been. Still, it is possible to observe the performance of other Latin American countries, activity by activity, and impute this to Mexico under alternative hypothetical rates of population growth, assuming that the losses from the Revolution had not occurred. This exercise is performed in Appendix B, below, and checks are made on the consistency of the estimated growth paths in terms of the country's potential savings and capacity to import.

Hypothetical growth paths have been estimated for three periods, 1910–25, 1925–30, and 1930–40. For each period the growth of output is based upon alternative estimates of the growth of population, production in agriculture, cattle raising, mining, petroleum, manufacturing, and transport. High and low estimates of population growth are used for the output of food and industrial crops for domestic consumption, and these two sets of figures are then added to alternative high and low estimates of output in other sectors, based upon trends in world demand for principal exports as well as on the performance of other Latin American countries on a commodity by commodity basis. The results are somewhat surprising. From 1910 to 1925 there is little evidence that per capita product would have increased more in the absence of revolution than it did in fact. This is largely because of the spurious increase in observed per capita figures resulting from the sharp reduction in population during the war and the postwar influenza epidemic. An increased rate of growth of gross domestic product resulting from our hypothetical range of estimates (3.5 percent to 4.8 percent per annum compared with the actual rate of 2.5 percent) is therefore offset against a higher rate of growth of population between 1910 and 1925 (1.1 to 2.3 percent as opposed to the actual 0.1 percent). Hence the annual rate of growth of per capita product would have been between 1.9 percent and 3.0 percent as compared with the actual value of 2.3 percent before 1925 (Appendix B, Table B.11).

The most notable difference between the hypothetical and observed behavior of the economy is for the years 1925 to 1930. There is evidence that the Mexican economy reacted much more sharply to the world depression at the end of the 1920s than other Latin American countries on a sector by sector basis. While Mexican GDP actually declined on the average of 2.6 percent per year between 1925 and 1930, our estimates based on performance elsewhere would have placed the decline at somewhere between 0.8 and 3.1 percent. Except in education and the banking system, there still had been little in the way of fundamental reforms in the social or economic structure of the country before 1930. Hence, it would be inappropriate to associate the greater sensitivity of output to the trade cycle with institutional changes in the domestic economy. On the other hand, it could be argued that the 1920s represented an "announcement phase" between the promise of reform and its fulfillment. At this time there was a great deal of uncertainty about what path future reform would take in mining, agriculture, and manufacturing. It was not yet clear what the new pattern of public investment in economic and social infrastructure would be. Such a climate of uncertainty undoubtedly rendered domestic expenditure much more vulnerable to exogenous disturbances than would have been the case in the absence of revolution and planned reform.

Our estimates for the years 1930–40 indicate that it is important to make a sharp distinction between the opportunity cost of announced reforms, in terms of economic activity foregone, and the effect of implemented reforms. It is difficult to show that from 1930 to 1940 the hypothetical growth of gross domestic product would have been any greater than it was in fact, according to the estimates in Appendix B. The actual rate of growth was 3.8 percent per annum compared to hypothetical rates of from 3.6 to 4.3 percent (Appendix B, Table B.11). In the absence of revolution and reform, gross domestic product in 1940 might have exceeded the actual level by as much as 12 to 61 percent. Even by the most extreme measure, per capita product still would have been only 18 percent above observed levels in that year (Appendix B, Tables B.9 and B.10). The hypothetical extremes for both total and per capita product were in fact achieved early in the 1940s as a result of the World War II boom.

These rough measures suggest that the economic costs of the institutional reforms in Mexico between 1930 and 1940 were relatively modest, but that significant economic and social opportunity costs are attributable to the violent years of revolution as well as to the announcement phase preceding the implementation of economic and social reforms. The process of internalization of the economy after 1910 had a high price in terms of lives lost, output foregone, capital destroyed, and new investment discouraged. Nevertheless the policies of these three decades laid the foundations for a pattern of subsequent economic growth in which those sectors would be encouraged that provided the greatest scope for absorption of the large and increasing supply of unskilled labor. This marked a sharp reversal from policies in the past, favoring the rapid growth of extractive industries and plantation agriculture regardless of the social consequences. Balanced growth of output for domestic as well as foreign markets permitted a broadening participation of the population in development, rising levels of real income and consumption for most, and a wider distribution of property ownership and economic responsibility than had ever before been experienced in the country. It should be emphasized that although the process of internalization of trade by public policy could be viewed as a logical outcome of postrevolutionary legislation, it would almost certainly have been less extreme had not the international trade depression of the 1930s occurred.

THE PERIOD OF DEVELOPMENT: 1940–65

The Years 1940–50

The first great wave of Mexican economic expansion ended around 1910. After thirty years of revolution, depression, and institutional reform, the economy once again entered a phase of rapid growth after 1940. Gross product rose during the 1940s at 6.7 percent per year while population increased at 2.8 percent (Table 1.4). This phenomenon was triggered by a sudden awakening of foreign demand for Mexican exports following the outbreak of World War II. Aside from the rapid rate of growth of total output, there was little about this third stage of Mexican development to recall the first. Too much had been changed by the Revolution for the Mexico of the 1940s to fit the image of a typical export economy entering a new expansion phase as external demand conditions once again became favorable. The experience of the 1930s demonstrated the high cost of overdependence on foreign demand. Mexico shared with most of Latin America a realization that in the future it would be essential to provide for greater balance between trade and autarchy as insurance against a recurrence of world depression. Since much of the present volume deals with an examination of post-1940 economic performance and public policy in this context, this and the next section confine themselves to a description of major trends as background for the more detailed material to follow.

The rate of growth of exports (in value terms) exceeded that of imports for the earlier years of the war. External demand produced a multiplier effect on domestic output beginning at below full employment levels. Though a number of sectors of the economy reached the limit in machine capacity on a one-shift basis fairly soon, in a number of industries such as textiles the continuation of a trend of rapidly increasing prices made it profitable to increase the number of shifts. Machines were run round the clock to supply the growing domestic demand for goods that could no longer be obtained abroad owing to wartime shortages. The inducement to growth from simultaneous increases in demand for Mexico's exports as well as import-competing goods proved far more powerful than had the deficit-financed increases in internal demand during the 1930s. Furthermore, post-1940 expansion took place in a different atmosphere. The policies of President Avila Camacho (1941–46) included an agreement on indemnification of the ex-owners of Mexico's petroleum industry, settlement of defaulted Mexican bonds, and encouragement of new foreign direct investment, particularly in manufacturing and commerce. Both domestic and foreign investors regarded the improved economic and political climate of the 1940s as a bellwether of even better things to come. All that was necessary was a guarantee that new investments to serve the domestic market would be protected once the favorable wartime conditions had ended.

The labor supply was relatively elastic throughout the 1940s, partly through underemployment in the 1930s and partly through a rapid and increasing rate of urbanization during the entire period. Real wages accordingly lagged behind increases in productivity, allowing a shift in income distribution between 1940 and 1945 toward profits and rent and away from wages and salaries. The welfare of the working class almost certainly improved during this period, although this was due to a shift in the occupational structure toward higher paying jobs rather than to increases in real wages in given occupations. The fact that abundant labor could be drawn out of subsistence agriculture at relatively low real wages meant that, although labor unions were increasingly active in the 1940s, wage rises were prevented from exceeding price increases in most sectors (see Chapter 2).

Output in the immediate postwar years 1946–50 was stimulated by increasing internal demand, thanks to a full-scale program of import substitution introduced by President Alemán (1947–52). Import controls were increased for consumer goods but were relaxed for capital goods, thus inducing a rapid inflow of machinery and equipment from abroad, paid for by foreign exchange earnings accumulated during the war years. The expansion of productive capacity was facilitated by a progressively undervalued exchange rate through 1948 that increased the marginal efficiency of investment through a reduction in the cost of imported producers' goods. The entire period was one of major increases in output per worker, both in agriculture and industry. It will be shown below that much of the growth in per capita output could be explained by increased domestic saving and investment. The economy benefited from a combination of (1) allocative gains from external trade, (2) improved technology embodied in imported capital goods which replaced the worn-out capital stock of the 1920s and 1930s, (3) a shift to new patterns of production in a number of sectors and particularly in commercial agriculture, and (4) gains from expanding internal trade and specialization. The latter influence, which became relatively more important as the years went by, was perhaps the predominant factor in the growth of the 1950s.

The human element is the unknown quantity in Mexico's post-1940 performance. Mexican entrepreneurs have been described as unique among their Latin American contemporaries. In his classic study, *Industrial Revolution in Mexico,* which deals primarily with the experience of the 1940s, Sanford Mosk focused upon the "new group" of Mexican businessmen, formed in the rough and tumble days of revolution and reform when success in any endeavor depended upon one's ability to reconcile immediate self-interest with the future aspirations of society. The new entrepreneur was a man who had made his peace with the government, accepted the need for social and economic reform, and tended to think in terms of the expansion of domestic as well as foreign markets as a basis for his own investment decision making. Foreign investment and technology, while regarded as vitally important to economic success, were subordinated to the desire for Mexicanization of private enterprise.

The government encouraged this type of economic nationalism. In spite of his vociferous wooing of American investment in the mid-1940s, Avila Camacho passed the 51 percent law calling for the ultimate Mexicanization of majority interests in most sectors of the economy.

Given a group of entrepreneurs responsive to increased domestic demand, rapidly rising profits, a fairly elastic supply of labor, and government policy favoring the growth of import-competing industrialization along with commercial agriculture, the most crucial bottleneck to growth during the 1940s was the rate at which machinery and equipment could be imported, set up, and put into production. The inflation of the 1940s reflected excess demand in sector after sector because of the lag between increased demand and capacity responses by producers faced with import, foreign exchange, legal, administrative, and other bottlenecks. It is not possible to isolate one or another constraint such as "savings" or "foreign exchange" as being solely responsible for the many lags between supply and demand. As subsequent chapters reveal, because of the importance of direct controls on trade, of credit rationing, and of lags in the adjustment of capacity to final demand, these constraints differed from period to period and activity to activity.

The 1940s were characterized by growth that was based, first on external, and then on internal stimuli. Manufacturing production led, growing at 8.1 percent per year; agricultural production followed at 5.8 percent; and mining and petroleum lagged, growing at only 2.5 percent (Table 1.4). This type of development could only be sustained for a time on the basis of import replacement. Ultimately, it depended upon a broadening of the internal market, making it essential that productivity gains be passed on to the population at large. Such dispersion of the benefits from growth did not develop in earnest until the 1950s, as a response to continuing construction of trunk and feeder roads, rural electrification, irrigation, and earlier investments in primary education. We shall see that these investments in social and economic infrastructure served to raise the productivity of rural producers and thereby to increase purchasing power throughout the country.

The Years 1950–65

The rate of economic growth of the 1950s was 6.1 percent per year, a performance that did not quite match the previous decade. Meanwhile, population growth accelerated, so that the rate of growth of per capita output fell from 3.9 percent for the 1940s to 3.0 percent between 1950 and 1960. From 1960 to 1965 the growth rate of GDP was 6.1 percent, but further acceleration of the rate of population growth (3.4 percent) reduced the rate of growth of per capita product to 2.7 percent (Table 1.4). The economy has continued to perform impressively, especially when one considers that the slack remaining from the Revolution and the depression of the 1930s, which had given an upward bias to the productivity gains of the 1940s, had been taken up. The forces for development in Mexico became progressively endogenous in terms of both supply and demand, and the foreign sector —while undeniably important as a source of gains from trade—could no longer be regarded as the principal engine of growth or as a sine qua non of sustained economic development. In the 1950s, import-competing production expanded at a more rapid rate than export production, partly because the external terms of trade moved against Mexico, and partly because shifts in factor availabilities and the rapid growth of domestic demand made internal markets more attractive than export markets for most economic activities. This process was abetted by public policy measures tending to promote increased regional specialization, internal trade, and factor mobility. In the 1950s, output increases were led again by manufacturing production (7.3 percent), followed by a resurgence of the extractive industries (5.3 percent) and agriculture (4.3 percent). The first half of the 1960s saw manufacturing growth accelerate to 8.1 percent per annum, with agriculture and extractive industries lagging at 4.3 percent and 4.2 percent, respectively (Table 1.4). For the first time in history, half of the population in Mexico was urbanized by 1960.

As Mexico became more productively self-sufficient, it continued to increase its ties with United States markets. Despite the imposition of direct controls on trade and the recent problems with the *bracero* program, goods and factors have moved with relative freedom across the border. From the northern and coastal regions of Mexico, truck crops increasingly were exported to American markets while American capital flowed south to provide commercial credit in agriculture, as well as long-term financing for industry. By the end of the 1960s, Mexican government bond issues were being floated on the New York (and European) security markets. The Mexican peso retained its par value with the dollar for more than ten years (from 1954 to the mid-1960s). The gross flow of foreign capital was temporarily disrupted during the balance of payments crisis in 1960–61, but it increased again in the following years, even though the share of borrowing for refinancing rose and the growing costs of debt service reduced the net inflow of funds to a minimum.

By the late 1950s, the government had expanded its influence on resource allocation through direct controls. Its agencies successfully encouraged the development of a number of new industries through flexible commercial policy measures, including a widespread quota system as well as selective credit controls. Continuing public investment in roads, irrigation works, electric power generating and transmission facilities, railroad modernization, subsidies of airlines, bus transport, and fuel costs, favored expansion in all sectors dependent on expanded internal and external trade.

Despite the rapid growth of manufacturing production throughout the period, productivity gains were not impressive in the 1950s (see Chapter 5). Mexico's newly expanded industrial capacity was not yet being utilized on a multishift basis as late as 1965. Much capacity was still being installed, while other plants had yet to be drawn into full production, owing to supply bottlenecks, quality shortcomings, noncompetitive prices, and, in certain cases, duplication of facilities and inadequate demand. Meanwhile, allocative inefficiencies owing to restraints on trade and imperfect factor mobility were disappearing rapidly; the quality of most product lines had improved; and distribution systems were being established to serve all regions of the country. The population as a whole was adjusting to new patterns of production and consumption, with important implications for future economic productivity and welfare. The structure of foreign trade has been changing (though slowly) as Mexico's comparative advantage shifts away from traditional raw materials and primary products toward exports of services (such as tourism) and manufactures. One sign of balanced growth in the decade since the mid-1950s has been the slow rate of increase in the price level. The rate of gross savings and investment continues to be high for Latin America (around 20 percent) and the labor supply remains quite elastic, though real wages have begun to rise in recent years.

Population growth continued to accelerate after 1950, as we have seen. The effect of this growth on the age distribution of population is dramatic. The share of the population in the working ages 15 to 64 has fallen steadily from 58 percent in 1930 to 55 percent in 1950 and 52 percent in 1960. Yet, over the same period, the share of the population engaged in economic activity has increased as a result of more women in the work force, improved general health conditions, and a probable decline in the rates of unemployment. The active share of total population, after declining slightly from 31 percent to 30 percent during the 1930s, rose to 32 percent by the 1950s (Table 1.2). The effect on this ratio of a rising proportion of children and elderly people resulting from accelerated population growth has been offset therefore by fuller participation of the middle-age groups in the work force.

Rapid population growth in recent years, rather than keeping pace with or surpassing the gains in output as occurred during the first century after independence, has been surpassed by the growth of total output. Because population growth has become associated with a shift in the work force from subsistence to commercial agriculture and urban employment, the mass of the population is beginning to share, now as never before, in the productive gains from technological change and capital formation brought about by higher rates of savings and investment. This has played an important role in the expansion of domestic markets in a parallel fashion with the growth of capacity in agriculture and manufacturing.

The domestic market is becoming the engine of growth in Mexico, with productivity of the mass of the population being the key to effective demand stimuli. Although gains in real income had an initial impact on the demand for consumer goods imports, local manufactures are increasingly able to compete with imported items. Given an initial degree of protection, the main requirement for success is that economies of scale be realizable. For this, it is essential to have as broad as possible a base of effective demand. This means that productivity gains must be spread throughout the economy. Although the present rapid rate of growth of manufacturing production is not providing sufficient demand for labor to permit an increase in the share of the work force in that sector, commercial agriculture is increasing its share of rural employment. This helps to diffuse agricultural productivity gains, and thereby to widen the market for manufactured goods. Subsequent chapters investigate the extent to which the Mexican experience illustrates the principle that expansion of the national market can be accomplished by a shift in population from low to high productivity occupations, even though the latter experience only modest increases in average productivity. In Mexico, labor has flowed from subsistence to commercial agriculture, from low productivity services and commerce to high levels of urban employment, and from artisanry to machine manufacturing. This transition has been facilitated by strategic government expenditures on rural and urban infrastructure. The Mexican case illustrates how economic growth and structural change can be interdependent and subject to important externalities calling for major public policy measures.

CHANGING LEVELS OF LIVING: 1900–40

How have living levels in Mexico responded to increases in production, income, and population growth during the last sixty years? The simplest measure of welfare is that of per capita product; it is also the most unrealistic, because it abstracts from distributive as well as noneconomic aspects of the change in social product over time. Gross domestic product may be used as a proxy for gross national product only when net factor income from abroad retains a constant share of GDP over the relevant period. Since consistent estimates of international factor payments have become available only since 1939 (Appendix D) and are still very questionable, this section resorts to the use of gross domestic product measures for long-period analysis as a proxy for gross national product. The evidence suggests that national and domestic income and product in real terms have tended to grow at approximately the same rate between 1939 and 1965. This was probably not the case for earlier years, however, since the analysis of Chapter 7 suggests that the net service of foreign borrowings was both negative and much higher as a share of GDP in 1910 than in 1940, owing to the greater importance of foreign debt service at the end of the Porfiriato. Hence gross national product probably grew more rapidly than gross domestic product between 1910 and 1940, after having grown more slowly over the course of the Porfiriato—a time when the country shifted first to a net importer and then to a net exporter of capital.[24]

24. A further adjustment of GDP could be made based on the secular behavior of the net barter terms of trade. This would permit national income to reflect changes in the real purchasing power of Mexican exports. One historical series on Mexico's net barter terms of trade (1937 = 100) shows them falling between 1905 and 1910 (124.3 to 92.7), fluctuating around a rising trend from 1910 to 1925 (136.7), falling in the period between 1926 and 1932 (145.0 to 70.7), recovering through 1937 (to 100.0), and then declining to 71.1 in 1941. United Nations, Economic Commission for Latin America (ECLA), *Economic Survey of Latin America 1949*. Table 4A, pp. 408–09. The terms of trade since 1940 first rose and then declined, so that by

With these qualifications in mind, per capita product is used as a proxy for per capita income in this section. This measure has followed an extremely varied path over the three major epochs of the twentieth century (Tables 1.1 and 1.4). Per capita product grew rapidly during the Porfiriato at a time when production, as we have seen, was shifting away from traditional agriculture and artisanry toward export crops, mining, and machine manufacturing. This pattern of growth tended to reduce the labor share of national income, since labor that had been employed fairly intensively in traditional pursuits was not absorbed effectively by modern mining, petroleum, or manufacturing industries or by commercial agriculture. The real income of the working class almost certainly lagged behind profits, interest, and rent during the decade from 1900 to 1910.

The period of revolution and recovery from 1910 to 1925 evidenced even more disturbance in the structure of the domestic economy. Traditional labor-intensive activities experienced setbacks in production owing to the recruitment of workers into the military and general disruption of the economy in the war years. Gross product grew at a slower rate than during the Porfiriato between 1910 and 1925; but net population growth was negligible, as we have seen, so that the statistical rise in per capita product during this period is misleading from a welfare point of view. The period of reform from 1925 to 1940 saw a number of opposing forces influence the level of economic welfare. Indicators of per capita product are even more precarious as measures of social well-being for the period. Along with internal reforms in education, political organization, and land tenure, the economy was exposed to a major collapse in export markets. All of this took place in a setting of tension and occasional armed clashes between church and state, liquidity crises, political uncertainty, and pressure from foreign creditors. These factors prevented the application of almost any kind of countercyclical economic policy, and output fell by as much as 18 percent between 1928 and

1963 they were at approximately the same level as at the beginning of the period. The average rate of growth of the net barter terms of trade was 4.6 percent per annum (1941–45), 0.8 percent (1946–50), −1.6 percent (1951–55), −3.2 percent (1956–60), and −0.1 percent (1961–63). Grupo Secretaría de Hacienda-Banco de México, Estudios sobre Proyecciones, "Manual de Estadísticas Básicas para Análisis y Proyecciones del Desarrollo Económico de México," Table 1-8, col. 3. These measures suggest that the secular behavior of the net barter terms of trade between 1900 and 1963 has been relatively constant despite wide fluctuations from period to period. For this reason we do not include this measure as an adjustment of long-run GDP.

1930 (12 percent below the 1925 level). Since population had grown somewhat by 1930, per capita product figures for that year are 18 percent below those of 1925, and the economy found itself operating well within the limits of full capacity with profits and rents squeezed even more than real income of the peasantry and working class.

Over the four decades from 1925 to 1965, there was a long cycle of change in per capita product which, after recovering from depressed conditions in the late 1920s and early 1930s, began a sustained rise through the 1940s, 1950s, and 1960s. The net result has been forty years of growth averaging 1.9 percent per year (Table 1.2). Manufacturing output per head grew by 3.8 percent per year, agricultural production by 1.6 percent, while per capita product originating in the extractive industries declined.

What has the aforementioned growth in per capita output meant for levels of living of the masses, and to what extent have at least some of the aspirations that inspired the Revolution been fulfilled since 1910? In Chapter 2 an attempt will be made to impute secular shifts in income distribution to changes in the sectoral, regional, and rural/urban pattern of employment and output.[25] An alternative method would be to quantify the increased participation of the population in activities generally associated with a higher level of living. Bearing in mind the difficulty of imputing welfare improvements to changes in isolated activities of the population, but lacking any better information for the long run, Professor James Wilkie has prepared indexes of seven characteristics which he terms reflective of general levels of living. These are the percentages of persons reporting themselves to be (1) illiterate, (2) speaking only an Indian dialect, (3) living in communities of less than 2,500 persons, (4) customarily barefoot, (5) wearing sandals, (6) regularly eating tortillas instead of wheat bread, and (7) without sewage disposal. Only the first three characteristics are available from the population censuses of 1910, 1921, 1930, and 1940. All seven are available for the years 1940, 1950, and 1960. Using 1940 as a base, an unweighted average of these indexes was derived to suggest changes in what Wilkie terms "regional poverty" in Mexico [26] (Table 1.5).

25. Budget studies from which Lorenz curves and Gini coefficients of income inequality could be derived have become available only since the 1950s, so that indirect methods of estimating distributional changes have been relied upon for earlier years.

26. James W. Wilkie, *The Mexican Revolution,* Chapter 9 ("An Index of Poverty").

Table 1.5
A Poverty Index for Mexico by Region
(1940 = 100)

	1910	1921	1930	1940	1950	1960
Total Mexico	124	115	109	100	86	72
North Pacific	131	121	107	100	87	74
North	131	122	112	100	88	76
South Pacific	111	108	103	100	90	82
Gulf	129	122	110	100	87	76
Center (less Federal District)	118	113	107	100	91	78
Federal District	179	145	126	100	79	79

Source: Wilkie, *The Mexican Revolution*, Appendix 1. The index is based on the unweighted average percent of the population reporting itself (1) illiterate, (2) speaking only Indian languages, (3) dwelling in communities of under 2,500 inhabitants (items 1 to 3 for years 1910–40), (4) regularly going barefoot, (5) regularly wearing sandals, (6) regularly eating tortillas rather than wheat bread, (7) lacking sewage disposal (items 1 to 7 for years 1940–60). More detailed figures for each category by state are available in the above volume.

The poverty index is derived from a simple average of the percentage of the population having each of the seven characteristics mentioned above. For example, in 1940 the simple average of all seven characteristics for Mexico was 46 percent. The range in averages was from 11.2 percent for the Federal District to 56.5 percent for the South Pacific. Following the South Pacific, the figures in descending order were Center (less the Federal District) 50.1, Gulf 54.9, North 40.0, North Pacific 37.3, and finally the Federal District, with by far the lowest percentage of "poverty" characteristics.[27]

Neither this nor any other proxy for social welfare is free from value judgments. Debates as to the appropriateness of each of the seven characteristics of poverty and their relevant weights could provide hours of activity for insomniac social scientists. Accepting the Wilkie index at face value, with appropriate qualification, as the best measure presently available of secular changes in social welfare, we have related annual percentage declines in "poverty" (a stock item) to increases in per capita income (a flow) in Table 1.6. The resulting pattern is far from symmetrical. While "poverty" shows a steadily increasing rate of decline since 1910, per capita income has risen,

27. Since the D.F. consists primarily of Mexico City and its suburbs, the index is biased downward in this case by inclusion of the percentage of population in communities of less than 2,500 as one of the seven characteristics. This is, perhaps, the weakest of the indicators in any case.

Table 1.6
A Comparison of Poverty Reduction and Per Capita Product Growth, 1910–60

	1910–25	*1925–40*	*1940–50*	*1950–60*
1. Cumulative annual percentage *decline* in the poverty index	0.7	0.8	1.5	1.8
2. Cumulative annual percentage *rise* in per capita product	2.4	0.0	3.9	3.0

Sources and Methods: 1. Taken from Table 1.5, assuming that the index fell steadily between 1921 and 1930 or by 0.6 percent per year, giving an estimate of 112 for 1925. (Since the period 1921–25 was one of rapid recovery in GNP, and 1925–30 was one of growth and then decline, this may slightly understate the decline in living levels by 1925.)

2. Taken from Table 1.4.

fallen, accelerated, and then decelerated. The comparison illustrates that the economist's usual qualifications about reliability of per capita income or product estimates as measures of general welfare are well taken. The living conditions of the very poor seem to have improved at a greater rate after 1925 than before, even though per capita measures show the opposite trend. In addition, the evidence tends to support the suggestion made later on in this study (see Chapter 2) that inequalities in income distribution widened in the 1940s and then narrowed in the 1950s as shown in Table 1.6. The poverty index falls more rapidly for the 1950s than the 1940s, although the growth of per capita product took the opposite trend. It follows from these tentative measures that rapid economic growth might well have been a necessary condition for major reductions in poverty (see the figures since 1940), although the data before 1925 indicate that rising per capita product was by no means a sufficient condition for rapid improvement in social welfare.

PRODUCTIVITY TRENDS AND THE SOURCES OF MEXICAN GROWTH

The growth of the Mexican economy since the Revolution, and the improvement in welfare that it entailed, may be attributable to two principal causes—increased inputs of manpower and materials and more efficient employment of previously existing means of production. In this section, total output is related to a weighted average of the three major inputs (land, labor, and capital) for the years 1925 to 1960 in order to estimate the share of increases in aggregate production attributable to increased use of land, labor, and capital. The aggregate results are subjected to detailed sectoral analysis in successive chapters. Initial efforts at estimating an aggregate production function for Mexico, using time series data, were not highly successful.[28] Problems of multicollinearity among the inputs of capital, labor, and land, as well as the complicated and unstable relationship among these factors over time and even within sectors (see, e.g. Chapters 3, 4, and 5), appear to have attributed far more than data problems per se to the estimating problem. For this reason the present section relies upon a Denison production function, in which an index of value added in constant prices is related to a weighted average of indexes of physical units of labor, reproducible fixed assets, and cultivated land employed since 1925. It is assumed for convenience that factors receive their marginal products and that, in the absence of positive or negative returns to scale, the rate of growth of gross domestic product would be a weighted average of the growth rates of the three major inputs; that the sum of these weights would be unity; and that the weight of each factor would equal its share in the functional income distribution of the economy.[29]

To estimate the expected growth of output under constant returns to scale, one need only calculate the growth rate of the three major inputs. Estimating the share of land, labor, and capital in total in-

28. One fairly good fit based on capital inputs alone was obtained in the process of estimating a simultaneous equation model of trade and growth for Mexico (1940–62). A. Maneschi and C. W. Reynolds, "The Effect of Import Substitution on Foreign Exchange Needs, Savings Rates and Growth in Latin America." The following production equation was fitted by three-stage least squares:

$$Y_t - Y_{t-1} = 2981 + 0.1403I_{t-1}$$

(first differ-   (2.419)   (2.335)
ence in gross   (lagged gross
domestic income)   investment)

The figures in parentheses are ratios of the estimators to their asymptotic standard errors and are analogous to *t*-statistics. The Bank of Mexico is presently working on a more elaborate growth model for projection purposes under the direction of Leopoldo Solís M., Chief of the Department of Economic Studies, based upon the 1960 input-output table, Banco de México, "Cuadro de Insumo Producto de México, 1960."

29. The reader will note that these are the assumptions of a Cobb-Douglas world in which the elasticities of substitution among factors of production are constant and equal to unity. It is not suggested that Mexico exhibits such behavior; rather that, if it did, the growth of output (assuming constant returns to scale) could be conveniently estimated from a few benchmark estimates of the major inputs, such as we possess.

come, and using these estimates as weights, one obtains a rate of growth that could be explained by the growth of inputs alone without any changes in productivity at all. This "explained" rate of growth is presented in row 5 of Table 1.7 for the period of reform (1925–40) and the two subperiods of development (1940–50 and 1950–60).[30] It is clear from the results that, even during the period of reform when there was no increase in per capita income, gross domestic product grew at twice the rate of the weighted average of inputs, a fact which strongly suggests increasing returns due perhaps to fuller use of capacity already in existence in 1925.[31] Similar results are obtained throughout the thirty-five years under consideration, the actual rate of growth averaging 4.3 percent while "explained" growth was only 2.3 percent per year.

What accounts for the "unexplained" growth that was as high as 3.3 percent per year during the decade of the 1940s? The gains in productivity reflected in the residual represent a combination of factors that includes returns to improved education and technical skills of labor, more productive machinery and equipment (where productivity gains are not reflected in the price of these goods), other real inputs for which our three variables are not effective proxies, disembodied technological progress, and a shift in factors of production toward more productive activities over time. In the earlier years, an additional element was the return to full capacity or "taking up of slack" in factor employment following the disturbance of revolution, reform, and world depression. A comparative study of productivity growth in Latin America for the years 1940–64 by Professor Henry Bruton illustrates the impact of the war years, which drew capacity into full employment in Mexico.[32] By his measure, the residual for 1940–45 was 6.7 compared with 1.2 for 1946–53. In all countries except Colombia (Argentina, Brazil, Chile, and Mexico), the share

30. The classic calculation of this type for the American economy was prepared by Edward F. Denison, *The Sources of Economic Growth in the United States and the Alternatives Before Us,* and "How to Raise the High-Employment Growth Rate by One Percentage Point." The same methodology is employed to compare productivity levels in eight European countries and the U.S. in Denison, *Why Growth Rates Differ.*

31. Note that the capital/output ratio appears to have fallen from a rather high level (4.2) in 1925 to 3.3 in 1940. Table 1.7, n.

32. Henry J. Bruton, "Productivity Growth in Latin America." The Bruton productivity residual for Mexico is 6.7 (1940–45), 1.2 (1946–53), 2.0 (1955–59), and 2.8 (1960–64). His calculations assume a relatively high capital share of value added for Mexico (.50 compared to our .25) and omit land as a factor of production.

Table 1.7
Mexican Economic Output, Inputs, and Productivity Trends
(compound annual rates of growth)

	1925–40	1940–50	1950–60	1925–60
Output				
1. Gross domestic product	1.6	6.7	6.1	4.3
Inputs				
2. Man-years of labor	1.0	3.6	3.1	2.3
3. Stock of fixed reproducible assets	(no significant trend)	2.8	5.5	2.3
4. Hectares of land in cultivation	2.3	3.6	1.0	2.3
5. Rate of growth attributable to inputs 2., 3., and 4.	0.8	3.4	3.6	2.3
6. Rate of growth "unexplained" by the above inputs	0.8	3.3	2.5	2.0

Sources and Methods: 1. The rates of growth of GDP are taken from Table 1.4.

2. The labor force statistics are for "economically active" population as indicated in the decennial population censuses without adjustment for age, sex, occupation, or education. The 1925 figure is based on an estimated population of 15.5 million for that year (an interpolation between the Gilberto Loyo estimate for 1921 and the 1930 census figure), to which a labor force participation rate of .324 was applied (from the 1921 census). The participation rate for 1900 was .377; for 1910, .352; and for 1930, .311.

3. Fixed reproducible investment estimates for 1940–60 are from Banco de México, Departamento de Estudios Económicos, "Alternativas de Estimación de la Inversión Bruta Fija en México, 1939–1962." The figure for 1925 is estimated by me, applying Cossío's assumed depreciation rate of 2.5 percent per annum to the capital stock for 1940 and using adjusted gross investment estimates for the years 1925–40 taken from an index in United Nations, ECLA, *Economic Survey of Latin America, 1949*, p. 414, "Quantum of New Capital Goods Available." (See Appendix D for details.) The resulting estimate of the capital stock for 1925 is not significantly different from that of 1940, implying a declining capital/output ratio of 4.2 for 1925 and 3.3 for 1940. The ratios are 2.3 for 1950 and 2.2 for 1960, respectively.

4. The figures for hectares harvested (hectares cultivated were not available in consistent form) are from Banco de México, Oficina de Estudios sobre Proyecciones Agrícolas, "Indices de los Rendimientos Agrícolas y de las Superficies Cosechadas, 1925–1962."

5. This figure is an average of inputs 2., 3., and 4. weighted as follows: labor, .70, capital, .25, land, .05. The weights are derived from functional income distributions cited in Studenski, *The Income of Nations*, p. 238, averaging the figures for countries in Mexico's income class (III) in 1955, in which capital received 24 percent of income (not including "mixed income") and labor 76 percent. These ratios compare with Denison's figures for the U.S. of .69, .22, and .09 for labor, capital, and land in 1909–13, and .73, .23, and .05, respectively, in 1954–58 (*The Sources of Economic Growth in the United States and the Alternatives Before Us*, C.E.D., 1962, p. 30). The

Table 1.7—*Continued*

sources of estimates of functional income distribution in Mexico are discussed in Chapter 2. Owing to the large "mixed income" component in these estimates, it is difficult if not impossible to separate out factor shares for the economy as a whole. Sectoral estimates for agriculture and industry are presented in the respective chapters. Subsequent to these initial calculations, it was pointed out by Paul David that the application of the capital share of national income as a weight (.25) biases downward the relative contribution of capital to output by omitting the depreciation share of both numerator and denominator. If the capital/output ratio in 1950 were 2.3 and the assumed rate of depreciation on the capital stock 2.5 percent per annum, the adjusted share of capital in GDP would be .29 (the addition of depreciation raises both numerator and denominator by 5.75 percentage points). On this basis the weights would become: labor, .66, capital, .29, and land, .05. The corresponding rates of growth attributable to these inputs become: 1925–40, 0.8; 1940–50, 3.4; and 1950–60, 3.7. Thus the only residual or "unexplained" rate of growth altered by this adjustment in weights is that of 1950–60, which falls from 2.5 to 2.4 percent per annum.

6. This figure is the residual of 1. minus 5.

of growth attributed to the residual was highest for the war years and fell sharply thereafter. Since 1949, Latin American productivity gains —including those of Mexico—have lagged behind most of the advanced industrial countries for which Bruton presents data (except for Canada and the United Kingdom). The unfavorable performance of this hemisphere he attributes in large part to the decline in efficiency of resource allocation and to the increased dependence on trade associated with postwar protection of consumer goods manufacturing abetted by low-cost producer goods imports. As a result, the structure of production became out of balance with changes in final demand, and this was reflected in rising prices and increased dependence upon imports.[33]

The Mexican pattern in Bruton's statistics tends to controvert his conclusions except between the war and immediate postwar years, since his productivity residual for Mexico rises steadily thereafter, from 1.2 (1946–53) to 2.0 (1955–59) and 2.8 (1960–64). Yet this has been a time of increasing protection of manufacturing. The problem may lie in his gross investment series, which apparently understates the growth of the capital stock (4.2 in the 1950s, compared with our figure of 5.5 percent per annum); but it is more likely to be found in the degree of aggregation underlying the production function used, which represents the whole economy as a single produc-

33. Ibid., pp. 1111–15.

tion unit. In subsequent chapters, production functions of a similar form are estimated for both agriculture and manufacturing for the three decades from 1930 to 1960. They disclose very different residuals in each case. Manufacturing shows an unexplained annual rate of growth of output of 1.9 percent (1930–40), 0.1 percent (1940–50), and −0.7 percent (1950–60) (see Chapter 5), while agriculture has a residual of 2.0 percent (1930–40), 1.1 percent (1940–50), and 1.9 percent (1950–60) (see Chapter 3). (Intersectoral shifts in factor employment explain much of the apparent discrepancy between high aggregate and low sectoral productivity residuals, a factor analyzed in detail in the following chapter.) This suggests that, while Bruton's argument may hold for manufacturing, it must be qualified to take into account sustained growth in agricultural productivity in Mexico, if not elsewhere in Latin America. The improvement in agricultural productivity between the 1940s and 1950s tends to offset the very low productivity residual in manufacturing. It provides a clear illustration of the importance of disaggregation in the analysis of disequilibrium systems such as exist in Latin America, where distortions in production relationships are likely to be severe.

THE ETHOS OF REVOLUTION

Observers of the Mexican development experience continually have emphasized that ideological and attitudinal factors associated with the process of revolution and reform are largely responsible for the country's rapid economic growth in recent years. This configuration of attitudes we shall term an "ethos of revolution," which may be said to have grown and then declined in importance over the long period since 1910. The ethos of revolution has been interpreted in different ways (both negatively and positively) by different social and economic groups and by different political administrations over time.[34] Indeed, it is too broad a term to permit meaningful analysis.

34. An anthology of Mexican attitudes concerning the survival of the revolutionary ethos and its behavioral corollaries is presented in Stanley Ross, ed., *Is the Mexican Revolution Dead?* An excellent and more recent description of this ethos as it is reflected in economic nationalism is provided by Manning Nash, "Economic Nationalism in Mexico," pp. 71–84. The ideological influences on public policy and particularly on federal expenditures by presidential administration are detailed in Wilkie, *The Mexican Revolution*, Part I ("The Federal Budget") and especially in Chapter 3 ("The Political Context of Budgetary Policy"), pp. 40–65.

The same holds for the term "economic nationalism." Such concepts must be transformed into their behavioral counterparts. Only then, and after testing their significance, can social science (1) predict the effect of radical social change and (2) prescribe alternative policies perhaps less costly than a revolution that might accomplish the same ends. Since major structural changes involve shifts in the distribution of income and wealth, they must somehow be explained in terms of an ethos sufficiently acceptable to permit their enforcement. In Cuba, a large share of the population left after the Castro Revolution; the remainder were mixed in their reaction to its effects, but enough were willing to work harder owing to the incentive effects of an ethos of revolution which served as a substitute for economic returns, to permit the economy to recover and grow despite a severe economic blockade. Structural change extended to the weights attached to the benefits derived from internal exploitation that shifted from the business and commercial class to the working class. A social ethic sufficient to permit sweeping structural changes may encompass economic nationalism, religion, racism, reaction against imperialism (different from nationalism, since this could include international confederations), and internal class warfare. In Mexico, economic nationalism and anticlericalism were added to rural class warfare (agrarian reform demands) to forge an ethos which was eventually extended to even the urban business and working classes. Perhaps this is because class warfare elements were less evident in urban than in rural areas prior to 1910, since Mexico was scarcely industrialized before the Revolution. Thus it was possible to build, from the outset, an industrial structure in which management was conditioned to a social ethic that demanded that social welfare be included as one objective of private decision-making.

One way of measuring the potential net impact of changing psychological factors on growth is to estimate the share of increases in output that are "unexplained" by as many conventional inputs (including land, labor, and capital) as can be measured. In the Mexican case the higher productivity residual appears not for industry but for agriculture. There are reasons to suppose that a progressive shift from inferior to superior technologies (as they became known to the peasants) may primarily account for the latter residual, and that increasingly efficient use of otherwise traditional inputs therefore explains much of the increase in agricultural output. Since there has been little or no residual in the most modern sectors of the economy, then would it be legitimate to suggest that psychological factors attributable, for example, to the Revolution, have had no part in the rapid growth of commercial agriculture and manufacturing?

The answer to the above is no, not necessarily. Although much of the growth took place through increased use of land, labor, and natural resources applied to changing technology, the process was accompanied by (and indeed enabled by) dramatic shifts in the structure of output (among sectors, between regions, and between rural and urban, as well as in skills of the labor force) and the propensities of individuals to respond to economic stimuli. Mexico achieved a near doubling of the savings rate over the course of a decade. The government was permitted to spend half of its income in capital formation and to channel an increasing share of private savings into public investment without wiping out the source of those savings. The state was able to acquire total or part ownership in a number of key industries and then to use them to ease bottlenecks in the production process (as well as to speed structural change by substituting public decision making for the lack of private initiative) without crippling the high and rising level of private investment.

It is hypothesized here that changes in the structure of the economy were brought about by public policies such as agrarian reform and the resulting redirection of attention to investments in rural infrastructure. These policies would have been neither proposed nor tolerated in the absence of the social and political changes accompanying the Revolution. The "ethos of revolution" is a catch phrase which embraces (1) changes in the political interpretation or weighting of social welfare functions; (2) willingness of property owners to tolerate a rising rate of expropriation of income if not assets; (3) willingness of private enterprise to accommodate its decisions to public policies, even when the latter are in direct opposition; (4) willingness of labor unions to restrain demands for wage increases in a belief that increases in product, achieved by preventing excess consumption, will be passed on in part to the state in the form of public savings to be invested for the good of the working class; (5) willingness of foreign investors to abide by local law with respect to their internal economic activities and thereby extend their private utility functions to accommodate the social welfare of the host nation to a greater extent than previously.

It is also hypothesized that private propensities to save, invest, and respond to changing market conditions in a peaceful manner (on the part of both labor and capital) were conditioned in part by changing expectations that improved over time and began to outweigh the negative aspects of radical social and political change. (The negative effects in the early years were substantial and are estimated in Appendix B.) Take, for example, the propensity to save. This depends upon expectations of future rates of return on capital discounted for risk. The resolution of political difficulties, however violent, together with imposition of a stable government, reduced risk discounts for given expected rates of return. The commitment of government to economic development with broader social participation, to policies of economic integration on a national basis in order to create a wide local market, and to export promotion policies that took advantage of foreign markets—all improved private expectations of future rates of return on capital. Thus did postrevolutionary regimes, particularly those after Cárdenas, improve propensities to save out of a given income.

Investment propensities were increased partly by shifting downward the risk discount by expansion of internal market (due to revolution-inspired decisions to attend to internal rather than external demand as a prime criterion of public policy), by state subsidies, by protection, and by identification of the state with business interests. These policies have been called "betrayal of the revolution" by critics of the post-Cárdenas administrations. Yet if the maximum amount of income is to become available to the masses through the role of the state (i.e. if the state ultimately identifies its interests with the masses, for political necessity if for no other reason), then maximization of the growth of output (by providing higher incentives for private investors through public policy) is entirely consistent with the goal of the Revolution. Maximization of social welfare, not expropriation for its own sake, is the purpose of revolution. Marx stressed expropriation only in order to return to the worker the means of production and thus to reduce his sense of "alienation." But modern technology is as alien to the shareholder as to the machine production worker. Making the worker a capitalist may infuse the production process with new ideas and alter the payoff ratio out of profits; but it will do little for the worker's psyche.

An analysis of what is contained in "ethos of revolution" should also include elements of convergence of individual welfare functions in such a way that welfare may be jointly maximized. While much conventional economic analysis depends on the assumption that the utilities of individuals are separable and independent, there is clearly an overlap for families, for social groups, and occasionally for whole societies, which cannot be ignored. How important this factor is in conditioning changing propensities of individuals to save, invest, and more efficiently allocate resources already in existence is debatable. The problem deserves more attention from social psychologists than it has received. Presumably some degree of what is called "solidarity" in certain ideological systems that pass as social-scientific can be generated during the development process. Probably it was operative for some classes (e.g. the agricultural) in Mexico, though studies such as Simpson's *The Ejido: Mexico's Way Out* suggest that a high degree of individuality and self-aggrandizement at the expense of the community continued after the Revolution and muddied the ideological waters of agrarian reform.

It may be possible, however, to use solidarity as an economic input (at least for a time) as leaders in the Mexican labor unions have used it with their workers for over a generation. By recalling early goals and the blood shed decades ago, they have forestalled rebellion in the ranks; but not without help from governmental subsidies; repressive state measures against dissidents; rising real wages (for individuals if not for occupations); better living conditions through social welfare expenditures on housing, education, and health; and a large "reserve army" of unemployed and semiemployed which reduces the effectiveness of strikes. The ethos of revolution may therefore help to explain part of the aggregate residual in Mexican economic growth, which has averaged 2.0 percent per year between 1925 and 1960 (Table 1.7). Certainly Mexico has performed as well as any major Latin American country since 1940, in terms of both output and productivity growth and has exhibited a greater degree of balance in the growth of agriculture and industry than most. The analysis of subsequent chapters will help to shed light on the extent to which material and ideological factors may jointly account for productivity increases in the Mexican economy. The following chapter provides a summary of the implications of general trends in economic growth for the distribution of output, employment, income, and population as a background for detailed treatment of agriculture, industry, foreign trade, and public policy since the Revolution.

Since the historical path of economic development in Mexico is only one of many that the country might have taken over the same period, each with its own implications for the growth of output, income distribution, and social welfare, the ultimate objective of the present analysis is not only to explain what has happened but to set this in a framework of alternative possibilities. This is particularly true in the case of a country that experienced such severe bloodletting and social disruption in the process of achieving a successful combination of economic growth and political stability. The economic losses that were sustained as a result of abrupt changes in the distribution of political and economic power and ownership of wealth were eventually recovered by an increase in the rate of growth that almost certainly would not have occurred without the Revolution. Whether the benefits actually compensated for the costs cannot be resolved in this volume. Such conclusions depend upon subjective judgments about social priorities which can be reconciled, if at all, only through the political process.

2

The Nature and Consequences
of Structural Change in Mexico:
1900–1965

What effect has Mexico's twentieth-century development had on the distribution of output, employment, and income? And what influence have the latter had on subsequent rates of growth? The present chapter deals with these questions in broad quantitative terms as background for more detailed sectoral analysis to come. It offers a statistical summary of changes in the structure of the Mexican economy for selected years between 1900 and 1965 in terms of the pattern of output, labor participation, and rural/urban income shares. The implications of these changes for income distribution, aggregate demand, and economic growth are discussed briefly, calling attention to a number of factors that receive special treatment in the following chapters.

Rapid economic growth in Mexico has taken place in an environment of widespread rural and urban poverty. There is even some indication that the gap between the very poor and those benefiting from economic progress has widened and that income inequality is positively associated with the rate of growth. By looking at the proximate sources of growth in productivity per worker by sector, as well as the pattern of growth of rural compared with urban output, evidence is obtained to suggest a long swing in income inequality associated with increases in the rates of saving and investment and output per capita since 1940. Most of the material in this chapter deals with real rather than monetary aspects of growth. Considerations of the influence of relative price changes on income distribution and resource allocation, the relationship between aggregate demand and the price level, and the role of financial intermediation in growth are therefore postponed until later.

The most striking change in the structure of production in Mexico between 1900 and 1965 has been a decline in the share of agriculture and an increase in manufacturing. In 1900, farming and animal husbandry accounted for almost 30 percent of gross domestic product, while manufacturing was the source of only 13.2 percent of output. By 1965, total agricultural production had fallen to 17.4 percent and manufacturing had risen to 25.3 percent (Tables 2.1 and 2.2). Extractive industries also declined in importance over this period. Although mining grew from 6.4 to 9.8 percent of GDP from 1900 to 1930, it fell sharply to 5.6 percent in 1940. By 1965, it accounted for only 1.7 percent of GDP. The share of petroleum, after falling in the 1930s and 1940s, reversed this trend and increased from 2.7 percent of production in 1950 to 3.2 percent in 1965.[1]

The pattern of output in the past sixty years shows a definite shift from rural to urban activities. The share in production of mining and the extractive industries has been reduced significantly, particularly since the reforms of the 1930s, although petroleum has recovered somewhat under nationalization. Total agricultural production has

1. Estimates of the value of production in Tables 2.1 and 2.2 are based upon indexes expressed in constant (1950) prices. As such, they fail to reflect relative price changes that may have had a significant effect on income shares over the long run. Although this is the only method by which GDP estimates may be derived for the early years 1900 and 1910, since value-added figures in current prices are unavailable for the earlier years, the study by El Colegio de México, *Fuerza de Trabajo,* does provide estimates of the gross value of production in agriculture, mining and petroleum, and manufacturing for 1900 and 1910. On the basis of these estimates, assuming that the sum of these three sectors plus government represented the same share of GDP in 1900 as it did in 1930 and that the proportion of value added to gross value of production was the same for each activity, the shares of agriculture, mining and petroleum, and manufacturing were 29.5 percent, 12.2 percent, and 12.9 percent of GDP respectively in 1900. In view of the precarious nature of these estimates, the best that can be said is that our figure for the mining share of output in 1900 (6.4 percent—Table 2.2) probably understates the relative importance of that sector as a source of income. This does not alter the trend in relative shares, however, since the El Colegio figures show a sharply rising proportion of mining production in GDP between 1900 and 1910. Alternative distributive shares based upon current prices for the years 1940–65 are presented in Appendix D.

Table 2.1
Structure of Production, 1900–65
(millions of 1950 pesos)

	Porfiriato		Revolution and Reform		Development		
	1900	*1910*	*1930*	*1940*	*1950*	*1960*	*1965*
Gross domestic product	8,540	11,825	14,946	21,658	41,060	74,317	99,700
Agriculture	–ᵃ	–	–	5,266	9,242	14,018	17,300
Crop production	1,218	1,344	1,962	2,730	5,999	9,178	11,600
Livestock	1,335	1,510	1,591	2,247	2,903	4,450	5,300
Forestry	–	–	–	265	263	254	300
Fishing	–	–	–	24	77	136	100
Manufacturing	1,131	1,620	2,489	3,889	8,437	17,116	25,200
Mining	547	1,044	1,458	1,209	1,243	1,648	1,700
Electrical energy	–	–	–	211	370	898	1,400
Petroleum	–	34	552	638	1,129	2,346	3,200
Construction	–	–	–	784	1,287	2,595	3,500
Transportation	264	330	793	974	1,988	3,638	4,300
Commerce	–	–	2,365	5,203	10,750	19,167	–
Government	–	–	543	668	1,294	1,985	2,700
Unclassified activities	4,045	5,943	3,193	2,816	5,320	10,906	40,400ᵇ

ᵃ Data not available.

ᵇ Includes Commerce for 1965.

Sources: 1900 and 1910 Agriculture: Index from Cosío Villegas, "Economic History of the Porfiriato" (manuscript), applied to figure for base year in Grupo Secretaría de Hacienda-Banco de México, Estudios sobre Proyecciones, "Manual de Estadísticas Básicas," Table 2-3.

1900–10 Manufacturing: Index from El Colegio de México, *Fuerza de Trabajo*, applied to figure for base year in Grupo Secretaría de Hacienda-Banco de México, "Manual," Table 2-3.

1930 Agriculture: Index from Banco de México, Oficina de Estudios sobre Proyecciones Agrícolas, "Indices de los Rendimientos Agrícolas" applied to figure for base year in Grupo Secretaría de Hacienda-Banco de México, "Manual," Table 2-3.

1930 Manufacturing: Index from *Trimestre de Barómetros Económicos*, No. 8, March 1948, applied to figure for base year in Grupo Secretaría de Hacienda-Banco de México, "Manual," Table 2-3.

Other 1900–30: Index of figures in *México: Cincuenta Años de Revolución*, vol. I ("La Economía"), Mexico: Fondo de Cultura Económica, 1960, Chapter 18, applied to figure for base year in Grupo Secretaría de Hacienda-Banco de México, "Manual," Table 2-3.

1940–65: Appendix Table D.5B.

Table 2.2
Structure of Production, 1900–65
(percents)

	Porfiriato		Revolution and Reform		Development		
	1900	1910	1930	1940	1950	1960	1965
Gross domestic product	100.0	100.0	100.0	100.0	100.0	100.0	100.0
Agriculture	_a	–	–	24.3	22.5	18.9	17.4
Crop production	14.3	11.4	13.1	12.6	14.6	12.3	–
Livestock	15.6	12.8	10.6	10.4	7.1	6.1	–
Forestry	–	–	–	1.2	0.6	0.3	–
Fishing	–	–	–	0.1	0.2	0.2	–
Manufacturing	13.2	13.7	16.7	18.0	20.5	23.0	25.3
Mining	6.4	8.8	9.8	5.6	3.0	2.2	1.7
Electric energy	–	–	–	1.0	0.9	1.2	1.4
Petroleum	–	0.3	3.7	2.9	2.7	3.2	3.2
Construction	–	–	–	3.6	3.1	3.5	3.5
Transportation	3.1	2.8	5.3	4.5	4.8	4.9	4.3
Commerce	–	–	15.8	24.0	26.2	25.7	–
Government	–	–	3.6	3.1	3.2	2.7	2.7
Unclassified activities	47.4	50.3	21.4	13.0	13.1	14.8	40.5[b]

[a] Data not available.
[b] Includes Commerce for 1965.
Source: Table 2.1.

fallen over the long run in relative shares, mainly because livestock production was curtailed by the disturbing conditions of the Revolution and agrarian reform between 1910 and 1940 and again in the 1940s by a severe epidemic of hoof-and-mouth disease. Crop production, however, maintained its long-run share of output (14.3 per cent in 1900, 14.6 percent in 1950)—largely as a result of the opening of new land to cultivation through investments in roads and irrigation systems. The share of crops in GDP, however, did decline to 12.3 percent in the 1950s.

Manufacturing has almost doubled its share of output since the turn of the century, with a much greater relative increase since 1950 than before, while construction, transportation, and commerce have held relatively constant. (The commerce index for 1930–40 must be regarded as highly speculative.) Government services have declined as a proportion of GDP over the long run. The overall pattern of behavior of the economy reflects changes in economically available resource endowments, as minerals have been depleted, new land has been made productive through technological change, and the labor force has multiplied, boosting the production of labor-intensive agriculture, commerce, construction, and services. Output has responded to a relative increase in internal as opposed to external demand and a higher income elasticity of demand for manufactures and services than for raw materials and primary products. The trend in production has been particularly responsive, since the Revolution, to public policies that have tended to favor commercial agriculture, manufacturing, and tourism over mining and the extractive industries. Some of these policies will be examined later on, although mining is touched upon only briefly as the present study focuses on leading rather than lagging sectors.[2] It will be shown that, in many cases, public policies have worked at cross purposes to each other with respect to given sectors and have been reversed over time so that no clear long-run pattern of suppression or encouragement of individual activities comes to light. Moreover, patterns of demand are difficult to separate from those of supply since reliable budget studies are unavailable except for recent years, and then only on a cross-sectional basis, whereas Mexican taste patterns have been subjected to major changes over time.

Changes in the pattern of employment have not always paralleled shifts in the structure of production since 1900 (Table 2.3). For example, although employment in agriculture and extractive industries declined in the long-run while the share of manufacturing and services increased, shorter period changes in output and employment were by no means symmetrical. The percentage of labor force in the agricultural sector appears to have risen slightly between 1900 and 1910, even when the 1900 figure is adjusted for overcounting of total employment and even though the share of agricultural production in GDP declined. By 1930, as expectations of land reform ran high and as other sectors of the economy experienced the disrupting influence of world depression, the share of the labor force in agriculture was

2. A comprehensive analytical history of the Mexican minerals sector is long overdue. An excellent economic history of the sulphur industry (1910 to 1966) appears in Miguel S. Wionczek, *El Nacionalismo Mexicano y la Inversión Extranjera,* Part 2. Marvin D. Bernstein, *The Mexican Mining Industry,* provides the most complete institutional treatment of contemporary Mexican mining (1890–1950) to date.

Table 2.3
The Structure of Employment, 1900–60
Distribution of the Labor Force by Major Sectors

	Porfiriato		Revolution and Reform	Development		
	1900	1910	1930	1940	1950	1960
1. Agriculture, Forestry, Fishing & Livestock Industry	61.9[a] (65.9)	67.1	70.2	65.4	58.3	54.1
2. Mining & Extractive Industries	2.1[a] (2.2)	1.9	1.0	1.8	1.2	1.2
3. Manufacturing, Construction, Electric Power, etc.	13.6[a] (14.4)	13.1	13.4	10.9	14.8	17.7
4. Services and Other Activities	22.4[a] (17.4)	17.8	15.4	21.9	25.7	27.0
5. Total	100.0	100.0	100.0	100.0	100.0	100.0

[a] These figures are based on the assignment of insufficiently specified workers (over 6 percent of the total in 1900) to "services and other activities." Keesing, in a reworking of the underlying data, suggests that the insufficiently specified personnel actually were not in the labor force and should be dropped from the total. If this were done, the total labor force in 1900 would be reduced by 311,826 to 4,819,225, and the share of employment in agriculture would rise to 65.9 percent, mining and extractive industries to 2.2 percent, manufacturing, etc. to 14.4 percent, while services, etc. would fall to 17.4 percent. The adjustment for 1910 is negligible since in that year only 65,847 were "insufficiently specified" (correspondence with D. Keesing, summer, 1968).

Source: Appendix Table E.2.

the highest of the entire period even though the agricultural share of output in 1930 was below that of 1900. Since 1930, the share of agricultural employment has steadily declined, particularly during the 1940s when crop production rose from 12.6 to 14.6 percent of GDP (although a decline in the share of livestock and forestry output more than offset the gains in crop production). Agricultural employment has fallen over the long run from 70.2 percent of the work force in 1930 to 54.1 percent in 1960. Manufacturing, construction, and electric power accounted for 13.6 percent of the labor force in 1900 and 17.7 percent in 1960. This rise was not steady, however, since the share fell to 10.9 percent in 1940. The major gains in manufacturing employment have taken place only in the past three decades. The virtual doubling of the share of manufacturing output from 13.2 percent in 1900 to 25.3 percent in 1965 (Table 2.2) is by no means matched in terms of labor absorption, since the employment share in manufacturing, construction, and electric power rose by less than 5 percentage points during the same period.

PROXIMATE SOURCES OF POST-1940 GROWTH

The increase in output per worker in Mexico between 1940 and 1960 revealed in Table 2.4 may be said to have resulted from two sets of

Table 2.4
Output per Employed Worker by Sector

	1940	1950	1960
Agriculture[a]			
Output (millions of 1950 pesos)	5,266	9,242	14,018
Labor force (thousands)	3,831	4,824	6,086
Output per worker (1950 pesos)	1,375	1,916	2,303
Manufacturing[b]			
Output (millions of 1950 pesos)	6,731	12,466	24,603
Labor force (thousands)	747	1,319	2,141
Output per worker (1950 pesos)	9,011	9,451	11,491
Services & Other[c]			
Output (millions of 1950 pesos)	9,661	19,352	35,696
Labor force (thousands)	1,281	2,129	3,027
Output per worker (1950 pesos)	7,542	9,090	11,793
Gross Domestic Product			
Output (millions of 1950 pesos)	21,658	41,060	74,317
Labor force (thousands)	5,859	8,272	11,253
Output per worker (1950 pesos)	3,697	4,964	6,604

[a] Agriculture includes crop production, livestock, forestry, and fishing.

[b] Manufacturing includes manufacturing, mining, electrical energy, and construction.

[c] Services includes transportation, commerce, government, and other activities.

Sources: Output data are from Table 2.1. Labor force figures are from Appendix Table E.2.

proximate causes: those associated with labor productivity growth in individual sectors and those related to shifts in labor from less to more productive sectors. In this section an estimate is made of the contribution of each set of forces to the total increase in labor output by looking at agriculture, manufacturing, and tertiary industries.[3] In

3. Agriculture includes value added generated by forestry, fishing, and livestock production; manufacturing also includes mining, petroleum, electric power, communications, and construction activities; tertiary activities or services refer to all other activities included in Mexican GDP.

order to separate the influences of productivity growth from the shift factor, an estimate was made of the increase in output per employed worker that would have occurred under the assumption of constant employment shares in these three main sectors for the two decades from 1940 to 1960. Employment shares at the beginning of each decade were used to weight observed gains in output per worker for each activity over this period.

Since one would expect labor to shift from less to more productive activities in response to wage differentials during the course of the decade, it is unlikely that the productivity gains achieved in the least productive sectors would have been as great had the initial share of the labor force been maintained in these sectors. At the same time, productivity gains in the most productive sectors might have been even greater had they not absorbed a greater share of the labor force over time. For example, one would not have expected agricultural output per worker in the 1940s to have grown as rapidly had the share of the labor force in this sector remained constant; diminishing marginal productivity of labor almost certainly would have influenced the results. On the other hand, the fact that manufacturing and services absorbed a rising share of the work force during the same decade almost certainly prevented increases in output per worker from being as great as they otherwise would have been owing to the same effect of diminishing marginal productivity. (This assumes that shifts in complementary factor inputs would not have been sufficient to offset the influence of the change in labor shares implicit in our hypothetical projection.)

With these qualifications in mind, the calculations have been made in Tables 2.5 and 2.6 for the 1940s and 1950s respectively and the results prove quite illuminating. For example, in Table 2.5 it appears that, had each sector maintained its share of the work force over the course of the decade and had observed productivity gains been realized nevertheless, the increase in output per worker for the economy as a whole would have been only 59 percent of the gain actually experienced during the 1940s. The shift factor accounted for 41 percent of Mexico's productivity growth during that decade, principally as a result of the movement of labor from agriculture to manufacturing and tertiary employment. Table 2.6 reveals that the shift factor was less important in the 1950s, accounting for only 24 percent of the growth in output per worker under our extreme assumptions. These calculations suggest that if the aggregate data may be relied

Table 2.5

Sectoral and Shift Factors Underlying the Growth in Output per Worker 1940/50

			Totals	Per-cent
Actual growth in output per worker (1950 pesos)			1,267	
Proximate sources of growth in output per worker:			*Totals*	*Per-cent*
Agriculture				
	ΔAa	354		
	ΔaA	−98		
	ΔaΔA	−38	218	17
Change in output per worker 1940/50 (1950 pesos) (ΔA)	541			
1940 share of labor force (a) × 100	65.4%			
Change in share of labor force 1940/50 (Δa)	−7.1%			
1940 output per worker (1950 pesos) (A)	1,375			
Manufacturing				
	ΔMm	56		
	ΔmM	297		
	ΔmΔM	15	368	29
Change in output per worker 1940/50 (1950 pesos) (ΔM)	440			
1940 share of labor force (m) × 100	12.7%			
Change in share of labor force 1940/50 (Δm)	3.3%			
1940 output per worker (1950 pesos) (M)	9,011			
Services				
	ΔSs	339		
	ΔsS	286		
	ΔsΔS	59	684	54
Change in output per worker 1940/50 (1950 pesos) (ΔS)	1,548			
1940 share of labor force (s) × 100	21.9%			
Change in share of labor force 1940/50 (Δs)	3.8%			
1940 output per worker (1950 pesos) (S)	7,542			
Estimated total change in productivity			1,270	100
Estimated change in productivity with no shift in labor force				
	ΔAa		354	47
	ΔMm		56	8
	ΔSs		339	45
	Total		749	100
Share of change in productivity attributable to the shift factor				
$\dfrac{1,270 - 749}{1,270}$				41

Note: The model employed in this and the following table (Table 2.6) is as follows:

where:

$Y_{ij} \equiv$ value added in sector i in period j
$N_{ij} \equiv$ employment in sector i in period j
$T \equiv$ total economy
$A \equiv$ agriculture
$M \equiv$ manufacturing
$S \equiv$ services

(1) $Y_T = Y_A + Y_M + Y_S$

(2) $\dfrac{Y_T}{N_T} = \dfrac{Y_A}{N_T} + \dfrac{Y_M}{N_T} + \dfrac{Y_S}{N_T}$

(3) $\dfrac{Y_T}{N_T} = \dfrac{Y_A}{N_A} \cdot \dfrac{N_A}{N_T} + \dfrac{Y_M}{N_M} \cdot \dfrac{N_M}{N_T} + \dfrac{Y_S}{N_S} \cdot \dfrac{N_S}{N_T}$

let:

$$A \equiv \dfrac{Y_A}{N_A}; \qquad a \equiv \dfrac{N_A}{N_T}$$

$$M \equiv \dfrac{Y_M}{N_M}; \qquad m \equiv \dfrac{N_M}{N_T}$$

$$S \equiv \dfrac{Y_S}{N_S}; \qquad s \equiv \dfrac{N_S}{N_T}$$

then:

(4) $\dfrac{Y_{Tt}}{N_{Tt}} = Aa + Mm + Ss$

(5) $\dfrac{Y_{T(t+n)}}{N_{T(t+n)}} = (A + \Delta A)(a + \Delta a) + (M + \Delta M)(m + \Delta m) + (S + \Delta S)(s + \Delta s)$

(6) $\dfrac{Y_{T(t+n)}}{N_{T(t+n)}} = Aa + \Delta Aa + A\Delta a + \Delta A\Delta a +$
$Mm + \Delta Mm + M\Delta m + \Delta M\Delta m +$
$Ss + \Delta Ss + S\Delta s + \Delta S\Delta s$

therefore:

(7) $\dfrac{Y_{T(t+n)}}{N_{T(t+n)}} - \dfrac{Y_{Tt}}{N_{Tt}} = \Delta\left(\dfrac{Y_T}{N_T}\right) = \Delta Aa + A\Delta a + \Delta A\Delta a +$
$\Delta Mm + M\Delta m + \Delta M\Delta m +$
$\Delta Ss + S\Delta s + \Delta S\Delta s$

This change can be divided into the sectoral and shift factors and combined factors as follows:

$$(7)_A \ \Delta\left(\dfrac{Y_T}{N_T}\right) = \overbrace{\Delta Aa + \Delta Mm + \Delta Ss}^{\text{sectoral factors}} + \overbrace{\Delta aA + \Delta mM + \Delta sS}^{\text{shift factors}}$$

$$+ \overbrace{\Delta A\Delta a + \Delta M\Delta m + \Delta S\Delta s}^{\text{combined factors}}$$

Source: Table 2.4.

Table 2.6

Sectoral and Shift Factors Underlying the Growth in Output per Worker 1950/60

			Totals	Per-cent
Actual growth in output per worker (1950 pesos)			1,640	
Proximate sources of growth in output per worker:				
Agriculture				
	ΔAa	226		
	ΔaA	−81		
	$\Delta a\Delta A$	−16	129	8
Change in output per worker 1950/60 (1950 pesos) (ΔA)		387		
1950 share of labor force (a) × 100		58.3%		
Change in share of labor force 1950/60 (Δa)		−4.2%		
1950 output per worker (1950 pesos) (A)		1,916		
Manufacturing				
	ΔMm	327		
	ΔmM	274		
	$\Delta m\Delta M$	59	660	40
Change in output per worker 1950/60 (1950 pesos) (ΔM)		2,040		
1950 share of labor force (m) × 100		16.0%		
Change in share of labor force 1950/60 (Δm)		2.9%		
1950 output per worker (1950 pesos) (M)		9,451		
Services				
	ΔSs	695		
	ΔsS	118		
	$\Delta s\Delta S$	35	848	52
Change in output per worker 1950/60 (1950 pesos) (ΔS)		2,703		
1950 share of labor force (s) × 100		25.7%		
Change in share of labor force 1950/60 (Δs)		1.3%		
1950 output per worker (1950 pesos) (S)		9,090		
Estimated total change in productivity			1,637	100
Estimated change in productivity with no shift in labor force				
	ΔAa		226	18
	ΔMm		327	26
	ΔSs		695	56
	Total		1,248	100

Share of change in productivity attributable to the shift factor

$$\frac{1,637 - 1,248}{1,637} \qquad 24$$

Source: Table 2.4.

upon, during the two decades since 1940 much of Mexico's impressive growth in per capita output is attributable to the internal flexibility of the economy whereby it was possible to transfer resources from less to more productive sectors of economic activity. Still well over half the growth in output per worker was due to gains within the sectors themselves.[4]

Output per worker in the economy as a whole increased by 34 percent in the 1940s and 33 percent in the 1950s, as may be determined from the data in Table 2.4. The sectoral performance was extremely uneven, however, particularly in the 1940s when agricultural output per worker increased by 39 percent, that of services by 21 percent, and manufacturing only 5 percent. In the 1950s, agricultural output per worker increased by 20 percent, that of services by 30 percent, and manufacturing by 22 percent. As a reflection of the importance of the shift factor in the second decade, none of the individual sectors showed as rapid a gain in output per worker as did the economy as a whole (33 percent). In the 1940s, however, only agricultural productivity growth exceeded that of the economy as a whole.

From the calculations in Tables 2.5 and 6, it is possible to divide overall productivity gains into their sectoral components. In the 1940s agriculture contributed 17 percentage points of the overall increases in output per worker (net of the negative shift factor). Manufacturing contributed 29 percentage points, while services contributed an impressive 54 percent. Although labor productivity in manufacturing and services did not begin to approach that of agriculture in the 1940s, the former sectors absorbed a much larger share of the increase in the work force than did agriculture, while at the same time maintaining a rising level of output per worker. The same pattern was repeated in the 1950s (Table 2.6). The net contribution of agriculture to overall productivity growth is only 8 percentage points, while that of manufacturing is 40 percent and services 52 percent. Once again it appears that the absorption of most of the net increase in the work force by urban employment has had a notable effect on the growth of output per worker in Mexico. The difference is that in

4. Further disaggregation might reveal increases in labor productivity due to shifts of labor from less to more productive employment within the main sectors. So far, the only sector for which it has been possible to estimate internal shift effects was agriculture. In this case less than 5 percent of the growth in productivity could be attributed to the shift of labor from less to more productive regions among the five major zones of cultivation (see Chapter 3).

the 1950s urban activities experienced more rapid increases in productivity than did agriculture. Thus the shift factor accounts for only 24 percent of overall productivity growth in that decade.

What might one conclude from these findings? First, it is evident that from one-quarter to one-third of the increase in output per worker was accomplished by a shift in employment shares from agriculture to manufacturing and services, even though the absolute number of workers employed in agriculture continues to rise. Urbanization in Mexico has been associated with rapid gains in output per worker, especially during the 1950s in both manufacturing and services. What cannot be estimated from the data is the extent to which observed gains in output per worker actually represent labor absorption into more productive activities. All that can be said from the data presented here is that, if it is correct, urbanization has not been inconsistent with rapid growth in labor productivity even in tertiary industries. The data does not say whether or not productivity gains in these activities have been passed on to the urban labor force as a whole.

The evidence that output per worker in tertiary activities has increased so rapidly in Mexico is quite remarkable because productivity performance of the service sector in other Latin American countries has tended to be quite unimpressive. The data in Table 2.4 shows output per worker in tertiary activities to have achieved a level of 11,792 pesos (1950 prices) in 1960 compared to 11,491 pesos in manufacturing and 2,303 pesos in agriculture. Output per worker in tertiary activities was five times that of agriculture in 1940, as it was in 1960, but the absolute gap between the two sectors has risen from 6,000 to 9,000 pesos. This is a characteristic that is also observed within both agriculture and services. Since agriculture continues to provide a subsistence livelihood to a large number of cultivators, while at the same time those employed in the more productive regions of cultivation are obtaining higher and higher real incomes, it is not unusual to find evidence of widening income inequality in the rural economy. Similarly, in the service sector those employed in menial occupations have not experienced major increases in real wages over the past three decades, while it is clear from the statistics that the income received in the form of interest, rent, and wages to skilled labor has grown impressively in terms of the volume of employment in this sector.

This overview of the proximate sources of productivity growth indicates merely the results of underlying forces of change rather than the forces themselves. The Mexican economy has indeed benefited from a shift of factors of production from less to more productive activities, but this shift has been made possible by massive investments in physical and human resources sustained over several decades. The policy framework of postrevolutionary governments has permitted relatively efficient resource allocation to take place within a setting of private and mixed enterprise. Labor and capital have been encouraged to seek employment in the most socially productive activities through the use of indicative planning measures and market leadership by public corporations in industries where few sellers exist. That is why there is little inconsistency between the evidence in this study for a minimum of "unexplained" productivity growth in agriculture or manufacturing, even though productivity growth in the economy as a whole has been quite favorable.

Indeed the productivity results of the Mexican experience are encouraging in that they show how considerable growth in per capita output may be experienced, without productivity miracles in individual sectors of production, simply by applying capital and labor to high productivity sectors and thereby changing the structure of production. This may be accomplished by providing a framework within which the greatest possible intersectoral and interregional factor mobility is facilitated so as to minimize the underutilization of physical and human resources and maximize the rate of formation of capital and skilled labor. Dynamic allocative efficiency is much more important in this respect than static efficiency. Nevertheless, the income distributive implications of this type of growth raise problems for countries with a large initial share of the population in subsistence agriculture. Until the turning point is reached at which the marginal productivity of unskilled labor begins to rise, absolute disparities in income per capita are likely to be aggravated and, with them, social and political tensions. Some of the income produced by the growth process must be used in the short run to relieve these tensions if economic progress is to be permitted to continue. During the Porfiriato, the growth of similar tensions ultimately contributed to a major sociopolitical explosion.

RURAL/URBAN INCOME SHARES: 1900–65

As the production and employment shares of the more industrialized sectors of the economy have increased, the rural shares have steadily

Table 2.7
Rural/Urban Income Shares
(percents)

	1900	1910	1930	1940	1950	1960	1965
Share of gross product imputed to rural areas	58	55	45	40	36	32	31
1. Agriculture[a]							
Share of total GDP	29.9	24.2	23.7	24.3	22.5	18.9	17.4
Rural GDP share	27	22	21	22	20	17	16
2. Extractive industries[b]							
Share of total GDP	6.4	9.1	13.5	8.5	5.7	5.4	4.9
Rural GDP share	2	3	5	3	2	2	2
3. Commerce & transportation[c]							
Share of total GDP	18.9	18.6	21.1	28.5	31.0	30.6	30.0
Rural GDP share	6	6	5	7	7	6	6
4. Manufacturing, construction, & electricity							
Share of total GDP	13.2	13.7	16.7	22.6	24.5	27.7	30.2
Rural GDP share	0	0	0	0	0	0	0
5. Government							
Share of total GDP	—[d]	—	3.6	3.1	3.2	2.7	2.7
Rural GDP share	0	0	0	0	0	0	0
6. Rent and others							
Share of total GDP	31.6	34.5	21.4	13.0	13.1	14.8	14.8
Rural GDP share	23	24	14	8	7	7	7

Distribution of Shares:
Share of total GDP from Table 2.2.
Rural GDP shares:

1. Agriculture–90 percent rural.
2. Extractive industries–35 percent rural based on 1950 input-output table wages and salary share of extractive industry value added.
3. Commerce and transportation–$\left(\dfrac{(3)}{100\% \text{ GDP} - (3)} \times \dfrac{1}{2} \dfrac{\text{rural share of GDP}}{\text{in other sectors}} \right)$.
4. Manufacturing, construction, electricity–all urban.
5. Government–all urban.
6. Rent and other (proportional to the percent of population in rural areas)–1900: .72; 1910: .71; 1930: .67; 1940: .65; 1950: .57; 1960: .49; 1965: assumed same as 1960.

[a] Includes agriculture, livestock, forestry, and fishing for 1940–65; includes only agriculture and livestock for 1900–30.

[b] Includes mining and petroleum.

[c] Commerce share for 1900 and 1910 assumed to be same as that for 1930; commerce share for 1965 assumed to be same as that for 1960.

[d] Data not available.

declined. Table 2.7 estimates the percent of gross domestic product received in the form of income by those living in rural areas since 1900. These figures are based on the assumption that no net transfers of income have occurred between urban (population greater than 2,500) and rural areas. Since there is considerable evidence that urban dwellers increasingly have subsidized their poorer relations in the countryside, tending to raise the relative income share of the rural sector over time above the measures in Table 2.7, this assumption is not entirely correct and probably results in a downward bias to the rural income share over time. Another assumption underlying the data is that those still employed in rural-based activities have not urbanized, although there is evidence that there has been a net shift of agricultural workers from smaller (under 2,500) to larger communities and that these are among the higher income recipients in agriculture. In this case our index is subject to an upward bias for those residing in rural areas. In addition, the data underlying the measures are expressed in constant prices assuming constant terms of trade between agriculture and industry. Since our rural/urban income estimates should in fact reflect the influence of relative price changes, these figures ought ideally to be adjusted by the terms of trade among the major production sectors. Such an adjustment has not been possible owing to the scarcity of meaningful national price indexes. From the evidence, it would appear that income distribution over the long run has tended to favor the urban population, although in recent years this trend may have been arrested (Table 2.8). In 1900, some 58 percent of gross domestic product went to income recipients in rural areas. This figure fell to 31 percent in 1965. Since no provision is made in the estimates for the real income derived from handicraft, artisanry, and other rural industries that gradually have been displaced by urban manufacturing, this downward trend may have been even greater over the past sixty years.

Most of the decline in rural income shares is attributable to the falling share of agriculture in gross domestic product. The falling participation of the rural sector in the value of commerce and transportation is based upon the assumption that income received from these activities is proportional to that arising from the other production sectors. It should be stressed that these figures represent relative rather than absolute levels of output and do not reveal the absolute improvements in welfare in both rural and urban areas, which have been considerable over the whole period.

The rural/urban income shares described above have been divided by population shares in Table 2.8 to provide an estimate of the posi-

Table 2.8
The Distribution of Gross Domestic Product and Population
Rural and Urban: 1900–60
(percents)

	1900	*1910*	*1930*	*1940*	*1950*	*1960*
1. Rural share of GDP	58	55	45	40	36	32
2. Urban share of GDP	42	45	55	60	64	68
3. Total	100	100	100	100	100	100
4. Rural share of population	72	71	67	65	57	49
5. Urban share of population	28	29	33	35	43	51
6. Total	100	100	100	100	100	100
7. Rural share of GDP ÷ rural share of population	81	77	67	62	63	65

Sources: Lines 1., 2., and 3.–Table 2.4.
Lines 4., 5., and 6.–Appendix Table E.3.

tion of rural income relative to total per capita income. One of the principal objectives of the postrevolutionary programs of agrarian reform and rural education was to reduce income inequalities between the city and the countryside. Our estimates shed some light on the effectiveness of this policy. If per capita income in rural and urban areas had been equal, the measures in row 7 of Table 2.8 would have been 100. Instead, our results show that in 1900 rural per capita income was 81 percent of the national average. As relative conditions in the countryside deteriorated during the last decade of the Porfiriato, the share by 1910 fell to 77 percent. During the years of revolution and reform, the relative income of rural dwellers actually worsened despite attempts by the government to redress the grievances of this important and militant segment of the population. Income in rural areas failed to keep pace with urban growth during the 1930s so that, by 1940, rural per capita income was only 62 percent of the national average. Although the rural share of population declined by six percentage points over the three decades from 1910 to 1940, this was insufficient to offset a decline of eleven points in rural income shares. Since 1940, however, the process has been reversed slightly as immigration from the countryside to the cities has been sufficient to offset the falling rural share of income. As a result, the ratio of rural to total per capita income gradually increased from 62 percent in 1940 to 65 percent in 1960.

These figures say nothing about the distribution of income *within* the rural and urban areas. Agriculture is characterized by a high degree of dualism between subsistence and commercial crop production and among the several regions of the country (see Chapters 3 and 4). In urban occupations there is also extreme inequality in income distribution between the large numbers of unskilled workers in construction and personal services and those employed in industry, banking, and commerce. Over the long run, income inequality almost certainly has increased within the rural sector as output per worker in subsistence agriculture has tended to lag behind that which took place in newly opened regions of commercial cultivation.[5]

TRENDS IN PERSONAL INCOME DISTRIBUTION: 1950–63

Statistics on income distribution in Mexico are difficult to obtain, since the budget studies on which they depend have been infrequent and notoriously unreliable. It is worthwhile, despite misgivings, to examine three of the best sets of estimates of personal income distribution for the years 1950, 1957, and 1963 in order to gain a rough idea of the pattern of distribution in this postwar period. What is perhaps most evident from the data in Table 2.9 is the degree of income inequality that Mexico apparently experienced. In 1950, for example, the lower three quintiles of the population received 24.6 percent of personal income. This share was said to be only 21.2 percent in 1957 and 21.5 percent in 1963. In comparison with the postwar shares of similar income groups in India (28 percent), in Ceylon (30 percent), in Puerto Rico (24 percent), in the United States (34 percent), and in the United Kingdom (36 percent),[6] Mexico is far below international standards. Indeed, by any of the three postwar measures shown, Mexico's income distribution remains less equal than that of India.

The budget study on which the 1963 estimates are based was independent from and considerably more reliable than that of the 1957

5. Leopoldo Solís M., "Hacia un Análisis General a Largo Plazo del Desarrollo Económico de México." See also pp. 101 and 102 below.

6. Simon Kuznets, "Economic Growth and Income Inequality." *American Economic Review: Papers and Proceedings,* May, 1955.

Table 2.9
Distribution of Personal Income, 1950, 1957, and 1963
(percent)

Deciles	Percent of Families[a]			1950			1957			1963		
	1950	1957	1963	% of Total Income	Cumulative Percentage Increasing	Decreasing	% of Total Income	Cumulative Percentage Increasing	Decreasing	% of Total Income	Cumulative Percentage Increasing	Decreasing
I	10.0	10.0	10.0	2.7	2.7	100.0	1.7	1.7	100.0	2.0	2.0	100.0
II	10.0	10.0	10.0	3.4	6.1	97.3	2.7	4.4	98.3	2.0	4.0	98.0
III	10.0	10.0	10.0	3.8	9.9	93.9	3.1	7.5	95.6	2.5	6.5	96.0
IV	10.0	10.0	10.0	4.4	14.3	90.1	3.8	11.3	92.5	4.5	11.0	93.5
V	10.0	10.0	10.0	4.8	19.1	85.7	4.3	15.6	88.7	4.5	15.5	89.0
VI	10.0	10.0	10.0	5.5	24.6	80.9	5.6	21.2	84.4	6.0	21.5	84.5
VII	10.0	10.0	10.0	7.0	31.6[b]	75.4	7.4	28.6[b]	78.8	8.0	29.5[b]	78.5
VIII	10.0	10.0	10.0	8.6	40.2	68.4	10.0	38.6	71.4	11.5	41.0	70.5
IX	10.0	10.0	10.0	10.8	51.0	59.8	14.7	53.3	61.4	17.5	58.5	59.0
X	5.2	5.1	5.0	9.2	60.2	49.0	10.1	63.4	46.7	14.5	73.0	41.5
	2.4	2.6	2.5	7.5	67.7	39.8	12.6	76.0	36.6	11.0	84.0	27.0
	2.4	2.3	2.5	32.3	100.0	32.3	24.0	100.0	24.0	16.0	100.0	16.0
Totals	100.0	100.0	100.0	100.0			100.0			100.0		

[a] The lowest income families are in decile I and the highest in decile X.
[b] This may be interpreted to mean that 29.5 percent of the total disposable income in 1963 was earned by the lowest 70 percent of the families, compared with 28.6 percent in 1957 and 31.6 percent in 1950.
Sources: 1950 and 1957–Navarrete, *La Distribucion del Ingreso*, Table 12.
1963–Banco de México, "Distribucion del Ingreso Familiar," Table 1.

calculations. The figures for 1963 show a slightly higher share of income earned by those in the upper half of the income groups, with the exception of those in the top 4.8 percent, the share of which was 39.8 percent in 1950, 36.6 percent in 1957, and 27.0 percent in 1963.[7] In other words, the shares of the lowest 50 percent and the top 5 percent of population appear lower at the end of the thirteen year period than at the beginning, while that of the middle groups rises. In view of changes in sampling methods and estimating techniques, the data do not admit any clear statement about trends in distributive shares.

The suggestion from Table 2.10 that the average level of absolute personal income of the top 5 percent of the population was lower in 1963 than in 1957 requires further investigation. There was systematic underreporting of income in all these budget studies, with the upper income groups' share biased downward in the samples. Thus, the sum of total income derived from a blowup of the unadjusted data appears to be much below the level of disposable income estimated independently from national accounting data. To compensate for this problem, the 1950 and 1957 data were adjusted before publication by applying arbitrary coefficients of underreporting to the sampling data. These adjustments were higher for upper than for lower income groups. As a result, the higher the income group in the published tables, the more subject the data may be to sampling error and hence the less useful for purposes of comparison. Estimates in the middle and lower range are much more reliable than those in the top decile. The data for the upper middle range (deciles VI–IX) show a share of 31.9 percent in 1950, 37.7 percent in 1957, and 43 percent in 1963. This supports independent evidence of increasing relative importance of the middle class in Mexico as a source of both savings and purchasing power, a factor that has played a cru-

---

7. All three estimates are subject to discrepancies between the aggregation of reported personal incomes from the respective budget studies and independent estimates of personal income by the Banco de México. Attempts to bridge the gap due to underreporting of family incomes require a high degree of conjecture regarding the distribution of underreporting among income classes. The estimates for 1950 and 1957 by Ifigenia M. de Navarrete, *La Distribución del Ingreso y el Desarrollo Económico de México,* are based upon an arbitrary percentage increase for each income class that rises progressively with the level of family income (conversation with me). The method employed by the Banco de México in the 1963 estimates has not been specified. In either case, there is no way to ascertain the degree of positive or negative bias that such assumptions build into the data.

Table 2.10
Distribution of Personal Income by Deciles,
1950, 1957, and 1963

	Percent of Families			Average Monthly Income (1957 pesos)[a]		
Deciles	*1950*	*1957*	*1963*	*1950*	*1957*	*1963*
I	10.0	10.0	10.0	247	192	223
II	10.0	10.0	10.0	311	304	223
III	10.0	10.0	10.0	348	350	279
IV	10.0	10.0	10.0	403	429	502
V	10.0	10.0	10.0	440	485	502
VI	10.0	10.0	10.0	504	632	669
VII	10.0	10.0	10.0	641	835	892
VIII	10.0	10.0	10.0	788	1,128	1,282
IX	10.0	10.0	10.0	989	1,658	1,952
X	5.2	5.1	5.0	1,621	2,233	3,234
	2.4	2.6	2.5	2,858	5,460	4,907
	2.4	2.3	2.5	12,329	11,765	7,137
Totals	100.0	100.0	100.0			
Averages				916	1,128	1,115

[a] Based on the wholesale price index of the Banco de México.

Sources: 1950 and 1957–Ifigenia M. de Navarrete, *La Distribucion del Ingreso y el Desarrollo Económico de México*, Table 12.

1963–Banco de México, Departamento de Estudios Económicos, "Distribución del Ingreso Familiar, Graph 6 and Table 1.

cial role in the expansion of the internal market for domestic manufactures since 1950.

Subsistence agriculture is still widespread in Mexico, and real per capita output for these poorest families has not risen significantly for the past fifty years. There is evidence that the marginal productivity of unskilled labor has not risen significantly over the long run despite major gains in overall agricultural productivity. Thus income distribution has become increasingly skewed not only in agriculture but in the economy as a whole. A fairly abundant supply of unskilled labor still exists that is willing to work at subsistence wages even though output per worker has multiplied throughout the economy. The distribution of personal income in 1963 by major activities (Table 2.11) indicates that, although 30.3 percent of disposable income was earned by families with average monthly incomes below 1,250 pesos, this was 47.1 percent in agriculture compared with only 29.5 percent in industry and 20.9 percent in services. Lorenz curve estimates based upon the 1963 budget study indicate that the

Table 2.11
Distribution of Personal Income by Sectors, 1963
(percent)

Income Class (pesos per month)	Total			Percent of Income by Income Class								
		Cumulative Percentage		Agriculture			Industry			Services		
		Cumulative Percentage			Cumulative Percentage			Cumulative Percentage			Cumulative Percentage	
	Per-cent	Increas-ing	Decreas-ing	Per-cent	Increas-ing	Decreas-ing	Per-cent	Increas-ing	Decreas-ing	Per-cent	Increas-ing	Decreas-ing
0–175	0.5	0.5	100.0	1.2	1.2	100.0	0.1	0.1	100.0	0.2	0.2	100.0
176–225	0.7	1.2	99.5	2.0	3.2	98.8	0.1	0.2	99.9	0.3	0.5	99.8
226–300	1.9	3.1	98.8	4.3	7.5	96.8	0.9	1.1	99.8	1.0	1.5	99.5
301–400	3.0	6.1	96.9	7.4	14.9	92.5	1.4	2.5	98.9	1.2	2.7	98.5
401–530	3.3	9.4	93.9	6.6	21.5	85.1	2.5	5.0	97.5	1.8	4.5	97.3
531–700	5.9	15.3	90.6	8.1	29.6	78.5	6.7	11.7	95.0	4.3	8.8	95.5
701–950	8.0	23.3	84.7	10.9	40.5	70.4	9.0	20.7	88.3	5.8	14.6	91.2
951–1,250	7.0	30.3[a]	76.7	6.6	47.1	59.5	8.8	29.5	79.3	6.3	20.9	85.4
1,251–1,700	9.6	39.9	69.7	5.9	53.0	52.9	12.5	42.0	70.5	10.3	31.2	79.1
1,701–2,200	9.3	49.2	60.1	10.6	63.6	47.0	7.8	49.8	58.0	9.2	40.4	68.8
2,201–3,000	10.9	60.1	50.8	10.8	74.4	36.4	8.8	58.6	50.2	12.1	52.5	59.6
3,001–4,000	9.0	69.1	39.9	6.7	81.1	25.6	9.4	68.0	41.4	10.0	62.5	47.5
4,001–5,200	7.7	76.8	30.9	5.4	86.5	18.9	9.4	77.4	32.0	8.2	70.7	37.5
5,201–7,000	7.7	84.5	23.2	6.0	92.5	13.5	4.8	82.2	22.6	10.2	80.9	29.3
7,001–9,200	3.9	88.4	15.5	1.0	93.5	7.5	2.9	85.1	17.8	6.0	86.9	19.1
Over 9,200	11.6	100.0	11.6	6.5	100.0	6.5	14.9	100.0	14.9	13.1	100.0	13.1

[a] As an example of the interpretation of this table, 30.3 percent of the disposable income in Mexico in 1963 was earned by families with average monthly incomes below 1,250 pesos.

Source: Banco de México, "Distribución del Ingreso Familiar," Table 2.

lowest 25 percent of families in agriculture received only 3.4 percent of personal income generated in that sector compared with 4.7 percent in industry and 5.0 percent in services. The lower 50 percent of families in agriculture received 13.2 percent of income in agriculture, 16.0 percent in industry, and 15.0 percent in services, compared with a national average of 14.0 percent.[8]

The data in Table 2.10 show that, despite rapid economic development since 1950, the average monthly real income for the lower 20 percent of the population appears to have been lower in 1957 than in 1950, although the 1950 share is approached in the 1963 estimates. On the other hand, the real income of the top 30 percent of the population may have been higher in 1957 than in 1950 with the exception of those in the highest two brackets. Independent budget study estimates of the Banco de México for 1963 confirm the high degree of inequality in income between rural and urban areas. The figures in Table 2.12 show that, although on the average 30.3 percent of total income in 1963 was received by families with incomes of under 1,250 pesos per month, the figure was up to 50.3 percent in rural areas compared with only 18 percent for urban dwellers. While monetary estimates fail to allow for differences in purchasing power of the peso in the cities and countryside, no reasonable adjustment prevents one from concluding that, if workers adjust expectations to average income differentials, the inducement to move to the cities continues to be great. Expectations of this kind are subject to qualification, as the share of employment in the lowest occupations (along with unemployment) in the cities rises over time. There is some evidence that this has been true for Mexico, since the employment share in "services and other occupations" between 1940 and 1960 rose by 7.8 percent (Table 2.3). Nevertheless, the growth of the corresponding share of output in these labor absorptive sectors greatly surpassed that of employment (23.2 percent) over the same interval (Table 2.2) causing the average output per worker in tertiary activities to grow rapidly. This factor is examined in greater detail in Chapter. 5.

The historical evidence regarding distributional trends in Mexico (Table 2.9) is worth reviewing in the light of a hypothesis, raised by Simon Kuznets, that developing countries will experience a "long swing in inequality":

8. Banco de México, Departamento de Estudios Económicos, "Distribución del Ingreso Familiar–México 1963," Table 3.

Table 2.12
Distribution of Personal Income with Urban-Rural Breakdown, 1963
(percent)

Percent of Income by Income Class

Income Class (pesos per month)	Total			Urban			Rural		
		Cumulative Percentage			Cumulative Percentage			Cumulative Percentage	
	Percent	Increasing	Decreasing	Percent	Increasing	Decreasing	Percent	Increasing	Decreasing
0–175	0.5	0.5	100.0	0.1	0.1	100.0	1.1	1.1	100.0
176–225	0.7	1.2	99.5	0.2	0.3	99.9	1.7	2.8	98.9
226–300	1.9	3.1	98.8	0.4	0.7	99.7	4.4	7.2	97.2
301–400	3.0	6.1	96.9	0.8	1.5	99.3	6.5	13.7	92.8
401–530	3.3	9.4	93.9	1.5	3.0	98.5	6.2	19.9	86.3
531–700	5.9	15.3	90.6	3.1	6.1	97.0	10.5	30.4	80.1
701–950	8.0	23.3	84.7	5.3	11.4	93.9	12.2	42.6	69.6
951–1,250	7.0	30.3[a]	76.7[a]	6.6	18.0	88.6	7.7	50.3	57.4
1,251–1,700	9.6	39.9	69.7	9.6	27.6	82.0	9.6	59.9	49.7
1,701–2,200	9.3	49.2	60.1	9.7	37.3	72.4	8.5	68.4	40.1
2,201–3,000	10.9	60.1	50.8	11.4	48.7	62.7	10.3	78.7	31.6
3,001–4,000	9.0	69.1	39.9	9.1	57.8	51.3	8.8	87.5	21.3
4,001–5,200	7.7	76.8	30.9	9.5	67.3	42.2	4.9	92.4	12.5
5,201–7,000	7.7	84.5	23.2	10.4	77.7	32.7	3.3	95.7	7.6
7,001–9,200	3.9	88.4	15.5	5.9	83.6	22.3	0.6	96.3	4.3
Over 9,200	11.6	100.0	11.6	16.4	100.0	16.4	3.7	100.0	3.7

[a] 30.3 percent is the percent of total income received by all families with incomes from 0 to 1,250 pesos per month.
76.7 percent is the percent of total income received by all families with incomes greater than 950 pesos per month.
Source: Banco de México, "Distribución del Ingreso Familiar," Table 5.

One might thus assume a long swing in the inequality characterizing the secular income structure: widening in the early phases of economic growth when the transition from the pre-industrial civilization was most rapid; becoming stabilized for a while; and then narrowing in the later phases. This long secular swing would be most pronounced for older countries where the dislocation effects of the earlier phases of modern economic growth were most conspicuous.[9]

The pattern of increasing and then decreasing income inequality is said to be particularly characteristic of economies with sharp differences in productivity between the traditional and modern sectors. Such has certainly been the case for Mexico since 1900, not only as between rural and urban activities but within agriculture itself, as described in detail in Chapter 3. According to Professor Kuznets, the long swing in income inequality is associated with similar movements in other variables, including (1) an acceleration and then deceleration in the rate of population growth, first through a fall in the death rate and then through a fall in the birth rate as development progresses; (2) a secular swing in the rate of urbanization; (3) a secular swing in the proportion of savings or capital formation to total economic product since the share of profits and rental income tends to be more skewed than that of wages and salaries; (4) a possible swing in the rate of foreign trade to domestic activities, presumably owing to the enclave aspects of export industries; and (5) a swing in the incidence of taxation that is first regressive, due to the importance of indirect levies on trade, and then progressive, as direct taxes are increasingly applied.[10]

In terms of the explanatory factors, the Mexican case provides mixed results. Population growth is still accelerating and taxation has yet to become progressive, while the rates of increase in urbanization and savings/investment are beginning to decline. In general, Mexico does seem to have shifted from increasing income inequality between 1950 and 1957 (continuing a trend which probably began as early

9. Kuznets, "Economic Growth and Income Inequality," p. 276. Kuznets experienced some difficulty in finding empirical evidence to support his hypothesis. This is partly due to the paucity of historical statistics on income distribution in the early stages of development of the industrial countries. His data for the U.S. (1929–50), United Kingdom (1880–1947), and Prussia (1875–1913) all indicate increasing equality rather than inequality for the respective periods (pp. 260, 261).
10. Ibid., pp. 276 ff.

as 1940) to fairly constant or perhaps decreasing inequality since the mid-1950s. While the statistical foundations of these observations are weak, as mentioned above, the Mexican experience does provide some tentative support for the Kuznets hypothesis.

The increase in income differentials in Mexico through 1957 was the natural result of a rising inequality in output per worker within the structure of production itself. A relatively abundant supply of unskilled labor existed that could be drawn from subsistence agriculture and service occupations into sectors with rising productivity during the development process, permitting wages to lag behind prices during the inflationary years of the 1940s and early 1950s. This served to slow the growth of real income for the working class, and real wages actually appear to have fallen in some occupations during the 1940s. The adverse welfare implications of this trend in real wages were to some extent offset for individual workers and their families by internal migration and movement up the employment ladder.[11] Rural families have been helped in recent years by farm price supports, and urban workers have received increased salary supplement benefits, state-subsidized consumer staples, social security, health, education, and other nonwage benefits. Nevertheless, those unfortunate persons who remained in the lowest occupational categories—peasant cultivators and unskilled urban service workers in particular—have experienced undoubted hardships and have forgone many of the benefits of rapid economic growth. Land redistribution through the agrarian reform may have mitigated these factors in earlier years by offering a sense of property ownership and dignity to the impoverished *campesino*. In a broader sense, the working class has been indoctrinated into a set of values that was termed the "ethos of revolution" in Chapter 1, an ethos that official party candidates, business, and labor leaders have used to identify aggregate economic growth with a generalized concept of social welfare. This ethos has paid undoubted dividends in the past by providing psychic income to offset losses in relative income shares for the working

11. Adolf Sturmthal accounts for the apparent contradiction between rising per capita income in the form of wages and salaries (1940–50) and falling real wages in terms of (1) a shift in employment from low wage occupations in agriculture to industry, changes in the structure of employment including: (2) a shift in employment toward higher skills within given industries, and (3) a shift in employment among industries toward those with higher productivities. "Economic Development, Income Distribution, and Capital Formation in Mexico."

class. But the period during which such ideological inputs may be drawn upon effectively cannot be expected to span more than a few decades. Most Mexican planners recognize that attention must increasingly be directed to improvements in the productivity and real income of unskilled labor if political stability is to continue.

PRICES, FACTOR COSTS, AND THE RATE OF INVESTMENT: 1940–65

Growing inequality in personal income distribution during the decade of development from 1940 to 1950 is associated with increased profit shares and a rise in the rate of gross investment from 10 to 15 percent of GDP. The first detailed estimate of income distribution by factor shares was made by a commission of the World Bank as reported in *El Desarrollo Económico de México,* 1953, Table 2. This study showed property income (profits, interest, and rent) increasing from 35.2 percent of national income in 1940 to 47.0 percent in 1950. Because the 1950 share was based upon preliminary figures, it was subsequently revised by the Bank of Mexico to 33.7 percent, reversing the trend.[12] Mexican economist Ifigenia Navarrete, in a now-classic work on income distribution, criticized this revision as relying on too low a margin for commerce in the 1950 input-output table.[13] Accepting a larger estimate for profits from commercial transactions, she concluded that "it is probable that an intermediate estimate (for total profits) is closer to reality." If the two alternative profit estimates are averaged, the property share of GDP for 1950 becomes 40.4 percent, a significant increase over that of 1940.

The wage and salary shares of income in the original Mixed Commission estimates fell from 29.7 percent in 1940 to 23.9 percent in 1950. The 1950 revision raised this share to 29.6 percent. The remaining components were net agricultural income (20.7 percent in 1940 and 19.8 percent in 1950, eventually revised to 26.1 percent) and nonagricultural mixed incomes (14.7 percent in 1940 and 9.5 percent in 1950, with the latter revised to 10.4 percent). Functional income distribution figures are not yet available for years after 1950 owing to the lack of an integrated set of national accounts, though estimates may be inferred from the 1960 input-output table of the Banco de México.[14] The table shows wages and salaries to be only

12. Banco de México, Nacional Financiera, and others, *Estructura y Proyecciones de la Economía de México,* Table 4, pp. 182–89, cited in Navarrete, *La Distribución del Ingreso,* p. 57.

13. Navarrete, *La Distribución del Ingreso,* p. 44 n., and pp. 56 and 58.

31.2 percent of GDP in 1960, or a slight increase over the revised 1950 figure. Profits, rents, and mixed incomes are unfortunately reported jointly in the table, making it impossible to compare these figures with those of earlier years.

Despite the statistical problems involved in any interpretation of functional income distribution, it is likely that the profit share increased substantially between 1940 and 1950 and remained relatively constant thereafter. Table 2.13 reveals the trend in money and real

Table 2.13
Legal Minimum Daily Wages, Rural and Urban,
for Selected Years: 1934–65

Year	1 Rural	2 Urban	3 Rural	4 Urban	5 Rural	6 Urban
	(current pesos per day)		(current U.S. dollars per day)		(index in 1950 pesos) (1950 = 100)	
1934–35	1.10	1.31	$ .31	$ .36	163	139
1940–41	1.28	1.85	.25	.36	134	138
1944–45	1.48	2.46	.31	.51	85	101
1950–51	2.82	3.93	.33	.45	100	100
1954–55	6.29	7.84	.53	.66	152	135
1960–61	8.45	11.46	.68	.92	158	153
1964–65	12.70	17.24	1.02	1.38	218	212

Sources and Methods: Columns 1 and 2 represent the weighted average of minimum wages by federal entity as obtained from Dirección General de Estadística, Comision Nacional de Salarios Mínimos, and assembled by José S. Alarcon.

Columns 3 and 4 are conversions of columns 1 and 2 at the official exchange rate for the average of each biennium.

Columns 5 and 6 are conversions of an index of minimum wages in current pesos based on 1 and 2 above by the wholesale price index for Mexico City.

minimum wages for both rural and urban areas since 1934. An attempt to estimate the share of value added in agricultural output implicit in rural minimum wage levels in Chapter 3 indicates that actual rural wages were considerably below the level of minimum wages in the 1930s, but that they have been approaching and even surpassing the legal minimum for most regions in recent years. As a result, the downtrend in real wages in agriculture between 1934 and 1945 is probably exaggerated, and the upward increase from 1950 to 1964 is understated, by using minimum wage figures.

14. Banco de México, "Cuadro de Insumo Producto de México, 1960." Since this was written, preliminary estimates of the post–1950 period have become available (see Appendix C).

Real wages for unskilled labor in both rural and urban areas probably did not increase between the mid-1930s and 1945, and there is some evidence that they actually declined during the early 1940s. The fact that price increases outstripped increases in money wages and salaries supports the functional income distributional evidence that profit shares rose during the 1940s. Similarly, the suggestion of fairly constant shares of profit plus mixed income in the 1950s accords with the more favorable performance of real wages in this period. An additional element in the dispersion of prices and costs in the 1940s was the behavior of real borrowing rates. The marginal cost of investable funds in real terms may even have been negative in some of the more inflationary years of the postwar period. For example, the wholesale price index in Table 2.14 is shown to have risen by more than 10 percent in 1950 and 1951, while the nominal rate of interest in these years averaged 11.3 percent. For those firms that were able to gain access to funds at this negligible real rate of interest and were able to employ labor at a constant or diminishing real wage rate, price increases represented a windfall that was reflected in excess profits, a high rate of private savings, and an increasing marginal efficiency of private investment in the postwar period. Since the mid-1950s, however, there is strong evidence that real borrowing costs have risen, adding to the cost pressures of rising real wages.

Additional support for the contention that profit shares increased during the 1940s is reflected in the notable increase in gross investment as a share of gross domestic product between 1940 and 1950, regardless of which of the four alternative measures of gross fixed investment one uses (Table 7.8). Estimate A, which is judged to be most reliable for purposes of this study, shows gross investment rising from 9.9 percent of gross domestic product in 1940 to 14.7 percent in 1950. This share continued to rise to 18.9 percent in 1955 and 21.3 percent in 1960, compared to earlier figures that show the 1960 share to be 13.6 percent (expressed in current prices).

Since all of the estimates show the investment share of GDP to increase by one-third to one-half over the first decade of development, and since the share of government direct investment in total investment did not increase during the period from 1940 to 1950, one must examine the effect of changes in the profit share of income on private savings and investment decisions in order to arrive at an explanation for the wave of investment that took place in the 1940s. Once rapid

Table 2.14

Liquidity, Price Level, and Interest Rates: 1940–64

Year	Money Supply[a] Total	Money Supply[a] Coin and Currency (millions of pesos, end of year)	Checking Deposits	Velocity of Circulation[b]	Corrected Figures (average during the year)	Rate of Interest[c]	Wholesale Prices[d] (1950 = 100)	Terms of Trade[e] (1950 = 100)	Exchange Rate (pesos per dollar; average)
1940	1,060.4	661.2	399.2	8.0			33.0	75.3	5.40
1941	1,269.5	797.3	472.2	7.5			35.2	62.7	4.86
1942	1,749.9	1,021.1	728.8	7.4			38.8	69.1	4.85
1943	2,672.9	1,477.5	1,195.4	6.1			46.8	80.7	4.85
1944	3,309.9	1,768.1	1,511.8	5.9			57.4	91.9	4.85
1945	3,539.5	1,657.9	1,881.6	5.8			63.9	99.6	4.85
1946	3,460.3	1,728.6	1,732.2	7.5			73.5	99.9	4.85
1947	3,438.7	1,753.8	1,684.9	8.6			77.8	109.0	4.85
1948	3,916.9	2,121.0	1,795.9	8.9		9.65	83.4	112.2	5.76
1949	4,352.4	2,378.4	1,974.5	8.9		10.58	91.4	105.9	8.02
1950	5,988.5	2,914.2	3,074.3	8.5	8.2	10.66	100.0	100.0	8.65
1951	6,800.9	3,457.8	3,343.1	8.2	8.3	11.41	124.0	105.6	8.65
1952	7,078.0	3,648.6	3,429.4	8.9	8.9	11.29	128.6	108.2	8.65
1953	7,652.9	3,863.6	3,789.3	8.0	8.3	10.57	126.1	106.6	8.65
1954	8,723.5	4,637.0	4,086.5	8.5	9.2	11.54	137.9	96.3	11.34
1955	10,516.7	5,084.0	5,432.7	8.9	9.3	11.41	156.7	93.8	12.50
1956	11,692.2	5,734.2	5,988.0	8.9	9.4	12.03	164.0	91.9	12.50
1957	12,493.4	6,093.5	6,399.9	8.9	9.9	12.59	171.0	86.4	12.50
1958	13,386.8	6,615.1	6,771.7	9.2	10.3	12.96	178.6	75.3	12.50
1959	15,434.4	7,250.5	8,183.9	8.8	8.8	13.36	180.7	75.6	12.50
1960	16,909.3	7,871.7	9,037.6	8.6	9.2	13.98	189.7	76.1	12.50
1961	17,889.6	8,275.4	9,614.2	8.5	9.9	14.53	191.4	75.9	12.50
1962	20,112.1	9,144.1	10,968.0		9.9	14.37	194.9	77.2	12.50
1963	23,474.3	10,263.8	13,210.5		9.4	13.70	196.0		12.50
1964						12.41			

a Coin, currency, and checking-deposit liabilities of Banco de México and deposit banks.

b Computed as ratio of annual gross national product to average money supply during year.

c Estimated as the average yield on the assets of private banking institutions, excluding legally required investments.

d Index of prices of 210 articles in Mexico City.

e Computed as ratio of annual index of export prices to annual index of import prices. Data for the years 1940–54 are taken from publications of the Economic Commission for Latin America; data for the years 1955–60 are taken from publications of Banco Nacional de Comercio Exterior.

Sources: *Annual Reports* of Banco de México and publications of the Banco Nacional de Comercio Exterior and CEPAL. This table corresponds to that in Brothers and Solís, *Mexican Financial Development*, p. 74, for 1940–60, except for the column of "Corrected Figures."

growth was well underway by the mid-1950s, it is likely that rising incomes of the middle class provided a growing source of investable funds without the need for further increases in the profit share of GDP. The capture of these savings for internal growth was facilitated by the rapid growth of financial intermediaries in a climate of free convertibility and price stability. Institutional reforms and attitudinal changes associated with the Revolution may well have provided the degrees of freedom within which increases in income inequality were permitted to take place since 1940. Indeed, there is some question that, in the absence of revolution and reform, the changes in the distribution of income and product over the past thirty years would or could have occurred without dangerous political and social repercussions.

3

Agrarian Revolution in Mexico:
A History of Agricultural Production
and Productivity, 1900–1960

THE AGRICULTURAL SETTING IN HISTORICAL PERSPECTIVE

Perhaps the most impressive aspect of Mexico is the land itself. Its geological magnitude dwarfs even the great architectural monuments that dot the landscape. The country is broken roughly into thirds by two great longitudinal mountain ranges, the Sierra Madre Occidental to the west and the Sierra Madre Oriental to the east. Between these two ranges and extending from the American border to below Mexico City is the high plateau, a tableland rising thousands of feet above sea level. Although this plateau is a desert in the north, its central regions have a temperate climate and are watered by seasonal rains.

To the east and west of the great mountain ranges lie tropical lowlands, the valleys of which reach like fingers into the high plateau. These regions, known as the *tierra caliente,* follow the contours of the coast and cover much of the southern third of the country. Here nature does nothing by halves and a turn of the season may bring flood or drought. A journey of a few miles takes one from subtropical rain forest to burning desert, yet even in such inhospitable climes there are remnants of well-developed cultures that depended for their growth upon the productivity of agriculture. The history of the interaction between agricultural development and urbanization in Mexico extends thousands of years into the past. Ruins throughout the country attest to the decline and fall of complex civilizations that were supported by productivity gains in agriculture. These early increases in productivity were mobilized by political and priestly hierarchies that appear to have used material and ideological persuasion as well as physical coercion to channel a growing agricultural surplus into the development of great cities.

As early as 5000 B.C. cave dwellers in the south-central Valley of Tehuacán were domesticating wild maize. The first records of agriculture in the Western Hemisphere trace back to these settlements. Recent excavations show that from 5000 B.C. to the time of Christ the people in this region of Mexico increased the length of an average ear of corn from one inch to four inches, apparently through selective seeding, irrigation, and other improvements in cultivation.[1] Agricultural development in Mesoamerica eventually permitted even higher stages of urban civilization. Archaeologists and ecologists have examined the remains of the great classic civilization of Teotihuacán that flourished during the first millennium A.D. Initial evidence suggests that by damming arroyos and terracing surrounding hillsides, the settlers of this valley were able to bring about increases in agricultural production capable of sustaining an urban population of as many as 100,000 priests, artisans, merchants, and other nonagricultural workers in the city of Teotihuacán itself (site of Mexico's great pyramids).[2] Centuries later, a high level of agricultural productivity in the Valley of Mexico was observed firsthand by the Spaniards under Cortez, who marveled at the "floating islands" (*chinampas*) which supplied food for the Aztec capital of Tenochtitlán.[3]

The interaction between agricultural development and urbanization may account not only for the rise of pre-Colombian civilizations but also for their decline. Increasing urbanization placed ever greater demands upon the rural sector for foodstuffs and raw materials. In exchange, urban dwellers were able to offer to the farmer the promise of security from invasion, theft, internal revolt, and divine interference and also works of art, literature, music, and simple manufactures. But before the Industrial Revolution the possibilities of exchange between cities and countryside were limited at best. The

1. The early maize culture of the Tehuacán Valley is described by Richard S. MacNeish in "The Origins of New World Civilization."

2. A preliminary analysis of the socioeconomic ecology of the classical civilization in the Valley of Teotihuacán is presented in William T. Sanders, "The Cultural Ecology of the Teotihuacán Valley."

3. For a description of agriculture in the Valley of Mexico at the time of the Conquest, see Charles Gibson, *The Aztecs Under Spanish Rule,* Chapter 11. A detailed ecological model relating improvements in agricultural technology to urbanization in Mesoamerica is found in Robert McCormick Adams, *The Evolution of Urban Society,* especially Chapter II ("Subsistence and Settlement").

rate of improvement in agricultural productivity could not be sustained by early civilizations for long periods of time. Indeed ecological research suggests that soil depletion and/or weed encroachment may well have reduced the level of agricultural productivity over time even for a stable population, especially in certain regions of Mesoamerica, such as Yucatán. And productivity gains in urban activities almost certainly did not arise to permit the rural/urban terms of trade to rise significantly to induce voluntary increases in man-hours devoted to cultivation. As the size of the military, administrative, priestly, and artisan classes grew relative to those employed in agriculture, the burden placed on the rural population for support of the burgeoning cities doubtless increased. In an effort to maintain their demands upon agriculture, it is likely that leaders of the pre-Colombian city states found themselves in ever more unstable political circumstances. Caught between expanding urban demand for food and rising rural resentment, the political administrators of the cities might well have succumbed to internal revolt if not external conquest, leaving their civilizations open to plunder, disintegration, and eventual destruction.[4]

In the perspective of Mexican history, the past sixty years are but a moment. Yet the experience of this half century, particularly in agriculture, holds out more hope for the eventual prosperity of the country than any of the great epochs of the past. Modern revolutions in agricultural and industrial technology have changed the conditions of production and with them the possibility of sustained growth. The future of the country is no longer likely to be subjected to a relentless cycle of growth and decline as defined in pre-Colombian cosmology. In this respect an examination of the behavior of the agricultural sector may provide important clues to the development of the rest of the economy. Agriculture is increasingly being placed first among the preconditions for successful economic development by students of development history. Productivity gains in agriculture provide, not only labor and raw materials for industrial growth, but also foreign exchange to provide importables unavailable locally and to relieve excess demand at growing points in the overall economy. If agriculture lags behind the growth of urban demand, relative prices may turn against urban activities and food imports increase at the expense of

4. This argument is developed somewhat further in my "Notes on an Agricultural Productivity Model to Explain the Rise and Fall of a Pre-Conquest Civilization" (unpublished, 1964).

imported capital and intermediate goods thereby retarding economic growth. To prevent this occurrence from taking place in Mexico, government administrators have adopted policies designed to steer a precarious course between rural and urban development with the objective of maximizing the rate of growth consistent with political stability. This chapter deals with the effect of these policies on agricultural production and productivity since 1900.

NATIONAL AGRICULTURAL OUTPUT TRENDS, 1900–60

Mexico in 1910 resembled a typical Latin American export economy based upon mining, livestock, and cash crop production, with output increases in these sectors directed primarily toward foreign markets. Income and product fluctuated with the international trade cycle. Scattered enclaves of commercial agriculture and mining were surrounded by a sea of subsistence cultivation in which a majority of the population was employed.[5] Such conditions were typical of Latin American countries at the turn of the century. Since the Revolution a new institutional framework has evolved, unique to Mexico, which draws upon the productive potential of a much greater share of the population than before. Government policies pursued during the past half century have expanded rural economic and social infrastructure in such a way as to increase the relative role of internal demand, despite the growing absolute importance of foreign markets to agricultural growth. Labor, which would otherwise have been underemployed, has been able to receive land through the agrarian reform

5. The term "subsistence" used here and elsewhere in the text is a relative concept. Mexican peasant farmers, even at the lowest levels of income and productivity, have always exchanged a significant share of their crops in local markets. Some of this produce inevitably found its way to large commercial centers. But in terms of the capacity of these cultivators to accumulate savings and raise their living levels, most have remained "subsistence" farmers. "Subsistence agriculture" is therefore applied in this volume to those peasant farms which have demonstrated a low and relatively constant output per worker and hence a relatively constant marginal productivity of labor over the long run. This condition is the result of the existence of large areas of land in Mexico that, although tending to remain extramarginal from the point of view of the exchange economy, have been inframarginal to the family units supported by them. After the Revolution agrarian reform helped to open up portions of this "extramarginal" land to small cultivators. Hitherto it had been in the interest of many commercial growers to restrict the use of this land so as to insure a large supply of cheap labor at peak periods of planting and harvesting.

program and to find markets for its produce as a result of expanded internal as well as external trade. The lessons from this experience are of value to other countries facing similar problems of excess demand for crop production and excess supply of rural labor.

Since 1900, the population of Mexico has increased by two and one-half times and agricultural production sixfold, while the share of population dependent upon the land has declined by almost one-third (see Table 3.1). This rapid growth in agricultural output per worker has permitted millions of peasants to be absorbed into other sectors of the economy, real per capita income and consumption to rise in rural areas, and the country as a whole to achieve a rising rate of savings and investment. Since Mexico experienced one of the most sweeping agrarian reforms in modern history during the same period, one is inclined to look for relationships between revolutionary changes in land tenure and agricultural productivity. (Those unfamiliar with

Table 3.1
Rural Population and Labor Force as Share of Total
(percents)

	1900	1910	1921	1930	1940	1950	1960
Rural population as share of total population[a]	71.7	71.2	68.8	66.5	64.9	57.4	49.3
Rural active population as share of total active population[b]	61.9[c] (65.9)	67.1	71.4	70.2[c] (67.9)	65.4	58.3	54.1

[a] "Rural" population is defined here and elsewhere as those living in communities of less than 2,500 persons.

[b] Rural active population includes workers in agriculture, livestock, forestry, hunting, and fishing.

[c] According to the Keesing estimates of rural active population as described in the note to Table 1.2, rural active population as a share of total active population would be 65.9 percent in 1900 and 67.9 percent in 1930.

Sources and Methods: The percentages are based on data from Population Censuses for stated years. These figures, which can be found in Appendix Tables E.1 and E.3, are of variable reliability; some censuses (such as that of 1921) are of doubtful quality, and others (such as that of 1910) are relatively reliable. Demographers, applying consistency checks, have adjusted the 1960 census figure for total population upward by 3.1 percent (from 34,923,000 to 36,003,000). See Grupo Secretaría de Hacienda-Banco de México, Estudios sobre Proyecciones, "Manual de Estadísticas Básicas," Table 9.1. Errors of undercounting typically occur in rural areas where census-taking occasionally becomes more thrilling than big game hunting; yet the reported figures include official adjustments of the returns that sometimes overcompensate for incomplete coverage.

the institutional aspects of Mexican agrarian reform may wish to read the summary in Chapter 4 at this point.) The analysis of this problem is complicated by the fact that this was also a period of technological revolution in Mexican farming. New methods of land reclamation permitted the irrigation of vast tracts of northern desert. The use of pesticides opened up much of the tropical lowlands to cultivation. Improved plant varieties and expanded use of chemical fertilizers greatly increased yields throughout the country (especially in wheat and maize) although much of the increase from these factors took place since the late 1950s. Thousands of miles of trunk highways and feeder roads were constructed, connecting rural areas with expanding urban and foreign markets. Primary education spread throughout the hinterlands, and labor skills in agriculture generally improved.

In explaining the growth of Mexican agriculture since 1900, it is necessary to estimate relationships between output and the changing level of both economic and social inputs. These production relationships have been influenced not only by shifts in technology but also by tenure reform, both of which have interacted to affect farmers' expectations and discounts for risk. This chapter represents a first step in the direction of isolating and analyzing the relationships between physical inputs and output by decade and by region. The next chapter deals with institutional influences on production through agrarian reform and associated policies. For purposes of analysis agricultural production is divided into five zones (North, North Pacific, South Pacific, Center, and Gulf)[6] with crop production

6. These five zones follow state boundary lines and are those used by the Dirección General de Estadística for the reporting of decennial agricultural census information. They comprise roughly similar geographical regions, although there are wide variations from state to state and even within certain states in terms of elevation, rainfall, temperature, ethnic composition, and living levels. The regions are defined as follows:

North: Coahuila, Chihuahua, Durango, Nuevo León, San Luís Potosí, Tamaulipas, Zacatecas.
North Pacific: Baja California Norte, Baja California Sur, Nayarit, Sinaloa, Sonora.
South Pacific: Colima, Chiapas, Guerrero, Oaxaca.
Center: Aguascalientes, Distrito Federal (Mexico City), Guanajuato, Hidalgo, Jalisco, Mexico, Michoacán, Morelos, Puebla, Querétaro, Tlaxcala.
Gulf: Campeche, Quintana Roo, Tabasco, Veracruz, Yucatán.

The census figures for agricultural production include crops consumed on the farm. In this study, forestry, animal husbandry, and fisheries are excluded except where specifically mentioned.

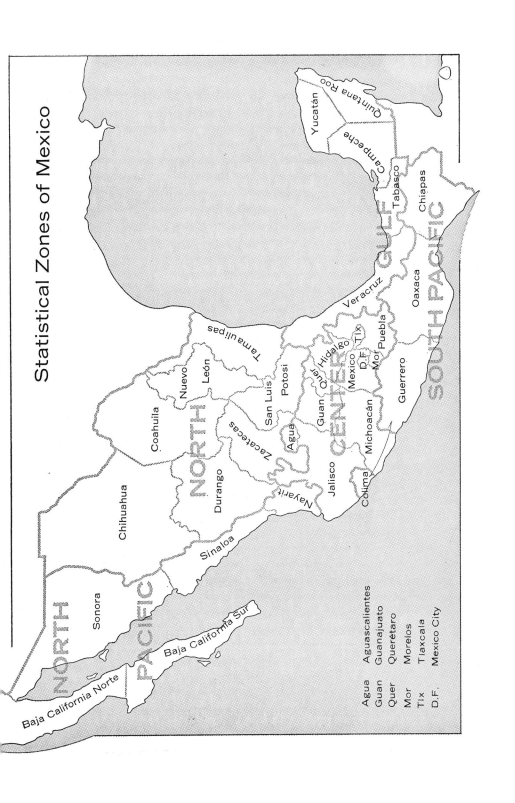

Statistical Zones of Mexico

Agua — Aguascalientes
Guan — Guanajuato
Quer — Querétaro
Mor — Morelos
Tlx — Tlaxcala
D.F. — Mexico City

figures for the bench-mark years 1900, 1907, 1930, 1940, 1950, and 1960. Official statistics of the Porfirian government are relied upon for the first two years and decennial agricultural censuses for the years since 1930. (The five zones are shown on the accompanying map.)

Agricultural factor inputs have also been estimated on both a regional and national basis since 1930. The figures on inputs and outputs are grouped in terms of the three major epochs of Mexican economic development since 1900, as outlined in Chapter 1. These periods evidence such wide differences in the pattern and rate of growth of crop production that they might have characterized three different countries (see Table 3.2). During the Porfiriato the growth

Table 3.2
Growth of Crop Production During the Major Periods
of Mexican Economic Development
(compound annual rates of growth)

	Porfiriato[a] 1877/1910	Revolution and Reform 1910/1940	Development 1940/1960
1. Total real crop production	0.6	1.1	6.3
2. Total population	1.4	0.9	2.9
3. Per capita crop production (1. minus 2.)	−0.8	0.2	3.4

[a] The period in the first column is 1877/1907. See Table 3.3, n. 3 for a discussion of the data for the years 1907–10.

Source: Data from Table 3.3 reperiodized.

of total agricultural production (crops, cattle, forestry, and fishing) failed to keep pace with that of population. Food crop production for domestic consumption lagged behind the rapid growth of agricultural exports. The latter, which included henequen, cotton, tobacco, coffee, and cattle, rose by 6 percent per year between 1877 and 1910 and accounted for a large share of Mexico's foreign exchange earnings, even though their combined terms of trade fell by 12 percent from 1900 to 1910 (after previous gains of an even greater amount). During this period an increasing share of the land was being shifted into the production of cash crops and cattle raising; the share of exports in total agricultural production rose from 4 percent in 1877 to 15 percent in 1907, and was perhaps as high as 19 percent in 1910.[7] With the trend away from food crop production for domestic

7. El Colegio de México, *Fuerza de Trabajo.*

consumption and toward exports, the relative price of foodstuffs rose by over 20 percent during the last decade of the Porfiriato.

This pattern was reversed during the years of sweeping institutional change from 1910 to 1940. After the decimating effects on population and cultivation of the revolutionary years 1910 to 1920, crop production began to recover and even surpass earlier levels of cultivation, so that from 1910 to 1940 output almost kept pace with population growth. The welfare implications of this process, from the point of view of rural dwellers who were formerly landless, is understated by the statistics. Although total crop production increased by only one-third between 1925 and 1940 (barely more than population growth that was already beginning to accelerate after the destructive effects of the Revolution), food crop production increased by one half and owner consumption of farm output rose dramatically between 1930 and 1940.

The years since 1940 have witnessed a reawakening of foreign demand for Mexican agricultural exports and a corresponding expansion of commercial agriculture, much of it on newly irrigated land. Food crop production has risen by 140 percent (1939–60) and total crop production by 184 percent, greatly exceeding population growth and permitting significant increases in per capita consumption, industrial inputs, and exports. This performance reflects a combination of new techniques of cultivation and massive public as well as private investment in agriculture. These investments were brought about partly through the increased commitment of the federal government to the rural sector following the Revolution. However, they have not been made in a balanced fashion either regionally or by tenure class. Indeed, much of the cultivation in Mexico remains tied to primitive techniques and is barely able to sustain those working the land. As a result, the sea of subsistence agriculture has not yet dried up, though the islands of commercial cultivation are encroaching upon it continually as a rising share of the rural population benefits from the agricultural revolution. There are not two agricultures in Mexico but many, and they overlap not only by region but even on individual plots, where a farmer may plant part of his land in cash crops and the remainder in traditional subsistence crops (such as maize and beans) as a primitive form of social insurance for himself and his family.

AGRICULTURAL DUALISM AND REGIONAL PER CAPITA OUTPUT

The recent history of Mexican agriculture is therefore one of a gradual transition from subsistence to commercial crop production. Although this process has touched most parts of the country, some regions have gained more than others. The regional pattern of agricultural production per rural dweller is shown in Table 3.3. These figures represent

Table 3.3
Regional Per Capita Agricultural Production
(1950 pesos per *rural* inhabitant)

Region	1899	1907	1930	1940	1950	1960
North	79	83	174	313	604	632
Gulf	231	256	278	345	425	662
North Pacific	157	85	474	413	937	1,323
South Pacific	67	102	110	141	340	423
Center	129	128	137	194	242	351
Mexico	125	128	178	243	405	533

Sources: Rural population figures are from Appendix Table E.3, with the 1907 figures interpolated from those for 1900 and 1910.

The value of crop production is based on the regional share of total value of crop production for 1899–1900 and 1907–08 in the Dirección General de Estadística, under the direction of Antonio Peñafiel, *Anuarios Estadísticos de la República Mexicana* for years 1900–07 (hereafter referred to as Peñafiel, *Anuarios*), and from corresponding figures in the four agricultural censuses since 1930. These value shares were applied to the overall index of crop production in 1950 pesos described in Table 3.7 to derive regional estimates in constant prices, with the exception of the 1940 figure which is taken from Rosenzweig, "Indices de los Rendimientos Agrícolas." This figure reflects a higher and somewhat more realistic output for 1940 than the value-added estimate of the Bank of Mexico, in terms of results of the 1940 census. To make the 1940 figure comparable to that in Table 3.7, one should scale the regional and national figures downward by a factor of 12 percent.

the farm value of all marketed and nonmarketed crop production per rural dweller. They give some indication of the extent to which output surpassed that level of cultivation (expressed in terms of real income) below which savings would be virtually nonexistent. By assuming a per capita output cutoff point for the generation of net savings in a region, one may obtain a rough indication of the extent of subsistence agriculture in Mexico at any point in time. I have set this figure at 150 pesos of 1950 value per annum per rural dweller.[8]

8. The current U.S. dollar equivalent of 150 pesos (1950 value) is ambiguous. At the 1950 peso/dollar exchange rate of 8.64, it represents $17.36 in

This subsistence threshold was purposely placed at a level which tends to underestimate the number of those with zero net savings (savings that are held longer than one crop year) so as to illustrate the breadth and persistence of rural poverty by using the most conservative possible figure. Budget studies are not yet sufficiently accurate to support the selection of one cutoff point rather than another. Far more research is required on rural income and expenditure patterns before one will be able to provide a more precise evaluation of the growth and welfare implications of regional inequalities in farm income and productivity.

Average output was below 150 pesos in three regions in 1895 and in all but the Gulf region in 1907. The four regions other than the Gulf contained 88 percent of the approximately 10.5 million persons living in communities of less than 2,500 inhabitants in 1907. If, as it is reasonable to assume, two-thirds of the rural dwellers in these four regions were supported by subsistence cultivation, then over 7 million peasants (half of the total population of Mexico) were for all practical purposes unable to add significantly to net savings or to constitute a significant market for manufactured goods as of 1907. Another 3 million peasants were only on the margin of commercial cultivation, and many of them might well have been included in the former figure, since the national *average* value of rural per capita crop production in 1899 was a mere 14 U.S. dollars (denominated in 1950 prices) and in 1907 was 15 dollars.

Since then the share of subsistence cultivation has fallen dramatically. In 1960 no region showed less than 40 U.S. dollars per

1950 dollars. Raising this amount to a 1965 value using the U.S. implicit GNP deflator (1965/1950 = 1.383) gives the current figure of approximately $24.00. However, if 150 1950 pesos are inflated by the Mexican implicit GNP deflator (1965/1950 = 2.472) and then converted to dollars at the official exchange rate (12.5 pesos/dollar), the current dollar value becomes approximately $30.00. In some instances official Mexican statistics employ the latter method of expressing current values of Mexican GNP and its components in dollars. A third possible approach, though extremely precarious, would be to convert Mexican values first to 1960 pesos and then to dollars at the estimated purchasing power parity rate of exchange of 8 pesos/dollar in 1960 rather than the official rate of 12.5 pesos/dollar in effect since 1954. See United Nations, ECLA, *A Measurement of Price Levels and the Purchasing Power of Currencies in Latin America, 1960–1962*, as quoted in ECLA, *Process of Industrialization in Latin America*, Table 1–6. The ECLA study estimates that in terms of relative purchasing powers there was a 36 percent undervaluation of the Mexican currency in 1960. In view of the alternative procedures and their wide-ranging results, the reader is warned to be certain of the basis for conversion of pesos to dollars wherever the latter appear in the literature on the Mexican economy.

capita output, or two and one-half times the national average of fifty years before. The region of lowest output in 1960 was the one with the highest share of rural population (41 percent)—the Center. Its companion in poverty, the South Pacific, had only a slightly higher output per capita. We may assume that 30 percent of the peasants in these two regions remain subsistence cultivators (almost certainly an underestimate) and that an additional 2.8 million may be added from other regions, so that the total number of those who have yet to enjoy the benefits of economic development is still well over 5 million.[9] This figure represents more than 10 percent of the current Mexican population, although it is approximately a million less than the number of persons supported by subsistence agriculture in 1907. Estimates such as this, while extremely rough, may be confirmed by the observations of any traveler to Mexico today. The history of extreme rural poverty is far from over. It may be another generation before that point is reached at which the productivity of marginal workers in agriculture begins to rise significantly.

The elimination of subsistence agriculture is partly dependent upon the expansion of commercial cultivation, and this in turn is reflected in rural output per worker. Commercial crop production has grown rapidly but in an unbalanced fashion since 1900. In every year since 1907 the two northern regions and the Gulf have held the top positions in rural productivity, while the Center and South Pacific have vied consistently for last place. The range of rural per capita output has widened between 1899 and 1960 according to Table 3.4. Today the average output of a rural dweller in the North Pacific is almost four times that of his counterpart in the Center. From these figures it is clear that, since the Porfiriato, the major gains in marketable crop production have been concentrated in a few regions; the Revolution, although it interrupted this trend in inequality, by no means ended it. From the point of view of engendering a high rate of savings and reinvestment, increased inequality might serve a useful purpose. And to the extent that productivity gains reflect scale economies

9. This definition of the level of "subsistence income" as a floor below which net savings are unlikely to take place may be subject to an upward adjustment over time since the zero savings point is doubtless a function of relative as well as absolute levels of income. In a rapidly growing economy such as Mexico, it may therefore increase as those elsewhere experience rising levels of income and consumption and as new commodities become available and desired by even the poorest peasant. The author is indebted to Moises Syrquin for this point.

Table 3.4
Rank Ordering of Regional Per Capita Agricultural Production

In Descending Order	1899	1907	1930	1940	1950	1960
1.	Gulf	Gulf	N. Pacific	N. Pacific	N. Pacific	N. Pacific
2.	N. Pacific	Center	Gulf	Gulf	North	Gulf
3.	Center	S. Pacific	North	North	Gulf	North
4.	North	N. Pacific	Center	Center	S. Pacific	S. Pacific
5.	S. Pacific	North	S. Pacific	S. Pacific	Center	Center

Range

Rural Per Capita Output of Region 1 as a Multiple of that of Region 5	3.4	3.1	4.3	2.9	3.9	3.8

Source: Table 3.3.

in the use of both land and capital, inequality may be an inescapable fact of economic life. In either case it carries with it a social cost that must eventually be recompensed in terms of better living conditions and broader participation of the masses in the benefits of growth.

Table 3.3 provides a picture of the general characteristics of agricultural dualism in Mexico and its behavior over the past sixty years. Despite pockets of prosperity and despite rapid rates of growth, the South Pacific and Center have remained at seriously low absolute levels of rural per capita output. This is the direct result of the failure of developments in commercial agriculture and urban activities to absorb subsistence cultivators at a sufficiently rapid rate to permit labor productivity at the margins to rise. The North, North Pacific, and Gulf regions, on the other hand, have maintained much higher average levels of per capita output. This is due to the success of commercial cultivation in these regions. The latter three regions now produce almost 60 percent of the total value of crop production in Mexico, although they accounted for only 43 percent in 1900 and 41 percent in 1907 (Table 3.5). The 60 percent of crop income from these regions now goes to 41 percent of the rural population (see Appendix Table E.2). This unbalanced regional growth of agricultural production is in part a natural phenomenon. Older sections of the country such as the Center (plateau) began to experience

Table 3.5
Regional Shares of Total Value of Mexican
Crop Production, 1899–1959
(percent by year of harvest)

Region	*1899*	*1907*	*1929*	*1939*	*1949*	*1959*
1. North	12	13	19	25	27	23
2. Gulf	23	24	20	19	16	17
3. North Pacific	8	4	16	11	15	18
4. South Pacific	8	12	10	10	14	15
5. Center	49	47	35	35	28	27
6. Mexico	100	100	100	100	100	100

Sources: Peñafiel, *Anuarios* for 1900, 1907; Agricultural Censuses of 1930, 1940, 1950, and 1960 for subsequent years. For 1900 and 1907 the shares represent 17 major crops constituting approximately 94 percent of the total value of crop production. For subsequent years the figures represent the share of total value of production of all crops included in the decennial agricultural censuses from 1930 to 1960.

severe diminishing marginal physical productivity of land and depletion through overcropping early in the century. In part, it is the result of regional inequalities in federal investment in rural economic infrastructure. The next section describes the growth of crop production and its relation to major inputs of land, labor, and capital in order to determine the balance in growth of inputs of land, labor, and capital and their relative influence on regional output and productivity trends.

REGIONAL AGRICULTURAL DEVELOPMENT, 1900–30

It is now possible statistically to examine the effect of the revolutionary and postrevolutionary periods on agricultural production, both nationally and regionally (Table 3.6). The Revolution did not disrupt for long the production of cash crops, though it had a sustained impact on basic food crops such as maize and beans. Commercial agricultural production continued earlier trends after the period of armed conflict was over, so that by 1930 the output of most of such cash crops as henequen, sugarcane, and coffee was well ahead of 1907 levels. Nevertheless, per capita product in agriculture fell by 18 percent between 1907 and 1929. Although this decline is less than that suggested by earlier indexes of rural output, it had a serious

Table 3.6

Growth of Regional Crop Production by Decade, 1899–1959

Region	1 1899/1907 (1899 = 100)	2 1907/1929 (1907 = 100)	3 1929/1939 (1929 = 100)	4 1939/1949 (1939 = 100)	5 1949/1959 (1949 = 100)
1. North	89	147	206	181	116
2. Gulf	110	107	121	144	216
3. North Pacific	60	318	104	177	292
4. South Pacific	145	98	138	220	174
5. Center	112	69	137	135	153
6. Mexico	108[a]	103	139	166	164

[a] The rate of growth of total agricultural production derived from these calculations for the period 1899/1907 (8 percent) is below that of El Colegio de México, *Fuerza de Trabajo* (Table 3.7, n. 1), as used elsewhere in this study (17 percent).

Sources and Methods: The indexes in columns 1 and 2 were computed by the author from the Peñafiel (1899 and 1907) and decennial agricultural census data (1929) for 17 major crops on a regional and national basis using the square root of the product of the Paasche and Laspeyres indexes to arrive at the Fisher ideal. As might be expected, the Paasche indexes were generally lower than the Laspeyres for the same period. For 1899/1907 the Laspeyres was 110.5 and the Paasche 104.7. For 1907/1929 the Laspeyres was 109.2 and the Paasche 97.0.

The indexes in columns 3, 4, and 5 are derived from Appendix Table E.6.

Note that the indexes in this table (and those in Table E.6) represent the increase in quantity of crop production and are not related to the regional distribution of agricultural value added presented in Table 3.3 in per capita form, although the value figures are taken from the same statistical sources.

impact on welfare, especially in view of its unequal regional incidence.[10]

Agricultural output per capita (total agricultural production divided by the total population of Mexico) rose from 1900 to 1907 by 13 percent and then fell between 1907 and 1929 by 22 percent (Table 3.7). It should be noted that 1929 was a relatively bad year owing to a recession in foreign demand and to a sudden increase in the pace of land reform under the interim administration of President

10. For example, the index of value added of total agricultural output in the sectoral breakdown of GDP 1895–1959 fell by 27 percent between 1907 and 1930 in Enrique Pérez López, "El Producto Nacional," included in *México: Cincuenta Años de Revolución*, pp. 587–89, whereas our index rises by 3 percent (Table 3.6). The Pérez López index was taken from an article by Humberto G. Angulo, "Índice de la Producción Agrícola," in which corn and beans (both of which fell in production between the two years by our measure) are very heavily weighted.

Table 3.7
Growth of Agricultural Production in Mexico
(compound annual rates of growth)

	1877/ 1900	1900/ 1907ᵉ	1907ᵉ/ 1925	1925/ 1940	1940/ 1950	1950/ 1960
1. Total physical crop productionᵃ	0.0	2.8ᵉ	0.0	2.7	8.2ᵉ	4.3
2. Total populationᵇ	1.5	1.1	0.1ᵈ	1.6	2.8	3.1
3. Agricultural production per capita 1.–2.	−1.5	1.7ᵇ	−0.1	1.1	5.4	1.2
4. GDP per capitaᵇ (1950 pesos)	0.6	3.1	2.3	−0.1	3.8	2.9

ᵃ Rates of growth from 1877/78 to 1907/08 are from El Colegio de México, *Fuerza de Trabajo*, p. 61 (expressed in millions of 1900 pesos). The rate of growth from 1907 to 1925 is based upon the sources for the index for all Mexico in Table 3.6 for the period 1907/1929, adjusted for changes between 1925 and 1929 by the figures from Banco de México, Oficina de Estudios sobre Proyecciones Agrícolas, "Índices de los Rendimientos Agrícolas," prepared by Fernando Rosenzweig and staff. This work supplies the basis for the 1925/1940 growth rate. Rates for 1940 to 1960 are from Grupo Secretaría de Hacienda-Banco de México, Estudios sobre Proyecciones, "Manual," Table 2–3 and are value-added indexes in constant pesos which conform to the official sectoral estimates of GDP.

ᵇ Appendix Tables E.1 and D.5B. The rate of growth of GDP for 1877/1900 and 1900/1907 is based on the rate of growth of four major components of GDP (agropecuaria, industria de transformación, industrias minero-metalúrgicas, and egresos del gobierno federal) expressed in constant prices as published in El Colegio de México, *Fuerza de Trabajo*, pp. 61, 105, 106, and 323.

ᵉ 1907 is used as the terminal year for the Porfiriato rather than 1910/1911 because of the lack of significant agricultural production figures for the years 1907 to 1910 except for crops exported. Nevertheless, estimates presented by Angulo, "Índice de la Producción Agrícola," p. 19, suggest that production fell by 4.8 percent from 1907 to 1910 for a small sample of basic food crops. This would provide an annual rate of decline of agricultural production from 1907 to 1910 of 1.3 percent and a per capita rate of decline of 0.2 percent, which is more consistent with earlier estimates.

ᵈ Growth rate for 1910/25.

ᵉ The growth rate for the 1940s is slightly exaggerated because 1940 was a bad harvest year.

Emilio Portes Gil (1929), which temporarily disturbed output in that sector. Hence the long-run experience from 1910 to 1930 is not quite as bleak as the growth rate based on the two years would suggest. Indeed, if one considers that the share of rural population fell from 71 percent (1910) to 66.5 percent (1930) while rural population grew by only 2 percent in absolute terms, agricultural productivity appears to have remained relatively the same before and after the period of armed conflict. Nevertheless, agricultural production remained unbalanced and regional inequalities actually intensified after the Revolution. Cash crops continued to grow during the 1920s, with little setback from political events. Yet the output of staples such as corn and beans, on which the mass of the population depended for nourishment, fell by 40 percent and 31 percent respectively between 1907 and 1929, at a time when the population grew by 9 percent.

In order to explain why the present estimate of crop productivity growth for the period 1907 to 1929 differs from findings of early studies such as that of Humberto Angulo (whose agricultural production index shows sharp declines between 1907 and 1929), one must disaggregate the index into its component crops. Of these seventeen crops, the two staples (beans and maize) registered absolute declines in output over the period, as did two important cash crops, tobacco and cocoa. Together, these four crops accounted for 46.2 percent of the total value of production of the seventeen in 1930 and 57.5 percent of the total value of production for the sample in 1900. Despite the behavior of these four commodities, the overall index showed no net decline in production between 1907 and 1929 because of impressive net increases in principal cash crops such as cotton, henequen, sugarcane (in the Gulf region), and coffee. The uneven pattern of crop production during this period carried with it important regional implications. For example, the center registered a decline in crop production of 31 percent (note Table 3.6) between the two years. Since this region contained 47 percent of the rural population in 1910 and 45 percent in 1930, its failure to match the behavior of the economy as a whole during the years following the Revolution meant that its impoverished peasants were forced to bear a disproportional share of the hardships of radical economic and social change.

It may be of interest to those analyzing the economic causes of the Revolution that between 1900 and 1907 production declined by 40 percent in the North Pacific. This region includes the state of Sonora, which was a center of revolutionary activity during the same period. Crops that led the declines in the North Pacific were beans, corn, tomatoes, potatoes, cotton, sugarcane, and wheat (the major food and cash crops). It is possible that the economic pressures associated with a shortfall in crop production in this region brought about increasing pressure on the Díaz administration—pressure which eventually polarized the opposition and led to a broad commercial agricultural basis for political revolution. The Center did not experience the same pattern of growth during the last decade of the Porfiriato. As population increased by 7 percent from 1899 to 1907 in this region, agricultural production grew at almost twice that rate. One may almost conclude that this most populous region of rural Mexico was better off in productivity terms immediately before rather than after the Revolution.

The regions of agricultural growth between 1900 and 1907 were the South Pacific, Center, and Gulf, in that order. It is interesting that the South Pacific, traditionally an impoverished area, led the growth rate during this period. Here agriculture was originally at such a low level of productivity that one may say it had no place to go but up. The high growth rate therefore tends to exaggerate the absolute gains in output per person. Furthermore, the gains in these three regions were not shared equally by all farmers. For example, in the South Pacific, although maize production did not show much growth through 1907, gains were realized in the cultivation of bananas, oranges, sugarcane, and beans. Except for beans, the increased production of these crops tended to be concentrated on plantations and large estates and, although this increased the demand for wage labor, there is little evidence that real wages in the region rose or that there was much improvement in the welfare of the majority of the rural population in subsistence agriculture.

The evidence for the years prior to the 1930s suggests that, although the Revolution interrupted the expansion of commercial agricultural production in Mexico and may have affected its regional distribution in favor of the North and Northwest, it did not end the process. Instead, the disturbance in rural Mexico during those early years was felt most, not by the *latifundista* and plantation owner, but by the smallholder whose livelihood depended on the cultivation of staples such as maize and beans. These crops declined, although not enough to offset the growth in cash crops. It is ironic that, before the actual implementation of agrarian reform law, it was the peasantry that appears to have suffered most from revolution, rural anarchy, and uncertainty about financing, market conditions, and tenure stability. Furthermore, the most densely populated regions experienced the greatest setbacks before 1930. It was the Center which sustained the major loss in rural output and productivity, and it is precisely this region which felt the strongest pressures for agrarian reform.

Zapata's movement arose in Morelos (South-Center) and tended to focus on this area as a base of operations, while Michoacán (Cárdenas's home state) and Jalisco also raged with internal disorder well into the 1930s. This was likewise the region with the most displacement of rural population to urban centers, as peasants and landowners fled from the turmoil in the countryside.

It is little wonder that agricultural production languished in the Center and South Pacific. What is surprising is the virtual isolation of agriculture in some regions (such as the North and North Pacific) from the immediate ill effects of the civil war and rural unrest. The data even suggest that the Revolution might have benefited agriculture in the North Pacific relative to other regions, since many of the new political leaders came from Sonora and were in a position to favor their locale in terms of land redistribution, rural credit, and public expenditures. Indeed, the North Pacific, which had lagged behind all other regions in the late Porfiriato, led the country between 1907 and 1929 by tripling production. In 1907 this zone accounted for only 4 percent of national crop production but by 1929 that figure had risen to 16 percent.

REGIONAL AGRICULTURAL DEVELOPMENT, 1930–60

The four agricultural censuses taken since 1930 provide a wealth of information on the rural sector. Table 3.7 reveals three major phases of expansion between 1925 and 1960: (1) the years of recovery from revolution and changing rural institutions as a result of the agrarian reform (1925–40); (2) rapid increases in output in response to abrupt increases in foreign and urban demand for food and industrial crops (1940–50), part of which was a return to full capacity after the depression; and (3) slower growth brought about by lagged supply responses to earlier investment in rural infrastructure (1950–60) despite declining rural/urban terms of trade in the 1950s (Table 3.8). Public investments in dams and irrigation systems have been extremely unbalanced regionally, tending to perpetuate and often to intensify the existence of regional inequalities in agricultural productivity even after thirty years of development. Meanwhile, the subsistence sector is gradually giving way to commercial crop production with accompanying gains in income and productivity and a rising supply of output (above that needed to sustain the rural population) that may be used for urban consumption, industry, and export.

Table 3.8
Agricultural/Urban Commodity Terms of Trade, 1925–60
(agricultural price indexes ÷ Mexico City wholesale price index)
(1925 = 100)

	1 Agricultural/ Urban Terms of Trade	*2* Food Products/ Urban Terms of Trade	*3* Primary Materials/Urban Terms of Trade	*4* Forestry Products/Urban Terms of Trade
1925	100.0	100.0	100.0	100.0
1930	93.6	99.8	72.3	101.0
1935	96.7	96.7	98.7	89.9
1940	101.5	103.4	99.0	80.1
1945	124.8	127.9	118.1	103.2
1950	134.6	125.0	163.8	87.8
1955	113.9	111.8	120.1	72.3
1960	117.1	121.0	107.9	92.6
(base year of each period = 100)				
1930–40	108.6	103.7	137.0	79.4
1940–50	132.7	121.0	165.6	109.6
1950–60	87.0	96.8	65.8	105.4

Sources: These series are composite commodity (net barter) terms of trade representing the ratio of farm prices of rural commodities to the wholesale commodity prices in Mexico City. The agricultural prices are from Agricultural Price Indexes– 1940 to 1960: Banco de México, Oficina de Estudios sobre Proyecciones Agrícolas, "Índice de Precios Agrícolas al Nivel del Productor y Quantum de la Producción Agrícola, 1939–1960," under the direction of Fernando Rosenzweig, (hereafter referred to as Rosenzweig, "Índices de Precios Agrícolas"). 1925 to 1935: worksheets provided by the same author. The numerator in column 1 is an average of the numerators in columns 2 through 4. The denominator in each column is the Mexico City wholesale price index, a combined index based on the following sources: 1925 to 1935: "Índices de Precios al Mayoreo en la Ciudad de México y en Estados Unidos," *Trimestre de Barómetros Económicos*, vol. 1, no. 2, September 1946. 1940 to 1950: Banco de México. 1950 to 1960: United Nations, Statistical Office of the United Nations, Department of Economic and Social Affairs, *Statistical Yearbook 1961*, p. 477. Since the Mexico City wholesale price index includes some agricultural commodities, the figures in this table tend to understate deviations of actual rural/urban terms of trade in either direction.

The shift from demand to supply-led growth in agricultural output between the 1940s and 1950s is reflected in the behavior of relative prices as summarized in Table 3.8. The rural/urban terms of trade, which had remained relatively constant between 1925 and 1940, rose 33 percent in the 1940s, followed by a decline in the 1950s. In each period the major factor affecting relative price changes in the rural sector was the behavior of foreign demand for Mexican primary materials. Shortages during World War II and the Korean period boosted commodity prices in foreign markets (particularly in the United States) that were passed on to Mexican suppliers (who are primarily price takers) in the form of high rates of return. Cotton production in particular benefited from these wartime conditions of demand. The relative price of primary materials rose 66 percent in the 1940s despite high domestic rates of inflation, while relative food prices rose 21 percent and forestry product prices 10 percent.

The post-Korean recession in the U.S. economy was transmitted to Mexico through commodity prices once again. During the 1950s, the internal terms of trade for primary materials fell by 34 percent, causing the rural/urban terms of trade to decline by 13 percent over the course of the decade (Table 3.8). Meanwhile the expansion of acreage in most crops had permitted supply increases which more than matched the growth of internal demand in the 1950s so that the relative price of food crops fell slightly as well. Mexican forestry, on the other hand, has tended to be a seriously neglected sector. Timber output has been far less than the country's rich supply of virgin forests would permit under a national conservation-minded program of exploitation. Much of the lumbering that does take place at present is clandestine, illegal, and wasteful. Supply is not keeping pace with demand and the forestry terms of trade have risen in the 1950s, going against the general trend of falling relative prices in agriculture. It should be noted that the farm prices of some staple commodities have been maintained at above equilibrium levels by the government marketing agency Compañía Nacional de Subsistencias Populares (CONASUPO), a recently established state marketing agency that acts to protect the rural producer and to subsidize food costs of urban consumers. Had it not been for CONASUPO supports for maize, for example, its price might well have fallen much more sharply in the 1950s and early 1960s.

The behavior of the rural/urban commodity terms of trade indicates that relative prices tended to shift in income toward rural dwellers in the 1940s and against them in the 1950s, although the net effect since 1925 has been relatively favorable to agriculture. Such a conclusion should be qualified by the relative productivity performance of the rural versus urban economy over the same period, since given price changes have differing implications if output per worker grows at different rates in agriculture as compared with manufacturing and services. The appropriate measure that includes the effect of relative productivity growth in the comparison of relative prices is the double factoral terms of trade.[11] This measure is simply the commodity terms of trade index (between rural and urban commodities) multiplied by an index of relative changes in output per worker (between agriculture on the one hand and a weighted average of manufacturing and services on the other). The data from Table 2.4 for the decades 1940/50 and 1950/60 has been transformed into a rural/urban productivity index, using the relative employment shares in manufacturing and services as weights for the denominator. Output per worker in rural occupations grew 21.1 percent relative to urban activities in the 1940s and fell by 5.3 percent in relative terms in the 1950s. These findings reinforce the trend in commodity terms of trade, since the double factoral terms of trade increase by 60.7 percent in the 1940s and decline by 17.6 percent in the 1950s. Productivity changes have therefore intensified rather than offset the relative shift in income toward rural areas in the 1940s and away from rural areas in the 1950s.

The fastest-growing region over the entire period since 1940 was the North Pacific (Appendix Table E.6), where crop production quadrupled. Its growth has accelerated steadily after a decade of virtual stagnation during the 1930s (Table 3.6). This region, adjacent to the American Southwest, has registered the greatest increase in land use with the smallest amount of land reform since 1940, although it experienced widespread land redistribution during the 1930s. Many of its farms are medium and large-scale private holdings that rely heavily on capital-intensive techniques of production. Some of the large holdings are also in the form of collective *ejidos* and these, too, tend to be highly capitalized. Detailed examination of the structure of inputs and outputs in the Sonoran economy suggests that the region enjoys a high rate of savings.[12] In 1950 it accounted for 15 percent of the value of agricultural production in Mexico and 7 percent of rural population, and in 1960 the figures were 18 percent and 7 percent, respectively (Tables 3.5 and E.2). Unlike the rest of Mexico, the period of most rapid growth for the North Pacific

11. Gottfried Haberler, *A Survey of International Trade Theory*, pp. 24 ff.
12. See Clark W. Reynolds, "La Capacidad para Financiar la Formación de Capital en Sonora," which relies upon the 1960 input-output table for Sonora, Banco de México, Departamento de Estudios Económicos Regionales, April 5, 1963.

was the decade of the 1950s, when the planting of wheat, beans, tomatoes, and cotton assumed boom proportions. New cotton production in the region was a direct response to the growth of American demand and the fact that Mexican suppliers were allowed beneath the U.S. price umbrella and were provided with crop loans from U.S. merchandising firms such as the Anderson-Clayton Company.

The South Pacific region has followed close behind the North Pacific in output growth ever since 1930. In that year this region had the lowest agricultural output per capita in Mexico (Table 3.3), while the North Pacific had the highest. Its growth rate of 429 percent over the three decades (Appendix Table E.6) is accordingly impressive. Though there has been relatively little investment in farm machinery, dams, or irrigation systems in the South Pacific and although its rural population has grown rapidly, per capita farm production has more than tripled, leaving the Center behind as the poorest agricultural zone in Mexico as of 1960. The decade of the 1940s, when the South Pacific led all other regions, was the period of most notable growth based on the expansion of coffee, cotton, banana, and cocoa production as well as staples such as corn, beans, and barley. In the next section it will be shown that most of the growth in the South Pacific is attributable to increased inputs of land and labor. While this was partly true for the North Pacific as well, the latter also depended on a twelvefold increase in capital stock (the capital/output ratio rising over the period from 0.9 to 2.5). In the South Pacific, capital stock grew at a slower rate than output over the three decades, the capital/output ratio falling from 0.3 in 1930 to 0.2 in 1960. Unfortunately this southern region, despite its impressive growth in percentage terms, has failed to bring absolute levels of rural income and welfare up to minimum standards (Table 3.3).

The North is a very heterogeneous region. It includes a portion of the vast and arid high plateau as well as fertile tropical lowlands along the Gulf Coast. With increased use of irrigation and pesticides, the latter zone has become very profitable in recent years, although agriculture in some parts of the northern high plateau remains among the worst in the country. A more detailed study of the region should take these dual characteristics into consideration, since the relative growth of production and productivity in the eastern (tropical) portion of the zone helps to explain why the North moved from fifth to third place in rural per capita agricultural production after the Porfiriato (Table 3.4). It led the nation in productivity gains in the

1930s and came in second over the course of the three decades, but has suffered severe setbacks in recent years (Table 3.9).

Table 3.9
Growth of Regional Agricultural Production
per Rural Dweller, 1930–60

Region	1930/1940 (1930 = 100)	1940/1950 (1940 = 100)	1950/1960 (1950 = 100)	1930/1960 (1930 = 100)
1. North	180	193	105	363
2. Gulf	124	123	156	238
3. North Pacific	87	227	141	279
4. South Pacific	128	241	124	385
5. Center	142	125	145	256
6. Mexico	137	167	132	299

Source: See Table 3.3.

The North region, while third in overall growth from 1930 to 1960, demonstrates the best and worst of Mexican agricultural development. Its growth rate actually has decelerated over the long run. During the 1950s, northern agriculture showed an annual rate of increase of only 1.5 percent compared to 5.1 percent for the nation. Capital formation in the North lagged behind all regions except the South Pacific during this period, and the cultivated land area increased by less than all regions but the Center. Almost the entire reduction in the rate of growth of the North is due to a 38 percent decline in cotton production after 1950, since this one crop accounted for 47 percent of the regional value of production in that year. The Laguna area around Torreon had been the heartland of Mexican cotton production ever since the completion of the North-South and East-West rail lines in the 1890s.[13] During the Cárdenas period of agrarian reform, the great commercial cotton plantations of the valley were expropriated and redistributed along with their valuable water rights. The new owners increased the use of well irrigation, which lowered the water table. Prolonged drought added to the difficulties of this erstwhile oasis, so that by the time the Korean War drove up raw cotton prices, production had shifted away from the Laguna to newly irrigated alluvial plains on both the east and

13. See Clarence O. Senior, *Land Reform and Democracy,* for a description of the Laguna region and its agricultural development problems through the 1940s. This information is summarized and brought up to date by Solomón Eckstein, *El Ejido Colectivo en México,* pp. 131–49.

west coasts. Recent agricultural gains in the tropical lowlands of Nuevo León and Tamaulipas have failed to offset diminishing production and productivity on the high plateau, thus causing the North to fall behind in recent years.

Fourth place in regional growth belongs to the Gulf where total output tripled between 1930 and 1960. The 1950s were the best years for this region. Growth of agricultural production was second only to that of the North Pacific (Table 3.6). As a result, the Gulf regained second place in per capita agricultural production as of 1960, a position from which it had been displaced in the 1940s by the rapid growth of the North. This coastal region has increased its land area under cultivation since 1940, with little public investment in irrigation until recently. However, since 1950 it has benefited from extensive highway and railroad construction that has opened it up to internal markets as never before. Since the region extends south from Veracruz to the Yucatán Peninsula and is primarily tropical lowland, it specializes in plantation crops and low-quality cattle production. Its agriculture has been export-oriented ever since the golden age of henequen.[14] During the 1930s, owing to depressed conditions in the world market, regional production per rural dweller grew by only 10 percent and the land area cultivated declined by 15 percent. Since 1940, however, a revival in world demand has been met by increased plantings of coffee, cocoa, tobacco, rice, oranges, and beans. The result has been an impressive increase in output, permitting the region as a whole (though not Yucatán) to shift its economic base from the henequen monoculture to the diversified production of cash crops. The share of henequen in the total value of production of the Gulf has fallen from 44 percent in 1900 to 39 percent in 1930, 13 percent in 1940, and 6 percent in 1950. Since this substitution was made possible through increased use of land and labor rather than capital-intensive methods of cultivation, the region affords an interesting example for those interested in labor-intensive growth and diversification of agricultural export economies, and deserves far more attention than it can receive in this study.

In last place among the five agricultural zones of Mexico is the region which fostered some of the great pre-Colombian civilizations— the Center. Indeed, this region has steadily been losing place to the periphery although production has tripled since 1930. Its share of

14. A cactus fiber of great value to the American cordage industry, during the last century that has been more recently losing place to synthetic fibers.

total output in 1930 (35 percent) was maintained until 1940 but fell abruptly to 28 percent during the 1940s and remained at that level through 1960 (Table 3.5). Its share of rural population has declined as well, though much more slowly, from 45 percent in 1930 to 41 percent in 1960 (Appendix Table E.2). As a result, rural per capita agricultural production in the Center, which was about average for the country in 1900, had fallen 23 percent below average in 1930 and 34 percent below the national figure in 1960. This is the zone with the largest cultivation of traditional crops. Corn and beans accounted for 62 percent of the value of crop production in 1900, and the share of these staples remained at 64 percent in 1950 even though some of this production was based on modern methods of cultivation for urban markets. Since the turn of the century, the share of these two crops in the output of the Center has far exceeded the national average (55 percent in 1900 and 41 percent in 1950).[15] As the rest of Mexico has diversified away from corn and beans, reflecting the displacement of subsistence crops by commercial agriculture, the Center has tended to move in the reverse direction. Nevertheless, some changes did take place in the 1950s as corn and beans fell behind the growth in cultivation of barley, alfalfa, wheat, sesame seed, coffee, and potatoes. To assist in the transformation of this region, the largest integrated river valley development in Mexico has recently been inaugurated. This project includes the entire basin of the Lerma, Chapala, and Santiago rivers, covers several states, and is patterned after the TVA as a source of urban and rural water supplies and electric power. Hopefully the trend of the past sixty years can be slowed, if not reversed here. Meanwhile the Center, and particularly its portions of the arid and badly eroded high plateau, remains the major problem area in Mexican agriculture.

PRODUCTIVITY GAINS IN MEXICAN AGRICULTURE, 1930–60

Much of the impressive growth of Mexican per capita output since 1930 has been due to the performance of agriculture. The growth of crop production has been described above. Remaining to be examined are the changing conditions of supply that have permitted this sector

15. These percentages reflect the share of corn and beans in the total value of production of the 17 major crops for 1900 and 21 principal crops for 1950. Thus their share of the total value of crop production would be slightly less than our figure for both years.

to respond so effectively to rising domestic and foreign demand while at the same time releasing a rising share of the population for employment elsewhere in the economy. These changing conditions of supply include increases in the land area under cultivation, the number of man-years applied to the land, private investments in plant and equipment, and public works that have transformed rural infrastructure in a number of regions. It is shown below that increases in land, labor, and capital between 1930 and 1960 have accounted for less than half of the real growth of agricultural production. The remainder may be attributable to one or more of the following factors: (1) changing rural technology; (2) increasing returns to crop production; (3) greater use of intermediate goods such as pesticides, high yielding seeds, and fertilizers; (4) better education of the work force and improved farm management; (5) changing attitudes and incentives of cultivators due to shifting rural social institutions; and (6) investments in rural economic infrastructure not included in our measure of fixed reproducible assets (such as public feeder roads, electric power, and telecommunications).

ESTIMATING THE INPUTS IN MEXICAN AGRICULTURE

An attempt is made in this study to relate agricultural output to its principal inputs—land, labor, and capital. Ideally, this could be done by estimating a set of production functions for the past sixty years by region and by crop. Unfortunately, annual data are available only for output and land area under cultivation but not for other inputs, except in the years 1930, 1940, 1950, and 1960, for which statistics are provided by state in the four Mexican agricultural censuses.[16] This information has been used to estimate an aggregate production function for each region having the assumed properties of unitary elasticity of substitution among the three inputs, constant returns to scale, and income distribution determined by each factor receiving its marginal product. This permits an estimate to be made of that level of output (value added) which would take place, based upon observed increases in land, labor, and capital if no productivity gains occurred. (A similar calculation was made for the economy as a whole in Chapter 1.) The difference between predicted growth and actual growth may then be associated with inputs other than land,

16. The censuses actually refer to the preceding crop years 1929, 1939, 1949, and 1959.

labor, and capital, including the effects of the agrarian reform as well as net gains in factor productivity.

The first step in this estimating procedure was to determine the amount of labor and land utilized and of capital stock existing in each of the four benchmark years since 1930. The results are detailed in

Table 3.10
Indexes of Major Agricultural Inputs and Output 1929–59
Regional and National

Region		*1929/39* (1929 = 100)	*1939/49* (1939 = 100)	*1949/59* (1949 = 100)	*1929/59* (1929 = 100)
North	Labor	110	130	125	178
	Land	125	142	126	223
	Capital	234	237	162	894
	Output	206	181	116	433
Gulf	Labor	106	127	129	173
	Land	85	179	148	223
	Capital	81	143	241	278
	Output	121	144	216	376
North Pacific	Labor	109	138	143	215
	Land	112	170	160	304
	Capital	110	516	226	1,290
	Output	104	177	292	537
South Pacific	Labor	106	128	139	189
	Land	106	183	140	271
	Capital	133	225	154	461
	Output	138	220	174	529
Center	Labor	103	121	121	152
	Land	99	125	109	135
	Capital	143	132	180	340
	Output	137	135	153	283
Mexico	Labor	106	126	127	169
	Land	105	144	127	192
	Capital	152	225	188	643
	Output	139	166	164	379

Definitions: Labor represents an index of the number of workers employed in agriculture, unadjusted for age or sex, as reported in the decennial population censuses.

Land represents an index of the number of hectares of land cultivated (though not necessarily harvested) as reported in the decennial agricultural censuses.

Capital represents an index of the value of fixed reproducible assets in agriculture, public and private, not including public roads or communications systems, expressed in pesos of 1950 purchasing power.

Output figures are taken from Tables E.6 and 3.6, the figures representing the crop years 1929/30, 1939/40, etc.

Appendix Tables E.2, E.9, and E.10, from which indexes have been derived by decade, as shown in Table 3.10. The term "labor" represents the total number of persons employed in agriculture. The data is taken from decennial population censuses, which are the only complete source of information available on those occupied in agriculture, including the self-employed. Ideally, these figures should be adjusted to account for improvements in rural education, changes in the age and sex composition of the work force, and intensity of employment, all of which presumably have influenced output. At present the net effect of these factors is captured along with all other unmeasured inputs in the productivity residual.

The number of hectares of land in cultivation is taken from the four agricultural censuses as reported by the peasants or their community representatives. Alternative annual estimates of land in use are available on the basis of regional samples taken by the Secretaría de Agricultura y Ganadería and reported in the *Anuarios Estadísticos* on a national basis except in the case of selected crops and given years for which state and regional totals are presented. The comparison of these totals with those of the censuses (Appendix Table E.9) shows them to be approximately the same for the years 1939 and 1959, although a 13 percent and 10 percent discrepancy exists for the years 1929 and 1949, respectively. The low 1929 figure may be due in part to sampling problems that arose during that time when the country was still in a state of rural unrest. The 1949 discrepancy is less explicable, suggesting that perhaps the increase in land use revealed by the census and employed in Table 3.10 is subject to an upward bias in the 1940s and a corresponding downward bias in the 1950s.

Public and private capital stock estimates in constant prices are prepared from independent sources. The former are based on recently published figures on annual gross investment of the federal government in agriculture since 1925 (a statewide breakdown is available only since 1959). These figures have been gathered and distributed regionally according to the cumulative number of hectares benefited by federal irrigation expenditures since 1925 (available on a statewide basis from the Comisión Nacional de Irrigación and the Secretaría de Recursos Hidraúlicos as reported by Adolfo Orive Alba).[17] The assumption implicit in this methodology is extremely crude—that regional federal investments in irrigation are propor-

17. Adolfo Orive Alba, *La Política de Irrigación en México*.

tional to the land area benefited and that other investments in agriculture by region are proportional to those in hydraulics (highway construction is not included in these figures and is discussed in Chapter 4). Nevertheless, this is the only method the author has found to disaggregate public investment figures for purposes of regional analysis. Private capital stock figures are taken directly from the censuses and are less subject to error. It is not clear whether the stated census values reflect original cost (with or without depreciation) or current value. If they were in fact reported in terms of original cost, then they should be reflated into 1950 prices and depreciated. This adjustment would slow the growth of private capital stock, increasing the productivity residual. It is doubtful, however, that they reflect original cost. The method actually used to convert the census figures to constant pesos relied upon a national rather than a regional price deflator (see Appendix Table E.10). Fortunately the calculations of productivity residuals in the next section, based on alternative value weights, indicate that the results are relatively insensitive to adjustments in the composition of inputs. This suggests that the estimates of factor inputs described above are useful for purposes of analysis despite the arbitrary assumptions on which they depend.

ESTIMATING THE GROWTH OF REGIONAL AGRICULTURAL PRODUCTIVITY

The method employed to estimate the growth of agricultural production by region and by decade for purposes of comparison with actual performance is identical to that which was applied to total gross domestic product in Chapter 1 (see Table 1.7). Cobb-Douglas assumptions permit a calculation of increases in value added [18] as a weighted average of rates of growth of labor, land, and capital inputs. The weights represent the respective factor shares of value added, which are equivalent to their output elasticities assuming that all factors are paid their marginal value product subject to constant returns to scale.

As there are no consistent data yet available on functional income

18. For the years before 1940, indexes of physical output are used as a proxy for value added of crop production owing to the lack of reliable data on intermediate inputs. For the years after 1940, the official GDP value-added index of crop production in constant prices is used, with regional physical output indexes adjusted in terms of this index assuming proportional changes in the share of value added to output for each region.

distribution within agriculture, several efforts were made to estimate distributive shares from the census data. The first attempt was to calculate the share of interest on capital, applying an implicit 15 percent rate of return on the value of private and public fixed assests. The wage share was derived in this case by assuming a constant marginal productivity of labor equal to the average output per rural worker in the South Pacific region in 1930 and applying this figure to the number of workers in each region for all years. Rents were then obtained as a residual after deducting the profit and wage share from value added in agriculture. The results for 1950 were wages 37 percent, profits 15 percent, and rent 48 percent of the value of agricultural production (the hypothetical "wage share" calculated by this method fell from 59 percent in 1930 to 37 percent in 1950 and rose again to 46 percent in 1960).

Since the first method of estimating the labor share was somewhat unrealistic in assuming that rural labor received its marginal product, that the marginal productivity of labor was equal in all regions, and that it was constant over time, an alternative measure was tried. It was assumed that the average worker in agriculture received the minimum wage (as published by the government by state for rural and urban workers since 1934).[19] The minimum wage figures were then multiplied by the man days of labor in agriculture. The results again proved disappointing, since the value of the hypothetical wage bill calculated by this method was greater than total value added in agriculture in the early years and almost 70 percent of value added in 1950.

A third attempt to calculate distributive shares was made by estimating land rents, adding to this the profit estimates described earlier, and taking wages as a residual. The basis for the rental share was an assumed rate of return of 10 to 15 percent applied to the declared value of crop land as reported in the agricultural censuses. But stated values turned out to be as high as five times the total value of crop production, causing some regions to show a rental share of 50 to 75 percent of value added based on the range of implicit rates of return chosen. Since each of these three estimating procedures was subject to highly restrictive assumptions, it was decided to assume arbitrarily three alternative wage shares of 40 percent, 50 percent, and 60 per-

19. The legal minimum daily wage was applied assuming 95 percent of the labor force, as reported in the census, to be gainfully employed on an average of 235 out of 365 days of the year at the minimum wage.

Table 3.11
The Growth of Mexican Crop Production, Inputs, and Productivity, 1929–39
(compound annual growth rates)

	Estimate A	*Estimate B*	*Estimate C*
North:			
1. Growth of output	7.5	7.5	7.5
2. Growth of inputs	3.6	3.4	3.4
3. Growth "unexplained" by inputs of labor, land, and capital			
(1 minus 2)	3.9	4.1	4.1
Gulf:			
1. Growth of output	1.9	1.9	1.9
2. Growth of inputs	−0.8	−0.6	−0.4
3. Growth "unexplained" by inputs of labor, land, and capital			
(1 minus 2)	2.7	2.5	2.3
North Pacific:			
1. Growth of output	0.4	0.4	0.4
2. Growth of inputs	1.0	1.0	1.0
3. Growth "unexplained" by inputs of labor, land, and capital			
(1 minus 2)	−0.6	−0.6	−0.6
South Pacific:			
1. Growth of output	3.3	3.3	3.3
2. Growth of inputs	0.7	0.7	0.7
3. Growth "unexplained" by inputs of labor, land, and capital			
(1 minus 2)	2.6	2.6	2.6
Center:			
1. Growth of output	3.2	3.2	3.2
2. Growth of inputs	0.6	0.6	0.7
3. Growth "unexplained" by inputs of labor, land, and capital			
(1 minus 2)	2.6	2.6	2.5
Mexico:			
1. Growth of output	3.4	3.4	3.4
2. Growth of inputs	1.2	1.2	1.2
3. Growth "unexplained" by inputs of labor, land, and capital			
(1 minus 2)	2.2	2.2	2.2

Sources: Actual growth of output and inputs from Table 3.10. The predicted rate of growth assumes a wage share of 40 percent (Estimate A), 50 percent (Estimate B), and 60 percent (Estimate C). The capital share is based on 15 percent returns on public and private capital (Appendix Table E.10) plus 5 percent depreciation on private capital, divided by the value of agricultural production (a physical output index tied to 1950 value added), thereby insuring that the share of value added in total crop production has not changed significantly over the entire period. This probably gives an upward bias to the output index, since intermediate inputs undoubtedly have risen on a share of the total crop production. The rental share is calculated as the residual of the wage and profit share from unity.

cent of value added in agriculture. To each alternative estimate (A, B, and C) was added the profit share estimated earlier plus a 5 percent depreciation allowance on private investment. Rents were calculated as the residual. Output was estimated based upon each of the three assumptions. Fortunately, except for the Gulf, the estimated rate of growth of output of each region proved relatively insensitive to the wage share of output, since labor and land inputs tended to increase at the same rate.

In Tables 3.11, 3.12, and 3.13 three alternative estimated rates of growth are presented based upon our indexes of labor, land, and capital. These estimated increases are subtracted from observed increases in output to provide alternative "unexplained" rates of growth for each period. These findings are analyzed in the next section to shed light on the economic factors that have been most important in generating productivity gains in Mexican agriculture over the past thirty years. One major conclusion to be drawn from Tables 3.11 to 3.14 is that aggregate analysis of Mexican agricultural development in which regional variations are not explicitly considered is almost certain to give misleading results. For example, the country as a whole experienced approximately the same productivity increases in each of the three decades; yet the regional pattern of productivity growth differed widely.[20] What conclusions might one derive from a look at the aggregate figures alone when even the total pattern of investment was not uniform over these periods (capital stock increasing by 50 percent in the 1930s, 125 percent in the 1940s, and 90 percent in the 1950s) and the regional distribution of factor inputs was extremely uneven?

It is not until regional breakdowns of the data are provided that one begins to obtain a meaningful picture of the contributory factors in Mexican agricultural growth. In Tables 3.11 through 3.13 the "unexplained" growth of production appears to have been extremely asymmetrical. For example, the South Pacific was the region of most impressive productivity gains over the whole period. It experienced a 2.8 percentage annual rate of growth of output unexplained by inputs

20. The concept "productivity" as used here and subsequently, includes the effect of a shift of labor and capital from less to more efficient regions, along with actual changes in technology within a region. The part of the national residual that reflects the positive effect of regional factor movements turns out to be extremely small. Internal shifts within given regions may have played a more important role in addition to the effect of increases in the productivity of individual farms.

Table 3.12
The Growth of Mexican Crop Production, Inputs, and Productivity, 1939–49
(compound annual growth rates)

	Estimate A	*Estimate B*	*Estimate C*
North:			
1. Growth of output	6.1	6.1	6.1
2. Growth of inputs	4.6	4.6	4.5
3. Growth "unexplained" by inputs of labor, land, and capital (1 minus 2)	1.5	1.5	1.6
Gulf:			
1. Growth of output	3.7	3.7	3.7
2. Growth of inputs	3.7	3.3	2.9
3. Growth "unexplained" by inputs of labor, land, and capital (1 minus 2)	0.0	0.4	0.8
North Pacific:			
1. Growth of output	5.9	5.9	5.9
2. Growth of inputs	9.4	9.3	9.1
3. Growth "unexplained" by inputs of labor, land, and capital (1 minus 2)	−3.5	−3.4	−3.2
South Pacific:			
1. Growth of output	8.2	8.2	8.2
2. Growth of inputs	5.0	4.6	4.3
3. Growth "unexplained" by inputs of labor, land, and capital (1 minus 2)	3.2	3.6	3.9
Center:			
1. Growth of output	3.1	3.1	3.1
2. Growth of inputs	2.2	2.2	2.1
3. Growth "unexplained" by inputs of labor, land, and capital (1 minus 2)	0.9	0.9	1.0
Mexico:			
1. Growth of output	5.2	5.2	5.2
2. Growth of inputs	4.2	4.1	3.9
3. Growth "unexplained" by inputs of labor, land, and capital (1 minus 2)	1.0	1.1	1.3

Sources: See Table 3.11.

Table 3.13

The Growth of Mexican Crop Production, Inputs, and Productivity, 1949–59
(compound annual growth rates)

	Estimate A	*Estimate B*	*Estimate C*
North:			
1. Growth of output	1.5	1.5	1.5
2. Growth of inputs	2.9	2.9	2.9
3. Growth "unexplained" by inputs of labor, land, and capital (1 minus 2)	−1.4	−1.4	−1.4
Gulf:			
1. Growth of output	8.0	8.0	8.0
2. Growth of inputs	5.9	5.8	5.7
3. Growth "unexplained" by inputs of labor, land, and capital (1 minus 2)	2.1	2.2	2.3
North Pacific:			
1. Growth of output	11.3	11.3	11.3
2. Growth of inputs	5.5	5.3	5.2
3. Growth "unexplained" by inputs of labor, land, and capital (1 minus 2)	5.8	6.0	6.1
South Pacific:			
1. Growth of output	5.7	5.7	5.7
2. Growth of inputs	3.4	3.4	3.4
3. Growth "unexplained" by inputs of labor, land, and capital (1 minus 2)	2.3	2.3	2.3
Center:			
1. Growth of output	4.4	4.4	4.4
2. Growth of inputs	2.0	2.1	2.3
3. Growth "unexplained" by inputs of labor, land, and capital (1 minus 2)	2.4	2.3	2.1
Mexico:			
1. Growth of output	5.1	5.1	5.1
2. Growth of inputs	3.2	3.2	3.2
3. Growth "unexplained" by inputs of labor, land, and capital (1 minus 2)	1.9	1.9	1.9

Sources: See Table 3.11.

Table 3.14
The Growth of Mexican Crop Production, Inputs, and Productivity, 1929–59
(compound annual growth rates)

North:
1. Growth of output 5.0
2. Growth of inputs 4.2
3. Growth "unexplained" by inputs
   of labor, land, and capital
   (1 minus 2) 0.8

Gulf:
1. Growth of output 4.5
2. Growth of inputs 2.7
3. Growth "unexplained" by inputs
   of labor, land, and capital
   (1 minus 2) 1.8

North Pacific:
1. Growth of output 5.8
2. Growth of inputs 5.6
3. Growth "unexplained" by inputs
   of labor, land, and capital
   (1 minus 2) 0.2

South Pacific:
1. Growth of output 5.7
2. Growth of inputs 2.9
3. Growth "unexplained" by inputs
   of labor, land, and capital
   (1 minus 2) 2.8

Center:
1. Growth of output 3.5
2. Growth of inputs 1.8
3. Growth "unexplained" by inputs
   of labor, land, and capital
   (1 minus 2) 1.7

Mexico:
1. Growth of output 4.5
2. Growth of inputs 3.2
3. Growth "unexplained" by inputs
   of labor, land, and capital
   (1 minus 2) 1.3

Note: The labor share for this table is Estimate B (50 percent) for each region; capital shares are from Table 3.11; rental share is a residual.

of land, labor, and capital (not including public investment in roads, schools, power, or communications; Table 3.14). Most of these gains occurred during the 1940s (Table 3.12), precisely when substantial road building took place, thus integrating the agriculture of this region with markets in the rest of the country and abroad. The statistics on regional highway construction are given in Appendix Table E.12. During the 1940s the South Pacific increased the amount of land in cultivation more than any other region in Mexico including the northern states; yet this occurred without much investment reported in physical units such as buildings, machinery, or irrigation works. Because a good share of the increase in output in the region was in plantation crops, capital formation took the form of clearing of land and planting of trees. As these activities make use of underemployed local labor, they represent a conservation of both foreign exchange and industrial output and are a conspicuous example of potential rural savings that can be mobilized in the form of labor-intensive investments once markets for cash crops appear.

The region of second highest productivity gains was the Gulf, another area not noted for a significant amount of physical investment in agriculture. Capital stock in the Gulf has grown 278 percent over the past three decades, the slowest rate of growth in Mexico and less than half the national average. The trunk highway and railroad line linking Veracruz to Mérida were not even begun until the 1950s. Our figures on regional output reflect this lag in transportation investment, since it was during the very years when the South Pacific was experiencing rapid productivity gains that the Gulf showed little or no unexplained growth (see Table 3.11). Once transport links had been created for this region, capital formation in the Gulf grew at the highest rate of any region in Mexico, and still a productivity residual of 2.1 to 2.3 percent remained.[21] It is significant that the two regions showing the highest unexplained productivity gains per-

21. One of the pioneer integrated river basin development projects of Mexico serves important areas of this region. An extremely imaginative, far-reaching, and costly undertaking, the Papaloapan (Butterfly) River basin was selected for a system of dams and roads to expand tropical agriculture and to bring isolated local peasants into the national economy. See José Attolini, *Economía de la Cuenca del Papaloapan; Bosques, Fauna, Pesca, Ganadería e Industria.* A preliminary assessment of the project by an American economist suggests that, owing to difficulties in planning which may have been associated with changing criteria of successive political administrations, the benefits that were hoped for have not been realized and performance was incommensurate with costs. (Thomas T. Poleman, *The Papaloapan Project.*)

formed most successfully immediately after transport links had been established with the rest of the country. Moreover, in each case these regions developed in a far more land- and labor-intensive way than the capital-intensive agriculture of the North and West.

The Center follows the Gulf in terms of growth of agricultural productivity (Table 3.14). It was the region with the second slowest rate of capital formation, and the only area in which the land/labor ratio actually declined over the past thirty years. Much of its cropland has been worked for thousands of years. While the total cultivated land area of Mexico increased 92 percent between 1930 and 1960, it increased only 35 percent in the Center. The growth of the rural labor force in the Center also has been the slowest in Mexico, rising only 52 percent in thirty years. It is little wonder that private investment has not been generally responsive and that the regional share of total value of production has fallen sharply. Yet, unlike the North, there is no indication of decreasing average productivity of capital, since productivity gains have accounted for half of the increase in output since 1930. As this region received a disproportionately high degree of public investment in economic and social infrastructure after the Revolution—in the form of roads, rural electrification, and schools—it is quite possible that the 1.7 percent annual productivity gains since 1930 are largely attributable to these other factors.

The North shows the fourth highest annual rate of growth of productivity during the last thirty years (0.8 percent). This long-run average should be qualified by evidence of a secular decline in productivity growth since 1940. In the 1950s the North actually experienced diminishing returns to the three basic factors of production as revealed by its negative productivity residual (Table 3.13). The rate of growth of capital formation in the North has decreased since the 1940s, while output in the 1950s lagged behind the growth of all three factors of production, including labor. Despite the fact that per capita output remains above that of the Center, the North and particularly the north-central portion of the high plateau shows the least favorable trend of any region.

Perhaps the most interesting finding of the analysis is that Mexico's richest agricultural region, the North Pacific, has had the lowest productivity gains over the long run. During the 1930s and 1940s its residuals were actually negative. Even after the impressive performance of the 1950s (between 5.8 and 6.1 percent annual growth in productivity), the regional gain for the whole period averaged a mere 0.2 percent (Table 3.14). Since the states on the northwest coast of Mexico have received the largest share of government investment in irrigation since 1940, these results are of some importance in assessing the role of regional public investment policy in Mexican agriculture. They suggest that either this policy was directed to absolute rather than to percentage gains in agricultural production, or that there might have been overinvestment in the North Pacific relative to other regions in Mexico.[22] When the low productivity gains of the capital-intensive North Pacific are contrasted with the high productivity gains in the labor-intensive South Pacific, there is some evidence from the data that labor- and land-intensive cultivation can yield much higher residuals than capital-intensive techniques.

The fact that capital formation in the North Pacific increased by over 400 percent, land inputs by 70 percent, and labor by only 38 percent in the 1940s, while output rose by 77 percent, illustrates that extremely capital- and land-intensive methods of cultivation were fostered by public policy in this region. Some of the returns to this investment evidently were deferred, since output increased by almost 200 percent in the North Pacific during the 1950s, although the capital stock rose by 126 percent and land by 60 percent during that decade. The different residuals for the 1940s and 1950s may well reflect the long gestation period for water resource development projects in the region. If society were willing to wait an indefinite amount of time for the return on rural investment, and if the net increase in productivity in this area occurred well in advance of the gains to investment in other regions despite the delay, one could be more positive about the relative efficiency of investment in the North Pacific. But even taking into consideration a five- to ten-year lag between investment and output, the results are not encouraging. One compensating factor is that propensities to save and invest out of increases in agricultural income of the North Pacific have tended to far exceed those of other regions because of initially high levels of per capita output relative to wage costs. Furthermore, the durability of dams and irrigation systems prolongs the period of productivity of a given amount of investment. The controlled climate cultivation that they provide permits not only a longer growing season but also greater increases in the productivity of fertilizer and high yield seed varieties

22. The latter suggestion is supported by the findings of Donald Freebairn, for both public and private investment in Sonora, "Relative Production Efficiency between Tenure Classes in the Yaqui Valley, Sonora, Mexico."

than could be obtained through dry farming or reliance on seasonal rainfall.

THE REGIONAL DISTRIBUTION OF RURAL PRODUCTION

Since agricultural production represents only two-thirds of the total income available to the inhabitants of rural areas, not counting that obtained from services, handicraft, commerce, and mining, the implications of agricultural development should be viewed in a broader context. It is clear from the statistics in Table 3.15 that the inclusion of livestock, forestry, and fishery production alters the level (though not the regional distribution) of rural per capita income. Although it was not possible to provide detailed time series for these other activities, Table 3.15 suggests that in the late 1950s important regional inequalities existed not only for crop production but for total rural production as well.

Since cattle raising and forestry traditionally have been concentrated in the North, this region receives a relatively large share of the total value of rural production, while the North Pacific and Gulf benefit from a high proportion of the value of fishery production (Table 3.15). Inadequate conservation policies and overcutting partly explain the relative stagnation of forestry production since 1940 (Table 3.16). This industry has been overwhelmingly concentrated in the North (Table 3.15) and its lagging production has tended to retard the growth of this region. Rapid increases in the fishing industry along the Gulf and North Pacific coasts are providing an important new source of income and foreign exchange for these areas. Fishing may eventually surpass the value of forestry production if the latter industry is allowed to remain in its present retarded condition (Table 3.16). Meanwhile, animal husbandry is experiencing a resurgence in output and productivity, the regional implications of which remain to be analyzed in future studies.

Our statistics indicate that regional disequilibria in total and per capita agricultural production are accentuated rather than diminished by the inclusion of cattle, forestry, and fishing. Both livestock and forestry production tend to be land-intensive, and cattle-raising promises to continue to grow in importance as a source of income in the North and North Pacific where open range predominates. Nevertheless, continuing encroachment of cropland into these grazing areas will almost certainly affect the northern livestock industry. As the

Table 3.15
Regional Gross Value of Agriculture, Livestock, Fishery, and Forestry Production—Crop Year (1959/60)
(million pesos of current value)

Region	Agricultural Production		Livestock Production		Forestry Production		Fishery[a] Production		Total Production	
	Amount	Percent	Amount	Percent	Amount	Percent	Amount	Percent	Amount	Percent
North	3,312	23	2,001	33	768	73	32	7	6,112	28
Gulf	2,443	17	878	15	78	7	161	33	3,560	16
North Pacific	2,581	18	751	12	24	2	252	52	3,609	16
South Pacific	2,151	15	650	11	97	9	31	6	2,930	13
Center	3,909	27	1,722	29	88	8	7	1	5,725	26
Mexico	14,396	100	6,002	100	1,055	100	483	100	21,935	100

Columns and rows do not always sum due to rounding.

[a] 1957.

Sources: All data, with the exception of that for fishery production, are from Dirección General de Estadística, *Cuarto Censos Agricola-Ganadero y Ejidal, 1960*, Table 23. Data on fishery production from Zamora, *Diagnóstico Económico Regional, 1958*. The statistics in this study were originally divided into seven regions that more accurately reflect Mexico's sharp geographical dissimilarities (Noreste, Altiplano, Nororiental, Pacífico Sur, Central Golfo, Ístmica, Sureste). The fishery data have been regrouped here into the five census regions to facilitate comparisons with the other sectors, the data for which were collected from a different source.

Table 3.16
Growth of Agricultural, Cattle, Forestry, and Fishery Production
(compound annual rates of growth)

	1900/ 1910	1910/ 1925	1925/ 1940	1940/ 1950	1950/ 1960
1. Physical Index of Crop Production[a]	2.8	1.0	2.7	8.2	4.3
2. Cattle Production[b,e]	1.2	0.5	2.2	2.6	4.4
3. Forestry Production[e]	–[d]	–	–	0.0	−0.3
4. Fishery Production[e]	–	–	–	12.3	5.9
5. Total Population[e]	1.1	0.1	1.6	2.8	3.1

Sources: [a] Table 3.7. The figure in column 1 is for the years 1900/1907. The rate of growth for 1940/1950 has an upward bias due to bad harvests in the base year.

[b] Cattle production figures 1900–40 are from Enrique Pérez López, "El Producto Nacional," *México: Cincuenta Años de Revolución*, Tomo 1, "La Economía," Fondo de Cultura Económica, 1960.

[e] All other data 1940–60 are from Grupo Secretaría de Hacienda-Banco de México, Estudios sobre Proyecciones, *Manual*, Cuadro 2.-3. (Table 3.7).

[d] Data not available.

[e] Table 3.7.

land values rise in this region, more attention is already being given to the growing of feed crops and improvements in breeding stock, especially in the beef cattle industry. Crop production and cattle raising are, therefore, both competing and complementary activities. Determination of the extent to which public investment in rural infrastructure has served to expand cattle, forestry, and fishery production requires a much more detailed analysis than is possible here.

Over the two decades since 1939, Mexican crop production increased almost threefold. Most of this growth was attributable to additional inputs of capital, land, and labor. In the 1940s, less than a quarter of the growth of value added remained unaccounted for by traditional inputs, and in the 1950s one-third of agricultural growth was unexplained. The experience of the 1930s was somewhat different, however, as two-thirds of the growth in crop production in this decade could not be accounted for by increased inputs. Since this was a time of recovery from depression, revolution, and sharp disturbances in the pattern of land tenure, the resulting rate of productivity growth would be expected to differ from that of later decades. Over the long run from 1929 to 1959, only 29 percent of agricultural growth was attributable to productivity changes. These results suggest that the sources of the remarkable performance of Mexican agriculture are by no means miraculous, that economic factors have been the proximate causes of growth. Yet the fourfold increase in public and private investment in agriculture since 1939 is itself a phenomenon that cannot be accounted for without considering institutional and attitudinal changes that are associated with the preceding Revolution and agrarian reform.

Agricultural productivity gains have differed widely among regions and over time and appear to have been somewhat independent of the pattern of factor employment and especially of the capital-intensity of production. For example, the region that was initially poorest showed the greatest net productivity gains, while the richest region showed the least. In part, increases in output have been due to the fuller use of land and labor in response to expanding demand created by improvements in transportation, commerce, and communications (such as in the Gulf and South Pacific). In part, growth has resulted from the opening up of desert land (such as in the North Pacific) which had negligible productivity before irrigation. In either case, favorable results depended upon the availability of profit-maximizing rural entrepreneurs. However uneducated in a formal sense, a large number of peasant farmers (many of whom obtained land through the agrarian reform) have responded shrewdly and quickly to market incentives. One cannot minimize the importance of these campesinos who, calculating their chances centavo by centavo, have employed every available means to better the conditions of themselves and their families. Although their response often has been qualified by the need for a minimum amount of income security, for which they have tended to keep part of their land in subsistence crops, most observers of the rural economy have remarked upon the rational and receptive attitude of the rural population to new economic opportunities.[23]

The evidence of this chapter suggests that no simple aggregate model is capable of explaining the impressive growth of Mexican agricultural production during the past fifty years. Each region must be analyzed separately in terms of its special circumstances of resource availability, climatic conditions, degree of integration with the

---

23. A recent history of one such peasant farmer which has already become a classic is Oscar Lewis's *Pedro Martínez*. A fascinatingly detailed analysis of a contemporary Mexican peasant community and its response to rural development incentives is contained in Michael Belshaw's *A Village Economy*.

rest of the economy, and population density, before one can generalize from the Mexican experience. In addition the importance of the human element in the campesino's response to economic stimuli suggests that more attention should be paid to social and psychological factors in development than economic analysis alone can provide. And with all of its success, Mexican agricultural growth cannot be disassociated from extreme income inequality. Although there has been considerable internal migration of agricultural labor from the less to the more productive areas of cultivation, little growth in rural per capita agricultural output since 1940 may be attributed to any permanent shift in rural population from regions of lowest to highest productivity. If, for example, increases in output per rural dweller (Table 3.3) from 1940–60 are weighted by the share of each region in total rural population in 1940, one arrives at an estimated increase in national agricultural output per rural dweller which is almost identical to the observed growth rate (97 percent). Rural migration almost certainly has permitted productivity gains to average more than would have been true under the assumption of no migration. Yet those regions with the highest initial level of rural per capita income have retained their relative position over the long run (see Table 3.4). This explains why rural personal income inequality remains so high, as shown in the budget studies cited in Chapter 2.

When agriculture develops in a rapid and unbalanced fashion, as in Mexico, and when a large though declining subsistence sector remains, one may expect the inequality of income to widen rather than narrow, at least during the transitional period of rural development. Our evidence suggests that even when a country has experienced major agrarian reform, this pattern of increasing rural inequality is difficult to avoid. The effect on rural welfare is clearly disadvantageous in view of the evident importance of relative income to the psychic well-being of the peasantry. As absolute income inequality increases, the rate of growth in real income of those at the bottom of the ladder will have to be greater than otherwise in order to compensate for the widening gap between the life they lead and that of their more fortunate fellow citizens. Policies associated with an "ethos of revolution" that stresses equality must be prepared to deal with the social and political problems that arise from sustained inequality in rural income. The advantages which such inequality may provide, in terms of rising rates of savings and investment and a correspondingly higher rate of growth of GDP, must be placed against the cost of increased rural unrest. This problem existed before the Revolution of 1910 and it remains present today. The following chapter shows how land redistribution helped to alleviate the problem in the past. It deals with important social, political, and institutional factors which have influenced the performance of Mexican agriculture and which help to account, not only for the "unexplained" portion of growth, but also for the extent to which agriculture has been able to respond so successfully to market stimuli over the past sixty years.

4

Land Reform, Public Policy, and
Mexican Agricultural Development[1]

Mexican agriculture has experienced three major land tenure alterations in the last hundred years, the first two imposed under quite different political regimes before and after 1910 and the third phase, since 1940, representing a more market-oriented response of rural institutions to public investment, technical change, and expanding urban and foreign demand for cash crops. The past is therefore rich in examples of the effects of land tenure change on agricultural production and productivity and of cases in which social as well as economic factors have altered the structure of land ownership and land use. The government has played a major role in this process of interaction by influencing both the pattern of asset ownership and the rate of return on investment in agriculture.

The preceding chapter showed how the growth of Mexican agricultural production after 1900 followed different trends (both regionally and by decade) in factor intensity, the level and composition of output, and productivity growth. This chapter will analyze regional crop production and productivity growth in terms of their relation to changes in land tenure associated with the agrarian reform program as well as the regional impact of investment in roads and irrigation systems. The implications of these results for employment, income distribution, and final demand will be discussed briefly, with special attention to the period since 1930. It will be shown that public policies in agriculture have contributed to the dualistic development of the rural sector of the economy. In conclusion, an assessment will be

1. The sequence of chapters 3 and 4 is designed to avoid prejudging the initial productivity analysis by setting it in an aprioristic institutional framework. It is recognized that some readers unfamiliar with agrarian reform in Mexico may prefer to read the descriptive section of this chapter before dealing with the analytical material in Chapter 3.

made of the effect of this dual policy of land tenure reform and public investment on the development of the national economy.[2]

Since late in the nineteenth century Mexico has included within its borders a wide divergence of agricultures. Its rural development can be understood only in terms of the gradual displacement of subsistence[3] by commercial cultivation, a process begun during the Porfiriato, interrupted and altered by the Revolution and agrarian reform, and accelerated in recent years. This process is outlined below:

Porfirian Enclosure

In the 1860s most of the land was devoted to the cultivation of crops either on large, virtually self-sufficient haciendas or on smaller plots, held by Indians and *mestizos,* which were barely capable of sustaining the peasant cultivator and his immediate family. The few exceptions

2. A number of previous studies have greatly contributed to our understanding of the role of agrarian reform in Mexican agricultural development. Although this is the first regional treatment of the problem for the period from 1930 to 1960, the author attempts to build on firm foundations by drawing freely upon a literature which includes: George McBride, *The Land Systems of Mexico;* Eyler Simpson, *The Ejido;* Marco Antonio Durán, *La redistribución de la tierra y la explotación agrícola ejidal;* Nathan L. Whetten, *Rural Mexico;* Ramon Fernández y Fernández, *Propiedad privada versus ejidos;* Lucio Mendieta y Núñez, *El problema agrario de México;* Luis Yáñez-Pérez, *Mecanización de la agricultura Mexicana;* Clarence O. Senior, *Land Reform and Democracy;* Edmundo Flores, *Tratado de economía agrícola;* Moises T. de la Peña, *El pueblo y su tierra;* and Solomón Eckstein, *El Ejido Colectivo en México.* Among the monographic literature I have particularly benefited from: Clarence A. Moore, "Agricultural Development in Mexico"; James G. Maddox, "Mexican Land Reform, A Report"; Edmundo Flores, "The Significance of Land-Use Changes in the Economic Development of Mexico"; Richard W. Parks, "The Role of Agriculture in Mexican Economic Development"; Banco de México, Office for the Study of Agricultural Projections (under the direction of Fernando Rosenzweig), *Projections of Supply of and Demand for Agricultural and Livestock Products in Mexico to 1970 and 1975;* and Leopoldo Solís M., "Recent Changes in the Structure and Behavior of the Mexican Economy."

3. The reader is referred to p. 92, Chap. 3, for the definition of "subsistence" used throughout the text. It is a relative concept, referring to the extremely low level of living earned by the peasant producer that makes net savings extremely difficult, yet it is consistent with observed historical evidence that a well-organized and active system of marketing and exchange has existed even in the poorest regions of rural Mexico since well before the Conquest.

to this rule included cattle ranches and plantations of sugar, cotton, and maguey.[4] Coffee, cocoa, and henequen plantations also were found in southern Mexico, but most of the cultivated land area was devoted to subsistence agriculture and there were only a few conspicuous islands of cash crop production.

Such a system produced very little beyond the essentials for survival. The rural economy generated no significant rural savings or investment and experienced correspondingly little growth of farm output per head. The administration of Porfirio Díaz regarded the condition of rural Mexico in the late nineteenth century as inconsistent with its goal of modernization. The existing land tenure system and the Mexican peasant were held jointly responsible for the backwardness of agriculture. It was assumed that most Indians and *mestizos* were innately lazy and unproductive, incapable of adapting to modern techniques of cultivation, unresponsive to economic incentives, and therefore unworthy to own or manage resources that could otherwise be employed to produce cash crops for urban and foreign markets. As a result the government supported what amounted to an enclosure movement, in which federal land and peasant communal holdings, as well as other private properties with clouded titles, were redistributed to land development companies and to individuals successful in gaining favor with the administration.[5]

This sweeping consolidation of rural holdings between 1880 and 1910 detached an ever-increasing number of peasants from the land and created a new class of agricultural wage laborers. Since the terms of trade for Mexican agricultural exports were increasing in the years before 1895, these gains were initially passed on in the form of rising real wages for the growing rural proletariat. During this period, the expansion of urban production improved the market for unskilled labor and helped to sustain the level of real wages in agriculture. As a result, the initial transformation of the rural sector from one of small-scale and feudal hacienda holdings to a commercial plantation system was less painful than it might otherwise have been. Yet those regions which were ultimately to spark the

4. A cactus from which a milky liquor is extracted and fermented into *pulque,* a cheap and popular alcoholic beverage now being replaced by beer.
5. The process of enclosure was preceded by the expropriation of church lands, begun in the 1850s and legalized by the Constitution of 1857, interrupted during the French occupation and resumed under the presidencies of Juárez and Porfirio Díaz. The anticlerical phase benefited primarily wealthy private landholders and set a precedent for the subsequent enclosure movement.

agrarian reform movement included states such as Michoacán, Coahuila, and Sonora, which had previously experienced a high degree of agricultural commercialization and land consolidation.[6]

It was not until after 1895 that the process of forced enclosure became associated with falling rural real incomes. The terms of trade for agricultural exports began to level off and then to decline by the turn of the century. Meanwhile, as artisans were replaced by machines and the urban labor supply began to exceed demand, workers were forced to move back to the countryside. Between 1900 and 1910 the urban/rural population ratio actually fell. Pressures began to mount for a return of those communal and private holdings which had been taken over by large-scale commercial cultivators. This cry for land represented a demand for greater economic security by the expanding rural population. It did not matter to those espousing a return to traditional tenure forms that general efficiency in agriculture might be sacrificed, since they were interested as much in its stability and distribution as in the level of income. Under the pre-Porfirian tenure system, a peasant and his family were at least able to eke out a subsistence from their own church, hacienda, or communally held village land. But the enclosure system, by drawing the peasants off the land, ended their independence from the exigencies of national and foreign markets. When these markets subsequently experienced falling prices, and when the demand for labor declined as well, the social cost of the enclosure system proved too great for political stability.

Postrevolutionary Reform

Shortly after 1910 the murmurings of rural discontent erupted into an explosion of violence which shook the countryside for almost a decade. President Madero was assassinated and the subsequent Carranza revolt against his self-appointed successor, General Huerta, widened into civil war. Political and military leaders split into factions competing for the support of the peasantry and distributing

6. An important discussion of the distinction between the *hacienda* and the *plantation* as economic and social units and their implications for peasant welfare is presented in Eric R. Wolf and Sidney W. Mintz, "Haciendas and Plantations in Middle America and the Antilles." See also Flores, *Tratado de Economía Agrícola*. Mexico illustrates the important political implications of a rapid and forced transition from hacienda to plantation agriculture. A full statistical analysis of similar characteristics in contemporary Brazilian agriculture is given by William R. Cline in a Ph.D. dissertation, "Economically Optimal Land Reform for Brazil."

weapons in the process[7] As a result, the masses were enabled to express their political will in terms of numbers of armed men rather than income or hectares of land, at which they were at a disadvantage. This provided a firm power base for the first major populist agrarian reform in the hemisphere since the North American expropriation of the Spanish-California land grants after 1849.

The Mexican agrarian reform had three principal phases: (1) anarchic reform, (2) decentralized institutional reform, and (3) centralized institutional reform.[8] The first phase involved the forced seizure of land by armed peasants and lasted from the beginning of the Revolution through the early 1920s. While it is impossible to determine the amount of land that changed and rechanged hands in this illegal manner, in terms of percentage of total hectares cultivated it probably was not large since, by the end of the 1930s, over 50 percent of the cultivated land had been transferred by legal means under the agrarian reform laws (Table 4.1). Some of this land, of course, had already changed hands under the anarchic phase so that the official decree simply recognized a fait accompli. The second phase refers to land tenure change by decree of the federal government but without centralized enforcement power or support of the judiciary, a process that continued from the end of the Revolution until the administration of Lázaro Cárdenas (1934–40). The third phase involved centralization of control of the institutionalized agrarian reform such that the president became able to count upon the support of the courts for his decrees and was capable of enforcing executive orders in almost all parts of the country. This phase dates from the mid-1930s to the present.

7. Robert E. Quirk, *The Mexican Revolution 1914–1915.*
8. If one were to generalize from Mexico's experience to that of other Latin American countries it would be useful to add an additional phase that now normally precedes the others, called the "announcement" phase. This is the period marking the beginning of political promises of agrarian reform during which expectations of tenure change are awakened. Such expectations are likely to have negative effects on rural investment and the efficiency of land use, lowering both output and productivity. These effects, in turn, may serve to increase the frustration of the peasantry and thus precipitate the "anarchic" phase. In Mexico (despite the initial support of some enlightened sectors of public opinion for land reform, including certain church liberals), there was little official announcement of reform before anarchy broke out in the countryside. In contemporary Latin America, however, there is still a chance to avoid the anarchic phase, and even the high social costs of the decentralized institutional phase, by moving swiftly from the announcement to the centralized institutional phase of tenure reform.

Table 4.1
Ejidal Hectares Cultivated as a Share of Total Hectares Cultivated, 1930–60
(000 hectares)

Region	1930	1940	1950	1960
1. North				
Ejidal land cultivated	311	1,144	1,428	1,629
Total land cultivated	1,672	2,353	2,946	3,711
Ejidal as % total	19%	49%	48%	44%
2. Gulf				
Ejidal land cultivated	136	348	715	1,021
Total land cultivated	829	631	1,239	1,833
Ejidal as % total	16%	55%	58%	56%
3. North Pacific				
Ejidal land cultivated	37	280	469	681
Total land cultivated	523	553	988	1,582
Ejidal as % total	7%	51%	47%	43%
4. South Pacific				
Ejidal land cultivated	93	325	529	773
Total land cultivated	779	772	1,477	2,066
Ejidal as % total	12%	42%	36%	37%
5. Center				
Ejidal land cultivated	509	1,790	2,170	2,404
Total land cultivated	3,462	3,562	4,214	4,590
Ejidal as % total	15%	50%	51%	52%
6. Mexico				
Ejidal land cultivated	1,086	3,889	5,312	6,507
Total land cultivated	7,265	7,870	10,863	13,783
Ejidal as % total	15%	49%	49%	47%

Source: Decennial Agricultural Censuses. Note that the figures for total land cultivated for 1930 and 1940 are slightly different from those in Appendix Table E.9. The differences are a result of the need to estimate ejidal and total land "cultivated" on a comparative basis, which required the summation of "superficie cosechada" and "superficie perdida" for both categories for each year. The result suggests that the totals in Table E.9 are slightly understated for both years. By no means all land distributed under the agrarian reform program was in ejidal tenure (see Table 4.3).

Each type of land tenure reform had unique implications for agricultural production and productivity, largely because of differing expectations about the certainty of tenure and because of the effect of these expectations on private incentives to work and invest in agriculture. The first two phases were characterized by a high degree of tenure insecurity, with accompanying low levels of investment and inefficient land use. In extreme cases there was actual soil depletion through overcropping and net depreciation of farm buildings and equipment. Opposition from the courts and local political leaders prevented the first postrevolutionary presidents from assuring the rapid transfer of secure title, even when this had been established by their own decrees. Hence neither previous nor current owners were able to predict with certainty when the land would actually change hands, and conditions in many parts of the country were virtually anarchic until well into the 1930s. The economic and social costs of the period from 1910 to 1930 may be measured in terms of agricultural output foregone and growth deterred. This was particularly evident in the Central region where rural unrest resulted in premature urbanization, soil depletion, deterioration of physical assets, and low levels of savings and investment, all of which slowed the pace of agricultural recovery after the Revolution. These costs must be set against the eventual benefits of agrarian reform in terms of more equitable distribution of the returns from land to the peasant; a higher own rate of return for his labor and hence more labor-intensive cultivation of peasant holdings, increased output per hectare in all regions, greater stability of rural incomes, wider participation of the rural population in national politics, identification of the peasantry with the developmental goals of the federal government, and freedom of the government to engage in large-scale investments in commercial agriculture once it had attacked the problem of land hunger.[9]

The third stage of agrarian reform represented an acceleration of land distribution from 1930 to 1940 accompanied by greater enforcement power of the government and increased security of tenure for the new occupants. Although there was a resurgence of land redistribution during the Lopez Mateos administration (1958–64), most expropriation occurred before 1940. Of the 30 million hectares of land redistributed between 1915 and 1960 (Table 4.2), 80 percent had already been allocated by 1945 (30,619,000 hectares).[10] Most of this redistribution occurred during the Cárdenas administra-

9. Today's slow progress in land reform legislation and implementation elsewhere in Latin America may perhaps appear less discouraging when one considers the length of time between the beginning of the Mexican Revolution (1910), the drafting of the reform articles of the Constitution (1917), the enactment of enabling legislation (1927), and the major period of enforced institutional agrarian reform (1934–40). The Mexican case illustrates that the longer the lag between the announcement of agrarian reform and its enactment, the greater the economic and social cost of uncertainty.

10. See Whetten, *Rural Mexico,* Table 19, p. 125.

Table 4.2
Total Land Area Redistributed Under Agrarian Reform Laws from 1915 to 1960
(000 hectares)

Region	Land with Regular Rainfall & Irrigation (1)	Land with Seasonal Rainfall (2)	Total Arable Land (3) = (1) + (2)	Noncrop Land (4)	Total Land Redistributed (5) = (3) + (4)
North	376	2,111	2,487	15,013	17,500
Gulf	245	1,630	1,875	3,672	5,547
North Pacific	184	613	797	2,974	3,771
South Pacific	128	1,353	1,481	2,935	4,416
Center	590	2,855	3,445	4,552	7,997
Mexico	1,523	8,562	10,085	29,145	39,230

Source: Dirección General de Estadística, unpublished work sheets from Secretaría de Agricultura y Ganadería. Data as of August 31, 1960.

tion (1934–40). As of 1933, the year before Cárdenas's election, only 7,625,000 hectares had been distributed.[11]

By the mid-1940s much of the smallholder agriculture that had been eliminated during the Porfiriato was restored. The new tenure unit or *ejido* averaged from two to three hectares during the 1920s and early 1930s, five to seven hectares during the middle and late 1930s, and seven to eight hectares through the mid-1940s.[12] Despite the questionable economic efficiency of such smallholdings, this was not an irrational policy in view of the pressing demands of the population for land as insurance against hard times. Economic security and political stability have long been associated with each other in

11. Simpson, *The Ejido*, Table 18, p. 612.

12. Whetten, *Rural Mexico*, p. 125. The term *"ejido"* is of Castilian origin and derives from the practice of assigning inalienable communal lands to Spanish villages. This practice was similar to the pre-Colonial corporate tenure system under the Aztecs and dates back to the Classical civilization of Teotihuacán. The establishment of the ejido in New Spain was much more extensive than its Spanish counterpart.

> In the Indian pueblos of Mexico, the ejido, from being a relatively small unoccupied space at the entrance to the village, broadens out and includes all of the communal agricultural land of the town. The ejido as it was conceived in New Spain is the Aztec *altepetlalli,* only slightly modified. It is also the prototype of the modern ejido reconstituted and recreated in the laws of the present day agrarian reform.

Simpson, *The Ejido*, pp. 13–14. See also McBride, *Land Systems of Mexico*, p. 166.

the minds of those who advocate small-scale agriculture, and political stability has been an important precondition to general economic development in Mexico. In the process of agrarian reform, the larger holdings were by no means eliminated but merely reduced in size, while the proliferation of smallholdings served to confirm the condition of dual agriculture in Mexico.

With one hand the government has advanced land redistribution in densely populated areas on the high plateau and in the south, and with the other has spent large amounts on irrigation projects in the north and west where water was needed to open up the desert. It has recognized agrarian reform as a political fact of life and has continued the process of land redistribution in small plots, while simultaneously channeling a growing amount of public investment into irrigation works to subsidize medium and large-scale private landholdings. In so doing it found itself able to meet the dual objectives of peasant welfare and agricultural growth.[13] One would find it difficult to prove that this dual policy in agriculture had an initially favorable effect on the rate of growth of crop production. Indeed, the uncertainties of agrarian reform in the early years may well have reduced agricultural output in several key regions, as shown below. Nevertheless, we shall also see why there is reason to conclude that the indirect benefits arising from agrarian reform had much to do with the subsequent growth both of the rural and urban sectors of the economy.

Agricultural Revolution

By 1940 the heyday of Mexican agrarian reform was over, at least insofar as massive distribution of ejidos was concerned. With the advent of presidents Avila Camacho (1940–46) and Miguel Alemán (1946–52), a third major phase in agricultural development was introduced. The country was faced in the 1940s with growing domestic and foreign demand for cash crops. In an effort to increase produc-

13. The question of the relative economic efficiency of the pattern of public investment expenditure in agriculture is treated at some length in Chapter 3. In most cases, and on the basis of reasonable social discount rates, individual projects proved well-justified in terms of private as well as social productivity. See, for example, David P. Barkin, "Economic Development in the Tepalcatepec River Basin," Ph.D. dissertation, and Richard T. King, "River Basin Projects and Regional Development." A somewhat less favorable evaluation of public investment in the Papaloapan basin is found in Poleman, *The Papaloapan Project.*

tion, the government distributed newly irrigated land in much larger units than before but in the form of private holdings rather than ejidos. Internal demand, which already had been stimulated by the expansionary fiscal policy of the late 1930s, swept forward in an export-led boom during World War II. Industrial capacity, idle since the 1920s, became strained; farm prices rose as the consumption of food and industrial crops expanded rapidly.[14] Large federal irrigation works were begun all over Mexico. We have seen in the previous chapter that, despite long gestation periods, these investments eventually played a vital role in expanding agricultural production. It is noteworthy that owing to the responsiveness of supply in the 1940s, the terms of trade for food crops (vis à vis industrial goods) increased only slightly, while output virtually doubled.

Favorable supply conditions in agriculture were accordingly a direct result of government agricultural policy, although not of the agrarian reform per se. By spending large sums on rural infrastructure from 1925 through the 1940s, the government effectively subsidized medium and large-scale commercial farms in the northern and coastal regions. These farms more often than not were private rather than ejidal holdings, and in many cases belong to those who were, or had been associated with, leaders of the Revolution. The owners of these lands, by taking advantage of new federal roads and irrigation systems; modern seeds, pesticides, fertilizers, and technology; and improved marketing conditions (some of which were the result of foreign investment); and by hiring cheap labor from the subsistence sector, were able to obtain high profits and rents. These men were often skilled entrepreneurs who tended to save and reinvest a large share of their income. While this behavior contributed to economic growth, it also served to widen the disparity in output per worker between the commercial and subsistence sector, causing a renewed drift of manpower away from the ejidos toward rural wage labor.

Although this process is similar to that which occurred during the Porfiriato, the government has continued its policy of land distribution, helping to forestall a repetition of the political disturbances of 1910, while price supports for basic crops have served to protect rural incomes from the effect of commodity price fluctuations or a decline in the terms of trade. Public transfers of investable funds

14. The rapid rate of inflation of the 1940s does not seem to be related to agricultural supply bottlenecks. See Marnie W. Mueller, "Structural Inflation and the Mexican Experience" (Ph.D. dissertation), Chapter 3.

Table 4.3
Total Area of Arable Ejidal Land Distributed and Cultivated as of 1960
(000 hectares)

	1	*2*
	Total Arable Land Distributed in	*Total Ejidal Land*
Region	*the Form of Ejidos as of 1960*	*Cultivated in 1960*
North	2,485	1,629
Gulf	1,812	1,021
North Pacific	1,095	681
South Pacific	1,622	773
Center	3,314	2,404
Mexico	10,328	6,508

Source: 1960 Agricultural Census: figures are for the crop year 1959/60. Note that the classification "arable land" (*tierra de labor*) in the census that is used in column 1 does not precisely coincide with that in Table 4.2, and land distributed under the agrarian reform program (Table 4.2) has never been solely in ejidal form, particularly since 1940. Those comparing Tables 4.2 and 4.3 will note that only 63 percent of the arable land (column 1) was actually cultivated (column 2) in 1960. It is therefore likely that the census overstates the amount of arable ejidal land.

from industry to agriculture have more than offset the flow of private savings from rural to urban areas, and the rapid growth of industry and services has expanded the demand for unskilled labor (Chapter 5). As the islands of commercial cultivation continue to grow, displacing the sea of subsistence agriculture, living conditions are improving for the average rural worker. In the meantime, the ejido system remains as a safeguard for the peasant who, when not in demand as a bracero in the north or a laborer in the cities, may return to his own plot of land, which remains inalienable under the Constitution.[15]

LAND REFORM AND ITS EFFECT ON AGRICULTURAL
PRODUCTION AND PRODUCTIVITY

The violent nature of Mexico's agrarian reform may or may not have been inevitable. But the poverty, oppression, and expropriation of the peasantry that took place during the Porfiriato made some redis-

15. In practice, the rental of ejidal holdings and creation of partnerships, although prohibited by law, does occur. This is to be expected since enterprising peasants, unwilling to leave land idle when the owners are working elsewhere, find ways to circumvent the letter of the law in order to better apply its spirit. Eckstein, *El Ejido Colectivo en México*, p. 489.

Table 4.4
Rank Ordering of the Rate of Growth of Per Capita Agricultural Production
(1930–60) and the Percentage of Ejidal Land to Total Land Under Cultivation (1950)
(Ranked in Descending Order)

1 *Rate of Growth of Agricultural Production per Rural Dweller (1930/60)*	2 *Share of Ejidal Land to Total Land Under Cultivation (1950 or 1960)*
1. South Pacific	Gulf
2. North	Center
3. North Pacific	North
4. Center	North Pacific
5. Gulf	South Pacific

Source: Column 1 from Table 3.9.
Column 2 from Table 4.1.

tribution of income and wealth unavoidable once the masses had been armed. Given the changes that did occur, what was the cost of agrarian reform and what were its benefits in terms of agricultural production and productivity?

Between 1930 and 1960 there was an almost perfect negative correlation between the regional growth of per capita agricultural production and the share of ejidal land under cultivation (Table 4.4). This suggests that the ejido system which emerged from the Revolution may have retarded agricultural development over the long run. However, the results for the years before 1930 are not so clear. For example, in 1930 the highest share of ejidal land in cultivation was in the North (19 percent). Yet from 1907 to 1930 the North also experienced the second highest rate of growth per capita product in agriculture (derived from Tables 4.1 and 3.4). The second slowest growth of rural per capita output during the same period occurred in the region with the next-to-lowest share of ejidos, the South Pacific. Furthermore, the North Pacific and the North were the regions with the greatest increases in per capita production between 1907 and 1930; yet the North had the highest and the North Pacific the lowest[16]

16. Perhaps it is not coincidental with these findings that many of the leaders in the 1920s came from the North Pacific (Sonora), including Presidents Obregón and Calles. On the other hand, President Cárdenas came from the Center (Michoacán) and depended on the peasantry for much of his political strength. During his administration (1934–40), land reform in the North Pacific was brought into line with the rest of the country, the ejidal share rising from under 10 percent to 51 percent (Table 4.1).

share of ejidos as of 1930 (19 percent and 7 percent, respectively). Therefore no simple relationship between growth of output and land reform emerges during this early period.

One reason for the lack of a clear relationship between the performance of output and early changes in land tenure is that the North had a very mixed agriculture even before the agrarian reform. Increased demand for cash crops through the 1920s offset the negative influence of expropriation. Per capita output increased rapidly in the commercial agricultural zones of the North and North Pacific before 1930 at the same time that the more densely populated regions of the Center, Gulf, and South Pacific lagged (Table 3.4). Furthermore, in the North and North Pacific, while cash crop production was rising, the output of staples such as corn and beans was poor and the bean harvest in 1930 was actually below that of 1907. Since considerably more land was redistributed in the North than in the North Pacific before 1930, it is significant that bean harvests declined much more in the North and corn production increased by a smaller amount. It would appear that, during the early phase of agrarian reform, peasant producers of subsistence crops suffered along with large landowners as a consequence of rural anarchy, violence, and economic uncertainty.

During the 1930s almost every section of the country was transformed by centralized institutional agrarian reform. The percentage of ejidal land rose from 15 percent to 50 percent of the cultivated area (Table 4.1). As land redistribution in the North Pacific increased more rapidly than in any other region, the rate of growth of rural per capita production in this region became negative. The North and Center experienced the least increase in the ejidal share of land cultivated but had the fastest growth rates (Table 4.5). As the pace of land reform intensified, a negative relationship between land redistribution and per capita output began to become apparent. Nevertheless other factors were also operating. World depression did much to curtail cash crop production in the North Pacific, North, and Gulf, independent of land tenure change.

Much of the increase in agricultural output of the Center and South Pacific during the 1930s represented a recovery of prerevolutionary levels of per capita product in subsistence agriculture. Therefore, one must examine the post-1940 figures for possible effects of land reform on rural productivity. The circumstances after 1940 are complicated, since it has been pointed out that private agriculture

Table 4.5
Rate of Growth of Per Capita Agricultural Production and the Increase in the Share
of Ejidal to Total Land Cultivated
(Ranked in Descending Order)

1	*2*	*3*	*4*
Rate of Growth of Agricultural Production per Rural Dweller		*Rate of Increase in the Share of Ejidal to Total Land Under Cultivation*	
1930/1940	*1940/1960*	*1930/1940*	*1940/1960*
1. North	North Pacific	North Pacific	Center
2. Center	South Pacific	South Pacific	Gulf
3. South Pacific	North	Gulf	North
4. Gulf	Gulf	Center	South Pacific
5. North Pacific	Center	North	North Pacific

Source: Columns 1 and 2 based on Table 3.2.
       Columns 3 and 4 based on calculations from Table 4.1.

received greater government encouragement than did the ejidos. Land expropriation and redistribution merely kept pace with the total expansion of cropland, except in the Gulf and Center where the share of ejidal land showed a modest increase over the two decades (Table 4.1).

Bearing these factors in mind, the evidence continues to favor the productivity performance of those regions having a relative increase in private holdings. Table 4.5 reveals a -1.0 rank correlation between the rise in regional per capita agricultural output and the rise in the ejidal share of land in cultivation between 1940 and 1960. While suggestive, this is far from sufficient evidence that ejidos were less productive than private farms, since allowance must be made for differences in the quality of soil, climate, degree of public and private investment, rural education, and proximity to markets of each tenure class as well as the contribution of each class to the overall productivity. In terms of most of the inputs cited, the ejidos have been at a disadvantage. But to what extent were complementary inputs not made available because ejidal tenure units were intrinsically inefficient and to what extent because they represented a threat to centralized political decision making?

The data does not permit more than inferential estimates of ejidal efficiency, though these suggest that over the long run those regions with a higher incidence of ejidal tenure experienced somewhat greater increases in "unexplained" productivity as calculated in the previous chapter. For example, the rank ordering of regional productivity residuals from 1930 to 1960 (Table 3.14) is identical to that of the share of ejidal land in cultivation by region as of 1950 or 1960 (Table 4.1) once the South Pacific is removed.[17] That region, however, showed the highest growth of productivity with the lowest share of ejidal tenure over the three decades. A more accurate measure of the potential relationship between the incidence of ejidos and productivity growth would be to rank the productivity residual for the period 1940 to 1960 by region and to relate this to the regional share of ejidal land. This has been done using the three alternative estimates of the residual; the rank correlation coefficients fall between -0.1 and -0.3, scarcely indicating that productivity growth since 1940 has borne any positive relationship to tenure class at a regional level of aggregation.

The long-run positive relationship, while tenuous, does tend to confirm independent evidence of more intensive land use by the small cultivator, whether ejiditario or private holder. The labor hours per hectare apparently increased for small farms relative to medium and large-scale holdings as the latter (whether collectively or privately held) shifted toward more capital-intensive methods of cultivation.[18] Since a precise estimate of the hours worked per man-year by region is unavailable, the productivity effect of this added labor appears in the residual. If the opportunity cost of rural labor were as low as regional wage levels suggest, then labor-intensive cultivation may

17. The author is indebted to Matthew Edel for making this point.
18. This is not to suggest that in cases where the peasant owned both private and ejidal land he did not work as hard or harder on his private smallholding. Rather it is illustrative of the fact that ejidal agriculture is a proxy for all *minifundia* in Mexico and that the relative increase in intensity of labor use helps to explain gains in output in regions where this type of agriculture predominates. Of course, these are not *net* increases since part of the gain in the output of smallholdings reflects a shift in labor time from other types of cottage activities such as pottery-making, weaving, and tortilla-making toward the cultivation and harvesting of crops, as farm prices relative to those of home-produced goods rose. For a theoretical discussion of this effect see Stephen Hymer and Stephen Resnick, "The Supply Response of Agrarian Economics and the Importance of Z Goods" (published as Hymer and Resnick, "A Model of an Agrarian Economy with Nonagricultural Activities," *American Economic Review*, vol. LIX, no. 4, Part 1, Sept. 1969). The expanding network of highways and feeder roads is gradually converting the nation from a constellation of small peasant markets and large urban enclaves into a single national market. Trade between town and country is rapidly expanding. Though the urban terms of trade seem to have been fairly constant between farm products and manufactures, they are probably rising in most rural areas as unit transport costs and retail margins decline for both "imports" and "exports".

have represented a more efficient use of Mexican resources, especially through the 1940s. Even in recent years there has been little shortage of unskilled labor in agriculture, while capital and other intermediate inputs have always been scarce.

An additional consideration is the necessity for making a sharp distinction between individual and collective ejidos. The former were generally small plots of land of inferior quality. These smallholdings stood in contrast to the larger estates from which they had been broken, in terms of crops grown, level of technology, and amount of investment in roads, irrigation systems, buildings, machinery, and equipment. The great plantations had frequently benefited from economies of scale in cultivation, harvesting, and processing. For example, the sugar mills of Central Mexico, which frequently dated back to the eighteenth or early nineteenth century, relied for a steady flow of cane upon hundreds and sometimes thousands of hectares of adjacent land. Large cotton plantations in the north were often farmed by families or corporations that had obtained control of local water rights and were therefore able to irrigate effectively even in dry years. Maguey and henequen also were cultivated on a land-intensive basis since they require a several-year growing season and new crops must be planted yearly to assure a regular harvest. When the land on these estates was subdivided into five- to ten-hectare plots, scale economies were lost, the advantages of central administration and long-term planning disappeared, and physical capital fell into disrepair.

The government was aware of the disruptive effects that the fragmentation of the plantations would have on crop production. In an effort to minimize these disturbances as well as to soften the blow to the original owners, the latter were permitted to retain 100 to 200 hectares of their choice. This usually included the nucleus of the old hacienda with its well, pump, storehouses, and buildings. Sometimes individual members of the family were permitted to retain an additional 100 to 200 hectares each, a provision that had the effect of keeping much of the hacienda intact. Often an owner could cause per-hectare productivity to increase as a result of a larger amount of capital, water resources, and trained personnel per unit of remaining land. The output of cash crops was therefore affected less than might have been expected under a more extreme form of expropriation.

An alternative method of retaining the advantage of large-scale cultivation while continuing the process of expropriation was the

Mexican innovation of the collective ejido.[19] The classic example of this new institution may be found in the Laguna region of North Central Mexico. A fertile basin centered in Torreon and overlapping the states of Coahuila and Durango, the Laguna accounted for half of Mexico's cotton crop in the 1930s. In 1936, after several years of agitation by day laborers in the region, Lázaro Cárdenas expropriated over a million acres of Laguna land in only forty-five days. The redistribution was far too hasty to permit optimal results. So many petitioners qualified for land that the original holdings were fragmented, with subsequent loss of scale economies.

Nevertheless, some 300 collective ejidos were formed in the Laguna in an attempt by the government to maintain efficient use of irrigation ditches, to apportion scarce water on an equitable basis, and to allocate federal loans. The form of the collectives varied from case to case but, in the majority, workers were paid weekly wages in anticipation of the harvest plus a share of profits net of deductions for new investment and Social Fund payments.[20] The National Ejidal Credit Bank, formed in the 1930s, concentrated most of its lending in a few regions and tended to favor the collective ejido. In 1936 the Bank allocated 36 million out of a total of 46 million pesos in loans to the Laguna.[21]

Although individually farmed ejidos generally have been regarded as less productive than private holdings,[22] there is less agreement about the performance of the collective ejido. The individual ejido was limited by its small size, the lack of education of its owner, the

19. See Eckstein, *El Ejido Colectivo en México,* for comprehensive economic and political analysis of the collective through the 1950s.

20. Ibid., pp. 123 and 131–49, in which there is a thorough discussion of collective ejidos in the Laguna region. Eckstein notes the resemblance between the organization of collective ejidos in the Laguna during the 1930s and the contemporary Israeli collective farms or *moshav shitufi* (pp. 120–21). Senior's *Land Reform and Democracy* also provides a provocative interpretation of the effect of this type of reform on political democracy in a peasant society.

21. Eckstein, *El Ejido Colectivo en México,* p. 140.

22. As we have seen, this finding is subject to numerous qualifications about the failure of the government fully to support the agrarian reform. Most writers argue that even the individual ejido would have been much more productive had land redistribution been accompanied by rural investment and technical assistance. Whether or not the scarce resources of the government would have produced higher marginal social benefits applied to the individual ejidos *as they existed* than to private commercial agriculture and collective ejidos (which received considerable public support in the 1930s), remains to be seen.

fact that it generally had poor land, little water, no technical assistance, and meagre amounts of fixed and working capital. On the other hand the collective ejido frequently included irrigated land, was centrally administered, and possessed considerable investments in buildings and equipment. The collectives also were favored by government loans until public policy shifted in the direction of medium-scale private agriculture in the 1940s. Simpson, Senior, and Eckstein all concur that collective ejidos, such as those in the Laguna region, were fairly productive; Eckstein even argues that they were more efficient than large private holdings but were discriminated against for political reasons after 1940.[23]

Eckstein shows that production in the Laguna, after declining during 1936–37, recovered earlier levels for wheat by 1937–38 and for cotton by 1941–42.[24] In his study he analyzed a sample of 2,133 census questionnaires from regions in which collective ejidos predominated for the years 1940 and 1950. The regions were first divided into ten high-income and six low-income zones. Results for the low-income zones showed individual ejidos to be more productive than collective ejidos, while both were surpassed by private holdings in terms of total production per unit of total inputs. But the results for the high-income zones were much more favorable to collective ejidos. In these regions collective ejidos were found to be more productive than either private holdings or individual ejidos. Eckstein found clear evidence of increasing returns to scale for the collective farms in the rich zones, but he also found there to be serious underemployment on ejidos in general, with a marginal productivity of labor for most that was not significantly different from zero.[25] His

---

23. Senior is somewhat less favorable in his analysis of tenure and productivity in the Lagna region, showing that ejidal productivity fell by more than that of private farms in both cotton and wheat between the 1930s and 1940s. This he attributed to cotton theft from ejidal to private land; diversion of irrigation water to private lands by bribed gate-tenders; greater use of wells by private owners (65 percent of the wells for 35 percent of the land area); greater fertility of private holdings, since the owner kept his choice of 150 hectares; larger and more efficient scale of private units; mechanization of 75 percent of private versus only 23 percent of ejidal farms; and relatively less credit for the ejidos.

24. Eckstein, *El ejido colectivo en México*, p. 142. He concludes from these findings that, "The fear that the Reform would destroy the productive capacity of the Laguna was definitively refuted. The new system had passed its first economic test, creating a strong stimulus for expropriations in other fertile regions."

25. Ibid., pp. 487–89.

conclusions, though relatively favorable to the collective ejido and unfavorable to the individual ejido, suggest that allocative inefficiency did arise from the creation of inalienable smallholdings.[26]

In conclusion, there is little question that between 1910 and 1940 Mexican agrarian reform kept the level of agricultural production within the limits of capacity, and even reduced those limits, most notably during the period of intense military activity from 1914 to 1916 and during the years of sweeping land expropriation in the late 1930s. Potential output was lost because landowners were dissuaded from planting or harvesting, rural infrastructure was allowed to deteriorate, many fled to the cities for personal security, some of the most productive large holdings were fragmented into inefficiently small units, and the inalienability of ejidal tenure perpetuated whatever allocative inefficiency resulted.

Yet a number of positive effects of agrarian reform helped to offset these factors and eventually contributed to a faster rate of growth. Even the smallest ejidos tended to utilize a larger amount of abundant local labor per unit of land than did medium and large private holdings, and certain of the collective ejidos proved more efficient in their use of capital than comparable private farms—particularly in the more productive regions. In addition, the rupturing of the old hacienda system tended to increase the per-hectare productivity of the reduced feudal estates by forcing owners to cultivate their remaining land more intensively in order to maintain previous levels of income and recover lost wealth. Those large holdings that survived the reform were forced to justify their continued existence in terms of productive efficiency and social justice if they were to reduce the risk of eventual expropriation.

The attitudes of many landowners underwent as great a transformation as the land system itself during the agrarian reform. Real estate came to be valued more as a factor of production than as a store of wealth or source of prestige. Such qualities of mind among rural entrepreneurs have always predominated in certain areas, par-

26. Ibid., p. 489. This type of "inefficiency" should be regarded as part of the cost of investment in rural social infrastructure necessary to permit other investments in economic infrastructure to take place. There is considerable evidence that most small ejidos were assigned extramarginal land, relative to that of commercial agriculture; yet they provided an important contribution to total output since they required little capital and made use of otherwise unemployed labor to produce food for local consumption that would have had to be supplied by the commercial sector in their absence.

ticularly in the North where the influence of the neighboring value system is most prevalent. But since the Revolution the commercial mentality often ascribed to the *norteño* appears to have spread throughout the country, partly as a concomitant of land redistribution and partly owing to the displacement of the traditional oligarchy by a new set of leaders from that very region. Finally, agrarian reform made it politically acceptable for the government to provide large-scale support for commercial agriculture. In a country where most of the land initially was held by a small percentage of the population, major public investments in agricultural development were politically unappealing and even dangerous. It would have constituted flagrant favoritism to use public revenues for the benefit of the small minority of rural rich before 1910. However, once land had been made generally available, it became possible for the government to invest heavily in rural infrastructure. Even when this investment directly benefited only a small share of the total number of landowners, it now could be justified in the name of "agrarian reform."

LAND REFORM AND PUBLIC INVESTMENT IN AGRICULTURE:
A DUAL STRATEGY

Unlike most countries in Latin America, Mexico has achieved both agrarian reform and revolutionary improvements in agricultural technology and output. The rate of growth of crop production virtually doubled between the Porfiriato and the period 1910/40 and was five times greater after 1940 (Table 3.2). As a result, even though population growth more than doubled between the pre-1910 and post-1940 period, per capita agricultural production, which had been declining during the Porfiriato, rose to 3.4 percent per year between 1940 and 1960. While it is true that most of this growth occurred during the postreform period of agricultural development, particularly in regions characterized by privately owned commercial agriculture, the revolutionary years before 1940 laid the foundation for this success.

It is not purely coincidental that the land redistribution of the 1930s was preceded by a slacking off of the demand for agricultural exports as a result of the depression, a fact which made the opportunity cost of land transfers much less than it would have been had general prosperity and high farm prices prevailed. At the very time when sharecroppers in the United States were being driven off their parched lands and forced to harvest the grapes of wrath, when food surpluses were being plowed under in an effort to raise prices, the Mexican peasantry was receiving increasing amounts of land at the expense of commercial growers. By redistributing income and wealth and improving political stability in the countryside the agrarian reform program represented a major investment in social infrastructure. In this respect it was distinct from the government's program of large public investments in rural economic infrastructure (dams, irrigation system, and roads) many of which were unrelated to the tenure reform program per se. Since only 20 percent of GNP was provided by agricultural activities in 1910 while 60 percent of the work force was so employed, it was possible to redistribute a significant amount of rural income and wealth through land reform without having a notable effect on total GNP.

At the same time, because Mexico possessed abundant amounts of unutilized land that only required irrigation to become productive, the government was able to commence irrigating and settling the more sparsely populated coastal and northern regions for the purpose of commercial cultivation. The policy of land redistribution, in the form of small ejidos, satisfied income security and distributive criteria essential to maintain political stability, while the policy of public investment satisfied productivity criteria designed to spur the rate of growth of agricultural production. The pressure on the government for urban welfare expenditures was kept down, since peasants who received ejidos did not move to the cities as readily as before and because agricultural production in the newly opened regions grew rapidly, providing food and raw materials for urban markets and export and minimizing the need for relief measures. Moreover, the growing number of commercial farmers with relatively high and rising incomes provided an expanding market for manufactured goods, and generated high rates of rural saving, both of which resulted in increased private investment in both agricultural and nonagricultural activities. From 1940 through the mid-1950s, the rural smallholdings served as a sponge of unskilled labor that could be squeezed to provide workers when needed for the growth of industry, services, and commercial agriculture at relatively constant real wages.

It has been shown that the land redistribution program per se did not involve large direct expenditures by the federal government. Although some compensation bonds were distributed to expropriated landowners during the 1920s, they covered only a fraction of the value of the land and their nominal values were wiped out in the inflation of the 1930s. By 1940 the government had completely abandoned the pretense of indemnification, so that the drain on the budget by the agrarian reform was felt only indirectly through agricultural taxes foregone and the relatively insignificant cost of public credit to *ejidatarios*. However, the second aspect of government policy in agriculture—investments in rural economic infrastructure—proved to be far more costly. Outlays for construction of highways and water resource development rose from one-quarter of the total value of federal investment from 1925 to 1935, to 44 percent between 1935 and 1945, and to 35 percent between 1945 and 1955, declining to 23 percent of federal investment after 1955 (Table 4.6).

Table 4.6
Percentage of Total Federal Investment in Irrigation and Roads, 1925–63
(percents)

	Proportion of Federal Investment in Irrigation	*Proportion of Federal Investment in Roads*	*Roads and Irrigation as Share of Total Federal Investment*
1925–29	14.1	8.5	22.6
1930–34	11.3	16.2	27.5
1935–39	18.6	26.6	45.2
1940–44	15.1	27.3	42.4
1945–49	16.5	19.9	36.4
1950–54	15.9	16.7	32.6
1955–59	11.9	13.9	25.8
1960–63	8.2	10.7	18.9

Source: Secretaría de la Presidencia, Dirección de Inversiones Públicas, *México Inversión Pública Federal, 1925–1963*, Mexico, 1964, Table 7, pp. 53–58 and Table 12, p. 119.

This expenditure, associated politically with the agrarian reform program, did more than anything else to bring about the rapid growth of crop production after 1940. The years 1935 to 1955 saw the government involved in a major transfer of resources from urban to rural activities, a fact that does much to explain the resulting balance in growth between agriculture and industry, a pattern uncharacteristic of most Latin American countries.

It is evident from the statistics in Table 4.6 that for the nation as a whole the expansion in land redistribution in the 1930s was accompanied by a very rapid increase in the share of irrigation and

highway construction in total public investment expenditure, the
share rising from 28 to 45 percent over the course of the decade.
Before 1940 regional government investments in rural economic
infrastructure followed a pattern similar to that of land redistribution.
A regional breakdown of federal irrigation activity is presented in
Table 4.7. Table 4.8 relates irrigation to total regional cultivation,

Table 4.7
Hectares of Land Benefited by Major Federal Irrigation Projects, 1930–58
(000 hectares)

	1930	*1940*	*1950*	*1958*
North	2	97	363	560
Gulf	0	0	5	53
North Pacific	0	37	402	839
South Pacific	0	0	21	24
Center	15	123	247	400
Mexico	17	257	1,038	1,876

Source: Orive Alba, *La Política de Irrigación en México*, Anexo 6 (see Appendix
Table E.10). Figures do not include "pequeña irrigación," which accounted for 5,000
hectares in 1940, 180,000 in 1950, and 360,000 in 1958.

Table 4.8
Hectares Benefited by Major Federal Irrigation Projects
as Percentage of Total Hectares Cultivated, 1939–59
(percents)

	1940	*1950*	*1958*
North	4	12	15
Gulf	0	0.3	3
North Pacific	4	39	53
South Pacific	0	1.4	1.2
Center	3	6	9
Mexico	3	9	14

Source: Data for hectares benefited by major federal irrigation projects is from
Orive Alba, *La Política de Irrigación en México*, Anexo 6, for the years 1939, 1949,
and 1958 (Appendix Table E.10). Figures on hectares cultivated are from the agricultural censuses for the crop years 1939/40, 1949/50, and 1959/60.

while Table 4.9 shows the regional pattern of road construction over
the same period. As of 1940 the North and Center contained three-
quarters of the ejidos in Mexico, 85 percent of the hectares benefited
by federal irrigation, and 78 percent of the roads paved between 1935

Table 4.9
Regional Construction of Paved Roads, 1935–60

	1	*2*	*3*		*4*		*5*	
	Percent of Total Land Area	*Percent of Cultivated Land (1950)*	*Construction of Paved Roads 1935–40*		*Construction of Paved Roads 1940–55*		*Construction of Paved Roads 1955–60*	
	%	%	km	%	km	%	km	%
North	41	27	1,429	39	3,897	30	2,536	28
Gulf	12	11	247	7	1,489	11	1,807	20
North Pacific	21	9	125	3	2,578	20	2,189	24
South Pacific	12	14	455	12	1,457	11	758	8
Center	14	39	1,438	39	3,543	27	1,708	19
Mexico	100	100	3,694	100	12,964	100	8,998	100

Sources and Methods: Column 1 *Compendio Estadístico:* 1962, p. 13.
Column 2 Appendix Table E.9.
Columns 3, 4, and 5: Data is compiled from the *Anuario Estadístico* and *Compendio Estadístico* for various years, using figures (some of which are conflicting) on kilometers of "caminos pavimentados" that may include some repaving, since the net advance in total federal paved roads in Mexico was 3,223 km from 1935 to 1940, 13,547 from 1940 to 1954, and 4,889 km from 1954 to 1959. (See *Anuario Estadístico:* 1958–59, p. 503.) City roads apparently are not covered by these figures, since the Federal District is reported as containing only 50 km of paved roads in 1960.

and 1940. After 1940, however, the regional patterns of public investment in agriculture and ejidal redistribution diverge sharply. During the 1940s the North and North Pacific received 81 percent of the newly irrigated land along with 50 percent of newly paved roads constructed (between 1940 and 1955), while the share of private to ejidal land in these regions grew rapidly. The situation did not change in the 1950s. Again 76 percent of the newly irrigated land and 52 percent of new highways constructed (1955–60) were in the North and North Pacific, while the share of ejidos in each of these regions by 1960 was much below that of 1940.

There is no way of determining with precision the economic cost of kilometers constructed and hectares irrigated on a regional basis for earlier decades, since a detailed regional breakdown of federal investment expenditures is not available for any year before the late 1950s. The pattern of regional expenditure in highway construction from 1959 to 1963 (Table 4.10) shows a very different regional emphasis compared to the 1940s and 1950s. For example, the Center, Gulf, and South Pacific received 68 percent of federal expenditures

Table 4.10
The Percentage of Total Federal Investment
Expenditure in Highways, 1959–63

Region	Percents
North	20
Gulf	19
North Pacific	12
South Pacific	14
Center	35
Mexico	100

Source: Same as Table 4.6. The percentages are averages of the regional shares for each year, 1959 to 1963; statewide breakdowns of public investment expenditure on roads were not available for publication for previous years.

on roads after 1959, whereas they had received slightly under 50 percent of mileage constructed in earlier years. This may indicate a declining emphasis on the North and North Pacific or it may simply reflect a higher cost per kilometer of highway construction in the central and southern portions of the country.

For whatever reasons, those regions with the highest concentration of ejidos (the Center and the Gulf) received a disproportionately small share of public investment in irrigation after 1940, although the distribution has improved in recent years. On the other hand, the share of these regions in highway construction has become somewhat more equitable. Between 1940 and 1960 the North and North Pacific (with 36 percent of the cultivated land in 1950) received over 50 percent of the new paved roads and 70 to 80 percent of newly irrigated land. Since then, however, these regions have received only 32 percent of federal expenditures on roads with major outlays going to the Center and Gulf. The evidence strongly suggests that until recently a dual strategy of agricultural development has been followed in Mexico, as an implicit if not explicit element of public policy. In highway construction and to a greater extent in irrigation, new lands and private holdings rather than ejidos have been favored by federal expenditure.

The probable positive effect of this strategy on rural savings has already been mentioned. Its favorable influence on total investment in agriculture may be deduced from the figures in Appendix Table E.10. Both before and after 1940 those regions with the largest amounts of public investment also evidenced the largest amount of private investment. For example, for the decade 1930 to 1940 the

North and Center received 85 percent of newly irrigated land and 78 percent of highways constructed (1935–40), along with the largest amount of private investment in agriculture. (It will be remembered that both the North Pacific and Gulf actually experienced net depletion of the private stock of capital during the 1930s.) From 1940 to 1960 the North Pacific and North received almost 80 percent of federally irrigated land, over 50 percent of newly paved highways, and accounted for 67 percent of net private investment in agriculture. Only in the South Pacific did private investment exceed federal irrigation expenditure between 1940–60, with the national ratio averaging one to three for the two decades. Evidently, the benefits from water resource development and road construction passed on to commercial growers in the form of high rates of return on capital made it profitable to invest large sums in private agriculture. Especially in a country like Mexico, with arid alluvial plains, rugged terrain, erratic rainfall, and long distances between population centers, such investments in rural infrastructure are costly and the benefits they provide are difficult to internalize. Under such circumstances the public sector is the logical source of funds for this type of investment, since the social expenditures will reap important social benefits.

Today many agricultures continue to exist side by side in Mexico. North Americans, accustomed as they are to the highly mechanized corporate farms of their own Southwest, are nevertheless impressed by the extent of scientific farming in northern Mexico. In the state of Tamaulipas, scores of new aircraft are parked along the highways ready to spray the cotton crops. In agricultural boom towns such as Hermosillo, Sonora, and Los Mochis, Sinaloa, gleaming glass-fronted showrooms filled with tractors and harvesters line streets that remain unpaved. Indeed the zeal of Mexico's commercial farmers occasionally appears to be excessive. In Sonora, private tube wells have lowered the water table and federal dams have blocked off the replenishing mountain streams, altering the ecological balance and threatening future production. Yet many of these growers now cooperate to conserve water by lining their irrigation ditches with cement and policing the amount of pumping in order to sustain production. As the large-scale commercial agriculture and truck farming for the United States market continues its southwesterly movement, production may be expected to shift still further into Mexico, accentuating past trends and opening up even more centers of relative prosperity.

At the same time, on the high plateau and in the far reaches of the

South, peasants continue to use the slash and burn techniques of their ancestors. Their crazy quilt patches of cultivation cover the mountainsides, startling visitors from Iowa who had been taught to believe that corn won't grow on hills. Ejidos predominate in most of this region and centuries of overcropping, deforestation, and erosion have taken their toll. Rainfall is seasonal and sporadic; yields are low in central and southern Mexico; and, except for a few lush river basins, the techniques of cultivation are reminiscent of Aztec times. A number of projects such as the Plan Lerma-Chapala-Santiago have been designed to transform these regions, but federal expenditures on economic infrastructure have had the general effect of moving the farm population from the center to the periphery of the country rather than of raising productivity in the center. Voluntary migration has already been extensive, as thousands of braceros have traveled north and west in pursuit of higher wages. Yet today almost as many Mexicans live at the level of subsistence cultivation as in 1910. Something must be done for these five to six million campesinos who have yet to share in their country's impressive growth. The agrarian reform helped to establish the political, social, and economic preconditions for regional and sectoral reallocation of labor and capital—a reallocation dependent upon the market mechanism and which until now has revolutionized much of Mexican agriculture. But in its continued neglect of the small cultivator, the agrarian reform program must be regarded as far from complete.

5

Urbanization and the Industrial Revolution in Mexico: 1900–1965

Mexico's industrialization process began in earnest during the late nineteenth century. Between 1877 and 1940 output steadily increased at an annual rate of 3 percent. Since then, the pace of industrial expansion has greatly accelerated, averaging 7.7 percent per annum from 1940 to 1960 (Table 5.1). Although post-1940 industrializa-

Table 5.1
Growth of Manufacturing Production During the
Major Periods of Mexican Economic Development
(compound annual rates of growth)

	Porfiriato 1877/1910	Revolution & Reform 1910/1940	Development 1940/1960
1. Total manufacturing production	3.1	3.0	7.7
2. Total population	1.4	0.9	2.9
3. Per capita manufacturing production (1 − 2 = 3)	1.7	2.1	4.8
4. Per capita agricultural production	−0.8	0.2	3.4

Sources: Row 1: Data from Appendix Table E.11.
Row 2: See Table 1.2.
Row 4: Taken from Table 3.2. The period in the first column is 1877/1907.

tion was more rapid in both Brazil and Venezuela, Mexico's manufacturing growth is noteworthy among Latin American countries, accompanied as it was by an expansion in the productivity and output of both agriculture and services. The share of manufacturing in GDP rose by 12 percentage points between 1900 and 1965 (from 13.2 to

25.3 percent), although the share of the labor force in manufacturing and related activities did not increase until after 1940, and then by no more than 4 percentage points between 1900 and 1960 (from 13.6 to 17.7 percent, Tables 2.2 and 2.3).

This alleged "miracle" of industrial growth will be shown instead to have been in large part the result of a vigorous response of private investors to changes in relative prices, abetted by favorable long term expectations to which government policy contributed. As the supply of capital and skilled labor increased, relative to land and mineral reserves, comparative advantage in terms of profit expectations shifted from resource-intensive activities such as mining and petroleum extraction to commercial agriculture and manufacturing. Any attempt to separate the effects of government policy from those of changes in underlying market conditions as they influenced the process of industrialization is unlikely to produce precise results, since these two sets of forces have been so interdependent over the past century. What began as a cluster of economically and culturally distinct regional markets has gradually evolved into a national economy, and this evolution has been influenced by a succession of public policies including massive government economic and social expenditures. In the process of national unification, the distribution of purchasing power has widened, tastes have been transformed, and a correspondingly greater potential for economies of scale in manufacturing production now exists. This expansion of effective demand, not unrelated to the growth of manufacturing itself, also depended upon the gradual displacement of subsistence agriculture by commercial farming and the development of highly productive tertiary activities. All these sectors have benefited from improvements in internal transport and communications supported by public policy.

The following section outlines the growth of national manufacturing production since 1900, the relationships between inputs and output, and their implications for industrial productivity by decade since 1930. Next are discussions of the pattern of regional industrialization and the effects of national economic integration on this process; the role of agricultural revolution and agrarian reform in the industrialization process; urbanization and the effect of industrial development on labor absorption; and the role of the service sector in the transmission of productivity gains from manufacturing to broader segments of the population. The relationships between public, private, and foreign investment in Mexican manufacturing are examined briefly, after which the relative intensity of postwar industrialization is compared with that of a hypothetical economy of similar income and population size.

MANUFACTURING PRODUCTION AND PRODUCTIVITY, 1900–60

Manufacturing was the sector least affected by the social and political upheaval of the Revolution. Although the rate of growth of agricultural production was considerably slowed during the period 1910–40, the rate of growth of manufacturing production, after declining from 1910 to 1925, picked up rapidly and exceeded prerevolutionary levels between 1925 and 1940.[1] In the long run, then, industry has grown prodigiously, its per capita output performance surpassing all major sectors between 1925 and 1965. Since manufacturing has drawn an increasing share of new investment over this period, and since the growth of the capital stock has been rapid as well, the relationship between the growth of output and factor inputs in manufacturing is worth examining in terms of possible patterns of productivity growth and their implications for the success of Mexican industrialization. A method of estimation of productivity growth through use of the production function residual similar to that applied to agriculture in Chapter 3 follows.

The statistical basis for a Denison production function estimate of Mexican manufacturing is presented in Table 5.2. The data are taken from a number of sources. Although industrial censuses have been conducted at five-year intervals since 1930, only those for the years 1930, 1950, and 1960 may be regarded as internally consistent and reasonably reliable, and even these differ greatly as to coverage. Hence the censuses may be relied upon only for relative measures of national and regional capital, labor, intermediate goods, and gross value of production. Independent time series estimates must be used to adjust the census data to provide comparable benchmark indicators of capital, labor, and value added in manufacturing for production function estimation purposes. Labor force estimates are drawn from population censuses of the respective years and may be considered reasonably accurate although no adjustment is made for age, sex, skill composition, or average number of man hours worked per year per person actively employed.

1. Statistical time series on value added in manufacturing are presented in Appendix Table E.11.

Table 5.2
Manufacturing Production, Employment, and
Fixed Reproducible Assets in Mexican Manufacturing

	1900	*1910*	*1925*	*1930*	*1940*	*1950*	*1960*
1. Total value added in manufacturing[a] (million 1950 pesos)	1,131	1,620	2,076	2,489	3,889	8,437	17,116
2. Total depreciated value of fixed reproducible assets in manufacturing[b] (million 1950 pesos)	–[c]	–	–	3,261	(5,095)[b]	11,727	25,664
3. Total manufacturing employment[d] (000 workers)	584	560	–	530	524	973	1,551
4. Capital value added ratio in manufacturing (2 ÷ 1 = 4)	–	–	–	1.31	(1.31)[b]	1.39	1.49

Sources and Methods:

[a] Appendix Table E.11.

[b] Estimates of the value of fixed reproducible assets in manufacturing for the years 1930, 1940, and 1950 are derived from capital/gross sales coefficients taken from the industrial censuses of 1929 and 1950, as presented in J. J. Bonilla G., "La Información Censal y su Aplicación al Análisis de los Cambios Estructurales de la Indústria en México" (thesis), pp. 82 ff. The ratios of capital/gross value of sales to value added/gross value of sales (from the same censuses) permit estimated capital/value added ratios for manufacturing. These ratios are then applied to value added in row 1 to arrive at the capital stock estimates in row 2. The 1929 capital/value added ratio was applied to 1930 and 1940 data. Although the relationship between capacity and output was less affected by the depression in manufacturing than in other sectors, the 1940 estimate may understate the capital stock and should be used with caution. The capital/gross value of sales ratios for manufacturing from the industrial censuses were: 1929: .855; 1950: .734; 1960: .985 (including mining). The value added/gross value of sales ratios were: 1929: .651; 1950: .529; 1960: .453. (For 1960 the value added figure is exaggerated since only "*materias primas consumidas*" were deducted as intermediate inputs from the gross value of sales. If fuels and half of "*otros gastos*" are also deducted, the ratio falls to .377, tending to increase the capital/value added ratio even more [see below].) The capital/value added ratios in manufacturing for the respective years implied by these ratios are presented in row 4 above, except for 1960 which was 2.17, resulting in a hypothetical level of capital stock of 37,142 million pesos. This 1960 ratio includes mining, since the data could not be separated conveniently in the industrial census (the corresponding 1950 ratio, including mining, was 1.58). The 1960 capital stock estimate eventually used in Table 5.2 is based upon an alternative procedure whereby gross investment in Table 5.9 for the years 1950–59 was accumulated, assuming the capital stock in 1950 to have been 11,727 million pesos and applying a 5 percent annual rate of depreciation.

[c] Data not available.

[d] Total manufacturing employment for 1940, 1950, and 1960 is taken from Banco de México figures derived from population censuses for the respective years. The figures for 1900, 1910, and 1930 are based on adjustments of the population census figures for those years by Keesing, "Structural Change Early in Mexico's Development." Keesing's study contains a detailed analysis of the Mexican occupational structure stressing the years 1895, 1921, and 1930. His figures for 1900 and 1910 may be contrasted with those of El Colegio de México, *Fuerza de Trabajo*, p. 48, which show 624,039 employed in manufacturing in 1900, and 613,913 in 1910.

Considerable difficulties arose in connection with the estimation of fixed reproducible assets in manufacturing. Since the total capital stock figures from the industrial censuses proved unreliable, the average capital/gross sales coefficients from the 1930 and 1950 censuses were applied to the average value added/gross sales figures to produce an estimated capital output ratio that was then applied to value added in constant prices from the GDP series for the respective years (Table 5.2). The 1940 estimate assumes the same capital output ratio for 1930 and 1940. While this contrasts with the assumption made in Chapter 1 that the capital output ratio for the economy as a whole declined between 1925 and 1940, it appears that much of the net investment that did take place between the two years occurred in manufacturing while private infrastructure in agriculture and the extractive industries was allowed to deteriorate before 1940. The problem of estimating the 1960 capital stock in manufacturing proved much more difficult. If the capital-output ratio of the census for that year (2.17) is applied to value added for that year, the stock that results turns out to be 37,142 million (1950) pesos, or 45 percent higher than the one eventually used (see Table 5.2, note b). Instead it was decided to cumulate the annual investment figures from Table 5.9 based on the 1950 stock estimate subject to a 5 percent annual depreciation rate, resulting in a 1960 stock of 25,664 million pesos (implicitly providing a capital-output ratio of 1.49, which is much more realistic than the one derived from the 1960 census).[2]

Having estimated capital and labor inputs for each of the four benchmark years, a weighted average of their respective rates of growth was obtained for each decade, based upon their share of value added at the end of the period. This provided a rate of estimated growth of manufacturing which could be compared with the actual rate of growth, in order to determine a residual for purposes of estimating the rate of productivity growth. The findings as presented in Table 5.3 are less than miraculous insofar as increases in manufacturing productivity are concerned. The residual for the 1950s is considerably less than one percent per annum, that of the 1940s is

2. It should be noted that if the same procedure is used to estimate the 1950 and 1960 capital stock based upon the 1940 value of 5,095 in Table 5.2 and the gross investment series for 1940–50 in Table 5.9 subject to 5 percent depreciation, one arrives at a hypothetical capital stock of 14,587 in 1950 and 27,371 in 1960. In this case the compound rate of growth of the capital stock is shifted up for the 1940s and down for the 1950s, altering the residuals in Table 5.3 in the opposite direction.

Table 5.3
The Actual and Estimated Growth of Manufacturing Production, 1930–60
(compound annual growth rates)

	1930/40	*1940/50*	*1950/60*
1. Growth of labor force in manufacturing	−0.2	6.4	4.8
2. Growth of capital stock in manufacturing	4.6[a]	8.7	8.1
3. Actual growth of manufacturing (value added)	4.6	8.0	7.3
4. Estimated growth of manufacturing	2.6	7.8	6.6
5. Growth "unexplained" by inputs of labor & capital			
(3 minus 4)	2.0	0.2	0.7

[a] Assumed equal to the rate of growth of output.

Sources and Methods: Rows 1., 2., and 3. are derived from figures in Table 5.2. Row 4 represents growth rates based on an index of inputs of capital and labor weighted by their respective share of value added in manufacturing for the final year of each decade. The weights for capital and labor are 1940 (.52; .48); 1950 (.61; .39); 1960 (.54; .46). The shares for 1940 and 1950 are from R. Ortiz Mena, et al., *El Desarrollo Económico de México*, Table 2, pp. 8–13. The 1960 shares were derived by the author from the Banco de México input-output table for that year. It should be noted that there is a slight upward bias to the capital share of value added in 1950. Had the 1960 distributive shares been used, the residual for the decade of the 1940s would have been 0.4 rather than 0.2.

negligible, and only in the 1930s do significant productivity gains appear. The tendency of the capital stock to grow more rapidly than labor inputs in each period causes the residual in manufacturing to be somewhat more sensitive to value weights than was true for agriculture. Furthermore, alterations in the level of capital stock in 1960 are bound to affect the productivity residuals. If base year rather than terminal year value weights are applied to the data in Table 5.3, the residuals for the 1940s and 1950s become 0.4 percent and 0.5 percent, respectively. If the 1960 capital stock implicit from the census data is used (37,142 million pesos) the residual for the 1950s based on end year weights actually becomes negative (−2.0 percent).

What is apparent from these measures of manufacturing productivity growth since 1940 is that there have been few windfalls during the process of industrialization. Most increases in output are attributable to additional inputs of capital and labor. Indeed, if a factor were added for the growth of labor skills, it is quite likely that most, if not all, of the residual for both decades would disappear. There is, of course, a reasonable chance that manufacturing production statistics are subject to a downward bias over time, since the output of new industries tends to be captured in the statistics only with a lag. The faster the rate of growth, the greater the tendency toward downward bias in the production series. Official manufacturing indexes for the 1940s have been revised upward progressively, and it is reasonable to suppose that this will eventually be done for those of the 1950s and 1960s as well. However it is likely that if a downward bias does exist, it will hold for factor inputs as well so that the residual will not be proportionately affected by any subsequent revisions in the data.

Even our favorable findings for the 1930s must be regarded as provisional until additional information about the pattern of manufacturing investment during that decade becomes available. At least two commentators wrote in 1928 that, although manufacturing output was somewhat larger than in 1910, the political, agricultural, industrial, commercial, financial, and social positions of the country were far below capacity and "much below the standard that is reasonably within the power of Mexico eventually to reach." [3] Manufacturing was favored by public policies in the 1930s as part of the Six-Year Plan of President Cárdenas. Import and export duties were raised and the exchange rate devalued. Government deficit spending helped to expand effective demand, especially in the cities. It is therefore probable that some of the excess industrial capacity of the late 1920s was more fully employed in the 1930s and that additional investment took place in certain areas of manufacturing.

Whether or not the 1940 capital stock in manufacturing is overestimated in Table 5.2, there is no question that a significant industrial base already existed at the beginning of the war which would allow manufacturing production to increase by 75 percent between 1939 and 1946 without any major new investment. [4] Much of this

3. Sterrett and Davis, *Fiscal and Economic Condition of Mexico*, p. 229.
4. Earlier indexes of manufacturing production greatly underestimated growth during the 1940s and confounded the analysis of economists such as Sanford Mosk whose work, *Industrial Revolution in Mexico* (1950), remains the classic study of the subject. Writers such as he found their personal observations of rapid and impressive industrial progress to be strangely unsupported by the official statistics. For example, the best index of industrial production available in the 1940s was that of the Secretaría de Economía, Dirección General de Estudios Económicos, *Trimestre de Barómetros Económicos*, no. 8, March 1948, pp. 36–57. It was based on the output of textiles, food products, construction, clothing, tobacco, paper, rubber products, and glass, and rose from 100 in 1939 to 125, 126, 132, 139, 140, and 136

growth in output was achieved by running machines two and three shifts. In this respect the "excess capacity" that existed in 1940 was not unlike that which exists today for most of Mexican industry, since few factories are operating more than one shift. Although the more labor-intensive use of plant and equipment caused machines to wear out sooner, it provided large profits during the war that were saved and later used to import more modern equipment, greatly updating the average vintage of the capital stock by 1950.

What is surprising is that the more modern and capital-intensive technology and more highly skilled labor force that have characterized the growth of manufacturing since 1940 have not been reflected in productivity gains. On the contrary, even the modest growth of productivity during the 1930s failed to continue in the 1940s, while increases during the 1950s were only slightly above the level implicit in constant returns to scale even without taking into consideration improvements in the quality of factor inputs (Table 5.3). This might be explained by the fact that the greater capital intensity of new industry has biased upward the capital output ratio due to a shift in the structure of production combined with the failure of new industry yet to achieve economies of scale. If all industries were experiencing increasing returns, but the average capital intensity of each were rising over time, the productivity residual for manufacturing might well be negative during periods of rapid growth.

Mexican manufacturing has yet to match the performance of agriculture, for which one-fourth to one-third of the growth since 1930 was unexplained by traditional inputs. Undoubtedly productivity gains are yet to be realized from economies of scale and from multishift operation, improved plant management, and greater competition, which in turn will depend on lower rates of protection against imports. Meanwhile the capital output ratio continues to rise. Since Mexico's industrialization has been very unbalanced regionally and since the rate of growth has varied widely among individual sectors, the following section presents a more detailed analysis of each of these factors.

---

in the years 1942–47 inclusive. A more recent index prepared by the Bank of Mexico from a broader sample of activities shows the growth to have been from 100 in 1939 to 139, 146, 157, 171, 175, and 170 for the years 1942–47 (Appendix D, "Mexican National Accounts and Historical Data"). It is possible that the *Trimestre de Barómetros* figures that have been used here for the years before 1940 (Table 5.2) are subject to a similar negative bias. At present, however, no alternative data are available.

REGIONAL MANUFACTURING DEVELOPMENT, 1930-60

Mexican manufacturing has increasingly tended to locate in the national capital and a few other major cities. In 1930 the Federal District accounted for 28 percent of manufacturing production. By 1950 this figure had risen to 38 percent (Table 5.4). The census of

Table 5.4

Regional Shares of Total Value of Industrial Production, 1930, 1950, and 1960
(percents)

Region	Manufacturing[a]		Mining & Manufacturing	
	1930	1950	1950	1960
North	23	14	28	23
Gulf	14	20	15	7
North Pacific	8	9	8	6
South Pacific	3	3	2	1
Center (excluding Federal District)	25	18	19	24
Federal District	27	38[b]	29	37
Mexico	100	100	100	100

[a] The first two columns exclude extractive industry except for petroleum and salt manufacturing. The figures from which these percentages have been derived can be found in Appendix Table E.12. See note to Appendix Table E.12 for an explanation of the reasons for the exclusion of extractive industries from the 1930 census figure.

[b] The shares of the Federal District in manufacturing in 1940 and 1955, based on the industrial censuses for those years, were 37 percent and 48 percent, respectively, according to Yates, *El Desarrollo Regional de México*, p. 49.

1955 showed that the top four manufacturing centers (Federal District, Monterrey-San Nicolás, Guadalajara, and Puebla) produced four times the value added of the next twenty cities combined (Table 5.6). The production of the Federal District alone was almost twice that of all the others. Since 1950 the growth of manufacturing production in Mexico City and its tributary towns in the states of Mexico, Querétaro, Hidalgo, Tlaxcala, Puebla, and Morelos (in the Center) has been more than double that of the North and North Pacific, which were the next highest in industrial concentration (Table 5.5). Paul Yates, in a critical evaluation of Mexico's general pattern of regional development, claims that over three-fourths of the increase in industrial value added between 1940 and 1955 was divided among the

Table 5.5
Regional Growth of Industrial Production, 1930–60
(compound annual rates of growth)

Region	1 *1930 / 1950*	2 *1950 / 1960*
North	3.5	4.7
Gulf	7.9	−0.5
North Pacific	7.3	4.6
South Pacific	5.9	2.9
Center (excluding Federal District)	4.5	9.8
Federal District	8.0	9.8
Mexico	7.2	6.8

Sources and Methods: The figures show the growth of regional value of production in constant prices estimated in the following manner. The 1930 figures used to compute the growth rates in column 1 are based on an application of the 1930 regional value shares in Table 5.4 to the author's estimate of national value added in manufacturing in 1930 of 2,489 million 1950 pesos. The 1950 figures were computed by applying the 1950 regional value shares in Table 5.4 for manufacturing alone to the 1950 value added for manufacturing (Table 5.2). The exclusion of petroleum in the national figures and inclusion in the regional shares biases these results according to the implicit assumption of regionally proportional value added. Column 2 is based upon the regional shares from Table 5.4 (including extractive industry) for 1950 and 1960 applied to the author's estimates of value added in manufacturing and mining (9,680 and 18,764 million pesos in 1950 prices). Because of the exclusion of mining from the first period, the growth rates in columns 1 and 2 are not strictly comparable. Petroleum was omitted in the column 2 value weights because of the lack of comparability between the national accounts concept and that of total value of production in the census. It was not clear what stages of petroleum extraction and refining were covered by the censuses' figures. Because of these problems, these regional rates of growth should be regarded as provisional, merely providing relative orders of magnitude.

Federal District and the northern states (53.1 percent and 23.4 percent, respectively).[5]

What has caused this concentration of industry? Mexico City owes its initial growth to historical factors. It has been the center of the country since the Aztecs first chose the Valley of Mexico for the site of their capital, Tenochtitlán, several hundred years before the Conquest. In contrast to the arid high plateau and the humid tropical lowlands, the Valley enjoys a temperate climate. Its large lake (now drained) once offered an ideal defensive position, as the center of Tenochtitlán was built on islands that could be reached only by man-

5. Yates, *El Desarrollo Regional de México*, p. 49.

Table 5.6

Gross Value of Industrial Production and Value Added in the Principal Cities, 1955

City	(State)	*Industrial Production*	*Value Added*
		(millions of current pesos)	
Mexico City	(D. F.)	38,867	14,820
Monterrey	(Nuevo Leon)	3,533	1,805
Mexicali	(Baja Calif.)	1,111	256
Guadalajara	(Jalisco)	959	503
Puebla	(Puebla)	856	418
Ciudad Madero	(Tamaulipas)	842	202
San Nicolás	(Nuevo Leon)	640	334
Matamoros	(Tamaulipas)	622	205
Torreón	(Coahuila)	614	212
Salamanca	(Guanajuato)	602	367
Chihuahua	(Chihuahua)	571	380
Sabinas	(Nuevo Leon)	496	264
Toluca	(Mexico)	427	186
San Luis Potosí	(S.L.P.)	418	240
Mérida	(Yucatan)	403	195
Reynosa	(Tamps.)	402	205
Orizaba	(Veracruz)	355	214
Saltillo	(Coahuila)	335	157
Gómez Palacio	(Durango)	329	105
Veracruz	(Veracruz)	295	163
Parral	(Chihuahua)	291	198
Hermosillo	(Sonora)	285	148
Fresnillo	(Zacatecas)	278	183
Zacatecas	(Zacatecas)	265	179
Santa Bárbara	(Chihuahua)	253	181

Source: Yates, *El Desarrollo Regional de México*, p. 217. The figures were derived from the 1955 industrial census.

made causeways. The fertile valley floor was well adapted to the cultivation of food crops such as corn and beans, and the surrounding mountains provided a shield against invasion.[6]

During the Colonial period the Spanish destroyed and rebuilt Tenochtitlán and converted it into Mexico City, the capital and political and economic heart of the viceroyalty of New Spain. Like vital arteries, the King's highways met at this point. No silver or any other major exports could leave the country without passing through the capital. Despite its separation from all of the principal ports of the

6. For an eloquent description of the economic ecology of the Valley of Mexico shortly after the Conquest, see Gibson, *The Aztecs Under Spanish Rule.*

country and despite the rugged terrain over which all of its commerce had to pass, Mexico City grew steadily. In 1900 the share of the Federal District in the total population was 4 percent. Since then this figure has risen progressively to 4.8 percent in 1910, 7.4 percent in 1930, 8.9 percent in 1940, 11.8 percent in 1950, and 13.9 percent in 1960.

Today many of the early attractions of the metropolis are gone due to overcrowding. More than 7 million people now live in the Valley of Mexico. The last remaining cropland is being rapidly converted into subdivisions, and the city is expanding up the hillsides and overflowing into the surrounding valleys. Now that Lake Texcoco has been drained and the country unified, the initial advantage of its situation is replaced by problems of sanitation, drainage, and the difficulties of construction on the porous soil of the old lake bed. Food, water, and industrial raw materials must be brought from ever-increasing distances. Nevertheless, Mexico City continues to attract new industry. Its mass market, easy access to labor, ready availability of suppliers and credit facilities, and the proximity of governmental regulatory agencies all represent advantages that typically accrue to a high concentration of manufacturing in major political and population centers in Latin America. In addition to the natural advantages of concentration, government policies have also tended to encourage industry to locate in Mexico City. The federal government has subsidized the distribution of wheat, corn, low-grade gasoline and diesel fuel, electricity, and natural gas, at prices favoring the Federal District.[7] Railroad rates use the capital as a basing point.

By measuring the relatively high per capita costs of urban infrastructure in the capital, Yates stressed the high price that society must pay for overconcentration of industrial investment in the Valley of Mexico. He concluded that these disadvantages have not been passed on to manufacturers in the form of rising costs, but rather have been offset by government policies which, for political or social reasons, are designed to keep the relative cost of living in Mexico City from rising too rapidly. Have these policies been optimal from the point of

7. Yates, *El desarrollo regional de México,* p. 127. The role of government subsidies for food, transport, water, oil, and electric power as they have favored the relative expansion of the Valley of Mexico region is focused upon by Laura Randall, "The Process of Economic Development in Mexico from 1940 to 1959" (Ph.D. dissertation). The economic costs of overcentralization are cited in terms of alleged income transfers from agriculture to manufacturing in the Mexico City area that accentuated rural/urban income inequalities and resulted in excess industrial capacity.

view of growth? Mexican industrialization has been extremely rapid. What would have happened to industrial growth in the absence of government subsidies to manufacturing in the capital city is far from clear.

It is not possible in this study to estimate whether or not the external social diseconomies outweigh the economies of industrial concentration in the Valley of Mexico by an amount sufficient to offset the net advantages to private investors who have located their plants in the area. These private advantages, while difficult to measure, are great. One of the principal shortages facing industry is the scarcity of skilled labor and managerial personnel. Industrial agglomeration permits a small number of administrators to operate several plants simultaneously, while many of these individuals hold post in government and education as well. In addition to the functional benefits from geographical concentration, there are other advantages based on the assumption that industrialization requires a collective mentality of change in which individuals are permitted to exercise their creativity with a minimum of restraint. Businessmen, whether they work for the state or private enterprise, seek the company of those with similar values. They thrive in localities where development already has occurred and is part of the way of life. Psychologically as well as materially, growth promotes growth.

If growth tends to be cumulative in major metropolitan areas, there is a danger that premature attempts to restore regional balance in industrialization would simply lower the expected rate of return in manufacturing and retard the process of development. This is not to say that explicit government policies promoting a high concentration of industry in the Federal District were optimal or should be maintained, especially in view of the present overcrowded conditions in the Valley of Mexico. Wage differentials have tended to rise between the capital and the surrounding regions of the Center, Gulf, and South Pacific, but labor migration has helped to narrow this gap. Until recently the government has supported migration by subsidizing all forms of internal transport, as well as food and other costs in Mexico City. Now, however, the cost of overcrowding in the capital is becoming increasingly oppressive for the working class and these disadvantages tend to outweigh the benefits of federal subsidies. As this is reflected in rising wage costs, industry is beginning to move away from the city toward labor surplus regions in the immediate vicinity. In the future, government policy can promote the continuation of this natural diffusion process by allowing manufacturing costs in the Valley of Mexico to reflect more adequately the high price of overurbanization.

As of 1955 most of Mexico's industrial production outside of Mexico City was located in the northern part of the country. Of the twenty-five leading cities listed in Table 5.6, fifteen were located in the North and two in the North Pacific (Mexicali and Hermosillo). Only four of the remaining cities were located in the Center (Guadalajara, Puebla, Salamanca, and Toluca), three in the Gulf region (Mérida, Orizaba, and Veracruz), and none were found in the South Pacific. The tendency of industry to concentrate either in the capital city or in the north of Mexico is explained to a large extent by the nature of industrialization in less developed countries. The first stages of industrialization are likely to represent the processing of raw materials and primary products for export and the production of machinery, equipment, and supplies to service the export industries. Most of the value of industrial production in the north of Mexico (including that of its second city, Monterrey) is of this nature. The rich mineral deposits of the Sierras and the fertile agricultural lands that have been brought into production during the past half-century through irrigation provide a natural base for processing industries. Many of these industries would not exist in the absence of foreign demand, particularly that of the United States.

A quite different type of industry has tended to locate in the Center, producing light manufactures primarily for domestic consumption. Given transport costs (which have tended to decline over time), profit maximization dictates that this type of industry develop in close proximity to sources of cheap labor and/or final demand. Although wage levels are considerably lower in the South Pacific and in the depressed agricultural and mining regions of the high plateau, effective demand tends to be concentrated in the vicinity of Mexico City. The allure of cheap labor in the outlying provincial towns has not been sufficient to offset the attractiveness of this enormous market where most of the products eventually must be sold. That the growth of "import-competing" industry in the Federal District is taking place at a faster pace than that of processing industries on the periphery is suggested by the data in Table 5.5. Between 1950 and 1960 industrial production in both the Center and the Federal District grew at a compound annual rate of almost 10 percent; manufacturing in the North and North Pacific lagged far behind; that of the South Pacific grew at only 2.9 percent per year; and the Gulf region showed no net gains over the decade.

The distinctions between industry in the North and Center are gradually disappearing, however. Unification of the national market is making it possible for petrochemical producers in the Center to service the northern regions in competition with those in the United States. Beer manufacturers in the North now are supplying consumers as far south as Oaxaca. Textile manufacturing plants that at one time might have located near the market in Puebla or Mexico City are being established in the labor-abundant Torreón-Gómez Palacio area, where agriculture is relatively depressed. As Mexican consumer goods manufacturing grows in competitiveness it will be able gradually to displace imports in the North. Meanwhile the expanding internal demand for raw materials and primary products will cause an increasing share of northern manufacturing to find its way into the national rather than foreign market. The regional process of industrialization in Mexico, originally quite separate and distinct, is beginning to converge gradually. As the economy continues to develop, final goods manufacturing and raw materials processing industries are being drawn together by new investment in the intermediate stages of production.

THE ROLE OF AGRICULTURE IN MEXICAN INDUSTRIALIZATION

Much contemporary economic analysis has focused on the relationship between agriculture and industry in the growth process. Numerous theories describe how technical or institutional change within agriculture is capable of producing a surplus of commodities and unskilled labor that may be drawn upon for the development of urban activities.[8] The data to support these arguments frequently are taken from the Japanese experience, in which labor-intensive applications of new techniques of cultivation transformed commercial agriculture in the past century.[9] Now that a considerable amount of information is available from Mexico, additional light is being shed on the

8. W. A. Lewis, "Economic Development with Unlimited Supplies of Labour"; B. F. Johnston and J. W. Mellor, "The Role of Agriculture in Economic Development"; J. C. H. Fei and G. Ranis, *Development of the Labor Surplus Economy;* W. Schultz, *Transforming Traditional Agriculture.*
9. An excellent analytical summary of the literature on the Japanese experience is presented in B. F. Johnston, "Agriculture and Economic Development."

mechanism whereby rural-urban transfers occur in a country with multiple agricultural technologies—capital-intensive expansion of wheat, cotton, and other field crops on irrigated land in the North and North Pacific as well as labor-intensive development of tropical agriculture in the Gulf and South Pacific. An example of issues found in the literature on the rural-urban transfer mechanism may be seen from the following:

> Rural welfare as well as over-all economic growth demand a transformation of a country's economic structure, involving relative decline of the agricultural sector, and a net flow of capital and other resources from agriculture to the industrial sector of the economy. Agriculture's contribution to the requirements for development capital is especially significant in the earlier stages of the process of growth; it will not be so crucial in countries which have the possibility of securing a sizeable fraction of their capital requirements by export of mineral products or in the form of foreign loans or grants.
>
> Although this paper has stressed the importance of agriculture's role in development, we part company with those who draw the inference that agricultural development should precede or take priority over industrial expansion. . . . It is our contention that "balanced growth" is needed in the sense of simultaneous efforts to promote agricultural and industrial development. We recognize that there are severe limitations on the capacity of an underdeveloped country to do everything at once. But it is precisely this consideration which underscores the importance of developing agriculture in such a way as to both minimize its demands upon resources most needed for industrial development and maximize its net contribution to the capital required for general economic growth.[10]

The Mexican experience lends support for at least some of these elements. Rising real incomes in rural areas have increased consumer demand. Improvements in rural technology have widened the market for fertilizers, pesticides, farm implements, and other intermediate goods that are being manufactured domestically on an increasing scale. Agricultural production itself has provided inputs for food and raw material processing industries. And most important,

10. Johnston and Mellor, "Role of Agriculture in Economic Development," pp. 590–91.

net foreign exchange earnings of agriculture since 1940 have been channeled increasingly into inputs for the development of urban activities.

If transmission of an agricultural surplus to industry is to occur, it is most likely to take place during periods of rapid technological progress in the rural sector. With sudden productivity increases, rural savings may exceed new investment opportunities so that agriculture would become a net lender to industry. Either the government could step in and tax away more than it spends in agriculture while running a deficit with industry, or the private banking system could channel rural net savings to net borrowers in other sectors of the economy. Any net flow of capital from agriculture will be reflected in a "balance of trade" surplus between agriculture and industry plus the rest of the world. Exports of agricultural goods and services to industry and abroad will tend to exceed imports into agriculture by an amount equal to the net transfer of savings out of the rural sector. A measurement of this balance of trade surplus may be estimated either in physical or financial terms.

Because of the statistical problems involved in estimating the flow of goods and services in and out of agriculture in the Mexican case, it has been easiest to look at the "capital account" of the sectoral balance of payments. This is done in Table 5.7 for public taxes and expenditures. Comparable data are not available for private intersectoral financial flows including transactions of bank and nonbank financial intermediaries. Tentative stock estimates from the Banco de México indicate that, in terms of the flow of funds through Mexican financial institutions, agriculture is a net lender.[11] However, much of the savings as well as working capital loans of commercial agriculture are placed abroad and are therefore missing in the statistics. Even so, there is considerable evidence that agriculture is a net lender abroad while industry is a net borrower. The data from which Table 5.7 is prepared indicate that, although the government spent a total of 19,088 million 1960 pesos in agriculture from 1942 to 1961 inclusive, the net flow of public revenues into agriculture over the same period was only 2,976 million 1960 pesos, or less than one percent of the value added produced in that sector during the same interval. It is not unlikely that net private savings in agriculture over the two decades exceeded private investment by considerably more than that amount because, as the data in Appendix Table E.10 indicate, the

11. Solís, "Desarrollo Económico de México," Table 5, p. 60.

Table 5.7

Net Flow of Funds through the Government to Agriculture, Industry, and Services
(millions of 1960 pesos)

Period	*Agriculture*	*Industry*	*Services*	*Industry and Services*
1942–45				
Expenditures—revenues	1,057.3	−4,233.7	4,619.1	385.4
1945–50				
Expenditures—revenues	746.9	−5,498.4	4,671.0	−827.4
1950–55				
Expenditures—revenues	189.2	−6,568.6	6,715.3	146.7
1955–60				
Expenditures—revenues	630.1	−10,998.0	11,706.9	708.9
1960–61				
Expenditures—revenues	353.4	−3,042.8	3,124.9	82.1

Source: Estimated from data in Solís M., "Desarrollo Económico de México," Section 3, and especially Table 7, p. 63. A minus figure indicates that more public revenues were collected from a sector than allocated to it. A positive figure indicates that more were channeled to a sector in the form of public expenditures than collected from it.

private capital stock in agriculture grew by 4,782 million 1960 pesos[12] or less than 2 percent of cumulated value added over the same period. Since private net savings in agriculture almost certainly averaged more than 3 percent of value added, pending further research it seems reasonable to conclude that a net outflow of savings on private account from the rural sector occurred well in excess of the net inflow of public expenditures.[13]

It will be recalled that much of the increase in agricultural production and profits was attributed to large-scale public expenditures in rural infrastructure. It is not surprising, therefore, that the public balance in agriculture has been positive throughout the twenty-year period covered by the table. Furthermore the annual net public expenditure in agriculture was greatest during the 1940s, precisely at the time when major public investment in dams and irrigation sys-

12. Assuming a conversion rate of 2.08 1950 pesos/1960 pesos based upon the Banco de México GDP implicit deflator.
13. Cf., however, the alternative conclusion of Solís, "Desarrollo económico de México," pp. 61–62, that "the affirmation that is frequently made that the agricultural sector has supported the development of the rest of the economy is not valid, insofar as it has received net income, since that which was obtained through the fiscal mechanism is greater than that transferred through the financial system."

tems was underway. The excess of government taxes over expenditures in industry has steadily increased. Meanwhile the service sector was a net user of public revenues of substantial proportions, receiving far more funds than agriculture since 1940.

The following sequence of financial flows is suggested from presently available Mexican statistics. The initial boom during World War II favorably affected income in both agriculture and industry. The government took advantage of this boom to increase the future growth potential of the rural sector. After the war, private savings in agriculture became increasingly available to finance continued industrial development. It is not likely that agricultural net savings would have been as great as they were between 1945 and 1960 had not the government used taxes from industry to finance rural infrastructure in the earlier years. Thus the flow of funds between agriculture and industry has been more complex in the case of Mexican development than most traditional two-sector growth models would suggest. In the early years financial flows from industry to agriculture by way of government brought about increases in output which permitted agriculture to eventually supply loanable funds to industry through the banking system and nonbank financial intermediaries.

While this process was occurring, there was a continued increase in net public expenditure on services including education, commerce, and transportation. Since 1955, the income generated in tertiary activities has provided a more important source of net private lending to industry than has that of agriculture. One additional element in the process of intersectoral flows should be mentioned at this point. Mexican agricultural development has provided an increasing source of foreign exchange earnings, as the agricultural sector has run an export surplus with the rest of the world. Thus, while agriculture may be a net importer from the rest of the domestic economy, it has a far greater balance of trade surplus with other countries.[14] This has permitted industry to be a net importer on foreign account, a process facilitated by the fact that a growing amount of agricultural savings in the form of foreign exchange is being captured by domestic financial intermediaries. The vital role of the latter in the process of intersectoral financial flows can only be touched upon here. The place of the public sector in the development of financial institutions in

14. Data illustrating this point for Sonora in 1960 appears in Reynolds, "La capacidad para financiar la formación de capital en Sonora" (unpublished).

Mexico and, in turn, their respective roles in the achievement of successful monetary policy, price stabilization, an increasing savings rate, and industrial investment are the subjects of a large and important literature.[15] Much remains to be done to stimulate the efficient spread of financial intermediation throughout the rural economy. Banking statutes still fail to permit rate differentials reflective of regional differences in financial market conditions, so that a large amount of rural savings continues to flow abroad. Agriculture could not have played as important a role in industrialization had not Mexican and foreign financial intermediaries helped to bridge the gap between lenders and borrowers in the two sectors.

URBANIZATION, LABOR ABSORPTION, AND INDUSTRIALIZATION

In addition to the flow of savings from agriculture into industry since 1940, a growing proportion of workers born in rural areas has become available for urban employment. The agricultural labor force increased by 2.5 million workers between 1930 and 1960 (Appendix Table E.2). Crop production virtually quadrupled during the same period (Table 3.14) so that rural employment grew much more slowly than output. Had labor productivity remained constant, the work force necessary to reach output levels actually achieved in 1960 would have been over 14 million farmers, or well over twice the number then employed in agriculture. (The economically active population in 1960 was only 11.3 million.) It is not likely, however, that labor productivity could have even been sustained at 1930 levels without additional investment in rural infrastructure. In the absence of public investment in agriculture, less new land would have become available and the average productivity of farm labor almost certainly would have declined. Labor would have been forced to move to the cities in search of jobs. A smaller crop surplus would have been forthcoming for their support. Had it been necessary to subsidize the consumption of these migrants, urban savings, investment, and the derived increase in labor absorption from these activities would have been far less than was actually the case.

If several million agricultural workers were released for urban employment by investment and technological change in agriculture, what

15. Antonio Campos Andapia, "Teoría de la intermediación financiera y las sociedades financieras privadas Mexicanas" (thesis); Bennett, *Financial Sector and Economic Development;* and Brothers and Solís, *Mexican Financial Development.*

importance did this push factor have on industrialization? As Table 5.2 reveals, there was no comparable rise in the demand for labor in manufacturing. On the contrary, the labor force in manufacturing (after apparently falling in the 1930s) increased by only 450,000 workers during the 1940s and by another half million in the 1950s. By 1960 the industrial work force was still only one-fourth that of agriculture. Most of the increase in urban employment has occurred in the service sector rather than in manufacturing. (The supporting statistics are presented in Chapter 2 and Appendix E.)

It is quite likely that investment subsidies, relatively low import duties on machinery and equipment, and a preference for the import of ready-made techniques from the United States and Europe have combined to bias factor employment in a capital-using direction.[16] Even making allowance for this bias, however, there is no indication that the most labor-intensive techniques in manufacturing would have been able to absorb the number of workers released from agriculture during the past three decades. In terms of the Mexican experience, dual models that stress labor supply aspects of agricultural development are rather misleading. It does not seem to be the release of labor that makes agricultural development so crucial to successful industrialization. The crucial element is rather the generation of savings that agricultural productivity gains provide (in the form of

16. One attempt to test the hypothesis that underdeveloped countries employ relatively capital-intensive technology in manufacturing, the so-called Hirschman hypothesis (A. O. Hirschman, *The Strategy of Economic Development*, Chapter 8) is presented in Edmar L. Bacha, "Comparación entre la Productividad Industrial de México y los Estados Unidos." The results of this study are inconclusive despite the fact that Hirschman makes a plausible theoretical argument for high substitutability between capital and skilled managers and administrators who are relatively less plentiful than capital in developing countries. Perhaps this is because Mexican industry, which contains a significant share of foreign direct investment, has been able to obtain foreign labor along with capital imports since World War II. The following comment lends support to this hypothesis:

In both Brazil and Mexico, the contribution of foreign capital to the provision of key industrial skills has been outstanding. In both countries there have been large government development banks which have played a major role in choosing the industries to be developed, and both have found that the most effective way of getting industrial know-how is via an equity participation. When the Mexican Nacional Financiera purchased know-how on a cash basis, it found that it had a high proportion of failures because foreign firms were not sufficiently committed to the success of the project.

Angus Maddison, *Foreign Skills and Technical Assistance in Economic Development*, p. 35.

food and raw materials) which may be transferred to industry, either directly or through foreign exchange earnings.

In order for labor released from agriculture to increase rather than slow the rate of growth of total output, there must be a demand for its services in other sectors of the economy. In the case of Mexico, a number of service activities have provided increases in demand sufficient to prevent large-scale unemployment and even to permit a modest rise in the real wages of unskilled labor. This demand has tended to concentrate in the retail trades, construction, and household employment—all of which are suited to the capacities of rural migrants who lack education and familiarity with urban technology. Employment in these occupations gives the worker a chance to acculturate, to familiarize himself with new habits of working and living which will equip him for higher skilled employment later on. Since increases in labor productivity in the lower skilled service occupations in Mexico have not been notable, these occupations should be regarded as transmitting rather than generating the gains in per capita output during the development process. Their principal function is to widen the market for those industries subject to increasing returns thus permitting productivity gains to take place in manufacturing. It is important that workers employed in service occupations have sufficiently high per capita income to bring this about. If too many workers were to move from agriculture to the cities, it is quite possible that this would force real wages in the urban service occupations to such a low level that they and their families would play little or no role in expanding the market for manufactures while previous employees would have even less purchasing power than before. Increased income and consumption inequality, associated with the low and falling marginal productivity of labor, would then serve to retard the growth of effective demand and slow productivity gains in industries subject to economies of scale.[17]

Premature migration of labor from the countryside might also slow the rate of growth of manufacturing by increasing the pressure for income subsidies in the cities. For example, if Mexican workers had been forced off the farms to seek urban employment too early in the process of industrialization, they would have swelled the ranks of

17. This point was made in an article by W. Paul Strassmann, "Economic Growth and Income Distribution," in which he compares the growth of Australia and Argentina in terms of their relative degree of income and consumption equality.

the unemployed and added to urban demands for food, clothing, and shelter without providing any correspondingly useful services. Income recipients in the productive sectors of the economy, instead of voluntarily employing these migrants in service occupations, would have been required to reduce their own consumption and savings to support the poor or to pass that burden along to the state. To the extent that the government would have been required to subsidize the income of these urban migrants, the rate of public savings would have declined or taxes would have had to increase. Either alternative almost certainly would have reduced the rate of total investment in the economy and slowed its rate of growth.

Fortunately for Mexico, premature urbanization of rural labor was partially forestalled by agrarian reform. Although much of the land redistributed in the 1930s was so poor or inaccessible that it was extramarginal from the point of view of the market, most of these smallholdings were nevertheless able to supply the subsistence needs of the owner and his family. Thus, land redistribution tended to place a floor on the marginal productivity of farm labor in Mexico. If urban incomes fell below the subsistence level plus the cost of moving to the cities, the peasant could always work his own plot of land and earn a subsistence wage. Once wages elsewhere rose above this subsistence floor, as has happened progressively since 1940, peasants could leave the land and seek alternative forms of employment.

In the rest of Latin America, rapid increases in the rate of population growth have seemed to create a surplus of rural labor. Except for a few regions in Central America, the Andes, and the Caribbean, this surplus is apparent, however, rather than real. Much of the land still available in these countries could provide productive employment for rural labor if prevailing tenure inequalities were eliminated by agrarian reform. Only in this respect did an "excess supply" of labor exist in Mexico in 1910. The unequal landholding system of that time prevented workers from gaining access to extramarginal land that could have provided them with a living wage. Today much of this land has been redistributed, preventing premature urbanization.

In addition to supplying output and labor to satisfy increasing urban demands, agricultural development in Mexico has helped to create a new class of rural consumers who now constitute a substantial share of final demand (Table 5.8). The results of a recent budget study show that 30 percent of total consumer demand for cloth-

Table 5.8
Structure of Total Demand by Employment Sector, 1963
(percents)

Sector providing main source of employment for principal wage-earner in family	Distribution of families[a]	Proportion of total expenditure including reported savings	Food, drink & tobacco	Clothing & shoes	Fuel, housing & other services	Vehicles, furniture & appliances	Insurance, mortgages & reported saving	Other expenditure
						Expenditures on		
Agriculture	43	30	36	30	20	31	16	24
Industry	21	23	24	22	25	16	35	22
Services	36	47	40	49	55	53	49	54
Total	100	100	100	100	100	100	100	100

[a] Share of families supported by a given sector does not match share of employment by sector owing to differences in the average size of households, percentage of wage-earners in households, and definitional problems, as well as aggregation.
Source: Budget study, Banco de México, 1963, in collaboration with U.S.D.A. agricultural projections survey.

ing, shoes, vehicles, furniture, and appliances comes from agriculture. A closer inspection than is possible from these data probably would reveal that most of the demand for these products is concentrated among a relatively small percentage of farm families located in the richest commercial growing regions of the country. Where incomes at the margin are so low in absolute terms, there is some chance that sustained rural income inequality may be associated with a growing market for manufactured goods at the expense of those remaining at the subsistence level.

MEXICAN MANUFACTURING INVESTMENT: AN ALLIANCE FOR PROFITS

Most of the growth of Mexican manufacturing production since 1940 is attributable to large amounts of private investment. This investment has caused the capital stock in manufacturing to double in the 1940s and again in the 1950s (Table 5.2). What is the reason for this performance? How important have been the relative roles of private entrepreneurship and public policy?

The decision to invest in Mexican manufacturing involves the same considerations as those which face an entrepreneur anywhere. These include expectations about the future level and rate of change in final demand, borrowing costs, costs of construction, machinery, and intermediate goods, availability of qualified personnel, and uncertainty as reflected in a risk discount applied to all of the foregoing. It is the higher discount for risk which sets apart the investment decision in countries like Mexico vis-à-vis the United States. The development process involves structural transformation of the entire economy during which innumerable imbalances in supply and demand are likely to occur. Disturbances in prices and costs will be correspondingly greater for a given exogenous shock to the system than those in a smoothly functioning, highly developed economy. This means that investors face a higher degree of uncertainty and require either a higher rate of return on capital or greater insurance against loss such as may be provided by the state.

Explicit support and protection of manufacturing by the public sector, by reducing uncertainty in the minds of potential entrepreneurs, may do more than any other single factor to raise the marginal efficiency of investment net of risk above the marginal cost of investable funds in the world market. Such a reduction in uncertainty would permit more investment for the same marginal rate of return on capital by lowering the risk discount. But it may not be possible in the early stages of industrialization to create expectations sufficiently favorable to cause a large amount of private investment at the going interest rate regardless of government policies and promises. It may be necessary under these circumstances either to subsidize the cost of loanable funds to potential private investors or to engage in direct public investment in manufacturing. If the weighted average of risk discounts of individual entrepreneurs is much above a reasonable level of uncertainty in manufacturing, government subsidization of private or public investment may be justified as a public good. On the other hand, there is the danger that manufacturers will become accustomed to below-equilibrium borrowing costs, import protection, or tax subsidies, and apply pressure for their continuation long after expectations improve.

Beginning with the administration of Lázaro Cárdenas and particularly since the presidency of Miguel Alemán, government and private industry have cooperated to mutual advantage in what might be termed an "alliance for profits."[18] The results have been successful in establishing a broad industrial base capable of providing sustained economic growth and a rising volume of exportable manufactured goods. But public policy, including investment subsidies, was not alone sufficient for successful industrialization. In the case of Mexican manufacturing, entrepreneurship was the initial condition for rapid and sustained rates of investment in manufacturing. Sanford Mosk, in his classic work on *Industrial Revolution in Mexico,* provided a detailed description of a so-called "New Group" of local industrialists which arose in the 1940s. These entrepreneurs showed a willingness to invest their own savings in the future of the Mexican economy once protection was provided from competing imports.

18. The close cooperation between important segments of the business community and government is documented and analyzed by Vernon, *Dilemma of Mexico's Development,* in terms of the relationship between *políticos* and *técnicos.* The latter are regarded as technicians who provide a professional bridge between the business community and policy-makers (*políticos*). The most insightful contribution of this volume is its recognition of the link between the two sectors, business and government, involving both economic and ideological ties. He notes that, just as the initially most antigovernment business organizations have come to accept and even expect government support, so some of the most vocally xenophobic opponents of foreign investment among Mexican businessmen are now dealing with U.S. and European firms (Chapter 8).

The attitudes, hopes, and fears of Mexican industrialists today can be understood only if we mark out one set of industrialists from all the rest. For the most part those classifiable in this special group are newcomers. Ten years ago they were unknown, and many did not emerge as industrial entrepreneurs until well after the Second World War was underway. They have no special name for their informal group, although the leaders often refer to themselves as "industrialists of youthful outlook" or as "progressive industrialists." For the sake of convenience I will refer to them as the New Group. It should be emphasized, however, that it is not their newness per se which distinguishes them from other industrialists in Mexico; rather it is the common outlook which they have on questions of industrial and national economic policy that sets them apart.

. . . .

The New Group is composed chiefly of owners of small manufacturing plants. Most of these plants, moreover, came into being during the Second World War to supply articles no longer available from foreign sources in sufficient quantities to satisfy the Mexican market. Thus the industries represented by the New Group are small and of recent origin. A third important characteristic is that they use Mexican capital. This sets them off from those new industries in which American capital is participating, whether in the form of investment or in supplying technical direction. . . . Above all, they fear competition from the United States. They want the Mexican market for their own, and they expect the Mexican government to see that they have it.[19]

In addition to the firms represented by this New Group, Mosk adds three other classifications of industries, "(1) industries that were important in the Mexican economy before the Second World War; (2) certain new large industrial ventures that have connections with American enterprises or American capital; and (3) older small-scale and handicraft industries that produce commodities for local markets." [20] At first none of the other three groups shared the highly protectionist mentality of the New Group as reflected in the policies of its primary organization, the Cámara Nacional de la Industria de

19. Mosk, *Industrial Revolution in Mexico,* pp. 21 ff.
20. Ibid., p. 24.

Transformación (CNIT). But since the 1950s, the New Group's attitudes about government support have become more widespread and its own fears of foreign investment have been gradually allayed. Mosk regarded the New Group as a potential force for Mexicanization of industry and the imbuing of local enterprise with a revolutionary spirit. In fact the gradual convergence between the objectives of the CNIT and other business groups reflects a general diffusion of values in which a "revolutionary ethos" or rhetoric of social concern and nation-building is becoming an integral part of the policy framework of much of Mexican industry.

The ready response of Mexican entrepreneurs to increased wartime demand, import-substitution policies of the government, and finally expansion of the internal market, have caused industrial capacity to multiply many times since 1940. Today Mexican manufacturing is relatively capital-intensive. Yet there is no positive relationship between the capital intensity of individual industries in Mexico and their labor productivity, as compared with American industry. On the contrary, the least capital-intensive activities in Mexico were those which showed the highest *relative* labor productivity (absolute labor productivity was of course positively correlated with investment per worker).[21] Edmar Bacha found that labor productivity in Mexico was only 32 percent of the U.S. level in 1960 (valued at the official rate of exchange), while Mexico's investment per worker was 42 percent of the U.S. figure. He proceeded to estimate the share of the difference in labor productivity "explained" by capital intensity by dividing the two ratios (32 percent/42 percent = 75 percent). It was pointed out by Einar Hardin and W. Paul Strassman that this calculation simply measured the relative output per unit of capital in the two countries.[22] By fitting the same data to CES and Cobb-Douglas production functions, these writers arrived at an alternative

21. Bacha, "Comparación entre la productividad industrial de México y los Estados Unidos," p. 669. The author's results are based on the industrial census of 1960, representing 62 percent of the value of industrial production in Mexico. The U.S. sample is from 1958 figures for firms representing 47 percent of value added in manufacturing (p. 659).

22. Einar Hardin and W. Paul Strassmann, "La productividad industrial y la intensidad de capital de México y los Estados Unidos." This material also appears in summary form along with an extended discussion of the effect of cultural values, education and training, supervision, and management on labor productivity in Mexico and Puerto Rico in Strassmann, *Technical Change and Economic Development,* Chapter 3, pp. 68–111, and Appendix B, pp. 316 ff.

estimate of the relative efficiency of labor in Mexican manufacturing showing this to be from 40 to 50 percent of the U.S. level in 1960. They noted, however, that, under present conditions of disequilibrium in the labor market, it would be wasteful of capital to pursue a policy that attempted to equalize labor productivity levels in the two countries, for example by adopting more capital-intensive methods of production in Mexico. As long as a relatively elastic supply of labor is available in that country at a subsistence wage, the two economies will remain in "disequilibrium" whenever unskilled labor abroad is paid more than a subsistence wage net of moving costs. Policies restricting the migration of Mexican labor have tended to perpetuate these disequilibria, permitting American workers to earn higher wages at the expense of their Mexican counterparts and American consumers. This is reflected in a loss of allocative efficiency in both countries brought about by the dual wage and employment structure.

Whether or not the prevailing technology in Mexican manufacturing in 1960 was optimal from the point of view of resource allocation, it was underutilized. Bacha estimates that two-thirds of industry was operating below capacity in that year.[23] One of the principal factors restricting the full employment of plant and equipment in multiple-shift operation was a lack of skilled labor and supervisory personnel. In this respect the Hirschman position is supported, since it appears to have been easier to import and install modern industrial machinery than to train and supervise the work force required to run it effectively. Because public and business education are expanding at a rapid rate, one may expect a steady increase in the supply of skilled labor which will permit higher productivity of presently installed industrial capacity. It is likely that the capital/output ratio eventually will fall below 1960 levels as a result of improvements in the quality of the work force.

Since the Mexican economy has passed through many crises during the past fifty years, potential investors at the beginning of the most recent period of growth had no reason to view the future with undimmed enthusiasm. There was no guarantee in 1946 that demand for domestic manufactures would remain at previous wartime levels, much less expand. Under the circumstances it was necessary for the government to improve entrepreneurial expectations and minimize the risk involved in new investment, if expansion of manufacturing

23. Bacha, "Comparación entre la productividad industrial de México y los Estados Unidos," p. 665.

for the domestic market was to continue. The government's response was swift and direct. A system of import licensing was introduced, along with an increase in tariff protection for local industry as detailed in the following chapter. In addition to receiving a high and sustained level of protection, industrialists were provided with tax concessions and investment subsidies, including a ceiling on the nominal rate of interest. As inflation continued this policy served to reduce the real cost of borrowing to a minimum. In addition rapid postwar development of financial intermediaries provided a broader base for the channeling of financial flows to industry, a practice which was encouraged by portfolio requirements imposed on *financieras* by the Central Bank.

We have seen that the profit share of national income increased rapidly during the 1940s and remained high during the following decade. Wage costs were kept down by the relatively elastic supply of labor from the service sector and agriculture, as well as by effective government control over the labor unions. Imported producers' goods costs were reduced through favorable tariff policy. Lagged revenue collection (more important during the early years of inflation), tax concessions for new industry, and underreporting of profits permitted the effective rate of taxation on profits to remain low. All of these factors tended to increase the rate of return on capital in manufacturing, although reliable figures on net profits are unavailable.

Although the initial wave of postwar expansion involved primarily national rather than foreign investment, U.S. firms increasingly sought government permission to place subsidiaries in Mexico to take advantage of the growing internal market. U.S. direct investment in Mexico between 1929 and 1959 first decreased and then increased. From a reported 682 million dollars invested in 1929 [24] and 480 million dollars in 1936, the total fell to 286 million dollars in 1943 following the expropriation of petroleum in 1938. By 1950, investment had risen again to 415 million dollars, a figure which increased to 739 million dollars in 1947 and 759 million dollars in 1959.

Forty-seven percent of U.S. direct investment in Mexico was in manufacturing as of 1959, compared to only 17 percent in Latin America as a whole. While over half of American investment in the hemisphere was concentrated in mining and petroleum, the figure for

24. This reported figure is considerably higher than the actual value of installed plant and equipment and cost of real property in that year because of the use of accounting procedures by foreign petroleum companies which included the value of reserves in total assets.

Mexico was only 22 percent. It is not surprising that U.S. investment in extractive industries has fallen off since the nationalization policies of the 1930s. What is unusual is the extent to which Americans have invested in manufacturing in Mexico in recent years. While U.S. manufacturing investment in Latin America increased between 1950 and 1959 by 80 percent or from 780 to 1,405 million dollars, in Mexico it increased at double that rate or from 133 to 355 million dollars. Indeed, almost all of the growth in U.S. investment in Mexico during the 1950s was in manufacturing.[25]

A comparison of the reported value of U.S. direct investment in Mexican manufacturing in 1959 with our earlier figure for the total capital stock in manufacturing (Table 5.2), converting the latter at the official exchange rate for 1950 pesos (8.64 per dollar), shows that in 1959-60 U.S. investors held claims on approximately 8 percent of total manufacturing capacity. The comparable figure for 1950 was almost 10 percent. Despite the steady increase in U.S. investment in manufacturing during the 1950s, its share of total investment in that sector has declined.

In addition to direct foreign investment in manufacturing, private industry has placed an increasing number of loans abroad along with public and private financial intermediaries, and the federal government. A large proportion of the proceeds of the loans has gone into the financing of manufacturing. The rapid postwar development of the Mexican economy, recent balance of payments equilibrium, and a stable exchange rate since 1954 have combined to improve Mexico's credit rating abroad. Unlike most countries in Latin America whose debt default in the 1930s is still remembered with disfavor in foreign bond markets, Mexico's problem is not in obtaining credit but in preventing an excess of borrowing. Already the share of debt service in the balance of payments is assuming proportions reminiscent of the last years of the Porfiriato.

THE RELATIVE PERFORMANCE OF POSTWAR INDUSTRIALIZATION IN MEXICO

In order to determine the relative effect of Mexico's industrialization policies, a comparison can be drawn between the actual levels of per capita output in fifteen major industries and what might have been

25. All of the preceding statistics are taken from U.S. Department of Commerce, Business Economics Office, *U.S. Business Investments in Foreign Countries,* pp. 89, 91, and 92.

Table 5.9
Gross Investment in Industry[a]
(millions of pesos)

	Current Pesos	1950 Pesos
1939	198	684
1940	208	654
1941	234	684
1942	165	462
1943	262	686
1944	438	983
1945	690	1,599
1946	1,010	1,842
1947	1,398	2,327
1948	1,612	2,261
1949	1,680	1,954
1950	1,872	1,872
1951	2,236	1,899
1952	2,389	1,830
1953	2,346	1,641
1954	3,079	1,900
1955	4,687	2,499
1956	5,312	2,589
1957	6,232	2,778
1958	6,997	2,965
1959	6,405	2,664
1960	7,732	2,891
1961	9,891	3,823
1962[b]	9,848	3,763
Total gross investment 1940–49		13,452
Total gross investment 1950–59		22,637

[a] Includes investment in mining, petroleum, electrical energy, and manufacturing. Does not include construction.

[b] Preliminary estimate.

Sources: Period 1939–49: Ortiz Mena, et al., *El Desarrollo Económico de México*, Table 14.

Period 1950–62: Nacional Financiera, S.A., Departamento de Estudios Financieros Division de Proyectos as presented in United Nations, ECLA, "El desarrollo industrial de México," Table 43, p. 140.

expected if Mexico had followed the pattern of a "typical" developing country. To do this, an estimate was made of the divergence of the structure of industrial production in both 1950 and 1960 from that of a hypothetical economy based upon data from thirty-eight countries in a study by Hollis Chenery, "Patterns of Industrial Growth" (*American Economic Review,* September 1960). In that paper Professor Chenery assumed that the pattern of per capita industrial production of a given country may be explained by per capita income and population size. Using the coefficients from his model, levels of output were estimated for fifteen Mexican manufacturing industries in both 1950 and 1960. These hypothetical figures were compared with actual per capita production in Mexico based on data obtained from the 1950 and 1960 input-output tables. All data have been converted into 1953 prices, using the wholesale price index as a deflator for comparison with results of the Chenery study (Table 5.10).[26]

In 1950 actual output exceeded predicted levels in twelve of the fifteen industries, suggesting that even then the Mexican economy was considerably more industrialized than might have been expected of a "representative" country of similar population and per capita income.[27] However, the 1960 results show only seven of the fifteen industries to be above expected levels of per capita output. Both World War II and the industrialization program of the Alemán administration (1946–52) had a definite effect on the structure of pro-

26. Much of the material in this section was prepared with the assistance of Saul Trejo whose results appear in Trejo, "Los patrones de crecimiento industrial."

27. The interpretation of these results is filled with pitfalls. Even if the composite economy were truly representative and free from the distortions of public policy, Mexico's comparative advantage undoubtedly differed from that of the average less developed country. For example, because Mexico was relatively rich in petroleum reserves due to the fortunes of geography, petroleum-processing and petrochemical industries show outputs far in excess of the composite economy, as observed in Table 5.10 for groups 10 and 11. Since public policy effects are not neutralized in the model, the coefficients of the composite economy reflect a general international tendency to favor import competing over export industries. Thus the absolute divergence of Mexico from the model understates the effect of public policy on Mexican industrialization, on the one hand, while failing to correct for deviations in comparative advantage favoring Mexican mineral and other natural resource-intensive exports on the other. The relative change in the ratio of actual to predicted output from 1950 to 1960 may more closely reflect the net effect of Mexican industrialization policy during the 1950s, to the extent that this policy differed from that of the sample.

duction, tending to increase the share of manufacturing much above the level that might have been expected in the absence of official support. In view of the debates which surrounded the government's decision to support Mexican industrialization at the expense of other activities, and specifically of small-scale agriculture, it is important to bear in mind that these statistical results say nothing about the relative efficiency of resource allocation or about the relative degree of government protection (including subsidization) of the various industries. In the next chapter this problem is dealt with in terms of the implications of industrialization policy for the demand for scarce resources including skilled labor, imported and domestic capital equipment, and imported intermediate goods.

Mexico's relatively high degree of industrialization failed to keep pace with the Chenery model between 1950 and 1960. Although per capita output in manufacturing remained above expected levels in 1960, the margin was much smaller than before (Table 5.10). The percentage by which actual exceeded predicted output was greater in all but one of the fifteen industries in 1950 than in 1960. Actual performance surpassed expectations in both years in only seven of the sectors, and for printing, wood products, and transport both years showed less output than the Chenery study would have predicted.[28] Of those sectors that received assistance in the form of government financing, subsidies, and protection—including chemicals, petroleum, and transportation equipment—we have seen that the latter failed to reach predicted levels by 1960 and all three showed a deterioration in their position relative to the composite economy between the two years. The machinery manufacturing industry which was ahead in 1950 fell behind in 1960 although there is independent evidence that machinery repair showed rapid growth. It would appear that the policies of protection for the machinery industry have not been sufficient to allow production to remain above predicted levels, suggesting that scale factors may have imposed limits on the growth of this sector.

Mexican manufacturing has grown rapidly, though not miraculously, except insofar as the achievement of sustained high rates of investment may be regarded as exceptional in a developing country. Much of the explanation for the continuing growth of manufacturing

28. These results combine changes in both price and quantity in individual sectors since the use of a single deflator fails to allow for relative price changes.

Table 5.10
Actual and Predicted Per Capita Output in Fifteen
Mexican Manufacturing Industries
(1953 U.S. dollars per capita)

	1950			1960		
	Actual	*Predicted*		*Actual*	*Predicted*	
Industry Group	*Output*	*Output*	*A–P*[a]	*Output*	*Output*	*A–P*[a]
1. Food & Beverages	16.97	9.62	+	21.06	14.77	+
2. Tobacco	1.45	1.36	+	1.58	2.08	−
3. Textiles	6.68	4.75	+	5.80	9.32	−
4. Clothing	4.57	2.09	+	4.99	4.04	+
5. Wood, etc.	1.51	1.58	−	1.98	2.83	−
6. Paper	3.23	0.58	+	1.58	1.91	−
7. Printing	1.10	1.51	−	1.52	3.04	−
8. Leather	1.35	0.33	+	0.79	0.61	+
9. Rubber	0.79	0.46	+	1.25	1.13	+
10. Chemicals	4.03	2.50	+	5.66	5.08	+
11. Petroleum	6.87	0.17	+	10.85	0.53	+
12. Nonmetallic Minerals	2.04	1.69	+	2.52	3.29	−
13. Metals	3.33	2.89	+	5.98	2.87	+
14. Machinery	1.95	1.18	+	3.08	3.76	−
15. Transport Equipment	1.15	1.52	−	2.52	3.98	−
Total of these industries	57.02	32.23	+	71.16	59.14	+

[a] *A* refers to actual output; *P* to predicted.

Source: Trejo, "Los patrones de crecimiento industrial." Actual output is based upon the 1950 and 1960 input-output tables prepared by the Departamento de Estudios Economicos, Banco de México converted to 1953 pesos and then to dollars. Predicted output is based upon the method used by Chenery, "Patterns of Industrial Growth." The Chenery study has since been enlarged, time series data for each country were added, and the categories in the sample were broadened, though similar changes do not appear in the Trejo analysis. Ref. Chenery and Taylor, "Development Patterns."

may be traced to the successful transformation of agriculture which has sustained a balance of trade surplus with the rest of the world and has prevented excess urbanization. In addition the service sector has absorbed increases in the labor force, has registered notable productivity gains, has widened the market for manufactured goods, and has therefore permitted the realization of economies of scale in a number of industries.

Given the importance of rapidly increasing internal demand to the growth of manufacturing since the initial World War II boom, another sine qua non for successful industrialization was the existence of a large number of entrepreneurs prepared to gamble on the future of their economy. The psychology of the Mexican businessman deserves to be analyzed in considerably more detail. Revolution and reform have played an important role in opening up business opportunities to a more representative cross-section of the population than is typical elsewhere in Latin America. Agrarian reform forced many of the landed gentry to seek employment in urban activities. Although there was almost no monetary compensation for expropriated land, many had accumulated savings that were invested in commerce, manufacturing, and urban real estate in an effort to maintain earlier levels of income. Others without previous wealth found that abolition of the Porfirian aristocracy left a vacuum at the top levels of society, a vacuum which began to be filled by those who proved successful as military leaders in the Revolution, in postrevolutionary politics and in business. The nouveaux riches among the business community found a far easier access to social prestige and acceptance after the Revolution than before. This establishment of a new aristocracy based on wealth rather than birth has done much to legitimize business activity as an avenue of success and power for ambitious Mexicans from all levels of society.

The government itself was active in supporting and in many cases subsidizing industrialization. Entrepreneurship and public policy have combined to create a modern and highly capital-intensive industrial sector that is only beginning to reflect its productive potential. The growth of Mexican industry has exceeded that of most countries of comparable population size and income levels. Foreign direct and indirect investment, which tended to follow rather than precede local investment in manufacturing, have assumed an increasingly important role in absolute—if not relative—terms since World War II. Despite the fact that foreign direct investment is subject to tighter control than in almost any other noncommunist country with the exception of Japan, public and private domestic and foreign investors have shown an increasingly cooperative spirit based on mutual advantage. This spirit is summed up here as an "alliance for profits" without which Mexican industrialization would scarcely have achieved its present success.

6

Changing Trade Patterns and
Trade Policy: 1900–1965

Poor country, so far from God and so close to the United States.

—Porfirio Díaz

Mexico has been a commercial center since pre-Colombian times. On their arrival Spaniards discovered great marketplaces and a high degree of specialization in production and exchange. Metalworking is said to have been brought from South America during the process of trade under the Mixtecs. Ceramics from Central Mexico have been excavated in early Guatemalan sites. By the Aztec period merchants were prominent in the social and political hierarchy, having accumulated fortunes from trade in feathers, metals and precious stones, artifacts, and foodstuffs. After the Conquest trade with Spain vastly influenced the distribution of production and wealth in Mexico and with it the rate of economic and population growth. During the nineteenth century, the liberalization of trade served to relieve bottlenecks in the process of production and to provide additional capital, skilled labor, and technology for the fuller utilization of natural resource endowments.

A nation's gains from trade are customarily explained in terms of the doctrine of comparative advantage, a theory which attributes the pattern of trade to regional variations in factor endowments and final demand. Since trade itself brings about changes in the availability of labor, capital, and intermediate goods, as well as the pattern of income and tastes, a trading nation's comparative advantage is certain to evolve over time and with it the future path of trade. In a world of perfect knowledge, pure competition, instantaneous adjustment, and stable expectations, private profits might be expected to reflect the natural state of comparative advantage, provided there were no externalities of production or consumption, taxes or subsidies, increasing returns, or private or public restraints on trade. But the greater the role of public policy in the economy, and the more prominent these other factors, the less private profits may be expected to reflect the economy's comparative advantage. The fact that Mexico has grown rapidly in the past century, that the production base has been transformed, and that much of this has been directly or indirectly attributable to public policy, makes any analysis of its trade and growth a problem of considerable complexity. Furthermore, much of Mexico's trade in recent years has taken place with her near neighbor to the north whose political and economic power afford a mixed blessing. The two countries are separated by only a river and a fence. Slightly over a hundred years ago half of the Mexican territory was annexed to the United States by force of arms under the administration of President Polk. Since then, Mexico's problem has been to maximize the gains from trade with the United States subject to the retention of political and economic independence. The effects of this struggle are mirrored in the history of her trade and commercial policy.

Mexico began the twentieth century as a capital-scarce, labor-abundant economy with underutilized land and mineral resources. Over time there has been considerable emigration of labor to the United States (especially on a seasonal basis) and large-scale importation of machinery and equipment, first to be used for the extraction of minerals to exploit the country's initial comparative advantage in natural resources, and more recently for the development of commercial agriculture and manufacturing. The modernization of mining required large investments (financed primarily by foreign loans) in railroads, electric power, and telecommunications before its potential comparative advantage became reflected in high private rates of return on capital.

Following the Revolution, pressures for nationalization and agrarian reform caused a shift in public policy. Government investments in rural infrastructure began to favor the expansion of commercial agriculture over mining. Rising rates of taxation combined with unfavorable conditions of foreign demand and threats of expropriation discouraged investment in the extractive industries. Over the past fifty years, relative rates of return on capital after taxes shifted from mining and petroleum toward agriculture and services (tourism in particular). This trend is mirrored in the pattern of trade that has evolved since 1910. Agricultural products have increased from 30 to 55 percent of commodity exports and minerals have fallen from 60 to 23 percent (Table 6.4). Although most of these changes did not take place until the 1940s, the policies that influenced them were introduced much earlier. And even so, these policies were only partially responsible for changes in the structure of the economy. Mexico's proximity to the United States has continually influenced the exchange of goods and factors of production. This intercourse has been subject to the control of Mexican policy-makers only within the degrees of freedom permitted by U.S.–Mexican relations. Just as the American market for Mexican goods and services has fluctuated, along with foreign lines of credit, the political policy space afforded to Mexican planners has also varied with the conditions of U.S. domestic and foreign affairs.

Because trade since 1910 has changed in response to market conditions as well as public policy, it is difficult to determine what would have happened had political events at home and abroad followed a different path. This is especially true since in many respects trade between Mexico and the United States is a residual activity in which surpluses are exported and shortages are made up by imports both on current and capital account. A modest change in the structure of supply and demand in either country can therefore have a major influence on Mexico trade flows. Investment in the mineral sector probably would have grown more rapidly between 1910 and 1940, in the absence of revolution. What is not certain is whether the net effect of agrarian reform on private investment in agriculture before 1940 was positive or negative.

Earlier chapters showed that after 1940 the emphasis in agrarian policy shifted from expropriation to the building of rural infrastructure. This change had a highly favorable influence on both public and private investment in commercial agriculture, permitting a sharp increase in commodity exports once foreign demand conditions were favorable. More recently, the government has become open to additional potential gains from trade in mining and petroleum, and attention has again turned to the extractive industries. The incidence of mineral taxation has been reduced since the early 1950s, although it is still much higher than in any other sector of the economy. While the government has altered the pattern of export trade through tax and expenditure policy, one of its major programs has been the promotion of industrialization since the mid-1930s, partly to provide employment and higher incomes for a rapidly urbanizing population and partly to relieve the demand for imported manufactured goods.

The following section provides a brief sketch of the evolution of Mexico's foreign trade since 1900. Next there is a description of the special character of her contemporary commercial policy, followed by a discussion of its effect on production and trade since 1950. The latter section estimates the extent to which "import substitution" has in fact taken place, by measuring the input requirements under alternative expansion paths. An evaluation of the effect of commercial policy on the demand for skilled labor, capital, and foreign exchange follows. Finally, the chapter touches on various influences on Mexican trade and development arising from her special circumstances as a neighbor of the United States.

THE PRESENT TRADE POSITION OF MEXICO
IN HISTORICAL PERSPECTIVE

The Mexican economy in 1910 was divided into numerous social and economic enclaves. Foreigners and a small number of nationals owned much of the nation's resources. Trade flourished before the Revolution, with exports leading the growth of total output between 1900 and 1910 (Table 6.1). The ratio of trade (merchandise exports and imports) to GDP was 19.5 percent in 1910 and remained fairly constant through 1950 when it was 21.3 percent (Table 6.2). Minerals and agricultural commodities accounted for 90 percent of total exports in 1900. Given the highly unequal income distribution resulting from this pattern of trade, resource allocation was probably quite "efficient" during those years. But efficiency in this narrow economic sense existed under conditions in which the majority of Mexican society was excluded from the benefits of economic growth. Economic growth through 1910 was associated with growing political dissatisfaction. The impressive expansion of traditional exports during the Porfiriato neither unified national markets nor broadened the distribution of income sufficiently to buy off social unrest, the consequence of which was eventual civil war.

The ensuing crisis had little effect on the pattern of trade. From 1910 to 1920, with only brief interruptions, mineral and petroleum exports flourished in response to the demands of World War I. By 1925, the ratio of exports plus imports to GDP had risen from 19.5

Table 6.1

Growth of Mexican Gross Domestic Product and Foreign Trade, 1900–65
(compound annual rates of growth)

	Porfiriato	Revolution and Reform		Development		
	1900–10	1910–25	1925–40	1940–50	1950–60	1960–65
1. Gross domestic product	3.3	2.5	1.6	6.7	6.1	6.1
2. Exports of goods and services[a]	4.5	(2.7–5.1)	−1.4	8.2	1.8	(4.1)[b]
3. Imports of goods and services[a]	1.3	(1.9–4.3)	−3.5	9.4	4.3	(3.0)[b]

[a] The data for the years 1900 to 1940 reflect exports and imports of merchandise only. The data after 1940 reflect exports and imports of goods and services.

[b] Estimate.

Sources and Methods: Row 1: Table 1.4.

Rows 2 and 3: The figures for 1900–10 are for (2) exports adjusted by terms of trade (capacity to import) and (3) imports in real terms from El Colegio de México, *Comercio Exterior de México, 1877–1911*, p. 163.

The data for 1910–25 actually cover the period 1909–10 to 1926 as presented in Sherwell, *Mexico's Capacity to Pay*, in which the value of exports reflects only the share of export earnings retained in Mexico (returned value). The larger of each of the growth rates is the growth of the value of trade in dollars. The smaller rates are based on the value of trade in pesos deflated by the wholesale price index in Mexico City.

The data from 1925 to 1940 are from United Nations, ECLA, *Economic Survey of Latin America 1949*, expressed in millions of 1937 pesos.

The figures for 1940–60 are from Grupo Secretaría de Hacienda—Banco de México, Estudios sobre Proyecciones, "Manual." Tables 1.1 and 1.3 and represent the "capacity to import" (2) and total imports of goods and services (3). The figures for 1960–65 are from recent unpublished sources of the Banco de México expressed in current (peso) values deflated by the implicit GDP deflator, thereby assuming constancy in the terms of trade.

to 21.8 percent (Table 6.2). As of 1926, the extractive industries accounted for 76 percent of total exports (Table 6.4). Nevertheless it was politically unfeasible after the Revolution to return to the pre-1910 policies of relative laissez faire with unrestrained foreign investment. Instead, a series of new laws increased the taxes on mining and petroleum. The proceeds of these taxes were designed to support public investments in education and public works in order to improve social welfare and to strengthen the internal market at the expense of profits on trade. Yet the tax policies of postrevolutionary administrations did not retard exports of agricultural, mining, and petroleum

Table 6.2

Estimates of the Merchandise Trade Share of Mexican Gross Domestic Product, 1910–65[a]

	1910 A	1910 B	1925 A	1925 B	1930 A	1930 B	1940 A	1940 B	1950 A	1950 B	1960 A	1960 B	1965 B
	(Million pesos—current value)												
Merchandise exports	260	294	682	682	459	458	960	960	4,339	3,789	9,233	7,896	12,491
Merchandise imports	195	206	391	391	350	350	669	669	4,403	4,807	14,830	14,831	19,503
Gross domestic product	2,330	2,497	4,902	3,621	3,960	4,318	7,108	7,995	41,060	41,060	155,867	155,889	246,200
	(Percentages of gross domestic product)												
Merchandise exports	11.2	11.8	13.9	18.8	11.5	10.6	13.5	12.0	10.5	9.2	5.9	5.1	5.1
Merchandise imports	8.3	8.2	7.9	10.8	8.8	8.1	9.4	8.4	10.7	11.7	9.5	9.5	7.9
Sum	19.5	20.0	21.8	29.6	20.4	18.7	22.9	20.4	21.3	20.9	15.4	14.6	13.0

[a] For estimate A the current values of merchandise exports and imports for 1910 are from Sherwell, *Mexico's Capacity to Pay*; for later years from Nacional Financiera, *50 años de revolución en cifras*. GDP figures in current values in estimate A before 1940 are based on the Reynolds estimates in millions of 1950 pesos in Appendix Table C.2, converted to current values using the wholesale price index for Mexico, D.F. of 19.7 for 1910, 28.7 for 1925, and 26.5 for 1930, with 1950 = 100. For 1940 and later years GDP figures are directly from *24*, Appendix Table D:1A.

For estimate B all figures are taken directly from Banco de México, "Producto bruto interno" (Gutierrez) pp. 114 ff. (See note to Table 6.3.)

The wide discrepancy in current value GDP estimates for 1925 and 1930 reflects alternative estimating procedures for the underlying physical production indexes (especially for agriculture) and different deflators used to transform estimates in constant prices (1950) to current values. The GDP estimates in constant prices used in this table (expressed in million 1950 pesos) are:

	1910	1925	1930	1940	1950	1960	1965
Est. A (Reynolds)	11,825	17,081	14,946	21,658	41,060	74,317	99,700
Est. B (Gutierrez)	11,650	14,816	15,540	22,889	41,060	74,317	99,616

products during the Obregón and Calles administrations (1920 to 1928). The provisions of the Constitution of 1917, which affirmed federal ownership of land and subsoil assets as part of the "national patrimony," were not taken seriously in most quarters. In commerce, British and American interests invaded the Mexican market. The foreign-owned share of total Mexican wealth may actually have increased between 1900 and 1929, though there is doubt about the intervening years.[1]

This increase in the foreign ownership of national assets was particularly true for traditional export activities. The violent years of revolution proved more harmful to the small, vulnerable Mexican enterprises in mining and petroleum than to the large, well-financed foreign firms that eventually absorbed many bankrupt small operators. The immediate postrevolutionary governments maintained a hands-off policy on American property in order to preserve precarious diplomatic relations with the United States and to minimize the threat of foreign intervention during the difficult period of debt settlement and reconstruction. As a result, American and British export industries were less damaged by the Revolution than those of the Spanish and Germans. Indeed, the former two gained at the expense of the latter and the small Mexican investor. This was a time when U.S. investors throughout Latin America regarded themselves as subject to American rather than foreign law and fully expected that U.S. diplomacy, including military intervention if necessary, could be called upon to champion their "rights."

In this respect the increased growth of imports from 1910 to 1925 would not have been possible had the government continued to service its outstanding foreign debt inherited from the administration of Porfirio Díaz. Debt default provided relief for the postrevolutionary balance of payments equivalent to a unilateral international transfer

1. Raymond Goldsmith, *The Financial Development of Mexico,* Table 7, p. 73. For an illuminating and detailed comparison of foreign investment in Mexican export activities in 1910 and 1926, as well as a comparison of the balance of payments of Mexico in these two years, see G. Butler Sherwell, "Mexico's Capacity to Pay, A General Analysis of the Present International Economic Position of Mexico," Washington, D.C., 1929 (typescript). Sherwell estimates that the share of gross value of exports returned to Mexico actually *declined* between 1910 and 1926 from 79 percent to 66 percent (my calculations from his figures) because of remittances of interest and principal on a rising foreign share of mineral investment. This would help to explain subsequent tax policies, government support of labor unions, and outright nationalization, all of which tend to increase the domestic share of income from export activities.

of purchasing power of several hundred millions of dollars. Efforts were made throughout the 1920s to achieve some settlement of this debt, and the U.S. Republican administrations of those years placed steady pressure on Mexico for compliance. Balance of payments relief was obtained at the expense of badly deteriorating relationships between the Mexican government and the international financial community—relationships which were not cemented until well into the 1940s.

By 1925 a paradoxical situation existed in that the Revolution,

Table 6.3

The Structure of Mexican Exports of Goods and Services, 1910–60

(Percent of recorded current values)

	1909–10	1926	1940	1945	1950	1955	1960	1964
A. *Goods*	97	94	75	64	66	65	58	58
Commodity exports	53	75	44	54	60	61	54	56
Gold and silver exports	44	19	31	10	6	4	4	2
B. *Services*	3	6	25	36	34	35	42	42
Internal tourism	a	0	8	9	13	10	11	13
Frontier tourism and other border transactions[b]	a	2	15	13	15	22	27	25
Emigrant remittances[c]	a	4	a	11	2	2	3	2
Other exports of services	3	1	2	3	4	2	2	2
Grand Total	100	100	100	100	100	100	100	100

[a] Included in "Other exports of services."

[b] "Other transactions" conceal certain commodity exports associated with tourism which, if they could be separated from the total, belong more appropriately under section A.

[c] After 1940 this figure represents bracero income returned to Mexico, as shown in Appendix Table D.3.

Sources and Methods: Data for 1909–10, 1926 are from Sherwell, *Mexico's Capacity to Pay*, pp. 6, 7, 39, 49, expressed in pesos. Data for 1940–64 are from Banco de México, Grupo Secretaría de Hacienda, Estudios Sobre Proyecciones, "Manual," Table 7.3 expressed in current dollars. Totals do not always agree due to rounding. Since the writing of this manuscript a new breakdown of data on merchandise exports and imports from 1892–93 to 1910–11 and exports and imports of goods and services from 1920–67 by sector of economic activity has appeared: See Banco de México, Departamento de Estudios Económicos, "Producto bruto interno y series básicas, 1895–1967," (prepared by M. Gutierrez R., Jan. 1969, I(E)69/15 mimeo.), note to Table 2. These data are expressed in current pesos and are reconcilable with the 1960 input-output table of the Banco de México. While the series provide a more complete and consistent coverage of the entire period, they do not significantly alter the analysis or conclusions of this chapter.

which had been partly a reaction against increasing economic dualism during the Porfiriato, resulted in an even more dualistic structure of trade and production than before. Table 6.4 reveals that mining and fuel exports, which represented 60 percent of traded goods in 1910, increased to 76 percent by 1926. Commodity exports as a share of GDP increased from 11 percent to almost 14 percent over the same period (Table 6.2). The implications for income distribution are

Table 6.4

The Structure of Mexican Commodity Exports, 1910–60

(percents)

	1909–10	1926	1940	1945	1950	1955	1960
1. Agricultural and forest products	30	21	20	35	52	57	55
2. Livestock and fisheries	8	2	4	6	5	5	12
3. Fuels and lubricants	0	33	11	3	5	6	3
4. Minerals	60	43	62	26	31	24	23
5. Manufactures and other products	2	1	3	30	7	7	8
6. Total	100	100	100	100	100	100	100

Sources and Methods: Data for years 1909–10 and 1926 are from Sherwell, *Mexico's Capacity to Pay.* Data for years 1940 to 1960 are from Appendix Table D.6, Part A.

evident, especially when one considers that the share of foreign ownership in mining and petroleum may well have increased by 1926 while the proportion of returned value to Mexico declined. Meanwhile, the situation in agriculture offered little or no improvement in rural income distribution. Although agrarian reform was gradually beginning to acquire force of law by the mid-1920s, not much land had yet changed hands by government decree. As a result, income distribution had not yet been strongly affected by agricultural policy, even though the share of commercial crops in commodity exports fell from 30 percent in 1910 to 21 percent in 1926 (Table 6.4).

The advent of world depression at the end of the 1920s drastically altered expectations. The failure of foreign markets and private enterprise to provide a stable source of growth made it increasingly likely that public policy in petroleum, mining, and agriculture would eventually turn against all foreign investors, including Americans. Foreign investment was the easiest and least costly area to attack —especially since the exports of these industries were already falling.

Had trade continued to flourish after 1929, the subsequent path of
Mexican commercial policy might well have been different. But the
onslaught of world depression and the blow it caused to Mexican
exports were forceful reminders of the country's vulnerability to
foreign trade and investment, thus reopening the case for nationalization and autarchy that had been introduced at the framing of the
Constitution in 1917.

Table 6.5
The Structure of Mexican Imports of Goods and Services, 1910–64
(percent)

	1909–10	*1926*	*1940*	*1945*	*1950*	*1955*	*1960*	*1964*
A. *Goods*	63	72	82	85	86	88	85	78
(1) Registered commodity imports (including imports to free zones)	—ᵃ	–	71	75	77	76	72	66
(2) Frontier importsᵇ	–	–	11	10	10	13	13	12
B. *Services*	37	28	18	15	14	12	15	22
(3) Tourismᵇ	–	3	4	2	1	1	2	5
(4) Service of foreign direct investment	22	13	11	10	9	7	9	11
(5) Interest on government debt	9	5	–	0.2	1.5	1	2	2
(6) Others	6	7	3	3	3	3	2	4
(7) Total	100	100	100	100	100	100	100	100

ᵃ Data not available.

ᵇ Much of row 2 represents Mexican border tourism, which should be considered
together with the data in row 3. For 1926, row 3 includes only frontier tourism.

Sources and Methods: Source of data for years 1910–11 and 1926, Sherwell,
Mexico's Capacity to Pay. Data for years 1940–64 from Grupo Secretaría de
Hacienda—Banco de México, Estudios sobre Proyecciones, "Manual," Table 7-5.
The current value figures on which these data are based, with slight modification
for rows 4 to 6, appear in Appendix Table D.3. In that table, rows 4 and 5 appear
under the heading "Factor income paid abroad."

Foreign investors who bore the brunt of the new government tax,
wage, and import policies reacted by withdrawing profits from the
country and slowing the rate of replacement of plant and equipment.
The result was falling exports, a negative response to wage demands,
and a growing impasse between foreign investors on the one hand
and the government and labor unions on the other. What had begun
as a gradual expropriation of the yield on foreign-owned assets

Table 6.6

The Structure of Mexican Commodity Imports, 1940–63

(percent of recorded current values)

	1940	1945	1950	1955	1960	1963
1. Consumer goods	28	28	18	15	11	14
2. Fuels and lubricants	3	3	4	8	4	3
3. Primary materials	41	40	42	37	41	38
4. Capital goods	28	29	36	40	44	39
(a) Construction equipment	6	5	7	6	5	4
(b) Agricultural equipment	2	2	4	5	4	2
(c) Industrial and mining equipment	13	17	21	23	25	27
(d) Transport equipment	7	4	3	6	10	5
5. Total	100	100	100	100	100	100
6. Unclassified frontier imports as a share of total commodity imports	13	12	11	15	16	18

Sources and Methods: Percentages in rows 1–5 are based on data in current pesos in Appendix Table D.7A. The figures for 1963 are provisional. Percentages in row 6 are based on data in current pesos in Appendix Table D.3 using total merchandise imports as divisor in all years; it should be noted that for the years 1945 and 1950 the totals in the two tables for nonfrontier commodity imports do not coincide. See Appendix Table D.7A, note a.

eventually became, at least in the case of petroleum, outright expropriation of the assets themselves. These actions tended to depress expected rates of return on capital from traditional exports relative to import-competing activities. Taxes applied to mining crippled Mexican and foreign-owned enterprises alike, so that mineral production never fully recovered. Petroleum production for the nationalized oil industry did not regain 1927 levels until 1949. Of the principal export metals over the 1925/29–1945/48 period, silver production declined by 46 percent, lead production fell by 15 percent, and copper production by 4 percent, with only that of zinc rising (44 percent).[2]

As elsewhere in Latin America, and particularly in Argentina,[3] Chile,[4] and Brazil,[5] the depression of the 1930s was responsible for

2. The most complete treatment of Mexican foreign trade between 1925 and 1948, from which these figures are taken, is presented in the United Nations, ECLA, *Economic Survey of Latin America 1949,* Chapter 9 ("Economic Development of Mexico").

3. See Carlos Díaz-Alejandro, "An Interpretation of Argentine Economic Growth Since 1930, Parts 1 and 2.

4. Paul T. Ellsworth, *Chile, An Economy in Transition.*

5. Werner Baer, *Industrialization and Economic Development in Brazil,* Chapter 2.

a major attempt to restructure production toward manufacturing and other activities to serve the domestic market. This process has subsequently become identified with the term "import substitution," though the strategy was initially designed as much to relieve unemployment as to substitute local products for importables. Public policy in Mexico, while it did result in some growth of manufacturing, as we have seen, was not met with the same enthusiasm among entrepreneurs as it was, for example, in Argentina (at least until Mexican trade conditions improved in the 1940s).[6] President Cárdenas's attempts to encourage domestic manufacturing in the 1930s were offset by his own agrarian and petroleum policies, which created an atmosphere of uncertainty among private investors. This situation was aggravated by the small size of the domestic market, a shortage of liquidity, lack of confidence in the peso, inflation, and balance of payments problems. Indeed, the stability of the government was itself in doubt as late as 1940 when backers of the opposition candidate, General Almazán, threatened to secure victory through force of arms. The General ultimately disavowed this support and accepted the election of the official party candidate, Avila Camacho.

If the Mexican government in the 1930s had been able to offset unfavorable expectations arising from the expropriation of commercial agricultural and petroleum properties with large expenditures on economic infrastructure and subsidies to import-competing industry, the process of import substitution might have commenced earlier. But since it was primarily dependent upon revenues from trade, and since the depression and reform program were responsible for sharp declines in foreign exchange earnings, the public sector was fiscally unable to provide industry with much tangible support. A deficit was run during the late 1930s, but its effect on demand was not sufficient to offset the stagnation and decline of traditional exports, nor did commercial policy do much to protect domestic producers. As a result, per capita product failed to show any perceptible increase between 1925 and 1940 (Table 1.4). Indeed, the share of exports plus imports in GDP rose rather than fell during the 1930s (Table 6.2).

From 1940 to 1950 the share of merchandise imports in GDP increased from 9.4 percent to 10.7 percent (Table 6.2), and the rate of growth of both exports and imports of goods and services out-

6. See Mosk, *Industrial Revolution in Mexico,* for a detailed analysis of the "new group" of entrepreneurs which arose in the 1930s and 1940s and its positive response to improved economic conditions after 1940.

stripped that of GDP throughout the decade (Table 6.1). Not until the 1950s did the growth of total output surpass that of imports and exports.[7] It appears that in order to reduce its ultimate dependence on trade, Mexico had first to increase its exports sharply in the short run, something which was only possible after the advent of World War II.

In the 1940s import substitution began in earnest. The restrictions on exports to Mexico imposed by the United States during the war, while less extreme than those applied elsewhere in Latin America (since imports from the United States did not require sea transport, and since Mexico was considered an extension of the U.S. war economy) meant soaring sales for Mexican manufacturers. A large supply of previously underemployed labor and underutilized capacity permitted firms to enjoy price increases far in excess of rising costs. Low effective rates of taxation permitted both exporters and local suppliers to retain excess profits.

This sudden growth of export revenues during the 1940s had a multiplier effect on the rest of the economy, and especially on the growth of manufacturing production, which was far greater than that of the expansionary policies of the 1930s. Export expansion loomed large in absolute terms and import leakages were temporarily reduced due to wartime trade restrictions.[8] By mid-decade, the growth of Mexican industrial production was severely straining capacity. Prices soared and inflationary profit margins provided firms with large amounts of internal funds for new investment, provided that they could be assured of a continued demand for their products and a stable source of essential machinery and raw materials once the war was over and U.S. and European export restrictions were removed. In the view of many Mexicans this threat had to be met by com-

7. Although indexes of physical exports and imports during the years 1925 to 1940 indicate net declines, this is misleading, since the rising relative prices of traded goods resulted in an increased share of both exports and imports in GDP during the 1930s and a rising share of imports from 1925 to 1940 (Table 6.2). Despite the nationalization of petroleum and much of commercial agriculture and the increased taxation of mining, the commodity export share in GDP in 1940 was greater than in 1910 and almost as large as in 1925.

8. Mexico has always had a very high income elasticity of demand for imported consumer goods and services. In recent years, import restrictions have tended to blur this fact, since recorded consumer goods imports have fallen as a share of total recorded commodity imports. At the same time the share of unspecified border transactions in total imports has risen sharply along with contraband (obviously missing from the reported figures) as a share of total imports.

mercial policy to prevent earlier gains from being lost through renewed foreign competition.[9]

After 1947, the government of Miguel Alemán (1946–52) took
steps to implement an extensive program of protection for domestic
manufacturing through a system of import licensing for almost all
categories of imported goods. Those industries that were to be favored
with protection received assurances from the government that other
requests for licenses to import competing goods would not be granted.
Tariffs were increased, though with a lag in terms of value of imports, until in 1947 legislation dating back to 1930 authorizing only
specific tariffs was amended to include ad valorem duties on most
articles. But because the primary objective of tariffs was revenue,
direct controls eventually became the basic weapon of protection for
new industries (see Table 6.7). Once a high degree of protection
could be assured, both Mexican and foreign investors vied to participate in the expanding Mexican market. Urban population and
gross domestic product were growing at rapid rates, while substantial
investments in rural infrastructure since the 1930s were beginning to
pay off, promising that agricultural supply problems that had already
begun to afflict other Latin American countries would not slow
Mexico's rate of growth by siphoning off foreign exchange for food
imports or tax revenues for urban consumption subsidies.

The structure of imports from 1940 to 1960 in Table 6.6 reveals
important changes in both supply and demand in Mexico, many of
which are attributable to protectionist policies since the war. While
the share of commodity imports in GDP has not declined since 1940

9. Major questions were raised in the late 1940s and early 1950s over the
advisability of increased protection to encourage continued Mexican industrialization. A number of foreign scholars, including Mosk (*Industrial
Revolution in Mexico*) and Tannenbaum (*Mexico, The Struggle for Peace and
Bread*), urged alternative policies favoring greater emphasis on the development of agriculture, transportation, electric power, and communications. This
point of view reflected a widespread fear that direct controls on trade and
industrial subsidies would produce imbalances in the structure of production
which, together with liberal monetary policy, would lead to severe inflation.
The Tannenbaum position was answered by Alemán's former Undersecretary
of National Economy, Manuel Germán Parra, in *La industrialización de
México*. Germán Parra combined economics with anthropology in a simplistic
morphology of development which argued that all societies must pass through
similar parallel stages of social, political, and economic change. On this basis
he concluded, along with many of his contemporaries, that industrialization
was an essential precondition for a mature Mexican society.

Table 6.7
Import Duties Collected Compared with the Value of Imports, 1939–61
(Million current pesos, except as otherwise indicated)

Year	Import duties collected[a]	Value of imports	Duties as percent of imports
1939	93.6	629.7	14.9
1940	90.1	669.0	13.5
1941	131.7	915.1	14.4
1942	95.5	753.0	12.7
1943	91.4	909.6	10.0
1944	128.1	1,895.2	6.8
1945	153.8	1,604.4	9.6
1946	231.2	2,636.8	8.8
1947	265.4	3,230.3	8.2
1948	321.2	2,951.5	10.9
1949	343.2	3,527.3	9.7
1950	432.3	4,403.4	9.8
1951	614.9	6,773.2	9.1
1952	632.1	6,394.2	9.9
1953	631.4	6,985.3	9.0
1954	757.9	8,926.3	8.5
1955	915.6	11,045.7	8.3
1956	998.0	13,395.3	7.5
1957	1,013.1	14,439.4	7.0
1958	1,312.6	14,108.0	9.3
1959	1,554.1	12,582.6	12.4
1960	1,752.6	14,834.4	11.8
1961	1,659.9	14,233.2	11.7
Sum: 1939–1961	14,219.7	147,843.3	9.6

[a] Excluding subsidies.

Source: Santillán López and Rosas Figueroa, *Teoría General de las Finanzas Públicas y el Caso de México*, p. 225.

and remains higher than in 1910, the proportion of consumer goods to total registered commodity imports has fallen from 28 percent in 1940 to 14 percent in 1963. This has reduced the slack in import requirements since most remaining imports represent capital and intermediate inputs essential to the growth of domestic production. The best opportunities for import substitution have already been taken and firms that now wish to enter the Mexican market, such as machinery or equipment manufacturers, tend to require a larger share of imported inputs than their predecessors.

The early stages of Mexican import substitution from 1940 to the mid-1950s were attended by severe inflation and balance of payments disequilibrium that required two major postwar devaluations. These problems have diminished more recently as domestic production has continued to replace traditional imports, a circumstance virtually unique in Latin America. Indeed, Mexico appears to have import-substituted more effectively than many other developing countries of similar size and wealth. This process has tended to alter comparative advantage in exports as well. The structure of exports has changed dramatically since 1940, partly as a result of public policy and partly in response to changing market conditions. The share of commodity exports in GDP, which declined somewhat during the 1940s, fell drastically during the 1950s (Table 6.2). The share of commodities in total exports of goods and services fell from 75 percent in 1940 to 58 percent in 1964, while tourism plus border transactions rose from 23 percent to 38 percent of total exports (Table 6.3). This decline in commodity exports is totally attributable to gold and silver, which decreased their share from 31 to 2 percent while other commodities rose from 44 to 56 percent. Both commercial policy and declining terms of trade deflected investable funds away from the expansion of traditional exports toward production for the domestic market. While the substituting industries themselves eventually may be expected to grow out of infancy into full-fledged exporters in their own right, this has yet to occur for most. In the meantime, the share in total exports of raw materials and primary products has been lowered by depletion of mineral reserves and by an expanding national market for these former export staples. This historical pattern has been observed not only in Mexico but in other countries as well, including the United States and Japan. The share of traditional exports of minerals and fuels has fallen from 73 percent of commodity exports in 1940 to 26 percent in 1960 (Table 6.4). Meanwhile, commodities such as cash crops primarily from the newly irrigated regions of the North and Northwest and a few manufactures have risen from 23 percent to 63 percent of exports during the same twenty-year period. Still, natural resource-intensive activities employing predominantly unskilled labor, such as commercial agriculture and tourism, account for the majority of exported goods and services.

While trade patterns reflect the evolution of comparative advantage, the very word *comparative* implies that Mexico's changing trade position has depended to a large extent on that country's relative standing in the historic development race. Before 1940, Mexican growth lagged behind most of Latin America, partly because of her traditionally impoverished agriculture and partly because of the Revolution and subsequent reform. Since 1940, however, the roles have been reversed; Mexico has moved into the leading ranks not only in Latin America but among all developing countries. We have seen that previous social and political reforms probably stimulated a more rapid pace of development after 1940 than would have occurred otherwise. Nevertheless, whatever conditions the Revolution and subsequent reform provided to shift public policy toward import substitution, they were not sufficient to bring about a major change in the structure of trade. Other factors, such as a rapid rise in income, effective demand for domestic goods, and capacity to import, also needed to be present before import-substitution policies could be implemented successfully.

Once these essential elements existed, the process began. Import substitution has been accompanied by a drastic decline in the share of commodity exports in GDP even as the commodity import share has stayed relatively constant. The resulting trade gap has been closed by increased exports of tourism, additional net foreign borrowing, and a shift toward the holding of domestic rather than foreign liquid assets by Mexican nationals. There is a growing possibility that in the future import-competing industries will become sufficiently competitive to begin exporting manufactured goods as well. As in the United States shortly after the turn of the century and more recently in Japan, there are prospects that Mexico eventually will become a net importer of raw materials and primary products and a net exporter of manufactures, but that day is still far in the future. The share of manufactured exports remains small though it has risen from 1 percent of total commodity exports in 1926 to 3 percent in 1940, 7 percent in 1950, and 8 percent in 1960. At the same time the country has become self-sufficient in a number of formerly imported crops, and a very sizable exporter of agricultural products which had long been exported in small quantities, cotton being a principal example. Wheat was a very important net import in the mid-1940s and early 1950s, but owing to the development and use of new seed varieties developed through research supported by the Rockefeller Foundation, plus the application of fertilizer and irrigation, Mexico achieved self-sufficiency in wheat cultivation by the early 1960s. She is presently exporting a considerable share of this crop, even though both population and per capita consumption of wheat have risen very rapidly in recent years.[10]

In the case of manufacturing, the automobile industry was highly protected and inefficient as late as 1962, with prices far above international levels. There were too many firms, too many styles, and too great a variety of parts to permit economies of scale, given the size of the national market. Following a government decree in the early 1960s calling for a high degree of integration of the industry, a number of manufacturers withdrew from the market and others made plans to restrict the number of models and to produce over 50 percent of the value of their automobiles in Mexico. Automobile prices are still well above those in the United States, but some firms—including the recently established Volkswagen subsidiary in Puebla—are making plans to compete in the U.S. market, installing capacity far in excess of Mexican demands. While Volkswagens are currently selling locally at about $2,300 (U.S.), plans are being made to reduce the export price below that of German-produced models in the American Southwest.

A number of manufacturing companies have similar objectives and look forward to serving foreign markets in the near future. One example, the local Rolls-Royce affiliate, has a franchise to export diesel engines to the rest of Latin America as soon as it achieves full production and can guarantee equal quality with British engines. The local engineers and supervisors of this company claim that Mexican labor is highly qualified to do precision machining and assembly of even the most complex motors. They assert that sales volume is the only obstacle to competitive pricing of Mexican production in the world market.

Meanwhile a number of "border industries" are being established in the free zone along the U.S./Mexican frontier. (This zone does not include the major Mexican cities bordering Texas and is confined primarily to Tijuana, Mexicali, and Nogales. These plants will take advantage of cheaper Mexican labor to produce textiles, solid state electronics, handicraft items, and other labor-intensive products. Between 1966 and 1967, sixty firms were established employing over

10. As in the U.S., Mexican wheat exports partly reflect internal price supports which at the present exchange rate are about 20 percent above world price levels.

4,000 Mexicans with the promise of doubling this number by 1968. The purpose of the border industries is to permit low-priced Mexican labor to compete with that of Hongkong, Taiwan, and other free zones in the production of goods for the U.S. market. At present these industries are prohibited from selling their products inside the Mexican frontier. These industries are also designed to compensate for unemployment caused by the termination of the bracero program in the U.S.

The preceding pages have briefly described attempts by the Mexican government to restructure the pattern of trade—its prewar frustrations, the gradual success of import-substitution policies since 1940, and prospects for the future evolution of Mexican trade. One of the principal implications is that import substitution is itself import-intensive. While the share of final goods imports has declined in Mexico, that of intermediate goods has risen by the same amount, resulting in a relatively constant proportion of total imports in GDP over the past fifty years. Structural changes in the economy have reinforced shifts in foreign demand to reduce sharply the share of traditional exports in GDP. Since there has been little change in the country's average import requirements, sustained growth has necessitated a major shift in the composition of exports. Favorable conditions of foreign demand fortunately have permitted an expansion of new natural resource- and labor-intensive exports. Since there is also a high internal income elasticity of demand for items such as cash crops and local tourism, the transformation of the export sector also permits some import substitution to take place. Despite the fact that its exports are likely to remain primarily labor- and natural resource-intensive for some time, Mexico is already on the threshold of a rapid expansion of labor-intensive manufactured goods for export to the United States once its import restrictions permit.

CONTEMPORARY MEXICAN COMMERCIAL POLICY

It was reported to the United States Tariff Commission in a postwar review of Mexican trade policy that:

Economic controls and commercial policies in Mexico differ from those of other Latin American countries principally in the greater extent to which they are employed to carry out a definite national program which seeks to improve the social and economic status of the Mexican people.[11]

One of the first major programs designed to accomplish these broad social objectives was the Six-Year Plan of the Cárdenas administration, first published in 1934. Unspecific as the plan was in describing programs for the implementation of policy, its intent was clear. Among other things the plan ". . . contemplated the reduction of the country's dependence on foreign markets, the encouragement of medium or small industries instead of large units, and the development of Mexican enterprises rather than foreign-controlled enterprises." [12]

One of the conditions for success of such a program is a major restructuring of the pattern of production with important implications for the pattern of trade. For this to be accomplished the economy must possess a high degree of internal flexibility. Rapid growth permits such changes to take place at the margin without seriously disrupting existing capacity. Otherwise, attempts to reallocate resources through public policy would tend to produce unemployment of labor and capital, losses in output, reduced incentives to save and invest, and balance of payments disequilibrium. The Mexican economy has shown considerable flexibility in recent years, partly because its export-led growth in the 1940s was so spectacular and partly because its institutions have been so adaptive. Thus the opportunity cost of highly protective commercial policy was almost certainly below that of most other Latin American countries attempting to industrialize during the same period. The rapid response of Mexican entrepreneurs to new investment opportunities, combined with readily available financing, have greatly contributed to this flexibility.

At the beginning of the 1930s commercial policy was relatively liberal. The principal instrument of protection was a specific tariff, broadly applied and averaging about 16 percent ad valorem from 1935 to 1939. Mexico's exports traditionally exceeded imports, net savings flowed abroad, and balance of payments problems were infrequent, except during periods of political emergency such as from 1914 to 1916. As a result, the peso/dollar exchange rate was almost the same in 1925 as in 1910. When Mexico abandoned the gold

11. United States, Tariff Commission, *Economic Controls and Commercial Policy in Mexico,* p. 8. This report includes a detailed description of Mexican commercial policy from 1930 to 1945.
12. Ibid., p. 17.

standard in 1931 the peso showed a slight decline relative to the dollar; but the U.S. silver purchase program initiated in December 1933 (a virtual guarantee to absorb all of Mexico's silver exports) helped to stabilize the exchange rate until that agreement was terminated in 1938, following expropriation of the petroleum industry.

An outstanding characteristic of the Mexican balance of payments in those early years was its stability. This was attributable to the openness of the economy and the lack of economic controls. Export fluctuations (which moved with and slightly ahead of the U.S. trade cycle) were followed closely by fluctuations in income and the demand for importables. With the exception of the periods from 1914 to 1916 and the late 1930s, trade deficits were short-lived and the exchange rate remained relatively stable. Balance of payments stability was purchased at the price of instability in internal income and product. Since the depression, the government has attempted increasingly to insulate domestic income from the unstabilizing effects of foreign trade while pursuing full employment and growth policies at home.

Tariffs were gradually increased in the 1930s and export duties were instituted, ostensibly to subsidize experimental collective farms but primarily for revenue purposes. The major source of government revenue was import duties, although their share of the value of imports declined through the early 1940s. During this same period the share of export duties in the value of exports rose as the government made an increasing effort to siphon off excess profits derived from the 1938 devaluation and from favorable wartime prices.[13] (See Tables 6.7 and 6.8) Both import and export duties were levied primarily for revenue purposes, although after 1934 they were expected to stimulate manufacturing as well, in accordance with the Six Year Plan. While balance of payments stability is still a top priority item, it has been increasingly subordinated to public expenditures designed to alter the structure of the economy in the direction of more rapid growth and full employment of the burgeoning population. Such expenditures have in turn placed periodic strains on the balance of payments which could be only partially offset by changes in commercial policy. Therefore wide fluctuations in the balance of payments still occur, although the trade cycle is now more attributable to endogenous than exogenous causes.

Policies used to protect the economy's balance of payments have

13. Ibid.

Table 6.8
Export Duties Collected Compared with the Reported Value of Exports, 1939–61
(Million current pesos, except as otherwise indicated)

Year	Export duties collected[a]	Value of exports	Duties as percent of exports
1939	47.7	914.4	5.2
1940	43.1	960.0	4.5
1941	38.6	729.5	5.3
1942	62.7	989.7	6.3
1943	117.4	1,130.2	10.4
1944	98.3	1,047.0	9.4
1945	113.7	1,271.9	8.9
1946	110.2	1,915.3	5.8
1947	122.9	2,161.8	5.7
1948	137.2	2,661.3	5.2
1949	457.0	3,623.1	12.6
1950	470.3	4,339.4	10.8
1951	669.8	5,446.9	12.3
1952	677.7	5,125.8	13.2
1953	588.5	4,836.2	12.2
1954	958.2	6,936.1	13.8
1955	1,446.4	9,484.3	15.3
1956	1,253.1	10,089.9	12.4
1957	1,045.4	8,826.5	11.8
1958	1,023.5	8,863.8	11.5
1959	945.6	9,037.6	10.5
1960	932.0	9,233.9	10.1
1961	807.3	10,049.2	8.0
Sum: 1939–1961	12,166.6	109,673.8	11.1

[a] Total export taxes collected, disregarding subsidies.
Source: Santillán López and Rosas Figueroa, *Teoría General de las Finanzas Públicas*, p. 226.

not included frequent manipulation of the exchange rate. Since 1940, Mexico has devalued only twice, in 1948–49 and in 1954. At other times the exchange rate has been kept within a very narrow range by operations of the Central Bank. Because of the long frontier with the United States, which affords ready access to dollar deposits, it has been impractical to abandon free convertibility of the peso, a factor that rules out foreign exchange controls as an instrument of commercial policy. Threatened and actual devaluations have periodically created much uncertainty among holders of liquid assets; as a result, the capital account of the balance of payments is exceedingly vulnerable to exchange risk. For this reason the government generally has considered the cure of devaluation to be worse than the illness and has relied on other measures to reduce any excess demand for foreign exchange which might arise. In 1938, a general increase in tariffs was employed to stabilize the balance of payments. In the late 1940s, expansion of direct import controls provided some relief, although devaluation was again necessary in 1954 as the economy attempted to absorb the short-run strains of import substitution plus the shock of falling demand for exports during the post-Korean trade cycle. By the late 1950s it became possible for the government to relieve balance of payments pressures by increasing long-term borrowing abroad while simultaneously tightening domestic credit controls.

In view of the political and economic disadvantages of devaluation, the promotion of domestic industrialization has had to depend on tariffs to some extent and quotas in particular to guarantee internal demand despite relative price changes between Mexico and the United States. Rafael Izquierdo provides a description of these aspects of commercial policy since 1940,[14] stressing the partial and short-term character of tariff and quota protection. He notes that import substitution was initially a by-product of Mexican commercial policy, the main objective of which was to relieve balance of payments pressures during the postwar period.

> The simple protectionist concept of import replacement at different times has been the rival of other objectives—notably maximizing government revenue, easing government procurement, encouraging foreign direct investment, holding down internal prices. . . .[15]

In Mexico, much of the import replacement which the private sector has undertaken has been a by-product of import prohibitions . . . used to handle balance-of-payments difficulties, of tariffs levied for revenue purposes, and of devaluations. Though the government has almost always given favorable replies to requests for protection, it has done so without due consideration of the type of product or its proportion of imported inputs, and without demanding the fulfillment of progressive integration programs. What might be called the natural theory of import replacement was widely accepted. If the internal market were pro-

14. Rafael Izquierdo, "Protectionism in Mexico."
15. Ibid., p. 275.

tected, invisible forces would inevitably appear on the scene to profit from the opportunities the government had created.[16]

What the record suggests is that pro-industrialization policies carried out since World War II have not always been designed to minimize import requirements or to maximize the efficiency of resource allocation. Import controls, on the other hand, have not always served the goal of maximum industrial growth. Indeed, most would agree with Izquierdo's contention that import-substitution policy has only recently been subject to general efficiency criteria. Although industrialization and import substitution objectives have sometimes conflicted, they have normally been complementary. Nevertheless it is not easy to justify numerous quotas and tariffs, which often have an ad hoc quality about them. This may be due partly to the divided attitude of private enterprise on the subject of protection as well as to the unequal political influence of management. Representatives of larger and particularly foreign firms normally advocate a minimum of direct import controls, a position supported by the Confederación de Cámaras Industriales (CONCAMIN). The smaller manufacturers, represented by the Cámara Nacional de la Industria de Transformación (CNIT), tend to back direct controls—including quotas and import licenses—somewhat indiscriminately. This apparent inconsistency is explained by the relative position of such firms in the production process. Assembly plants turning out final products with imported components benefit from a minimum of controls on intermediate goods. The small domestic component manufacturer, on the other hand, is generally a vigorous protectionist since he feels the internal advantage derived from higher prices for his own products is greater than the loss from generally higher prices for manufactures. In certain respects, both groups ignore the social diseconomies that arise from their private advantage. Meanwhile the government walks a tightrope between them, keeping a wary eye on the public interest.

As to the choice between tariffs and quotas, economists tend to favor the former on efficiency grounds. Mexican policy-makers seem to prefer quotas, however, on the grounds that inelastic demand for intermediate goods coupled with a local willingness to pay a large premium for foreign goods make tariffs ineffective in restricting imports. It is claimed that, in order to protect domestic producers adequately, tariffs alone have to be so high that they would in effect be-

16. Ibid., p. 287.

come quotas. Mexican tariff protection traditionally has been low among Latin American countries. As of 1954, the average receipt of duties on raw materials was 5 percent ad valorem, 10 to 15 percent on capital goods, and 50 percent on consumer goods, with luxury goods paying approximately 100 percent.[17] A comparison of the average tariff level of the 1930s (16 percent)[18] with the present share of duties in the value of imports (Table 6.7),[19] fails to show any notable increase in the average incidence of tariff protection during the past two decades, at least on those goods for which tariffs are not prohibitive. On the other hand, the effective protection against all potential importables has increased far more, as a forthcoming study by Gerardo Bueno will suggest.[20]

Quotas are now applied to about 80 percent of Mexican imports, including almost all manufactured goods but few primary products. Import licenses are granted whenever an article of comparable quality cannot be obtained locally in a fairly short period of time at a "reasonable" price.[21] With few exceptions, eligible applications for import licenses are processed within a period of four to five weeks. Those wishing to import a particular item normally obtain advance information as to its legitimacy from the Ministry of Industry and Commerce, which is in charge of import licensing. (The Ministry of Finance is responsible for tariff policy.) An actual license application is not submitted until the goods have arrived in customs. Because there is generally a lag of several weeks in processing an application, plus an additional wait of at least a week before the imported item may be received from customs, the present system of direct controls adds annual inventory charges equal to the interest on approximately 8 to 10 percent of the annual value of imports. This amounted to over 10 million dollars in 1960.[22]

17. Ibid., p. 254.
18. United States Tariff Commission, *Economic Controls and Commercial Policy in Mexico,* p. 10.
19. This table of course does not include the incidence of restrictive tariffs and therefore understates the degree of protection. The weighting procedure used for the U.S. Tariff Commission estimates is not specified.
20. See n. 24, p. 223.
21. According to government officials, the definition of "reasonable" is becoming more restrictive. Whereas simple availability was the primary consideration a decade ago, today licenses are beginning to be granted for those goods the domestic price of which is more than 100 percent above that of comparable imports before taxes.
22. Representatives of the Ministry of Industry and Commerce have already undertaken a major program designed to computerize license applications.

The great flexibility of the licensing system makes it a potential two-edged sword in the hands of those administrators skilled enough to wield it efficiently. Firms that comply with the broad criteria for domestic industrialization are assured that licenses will not be issued for similar imports.[23] More mature firms that have already gone through a several-year probation period and still do not produce at reasonable prices or provide adequate service to the customer may be threatened by government retaliation in the form of newly granted licenses for competing imports. This threat, together with internal competition among producers, is designed to reduce the danger of monopoly profits and restraints on trade that have otherwise resulted from the quota system. It is not clear whether the possibility of granting import licenses to break local monopolies is a more effective instrument of antitrust policy than the threat of tariff reduction.

The difficulty with direct import controls such as the Mexican licensing system is their arbitrary nature, as well as the high cost of administration. Each item a firm wishes to import requires an application that must be approved by the Ministry of Industry and Commerce. This places a costly drain on management time in addition to the inventory costs mentioned above. Moreover, there is no guarantee that import permits will be awarded in accordance with efficiency criteria (other than those of availability, quality, and occasionally price). Under the present discretionary system of controls, political influence may be more easily applied than under a system of tariffs and/or exchange devaluation. Furthermore, the issuance of licenses permits importers to earn excess profits that are only partly offset by duties and direct taxation, again tending to misallocate resources. One must resort to a statistical investigation of the effectiveness of Mexican industrialization and its welfare implications before drawing

---

Nevertheless, value-laden decisions as to which items may or may not be admitted are not readily relegated to machines. It is likely that the waiting time will not be reduced by much more than two weeks. The advance issuance of blanket licenses to import is resisted at present because of the government's desire to maintain tight short-run controls for balance of payments reasons. In lieu of foreign exchange control this policy makes some sense. Much of the criticism of the licensing procedure is directed not at the final decisions, which are generally favorable, but at the waiting time and manpower costs that the application process entails. Many companies retain one or more officers who must spend a large percentage of their time applying for licenses and clearing imports through customs.

23. The term "similar" is subject to wide interpretation and offers less security to the local producer than most firms interviewed would prefer.

any final conclusions on the choice of policy instruments adopted to this end.

THE EFFECTS OF COMMERCIAL POLICY ON THE STRUCTURE OF PRODUCTION AND TRADE SINCE 1950

To determine the amount of protection that domestic producers receive from commercial policy, or to estimate response to this protection, is a virtually impossible task. As mentioned above, Mexican commercial policy since 1950 has included exchange devaluation, import and export duties, and direct controls that now provide the major form of protection. In addition to trade policy, relative prices have been affected by numerous other government activities, making it difficult to separate out cause and effect in the resource allocation process. Those who have attempted to determine the impact of commercial policy on import substitution in other countries have tried to measure the degree of "effective protection" that local producers receive in terms of the net tariff component of value added after removing the offsetting effect of duties on intermediate imports.[24] While this procedure is well suited to those countries that rely primarily on tariff protection, in cases like Mexico's such calculations are partial at best since the predominance of quotas often distorts prices by more than the tariff component. Effective protection in this case would be more closely approximated by comparing domestic prices with unit values of traded goods in the world market. Even this calculation involves the implicit assumption that all differences between domestic prices and the prices of traded goods are attributable to commercial policy per se—a weak argument in the Mexican case where differential subsidies and tax allowances are widely applied for the promotion of industrialization.

In Chapter 5 an examination was made of the way in which the postwar growth of Mexican manufacturing industry differed from what might have been expected of a hypothetical internationally "average" developing country of similar size and income. There was no explicit treatment of the import requirements for import substitution at that point. One study that expressly examines this problem

24. For an application of this type of analysis to developed countries, see Bela Balassa, "Tariff Protection in Industrial Countries." This author is currently directing a similar study of selected developing countries. The portion dealing with Mexico, by Gerardo Bueno of the Nacional Financiera, was in progress at the time of this writing.

was prepared by the Nacional Financiera under the direction of Professor Alan Manne.[25] This report examined the possibilities of substitution between imports and domestic manufactures for twelve major sectors of the Mexican economy. It then provided a detailed treatment of the possibilities of substitution in twelve specific machinery industries, allowing for scale requirements and comparative costs based on U.S. standards. Results of the detailed analysis indicate that nine of the twelve machinery industries selected could be efficiently established in Mexico. (The exceptions are turbines and generators, ships, and locomotives.) The preliminary figures show that by 1972 several industries would have markets far in excess of optimal U.S. firm size, including mining and construction machinery, metal cutting and many metal-forming machine tools, other cutting tools, jigs and fixtures, machinery for special industries, and power transmission equipment. However, the degree of disaggregation in the report is insufficient to reflect actual scale conditions in particular product lines since value rather than volume units were used in the estimates; accordingly, the report, while presenting highly suggestive initial results, calls for further research on the subject.

Aside from the analysis of the individual machinery industries, one of the more interesting findings of the more general portion of the Nacional Financiera study was that most potential substitution could be restricted to a small number of commodity imports (particularly iron ore, semikraft paper, sodium carbonate, kerosene, diesel oil, and jet fuel). Sharply increasing the degree of protection on both intermediate and final goods would not have much effect on the amount of intermediate import substitution, although it would raise costs and particularly capital requirements. At a 6 percent projected rate of growth of GNP and allowing for 20 percent protection, import requirements for twelve key sectors of the economy would decline by 7 percent. With an infinite degree of protection (which assumes local production of all possible importables regardless of price) foreign exchange requirements would fall by only 25 percent, the trade-off being between imported inputs and the efficiency of domestic production as measured by total costs plus capital requirements. With 20 percent protection, costs for the twelve sectors as a whole would rise by 4 percent and capital requirements by 5 percent; with infinite protection, costs would rise by 6 percent and capital requirements by 19 percent.

25. Alan S. Manne, "Key Sectors of the Mexican Economy, 1962–72."

An important finding of the study was that almost 70 percent of the intermediate imports in the twelve key sectors of the economy were complementary to import substitution. That is, as import substitution increased, these intermediate imports would increase as well. In an extreme case under conditions of complete protection, imports of intermediate goods in the petroleum, petrochemical, and heavy chemical sectors would increase from 86 to 96 million dollars. In fact, a general rise in imports complementary to domestic machinery production of from 259 to 278 million dollars would occur were that sector provided with complete protection. This is a clear example of the narrow space within which Mexican policy-makers must operate in order to replace imports, now that the simplest industries have been integrated. Those sectors showing the greatest possibility for import substitution were paper and petroleum. In the case of petroleum, the aggregate output of that sector is already well in advance of international standards (Table 5.10) but there is still considerable scope for expansion of the industries mentioned above.

THE EFFECT OF INDUSTRIALIZATION
ON THE DEMAND FOR IMPORTS

In Chapter 5 it was shown that in both 1950 and 1960 output in most Mexican manufacturing activities exceeded expectations. These findings said nothing about the efficiency of import substitution policy. It is theoretically possible for the government to promote hothouse industries which, even though they replace final goods imports, are prodigal in their use of intermediate imports, leaving the country worse off than before. In order to evaluate the government's industrialization program during the 1950s, it is necessary to examine the effect of the resulting growth path on the country's overall import requirements. While it has not been possible to do this in detail for the fifteen subsectors of manufacturing in Table 5.10, calculations have been made for the economy as a whole (Tables 6.9 and 6.10). Initial results indicate that Mexican import substitution policy has been remarkably effective. Not only final goods but also intermediate goods imports have fallen sharply as a share of total value of production. This has permitted the rate of growth of gross domestic product to outstrip the much slower growth of exports without creating major balance of payments problems or requiring a devaluation after the early 1950s. Total imports fell from 13.5 percent to under 10 percent

Table 6.9
Structure of Mexican Production and Intermediate Imports, 1950

	Value of Production		Value of intermediate imports	
	Million pesos	*Percent of total*	*Million pesos*	*Percent of production*
Industry group	*1*	*2*	*3*	*4*
1. Agriculture, cattle, forestry & fisheries	11,357	19.5	113	1.0
2. Mining & quarrying	1,682	2.9	87	5.2
3. Petroleum extraction & refining	1,680	2.9	191	11.4
4. Food products, beverages, & tobacco	7,131	12.2	424	5.9
5. Textile, clothing, & leather goods	5,083	8.7	209	4.1
6. Wood products & furniture, paper, printing, & publishing	1,750	3.0	130	7.4
7. Chemicals, rubber & plastics	1,962	3.4	375	19.1
8. Nonmetallic minerals mfg.	648	1.1	30	4.6
9. Basic metals industries	1,265	2.2	78	6.2
10. Metal products mfg. & repair	1,548	2.7	288	18.6
11. Construction	3,000	5.2	419	14.0
12. Electricity	599	1.0	40	6.7
13. Commerce	10,698	18.4	112	1.0
14. Transportation	2,941	5.1	139	4.7
15. Services	6,885	11.8	228	3.3
Total	58,229	100.0	2,863	4.9

Source: Reynolds, "Changing Trade Patterns and Trade Policy in Mexico" (mimeographed). The statistics were prepared with the assistance of Ibrahim Samater, using data from the 1950 and 1960 input-output tables of the Banco de México.

of gross domestic product between 1950 and 1960, according to Mexican input-output tables for the respective years.[26] While these estimates probably exaggerate the decline, independent figures show merchandise imports alone to have fallen, as a share of GDP, from 10.7 percent to 9.5 percent between 1950 and 1960 (Table 6.2).

26. Import figures in the input-output tables for 1950 and 1960 are somewhat ambiguous. The Bank of Mexico value of merchandise imports, including *fronteriza* imports (those entering the fifteen-mile frontier zone which are unclassified), is approximately equal to the total import figure in the 1950 input-output table but is considerably in excess of the 1960 input-output value of total imports. If frontier imports are excluded from the Banco de México figures, the result approximates that of the 1960 input-output table. The 1960 input-output table therefore appears to understate total import requirements by approximately 18 percent. While important, this qualification does not seriously alter our conclusions about import substitution among intermediate goods, since most *fronteriza* imports are final goods.

Table 6.10
Structure of Mexican Production and Imports, 1960

| | Value of Production (million pesos) | (percents) | Value of Direct Intermediate Imports (million pesos) | Direct Intermediate Imports as Percent of Total Value of Production by Sector | Direct & Indirect Intermediate Imports (percents) | Direct Intermediate Imports with 1950 Coefficient and 1960 Structure (million pesos) | Direct Intermediate Imports with 1960 Coefficient and 1950 Structure (million pesos) |
	1	*2*	*3*	*4*	*5*	*6*	*7*
1. Agriculture, livestock, forestry & fisheries	32,166	14.0	548	1.7	2.6	322	760
2. Mining & quarrying	4,311	1.9	61	1.4	3.6	224	93
3. Petroleum extraction & refining	9,586	4.2	700	7.3	14.0	1,093	485
4. Food products, beverages, & tobacco	29,455	12.8	567	1.9	4.0	1,738	531
5. Textile, clothing & leather goods	12,957	5.7	599	4.6	9.1	531	917
6. Wood products & furniture, paper, printing, & publishing	5,603	2.4	440	7.8	10.0	415	536
7. Chemicals, rubber & plastics	8,781	3.8	1,664	18.9	–	1,677	1,473
8. Nonmetallic minerals mfg.	2,528	1.1	156	6.2	11.9	116	156
9. Basic metals industries	4,690	2.0	366	7.8	11.3	291	393
10. Metal products mfg. & repair	10,502	4.6	1,934	18.4	21.1	1,953	1,139
11. Construction	13,938	6.1	921	6.6	8.7	1,951	786
12. Electricity	2,205	1.0	107	4.9	7.4	148	112
13. Commerce	53,539	23.3	119	0.2	1.2	535	84
14. Transportation	8,040	3.5	482	6.0	8.4	378	701
15. Services	30,994	13.5	429	1.4	2.9	1,023	378
Total	229,295	100.0	9,093			12,395	8,544
Share of intermediate imports in total value of production			(3.97%)			(5.41%)	(3.73%)

Source: Reynolds, "Changing Trade Patterns."

The changing share of *intermediate* imports in total value of production (value added plus interindustry demand) is presented in Tables 6.9 and 6.10. The total value of production in Mexico (not value added) is disaggregated into fifteen sectors that use data from the input-output tables for the corresponding years. The changing composition of output and import demand reflects the reaction of the economy to changes in conditions of supply and demand, many of which are directly attributable to import substitution policy. Although one cannot isolate the direct effects of commercial policy on changes in the structure of trade and production, the net effect on demand for intermediate imports has been quite favorable. The share of intermediate imports in total value of production fell from 4.9 percent to 4.0 percent between 1950 and 1960, a reduction of almost 20 percent. If these years may be said to indicate a trend, this reflects a decline in two factors—the share of intermediate imports in intermediate production and the share of final imports in final demand. The former fell from 13.2 percent to 10.7 percent over the decade, while the latter (adjusting the 1960 import figure upward for evident omissions in the 1960 input-output table) fell from 6.5 percent to 5.5 percent of gross value added in the economy.[27]

Nine of the fifteen subdivisions of Mexican GDP showed a decline in the proportion of intermediate imports to total value of production over the decade. The most important were food products, commerce, and services, which together accounted for over 42 percent of the value of production in 1950 and almost 50 percent in 1960. The decline in intermediate import requirements of food processing industries is a dramatic illustration of the possibilities that countries like Mexico have for the forward integration of raw material and primary

27. In a similar study by Richard T. King, "Rationale and Limitations of the Mexican Import Substitution Policies," the proportion of intermediate imports to intermediate production of goods and services was calculated for 21 sectors of production. In this study, the share fell from 13.2 percent to 10.4 percent, which is almost identical to the figures presented above. King's justification for using only *intermediate* production as a base was that intermediate imports were more closely related to the former than to value added. In the present study it was felt that an advantage would be gained by observing the shift in demand for intermediate imports as a function of total demand in the economy including final demand for goods and services, since the welfare implications of public policy are reflected in value added. Regardless of the comparison used, the relationship between final demand and intermediate demand has not changed sharply during the decade, making the conclusions quite consistent.

product-producing sectors in which they clearly possess a comparative advantage. Import requirements as a percentage of production also declined sharply for mining, petroleum extraction and refining, and construction, further illustrating the principle that comparative advantage first appears in the processing industries.

On the other hand, manufacturing as a whole did not show a net reduction in intermediate import requirements. On the contrary, four of the seven manufacturing sectors (4 to 10 inclusive) increased their average import requirements. Textiles, wood and paper products, chemicals and plastics, and basic metals industries increased their share of imports in total value of production from 9.1 percent to 11.4 percent over the decade. Activities engaged in the repair and manufacturing of machinery and equipment showed no perceptible change in their relatively high proportion of imports (18.6 and 18.4 percent in the two years). However, independent estimates of machinery and equipment manufacturing and imports do indicate a sharp rise in the proportion of machinery and equipment produced in Mexico.[28] The intermediate import requirements of manufacturing as a whole were 7.9 percent in 1950 and 7.7 percent in 1960. This suggests that the policies mentioned earlier, which provided for relatively rapid growth of manufacturing, probably tended to offset the general decline in intermediate imports as a share of GDP. Among the six sectors that showed an increase in intermediate import requirements, the most important were agriculture, textiles, and transportation. Table 6.10 reveals that imported agricultural inputs in 1960 were over 200 million pesos greater than they would have been had 1950 relationships obtained.

What would the demand for intermediate imports have been in 1960 had import coefficients remained the same as in 1950? If the economy had produced the actual volume of 1960 production with sectoral import requirements at 1950 levels, intermediate imports in 1960 would have risen by 36 percent, or from 9 to over 12 billion pesos. Since this would have implied less import substitution, final goods imports would almost certainly have exceeded 1960 levels as

28. Estimates of the Bank of Mexico indicate a fall and subsequent rise in the internal production of machinery and equipment as a share of total demand for capital goods, from 46 percent in 1940 to 43 percent in 1950 and 53 percent in 1960. (Banco de México, Departamento de Estudios Económicos, "Alternativas de estimación de la inversión bruta fija en México, 1939–1962," Table 14.)

well. It is, of course, incorrect to assume that the structure of production would have remained the same either in absolute or relative terms had the actual import substitution in intermediate goods not occurred. In fact both market and policy-induced changes in the conditions of supply and demand combined to shift the structure of production toward *more* import-using sectors.

Even though all of the seven manufacturing sectors in Tables 6.9 and 6.10 that increased their share of the total value of production had declining intermediate import coefficients, this was not sufficient to offset their higher average demand for imports. This is illustrated by comparing columns 3 and 7 in Table 6.10. Had the 1950 structure of demand obtained in 1960, imports would have been 550 million pesos below actual levels. This provides an important lesson for import-substituting countries, since the substitution gains within individual sectors may be offset by the fact that the average share of imports in these sectors is itself relatively high. As demand shifts in the direction of import-competing industries, average intermediate import requirements may actually *increase* even though each individual sector is reducing its requirements. The question is whether imports increase more per unit of final demand before or after so-called import substitution takes place. This depends upon the import component of value added, but since data is not yet available on final goods imports by similar input-output categories, such calculations cannot yet be made for Mexico. Whatever the result, the situation may be favorable for long-term development, to the extent that structural changes in the economy are consistent with comparative advantage and promote exports as well.

During the 1950s the majority of finished goods imports were replaced by domestic products; locally produced intermediate goods have been gradually substituted for importables; and exports such as cotton and wheat have grown. The effect has been to spur the rate of industrial growth and to reduce overall import requirements as a share of GDP by 37 percent. Yet shifts in domestic demand proved to be heavily import biased. Some of these shifts may have been attributable to the pattern of growth itself that favored industry over other activities and led to increased inequality in income distribution. The principal export sectors—agriculture, mining, and services—all had relatively low intermediate import requirements. The relationship between Mexican import substitution and the demand for other scarce factors, including skilled labor and capital goods, is examined below.

THE EFFECT OF COMMERCIAL POLICY
ON THE DEMAND FOR SCARCE RESOURCES

The three principal arms of Mexican commercial policy, import and export duties, licensing, and devaluation of the exchange rate (or the lack of it), have had varying and occasionally offsetting effects on the pattern of resource allocation. This is best illustrated by dividing Mexico's recent experience into three periods, 1941-48, 1948-54, and 1954-present. By separating total domestic production into export activities, import-competing industries, and industries producing nontraded (home) goods, the effect during the three periods of commercial policy on the allocation of resources among these sectors may be examined.[29]

From 1941 to 1947 the Mexican exchange rate was maintained at 4.85 pesos per dollar. The share of export duties in the value of exports rose during the war years and then fell again in the immediate postwar period (Table 6.8), while import duties as a share of imports declined over time (Table 6.7). Although import licensing received government approval in the early 1940s, it was not widely applied until 1947; before then, duties on exports and imports had provided the major form of protection. Since the incidence of both import and export duties was falling during this period (with the exception of the early 1940s), commercial policy tended to slow down the rate of expansion of import-competing vis-à-vis export activities.[30] Relative price changes had a similar effect, since export prices rose far more rapidly than those of importables and even more rapidly than domestic prices in general once the effect of the devaluation of 1948 is in-

29. While recognizing the identification problem involved in attempting to assess the effect on supply incentives of relative price changes (which themselves may affect changing conditions of supply rather than demand), this section suggests *probable* supply effects induced by the three types of commercial policy: duties, quotas, and exchange devaluation. "Home goods" became a more inclusive category as the implementation of direct import controls placed embargos on an increasing number of commodities.

30. It is assumed here that relative price increases resulting from commercial policy as well as conditions of excess demand are positively correlated with relative rates of return among the three branches of Mexican industry. Clearly, the pressure on relative prices from various aspects of commercial policy does not necessarily reflect the *net* change in relative prices that actually occurred in the economy. We are just discussing in this section those elements among the many pressures on relative prices that may be attributable to known applications of commercial policy.

cluded (Table 6.12). This suggests that in regard to actual changes in commercial policy from 1941 through 1947, the government did little to improve the climate for investment in import-competing activities, aside from making loud encouraging noises.

After 1948, however, conditions arose that required a much more positive program of foreign exchange conservation. The years from 1948 to 1954 represented the greatest sustained pressure on the Mexican balance of payments in history. Every device in the policy-maker's bag of tools was called into play to reduce imports and increase exports. High and increasing levels of economic activity during the 1940s and early 1950s, spurred by booming wartime export markets and sustained by government deficit financing, had produced a backlog of import demand that rapidly drained foreign exchange reserves after the war. As a result the long-awaited import-licensing system was finally implemented for a broad range of commodities. Also, ad valorem duties were added to specific tariffs for most articles. As Tables 6.7 and 6.8 reveal, the incidence of both export and import duties rose sharply following the 40 percent devaluation of 1948. Devaluation favored both import-competing and export activities,

Table 6.11
Relative Price Changes Between Mexico and the U.S.
and Exchange Devaluation, Specified Periods, 1941–63
(percent)

	1941[a]/48	*1948/54[b]*	*1954/63*
1. Change in the Mexican price level	+149	+63	+60
2. Change in the U.S. price level	+69	+13	+20
3. Change in the peso-dollar exchange rate	+40	+46	0
4. Rise in relative prices: Mexico ÷ U.S. adjusted for exchange devaluation	+5	−1	+33

[a] 1941 is used as a base since the somewhat higher Mexican exchange rate in 1940 reflected unsettled conditions of the late 1930s and could not be regarded as an equilibrium rate. The peso/dollar rate between 1940 and 1941 fell by 12 percent. This column includes only the 40 percent devaluation in 1948.

[b] This period includes the devaluations of 21 percent in 1949 and of 31 percent in 1954, which placed the dollar value of the peso 46 percent below that of 1948.

Sources: Row 1: GDP deflator, Banco de México.

Row 2: GNP deflator, U.S. Department of Commerce, Office of Business Economics.

Row 3: Nacional Financiera, *50 Años de Revolución Mexicana en Cifras*, 1963, p. 115. Exchange devaluations were only in 1948/49 and 1954.

Row 4: $\dfrac{[(\text{row } 1 + 100) \div (\text{row } 2 + 100)] \times 100}{\text{row } 3 + 100} - 100 = \text{row } 4$

Table 6.12

Relative Changes in the Prices of Mexican Home Goods Versus Exportables and Importables, and Changes in the Terms of Trade, Specified Periods, 1941–63

(percent)

	1941/48	*1948/54*	*1954/63*
1. Change in relative prices of Mexican home goods ÷ internal price of exports	−16	−13	+36
2. Change in relative price of home goods ÷ internal price of imports	+27	−25	+16
3. Change in Mexican terms of trade	+52	−14	−15

Sources: Row 1: Mexican GDP deflator (Table 6.11, row 1 ÷ index of implicit prices of exports [peso value of imports ÷ volume index]) from Grupo Secretaría de Hacienda—Banco de México, Estudios sobre Proyecciones, "Manual," Table 1-8.

Row 2: Mexican GDP deflator ÷ index of implicit prices of imports, Ibid.

Row 3: Index of implicit unit value of exports in pesos ÷ implicit unit value of imports in pesos, or $\left(\dfrac{\text{row } 2 + 100}{\text{row } 1 + 100}\right) - 100 = \text{row } 3$.

though the terms of trade between 1948 and 1954 failed to reinforce this favorable effect on exports despite a brief upswing during the Korean War. Meanwhile, increased tariffs and quotas greatly enhanced the profitability of import-competing and home goods production. Though all policies had the effect of placing additional pressure on the price level, a comparison of Tables 6.11 and 6.12 reveals that, while domestic prices rose 63 percent, 50 percent faster than those abroad (U.S.), the devaluations of 1948-49 were effective in causing home goods prices to decline by 25 percent relative to imports, and 13 percent relative to exports (Table 6.12, rows 1 and 2).

The abrupt increase in tariffs and direct controls after 1947, in addition to devaluation, was insufficient to prevent serious balance of payments disequilibria after Korean War markets collapsed in 1953. Once again internal prices rose, but more moderately this time, with the rate of increase decelerating through 1963 (excepting 1960). Although one would have expected the 1954 devaluation to shift again the price of exports and import-competing goods above those of home goods production, Table 6.8 shows just the opposite. Meanwhile the balance of payments on current account became slightly favorable in 1955, while on capital account the net inflow in dollars for the years 1955-57 was two and one-half times that of the previous three years, causing a net increase in reserves from 1955-57 of 247 million dollars (Appendix Table D.3A). Recently, however, the relative advantage gained from devaluation has tended to disappear. Prices in Mexico increased 33 percent over those in the United States between 1954 and 1963 (Table 6.11). The real question is whether the 1954 devaluation undervalued the peso sufficiently to offset subsequent price rises. The history of the 1954 devaluation is shrouded in debate. The government of Ruíz Cortines (1952-58) consistently defended both the timing and magnitude of devaluation. Economists in the Mexico City office of ECLA attacked the policy in a major analysis of the structure of Mexican trade.[31]

In dealing with the natural tendency of Mexican development to produce external disequilibrium, this ECLA study considers devaluation among other policies that may be applied to correct these disequilibria. The conclusions stressed that:

> the increasing dependency on imports of intermediate goods which is typical of the initial phases of industrialization also characterized the case of Mexico, or so it may be inferred from the disproportionate expansion of imports of raw materials and semiprocessed imports in relation to aggregate consumption.
>
> . . . external disequilibria were aggravated when development was accompanied by a concentration of income, owing to the fact that import demand for consumer goods originated primarily in the medium- and high-income brackets. This was associated with a high income-elasticity of demand for durable consumer goods.

and

> . . . demand for capital goods also grew disproportionately once the periods of contraction or stagnation were superceded by modern development. This characteristic feature of the economic development process is also illustrated by the change in import-elasticity.[32]

While acknowledging that the 1954 devaluation might have stimulated certain export items (such as cotton) and fostered import substitution of easily produced manufactures, the study attempted to discourage similar policies in the future by saying:

31. United Nations, ECLA, *External Disequilibrium in the Economic Development of Latin America,* vols. 1 and 2.
32. Ibid., pp. 76, 77.

On the whole, however, export prospects were very restricted, and it is problematical whether even commodities whose export trends show a sharp upward trend will be able to imitate the exceptionally rapid development of cotton which finally reached an inflexion point when the foreign cotton policy of the United States underwent a change in 1956.

For these reasons, there appears to be little likelihood that future devaluations will serve to attenuate the disequilibria produced by a contraction of demand and intensified income concentration. In contrast to the effect of adjusting the exchange rate, a re-direction of productive resources according to the development trends in demand and capacity to import would enable structural changes in supply to take place more gradually, and thus reduce the possibility of a disequilibrium in the balance of payments. In other words, if investment were so planned that the requisite rate of import substitution was obtained, this would largely help to eliminate or reduce the trend towards external disequilibrium, without imperilling the free exchange regime prevailing in Mexico.[33]

This study was criticized at the time for implicitly suggesting that the peso had been undervalued. Yet it contains much worthwhile and surprisingly up-to-date analysis, including what proved to be a fairly accurate forecast of the 1965 balance of payments. One of its principal assertions was that U.S. travel in Mexico was price-inelastic. If true, then the undervaluation argument followed, since exchange policy could be shown to have lowered potential tourism revenues after 1954. (Relative Mexican price increases since 1954 would have tended to increase these revenues by the same logic.) There is some question as to the price elasticity of demand for tourism in Mexico. It is quite possible that American tourists, shopping for bargain travel, favored Mexico far more than would have been the case had post-1954 prices continued to rise without devaluation. This is a subject that deserves considerably more attention from future research.

The allegation of undervaluation of the Mexican exchange rate after the 1954 devaluation may receive some support from a recent ECLA study of purchasing power parity in Latin America, which shows that the legal rate was 36 percent below the parity rate for

33. Ibid., p. 77.

Mexico in 1960.[34] Since this measure includes a large share of non-traded goods, it is not designed to reflect an "equilibrium" exchange rate. Still, it does help to explain why Mexico has weathered 13 years of relative price increases without another devaluation (Tables 6.11 and 6.12). Undervaluation, if it did occur, might prove to have been an important precondition for the successful application of monetary policy in Mexico, by minimizing exchange risk for a number of years.

Since 1954 almost the entire burden of commercial policy for import substitution appears to have fallen on the licensing system. There has been no subsequent devaluation; the incidence of export duties has remained relatively constant; and the share of import duties in imports has risen only slightly (Tables 6.7 and 6.8). The allocative effects of these policies have tended to favor import-competing and home goods production at the expense of traditional exports.

Traditional economic theory argues that, under certain conditions (the most relevant being free competition, no increasing returns to scale, and an initially acceptable income distribution), the unfettered flow of trade will maximize welfare. Obviously, any assessment of Mexican commercial policy in general and industrialization in particular must come to grips with the basic issue: were the "gains from trade" that were lost in the short run through the distortions of commercial policy regained in the long run through a higher rate of growth of income and product? One must also determine how the distributional effects of commercial policy (including government disposition of tariff revenues) affected total welfare. Only a few aspects of this question are touched upon here. The following paragraphs examine the impact of import substitution in the 1950s on the demand for capital goods, capital goods imports, skilled labor, and direct plus indirect intermediate imports.

We have seen that nine out of fifteen major sectors of the Mexican economy reduced their average intermediate import requirements between 1950 and 1960 (Tables 6.9 and 6.10). Six of the nine also proved to be relatively light users of capital as of 1960 (Table 6.13). These results and their components show that import substitution

34. United Nations, ECLA, *A Measurement of Price Levels and the Purchasing Power of Currencies in Latin America, 1960–1962*, as quoted in United Nations, ECLA, *Process of Industrialization in Latin America*, Table 1–6. This study indicates that in terms of relative purchasing powers, the peso in 1960 would have been valued at eight to the dollar rather than twelve and one-half according to the official exchange rate.

Table 6.13

Output Capital Ratios by Sector, 1960

(million current pesos except as otherwise indicated)

	Gross value of production (1)	Stock of fixed reproducible assets (2)	(1) ÷ (2) = (3) (3)
1. Agriculture, livestock, forestry & fisheries	32,166	53,258	.604
2. Mining & quarrying	4,311	5,524	.781
3. Petroleum extraction & refining	9,586	16,127	.594
4. Food products, beverages, & tobacco	29,455	21,180	1.391
5. Textile, clothing & leather goods	12,957	8,318	1.558
6. Wood products & furniture, paper, printing, & publishing	5,603	6,046	.927
7. Chemicals, rubber & plastics	8,781	8,836	.994
8. Nonmetallic minerals mfg.	2,528	4,187	.604
9. Basic metals industries	4,690	8,485	.553
10. Metal products mfg. & repair	10,502	11,472	.915
11. Construction	13,938	6,372	2.187
12. Electricity	2,205	14,747	.150
13. Commerce	53,539	52,194	1.026
14. Transportation	8,040	42,520	.189
15. Services	30,994	29,506	1.050
	229,295	288,772	.794

Source: Column 1 from 1960 input-output table, Banco de México.
Column 2 from Solís M., "A Projection of the Development of the Mexican Economy in the Coming Decade" (mimeographed paper), Table 3, p. 16.

first took place in activities that were not capital-intensive either in terms of domestic or imported capital requirements. A Bank of Mexico ranking of sectoral coefficients for imported capital requirements in 1960 shows that only three of the nine import-substituting sectors have above average imported capital/output ratios (machinery and metal products, electricity, and chemical and rubber products).

Just the opposite is true of the relationship between human capital requirements and import substitution. Five of the nine import-substituting sectors in Tables 6.9 and 6.10—representing 56 percent of the value of production in 1960—have above average labor skill requirements. (The exceptions were food processing, commerce, construction, and mining.) [35] These findings are consistent with Hirschman's hypothesis that human capital is initially the scarcest factor, to the extent that those industries which developed since 1950 were at a comparative disadvantage with those which import substituted before that year. These results argue for the importance of formal education and on-the-job training if programs of industrialization are to succeed in the long run.[36]

Finally, the effect on overall demand for intermediate imports that would arise from a change in the value of production of each of the 15 sectors was estimated using the 1960 input-output table. As of 1960, six of the nine import-substituting sectors had below average direct plus indirect intermediate import coefficients. On the other hand, the three sectors that were import-intensive (metal products manufacturing, chemicals, rubber and plastics, and petroleum extraction and refining) had above average direct plus indirect import requirements. In the Mexican case, direct intermediate import requirements provide a good proxy for indirect requirements, since the rank correlation of direct plus indirect import requirements with the former is $+ .92$.

TRADE BETWEEN THE UNITED STATES AND MEXICO

The role of foreign investment in Mexican manufacturing was touched upon in Chapter 5. An adequate treatment of the positive and negative economic effects arising from Mexico's relationship to the United States would require a volume in itself. For such a study the interplay of political, social, and economic factors in the trade of the two countries should be dealt with as a set of interdependent relationships. Howard F. Cline, in an epic treatment of this problem, *The United States and Mexico*,[37] has stressed the ascendancy of economic over political ties in recent years:

> In the Era of Good Feeling which has marked relationships
> between the United States and Mexico since 1940, economic

35. The rank ordering of skill requirements used in this study was prepared with the advice of Donald Keesing, using data from Morris A. Horowitz, et al., *Manpower Requirements for Planning*. The indicators used refer to the number of professional and technical personnel per thousand employed workers, using an unweighted average for eight countries (United States, Canada, West Germany, England and Wales, France, Sweden, Netherlands, and Belgium).

36. Donald B. Keesing, "Labor Skills and Comparative Advantage."

37. Harvard University Press, 1953; rev. ed., Atheneum, 1963.

rather than political matters have been in the forefront. The flow of capital, goods, ideas, and men from the northern republic to the southern has been an important element in the economic and industrial revolution taking place in Mexico. However, that interchange has raised some new problems between the two countries. None of these is serious. As President Alemán reported to his Congress on September 1, 1951, "Our relations with the United States have developed on a plane of mutual understanding." [38]

What was true in the early 1950s still holds today. Market ties have proved so mutually advantageous that they have helped to overcome most of the political difficulties that grew out of the Revolution and the preceding history of border clashes, war, and annexation. The difficulties that have arisen from foreign trade and investment are modest, and Mexico has developed a high degree of autonomy in dealing with her neighbor. This section outlines a few of the more crucial economic relationships as they are reflected in the level and rate of change of Mexican–U.S. trade.

The United States became Mexico's major trading partner shortly after Independence. Trade between the two countries has flourished ever since. The share of Mexican merchandise exports destined for the United States rose to 90 percent during World War II, averaging around 75 percent for the rest of the period from 1937 to 1960 (Table 6.14). The U.S. share in Mexican imports has generally been higher, averaging over 80 percent until 1955, after which it declined slightly (Table 6.15). If trade in invisibles were added, the U.S. share of Mexican trade would rise still higher. In view of these figures and given the relative size of the U.S. economy, it is not surprising that until recently Mexican GDP has tended to parallel the American business cycle. (See Chart 6.1). A comparison of annual changes in GNP of the two countries between 1900 and 1965 shows an extremely close relationship. In thirty-nine of the fifty-four years for which comparisons can be made, the direction of change for both countries was of the same sign, and in only fifteen was there a negative relationship. When U.S. GNP is lagged one year, there are thirty-two years with the same sign and twenty-one with the opposite change in the level of output. However when Mexican GNP is lagged,

38. Ibid., p. 387. In a later book, *Mexico: Revolution to Evolution, 1940–1960,* Cline reasserts this position (pp. 304–08).

Table 6.14
The Share of the U.S. in Mexican Commodity Exports
(million pesos)

Year	*1* *Total Exports*	*2* *Exports to the U.S.*	*3* *(2)* ÷ *(1)* × *100*
1937	892	502	56.2
1938	838	565	67.4
1939	914	679	74.2
1940	960	859	89.4
1941	730	665	91.2
1942	990	905	91.4
1943	1,130	992	87.8
1944	1,047	890	85.0
1945	1,272	1,062	83.5
1946	1,915	1,366	71.3
1947	2,162	1,655	76.6
1948	2,662	2,005	75.3
1949	3,623	2,851	78.7
1950	4,339	3,747	86.4
1951	5,447	3,837	70.4
1952	5,126	4,027	78.6
1953	4,702	3,495	74.3
1954	6,918	5,131	74.2
1955	9,512	7,136	75.0
1956	10,090	7,162	71.0
1957	8,826	6,703	75.9
1958	8,864	6,894	77.8
1959	9,038	7,744	85.7
1960	9,233	7,155	77.5

Source: Banco Nacional de Comercio Exterior, S.A., *Comercio Exterior de México 1940-1948*, as presented in Aspra Rodríguez, "La Transmisión de las Fluctuaciones Cíclicas a la Economía Mexicana" (thesis), Table 9. (Owing to the different source, there are slight discrepancies between the figures in this table and those in Table 6.8).

the figures are improved, with thirty-nine years showing a plus and only fourteen a minus relationship.[39] It is likely that changes in Mexican

39. The figures for U.S. GNP for 1909 through 1965 are from the *Survey of Current Business*, U.S. Department of Commerce, Office of Business Economics as found in *Long Term Economic Growth 1860–1965*, U.S. Department of Commerce, Bureau of the Census, October 1966, pp. 166 and 167. The U.S. figures for 1900–08 were calculated by applying the yearly growth rates for this period for GNP estimates from John W. Kendrick, *Productivity Trends in the United States*, National Bureau of Economic Research as found in *Long Term Economic Growth 1860–1965*, p. 166 to the OBE series. The figures for

Table 6.15
The Share of the U.S. in Mexican Commodity Imports
(million pesos)

Year	1 Total Imports	2 Imports from the U.S.	3 (2) ÷ (1)
1937	614	381	62.1
1938	494	285	57.7
1939	630	416	66.0
1940	669	527	78.8
1941	915	771	84.2
1942	753	655	87.0
1943	910	805	88.5
1944	1,349	1,153	85.4
1945	1,604	1,322	82.3
1946	2,637	2,204	83.6
1947	3,230	2,856	88.4
1948	2,951	2,560	86.7
1949	3,527	3,068	87.0
1950	4,403	3,716	84.4
1951	6,773	5,520	81.5
1952	6,394	5,293	82.8
1953	6,985	5,804	83.1
1954	8,926	7,183	80.5
1955	11,046	8,762	79.4
1956	13,395	10,497	78.4
1957	14,439	11,121	77.0
1958	14,107	10,862	77.0
1959	12,583	9,174	72.9
1960	14,830	10,689	72.1

Source: Banco Nacional de Comercio Exterior, S.A., *Comercio Exterior de México 1940–1948*, as presented in Aspra Rodríguez, "La Transmisión de las Fluctuaciones Cíclicas a la Economía Mexicana," Table 6.

GDP have preceded those in the United States because raw material and primary product exports have provided the major link with U.S. final demand. Since the demand for these products tends to lead the cycle in the United States, and since its impact on Mexican income has until recently been relatively rapid and direct, the turning points in the Mexican trade cycle preceded those in the United States in 1928, 1932, 1936, 1951, and 1953.

Mexican GDP for 1900–24 are from *México: Cincuenta Años de Revolución*, Vol. I, pp. 587–89. The figures from 1925 to 1965 are my estimates, which can be found in Appendixes C and D.

Chart 6.1.

Comparative Growth of Mexican and U.S. Economies, 1900–65

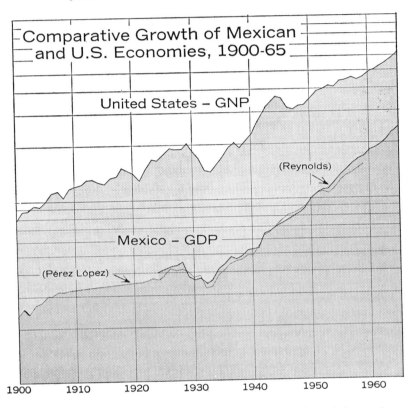

Sources and Methods: The two Mexico series are based on indexes where 1950 = 100. The lighter lines indicate where data were not available (for the Pérez López series between 1910 and 1921 and for the Reynolds series between 1900 and 1910, and 1910 and 1925). The U.S. series is in billions of 1958 dollars.

Mexican GDP (Reynolds): A description of the sources and methods of computation for the author's estimates of GDP can be found in Appendixes C and D.

Mexican GDP (Pérez López): Pérez López, "El Producto Nacional," *Mexico: Cincuenta Años de Revolución,* Vol. 1, pp. 587–89.

U.S. GNP: The figures for 1909 through 1965 are from the *Survey of Current Business,* U.S. Department of Commerce, Office of Business Economics, as found in *Long Term Economic Growth 1860–1965* (U.S. Department of Commerce, Bureau of the Census), pp. 166 and 167. The figures for 1900–08 were calculated by applying the yearly growth rates during this period for GNP estimates from John W. Kendrick, *Productivity Trends in the United States,* National Bureau of Economic Research, as found in *Long Term Economic Growth 1860–1965,* p. 166 to the OBE series.

As the Mexican economy has developed, it has become less dependent upon the exogenous impact of foreign demand as a source of internal instability. The following chapter reveals that government investment has become increasingly important as a source of instability, relative to exports, so that the six-year cycle of public expenditure is now perhaps the single most important destabilizing influence in the economy. Export diversification and the increasing importance of tourism as a source of foreign exchange have tended to smooth out the effect of fluctuations in foreign demand. This is revealed by recent research on the transmission of the U.S. trade cycle to the Mexican economy between 1937 and 1960,[40] some of the findings of which are repoduced in Table 6.16 During the period 1937-40 Mexican exports and U.S. industrial production showed a correlation of +.81, with exports lagged two quarters. In the same period exports and industrial production in Mexico showed a correlation of + .62 when the latter was lagged two quarters.

During the war years 1941–45, the two economies moved closely together. Mexican exports showed a + .82 correlation with U.S. industrial production for the same three-month period, and Mexican industrial production had a high correlation (+ .80) with unlagged exports. This situation continued during the immediate postwar period (1946–50) with unlagged exports and U.S. production highly correlated (+ .82) and with Mexican production following exports by two periods (+ .72).

The period that included several years of balance of payments crisis accompanying the Korean War cycle, 1951–55, shows no significant relationship between U.S. industrial production and Mexican trade, since the best fit for the two variables is + .33 (Table 6.16). Similarly, the previously close tie between Mexican exports and industrial production no longer appears, since in the period 1951-55 no correlation between the two variables surpassed + .50. There is some possibility that the 1954 devaluation reduced the significance of the results for this five-year interval by severely altering U.S.–Mexican trade relationships in the short run. Between 1956 and 1960 Mexican exports again become closely associated with U.S. industrial output (+ .83 unlagged). But the diversification of Mexican production, growing independence of public revenue and expenditure from the export cycle, and the rising importance of American investment

40. Luis Antonio Aspra Rodríguez, "La Transmisión de las Fluctuaciones Cíclicas a la Economía Mexicana," thesis.

Table 6.16
The Relationship Between U.S. Industrial Production,
Mexican Exports, and Mexican Industrial Production
(coefficients of correlation)

Period	Quarters Lagged[a]	Mexican Commodity Exports Correlated with U.S. Industrial Production	Mexican Industrial Production Correlated with Mexican Commodity Exports
	−2	0.81	0.26
1937	−1	0.42	0.21
to	0	0.18	0.45
1940	+1	0.07	0.42
	+2	0.04	0.62
	−2	0.57	0.75
1941	−1	0.62	0.76
to	0	0.82	0.80
1945	+1	0.52	0.77
	+2	0.48	0.72
	−2	0.35	0.64
1946	−1	0.69	0.50
to	0	0.82	0.06
1950	+1	0.79	0.48
	+2	0.48	0.72
	−2	0.32	0.20
1951	−1	0.26	0.42
to	0	0.18	0.40
1955	+1	0.33	0.01
	+2	0.23	0.50
	−2	0.01	0.47
1956	−1	0.10	0.41
to	0	0.83	0.46
1960	+1	0.72	0.30
	+2	0.68	0.37

[a] The figures in this column have a negative sign when the dependent variable follows the independent variable and vice versa.

Source: Aspra Rodríguez, "La Transmisión de las Fluctuaciones Cíclicas a la Economía Mexicana," Table 10.

as a stimulus to final demand, all contributed to make the simple relationship between Mexican commodity exports and local industrial production insignificant in this period.

Although the U.S. trade cycle has diminished in relative importance as a source of instability in the Mexican economy, commerce between the two countries remains vital to the growth of the latter.

Had the American market been more geographically remote and had U.S. entrepreneurs been less familiar with the favorable prospect of their southern neighbor, Mexican exports and foreign investment most certainly would have been less since 1940, though it is easy to exaggerate the net positive influence of such factors by ignoring their costs. How much has growth of the Mexican economy depended on proximity to the United States, and what economic and political costs has this entailed? Measures of this kind must necessarily be rule of thumb. Recognizing the rough order of magnitude of such an evaluation, there are two major aspects to the question: (1) what would the level of GNP have been in Mexico on a year by year basis without its location on the U.S. border, and (2) how would the rate of growth of output have been affected by the results of (1) plus the incremental capacity to import resulting from the proximity effect on the inflow of savings from the United States over the long run?

To answer (1), one must measure the slack in the economy taken up by "vent for surplus" exports that arose out of the proximity factor alone, since trade with the United States would have existed even if Mexico were not on the border, and since other countries would have filled part of the gap if its location were different. This net addition to value added cannot be greater than the share of exports to the United States minus intermediate imports, and it is doubtless much below that amount. Mexican exports of goods and services have averaged under 15 percent of GNP between 1940 and 1965 (Appendix Table D.1A), and total exports to the United States represent from 80–85 percent of that figure. Since the domestic value added share of Mexican exports net of direct plus indirect intermediate imports is from 95 to 97 percent (based upon the coefficients in Table 6.10 column (5) weighted by the average composition of exports), it may be supposed that Mexico has received an average of 12 percent of GNP from exports to the United States (15 percent × 82.5 percent × 96 percent) since 1940. Of these exports (including tourism) that share which reflects *proximity* alone, owing to lower transport cost, greater information, and net favorable treatment from U.S. merchants and government because of Mexico's location cannot have exceeded one-half, i.e. 6 percent of GNP, and was probably lower.[41]

41. A discussion of some aspects of the effect of proximity to the U.S. on Mexican exports appears in William O. Freithaler, *Mexico's Foreign Trade and Economic Development.* He notes that while considerable border trade

Of that 6 percent of total value added accounted for by proximity to the United States, only that share which equals the value added representing fuller employment of national factors of production should be counted. This equals the difference between the market price and the efficiency price (or "shadow price") times quantity of land, labor, and capital employed in additional exports plus real increments in value added through fuller employment of national factors in other activities through the multiplier effect of such incremental exports. Mexico's exports of commodities and tourism undoubtedly absorbed considerable land and labor that would have been underemployed otherwise; by the most extreme assumption of factor redundancy, perhaps only one-third of the 6 percent of value added mentioned above would have been produced in the absence of U.S. trade, leaving 4 percent of GNP remaining as the highest possible static gain from proximity to the United States attributable to vent for surplus.

On the other hand its location resulted in a high and rising level of Mexican tourism to the United States, as well as legal and contraband consumer goods imports which reduced both domestic aggregate demand and the capacity to import capital goods. Ceteris paribus this could have resulted in a lower level of output than might otherwise have existed. An offsetting factor is the possible net gain in technical efficiency attributable to proximity to the United States. This is explained by better information flows, the demonstration effect of a highly productive neighbor, and the availability of essential inputs on short notice (through legal or clandestine channels) to maintain plant and equipment in operation at a high level of productivity. Such influences cannot be measured but probably served to offset the losses on the import side.

As for a "brain drain" arising from the location factor, this seems

---

is largely a function of location, most of Mexico's net tourism receipts are derived from expenditures in the region of Mexico City because of direct air transport of visitors to the capital from foreign countries. Freithaler also shows that the regional impact of exports of both goods and services tends to intensify regional income inequalities by favoring the North and Mexico City areas at the expense of the southern regions of the country. While exports of cotton and sugar have been favored by special U.S. treatment in recent years, those such as shrimp and coffee have reflected Mexico's increased competitiveness with U.S. and Brazilian suppliers, respectively. (Most commodity exports, with the exception of sugar, coffee, and cocoa, are produced in the North and North Pacific.) (Freithaler, Chap. 4.)

to have been less serious for Mexico than for other developing countries, since relative wages and living conditions were so favorable for skilled labor in their homeland that few well-trained Mexicans have been tempted to migrate to the United States. On the other hand there has been a steady outflow of unskilled labor to the United States along with seasonal migration, offset by net immigrant remittances averaging about 2 percent of export revenues since World War II (and as high as 11 percent in 1945). If the opportunity cost of this labor were negligible (equal to subsistence income), GNP could have been slightly lower but per capita output and foreign exchange earnings higher through this aspect of proximity. In welfare terms, Mexicans have doubtless derived considerable benefits from this convenient vent for surplus labor whose marginal productivity at home is extremely low.

What about the effect of proximity on the growth rate mentioned in aspect 2 above? We have seen that perhaps 4 percent of GNP per annum would have been lost in the absence of proximity to American markets. Of course this proximity added to instability of GNP, though at a decreasing rate since 1940, as we have seen. The effect of instability on investment incentives, technical efficiency, and growth are still matters for debate among economists, but it is almost certain that the average degree of employment of factors of production will decline over the long run as the degree of instability rises. Offsetting this may be the "weeding out" of less efficient producers by the trade cycle as well as a higher long-run investment propensity. The latter has two bases: first, the positive elasticity of expectations of entrepreneurs which is higher in upswings than downswings; and, second, the irreversibility of capital formation which causes capital stock to rise more rapidly over time as the cycles in demand offer greater possibilities for occasionally operating at excess profit levels. In terms of exchange risk, the destabilizing aspect of proximity probably had a negative effect on the holding of financial assets in Mexico rather than abroad since the former currency tended to be more vulnerable to swings in trade.

Although GNP might have been lowered by a few percentage points under the assumption of a more remote geographical location relative to the United States, foreign exchange earnings would have fallen by a much larger share—perhaps as much as 40 percent (representing a decline in the export share of GNP from 15 percent to 9 percent). While some of the factors disemployed would have gone into the production of import-competing goods or alternative exports as the terms of trade shifted against Mexico through the loss of proximity to American markets, and while import requirements might have fallen slightly along with GNP, and while Mexicans might well have spent less on border tourism and consumer goods as mentioned earlier, the net loss of capacity to import on current account might conceivably have approached 5 percent of GNP.

In addition, Mexico has been a net borrower from the United States of considerable proportions. Since 1940 the overall net inflow of long and short-term capital (excluding interest and dividend payments) amounted to a total of $3,117 million dollars, with the total net inflow of short-term borrowing being negative (– $55 million) and the net inflow of long-term capital being $3,172 million (Appendix Table D.3A). If it is assumed that as much as one-third of this amount came from the United States due to proximity alone, then $1,039 million was added to Mexico's total capacity to import from goods and services of $27,296 million dollars between 1940 and 1964 (converting 341,198 million 1960 pesos cumulated from Grupo Table 1–3 at the current exchange rate). In other words, 4 percent was added to the capacity to import over the two decades through the proximity effect on capital account.

If the extreme assumption were made that all of these funds were spent on imported capital goods as net additions to the capital stock, then the latter would have grown by $1,039 million dollars less between 1940 and 1960, without U.S. proximity. Using the figures from Chapter 1 (a capital stock of 71,830 million 1950 pesos in 1940 and 161,616 million pesos in 1960) and converting the $1,039 million at the 1950 exchange rate, the capital stock would have risen by only 89,786 − 8,980 = 80,806 million pesos, reducing the compound annual growth rate over the two decades from 4.1 percent to 3.8 percent. The expected growth of output (estimated as in Table 1.7) would have fallen from 3.5 percent to 3.4 percent per annum, or by one-tenth of one percent due to the capital account effect of proximity.

The current account effect of proximity on growth is even more difficult to assess. If capacity to import had fallen by one-third (5 percent ÷ 15 percent) and if capital goods imports had fallen by one-half of this amount, this would have more seriously affected the growth of the capital stock. Adopting the same methods used above, the capital stock under the most extreme assumption of no local replacement of these imports might have risen by only 80,806 − 39,-326 = 41,480 million 1950 pesos, reducing its compound growth rate from 3.8 percent to 2.3 percent per annum. The expected rate of growth of GDP would then have fallen from an initial 3.5 percent, or from 3.4 percent after accounting for the effect of proximity on net capital flows, to 3.1 percent per annum. By these rough calculations, and without considering the influence of such a reduction in capital formation on the productivity "residual" (the initial unexplained residual for the two decades was 2.9 percent per annum), output growth might have fallen by as much as four-tenths of one percent less per year. Almost certainly, domestically produced capital goods would have supplied a considerable amount of the excess demand for producers goods imports caused by any such major shortfall in capacity to import. However, locally produced capital goods would have been less productive, raising the capital/output ratio and therefore the rate of savings and investment required to achieve a given rate of growth.

One can only speculate as to the influence of proximity on the aggregate and sectoral productivity residuals ("unexplained" increments in output). It has been shown in earlier chapters that the aggregate GDP residual since 1940 greatly exceeded that of industry and agriculture, owing in part to the shift of workers from rural to urban employment at much higher initial levels of output per worker and in part to significant growth in output per worker in transport, commerce, services, and other tertiary activities. Service income certainly benefited from major investment in tourism, much of which represented capital formation by American citizens in facilities to serve Americans (just as a good share of Miami's growth represents the investment of New Yorkers to serve New Yorkers). But most of the growth in tertiary income represented increments in the level and share of value added through unification of the national market, a higher degree of specialization in the process of production and exchange, and great advances in financial intermediation. Such activities resulted from investment in roads, sources of energy, and telecommunications as well as governmental subsidization of fuel, electric power, and transport. Little of this was due to proximity and, in the case of railroads, petroleum, and electric power, U.S.-owned assets were actually nationalized before major expansions took place in the postrevolutionary period.

Some Mexican economists such as Jose Luis Ceceña (*El capital-*

ismo monopolista y la economía Méxicana, Cuadernos Americanos, 1963) would argue that foreign investment has slowed rather than accelerated Mexican development and should be discouraged.

As they advance, Mexico and Latin America encounter great obstacles which impede progress and distort the economy, making whatever growth which does occur very costly in terms of energy and national sovereignty.

The greatest of these obstacles is monopoly capital, principally North American, which is constraining the nature, extent and rate of our development. The dominion which monopoly capital of the United States has over our economic activity and which is exercised through diverse channels, principally through direct investment and control of foreign trade, acts as a "straitjacket" within which our development becomes unbalanced objectives of improvement of the general welfare and national independence.[42]

American firms, on the other hand, complain that they are subjected to discrimination in favor of Mexican competitors. A comparison of foreign and locally owned manufacturing enterprises in Mexico (1963) indicates a much higher capital/labor ratio for the former (80,400 pesos of fixed assets per worker in a sample of 510 foreign firms compared with 59,746 pesos per worker from the national industrial census of 1960). Yet the share of capital in value added for the foreign firms was 57.3 percent compared with a share of 67.5 percent for capital in all Mexican industry.[43] Since the capital-value added ratio for the foreign firms in this sample was 3.4 in 1963 compared with the national figure of 2.2 (Table 5.2), it is clear that the reported average rate of return on capital was less for foreign investors than for industry as a whole in Mexico.

The proximity issue clearly cannot be resolved in this volume. Apart from the immediate economic consequences, life in the shadow of the American giant has had severe political, social, and even ideological influences which in turn have affected economic performance. Octavio Paz, in *Labyrinth of Solitude,* conjured up the spirit of *la Malinche* (a reference to Cortéz's Indian wife) to characterize his na-

42. Jose Luis Ceceña, *El Capitalismo Monopolista y la Economía Mexicana,* pp. 17 ff.
43. Bosco A. Muro Gonzalez, "Una Función de Producción para la Indústria Manufacturera Mexicana 1963" (unpublished manuscript).

tion's willing submission to intruders since the Conquest. But post-revolutionary history has revealed that Mexicans are wresting control of their destiny through an increased internal share of savings and investment and a higher degree of political autonomy. Expropriation of foreign assets helped change the nation's self-image in a positive direction and eventually permitted U.S.–Mexican relations to achieve a degree of equality never before experienced by the latter. Yet Mexico's most violent political-economic changes occurred at times when the United States was governed by liberal administrations (Woodrow Wilson and Franklin D. Roosevelt) and was on the verge of foreign war. Furthermore, the cost of such confrontations was considerable in the short run in terms of trade and capital foregone.[44] This study suggests that, although the short run costs of protection from trade and foreign investment may have been substantial, Mexico's long-run growth and resulting trade with the United States will almost certainly prove far greater than would have been the case under the laissez-faire conditions which existed in 1910.

LESSONS FROM THE MEXICAN EXPERIENCE

Mexico's is a case of import substitution that has thus far been conspicuously successful, although the transformation of the structure of production that brought this about involved tremendous strains on the economy, society, and balance of payments. It is noteworthy that the country was unable to industrialize rapidly in the 1930s while at

44. A comparative study of the effect of U.S. proximity on Mexican and Canadian trade and development in terms of their quite different commercial and diplomatic histories would be useful to those seeking to generalize from two cases of successful growth with industrialization. Mexico, although economically and politically weaker at the outset, has been more aggressive than Canada in protecting her interests. An illuminating discussion of Mexico's treatment of foreign investment as it bears on Canadian policy appeared in the *Toronto Star* on April 24 and 27, 1967, by correspondent Norman Gall under the title, "Uncle Sam's Other Neighbor: How Mexico tackled Foreign Ownership and the Price It Paid" (pp. 1 and 19, respectively). He writes, "Mexico has paid a price for nationalism—a price Canadians have never appeared willing to meet. A Mexican banker says: 'Mexico is industrializing at a great sacrifice, both in terms of price and quality.' Canada has not been willing to do this—possibly could not do it, because of its exposed and large international trading position. Canada, while grumbling over foreign control, has accepted foreign money on almost any terms rather than make any move that might raise costs or lower living standards." (April 24, 1967, p. 1.) See also a *Fortune* article, September 1965 "We're Bullish in Mexico," for a critique of Mexico's "hard line" on U.S. direct investments.

the same time reforming the rural sector, and that export revenues ultimately proved indispensable to the process of industrial growth. Although intermediate imports in 1960 were 37 percent below the level that would have obtained under the 1950 structure of production, commodity imports as a share of GDP fell by only two percentage points over the decade and actually rose during the 1940s. "Import substitution" therefore proved import-intensive.

The allocative effects of commercial policy had a negative influence on the expansion of traditional exports. As a result, the share of commodity exports in GDP fell by three percentage points in the 1940s and by almost five percentage points in the 1950s. Had it not been for a transformation in the pattern of exports from minerals toward cash crops and a few manufactures, this decline would have been even sharper. The resulting commodity trade gap was partially offset by expanded exports of services, particularly tourism. These new exports benefited from dams, highways, and other investments that also favored import substitution in both industry and agriculture, so that public policy served to expand trade even as it discouraged traditional mineral exports.

In the final analysis, the effectiveness of import substitution policies will be measured by the international competitiveness of domestic industry in terms of price, quality, and product mix. Once competitiveness is achieved, some "import-competing" activities will become transformed into net exporters. For certain crops such as wheat and maize, this already has occurred. In mining, the movement has, if anything, been in the other direction. Almost all of the mineral production of Mexico was exported in 1910, while today only half of the output is traded. In this case, domestic demand increased more rapidly than foreign demand, increasing domestic prices of raw materials (net of transport costs) relative to those abroad. As for the service sector, the continued rapid increase in revenues from tourism is consistent with evidence that, at the present exchange rate, Mexico's cost of food, travel, hotel services, and handicrafts remains well below that of the United States, despite relative price increases since the last devaluation in 1954. It should be noted, however, that the net gain from tourism (once Mexican border expenditures have been deducted) is a much smaller amount than gross tourist revenues, and the gap is narrowing year by year.

In manufacturing, import substitution certainly has occurred within most sectors, but changing conditions of demand among the subsectors have tended to prevent overall import requirements in manufacturing from falling. Meanwhile certain goods such as television sets, shoes, cotton textiles, handicraft articles, plastics, furniture, and glassware are beginning to be sold at prices competitive with U.S. products and are even replacing contraband imports. Border industry articles that are being produced only for export are also highly competitive. There is every indication that Mexican manufactured exports will expand rapidly in the future, provided they are not faced with increasingly restrictive policies on the part of other Latin American countries and the United States.

The ability to generalize the Mexican experience to other developing countries is limited by a number of particularistic features. A cursory examination of the influence of proximity to the United States indicates that this could have increased the growth rate of GDP by as much as one-half of one percent per annum and the absolute level of GDP by up to 4 percent. The role of tourism (itself a product of public policy), size of the market, effect of the Revolution and subsequent reforms on income distribution and entrepreneurship, and—perhaps most important—commitment of the government to social progress and national autonomy have all been discussed briefly, though each deserves a volume in itself.

Perhaps the key issue raised by this chapter, and one yet to be resolved, concerns Mexico's success in avoiding many of the pitfalls that one customarily associates with widespread controls on trade. Several hypotheses may be proposed in this regard. Tariff levels have been low and relatively uniform, reducing this source of price distortion. Quotas have remained flexible and may be raised or lowered according to the extent to which local suppliers satisfy price, quality, or delivery-time criteria. This tends to reduce the nontariff component of protection. The six-year-cycle of public administrations, including those responsible for commercial policy, limits the duration of favoritism if and when it exists. Government enterprises may enter any market in which prices and costs diverge unduly, or in which the latter reflect a high degree of technical inefficiency. The threat of competition from contraband exists for those commodities whose prices move far out of line with those abroad. Local entrepreneurs may easily benefit from the examples of prior successes and failures in the U.S. Foreign direct investors are subject to the threat of rising taxes and broader application of the 51 percent ownership law if their performance does not meet policy-makers' specifications. All of these factors undoubtedly play a role in the minimization of distortions in the production process and the inefficiency that this entails. The extent to which the lessons they suggest are transferable to countries with much different resource endowments, size, and location, as well as alternative social and political structure, must remain in doubt. Nevertheless we have evidence that at least one country has achieved major changes in the structure of production, along with rapid growth, by following a variety of highly unorthodox economic policies.

7

Public Finance
in Postrevolutionary Mexico

INTRODUCTION: AN ANALYTICAL PERSPECTIVE

Earlier chapters have dealt with the role of government in agriculture, industry, services, trade and foreign investment. Land was expropriated by presidential decree and redistributed to a maximum number of landless families, broadening the political and economic base of society, relieving pressure for income redistribution and urbanization, and increasing the government's freedom of action in more growth-promoting directions. Taxes were used to build roads, dams, and irrigation systems that opened up vast new territories to commercial cultivation. In industry the government set up its own firms whenever it considered private enterprise to be lacking or against the public interest.

In the private sector manufacturers were allowed increased protection against foreign competition, in exchange for which they were expected to improve their efficiency and eventually to reduce prices to international levels. In finance, private bank and nonbank intermediaries were encouraged to expand along with the state-owned Nacional Financiera, a remarkably successful industrial development bank. Government control of financial intermediaries through the Central Bank was used to divert funds from construction, commerce, and real estate speculation toward industry. The growth of internal transport, communications, and trade was facilitated by public expenditures on roads, power, telecommunications, and fuels. Foreign direct investment was increasingly subjected to government regulation affecting its direction and yield, and borrowing abroad was also placed under supervision of the Central Bank.

As a result of the changes wrought by the period of Revolution and reform, the demands placed upon recent governments have been quite different from those facing pre-Revolutionary administrations. The public has demanded more emphasis on social infrastructure and income equality than is customarily true in Latin America even today. On the other hand, the capacity of the Mexican government to intervene in the economy in banking, commerce, agriculture, and manufacturing has proved to be greater than that of most developing countries. With greater demands upon it, but also with greater freedom to act, the Mexican government has been uniquely challenged to provide both economic growth and rapid improvement in social welfare. This chapter deals with the response to this challenge in terms of tax and expenditure policies. Some of the statistical series employed go as far back as 1935, and a few extend beyond 1962. The analysis therefore covers over two decades of fiscal growth under a mixed enterprise system, revealing both strengths and weaknesses. Interpretation of these data faces a number of difficulties in addition to incomplete specification of social and political aspects of fiscal performance, which include:

(1.) Discrepancies between ex post and ex ante tax and expenditure policies as revealed by the growing gap between planned and actual budget levels. These discrepancies make both quantitative and qualitative imputations of fiscal intent extremely difficult to determine.[1]

(2.) The steady increase in licensing and other forms of direct controls as instruments of indicative planning of private expenditure that have played an important role in altering the pattern of resource allocation and the rate of investment since 1940.

(3.) Ambiguities in the construction of certain key economic indicators, including gross and net investment and the functional and personal distribution of income, the knowledge of which is essential to determination of the impact of taxes and expenditures on the level of output, distribution of income, and rate of growth.

(4.) The growing relative importance of monetary policy in Mexico which, while making fiscal policy more effective through stabilizing the price level, also acts as a substitute for taxation by permitting the government deficit to be increasingly financed through the transfer of private savings to public investment.[2]

1. A detailed analysis of planned and actual budgets by economic and social category since the Revolution is presented by historian James Wilkie, *The Mexican Revolution,* Part 1.

2. A number of works deal with the history of Mexican financial institutions and monetary policy. These include Brothers and Solís M., *Mexican Financial*

Characteristic of so many developing countries, the Mexican economy may be regarded as a dynamic disequilibrium system in which markets in excess demand coexist with those in excess supply for considerable periods of time, partly because of lags in the market adjustment mechanism and partly because of government regulation itself, but mainly because the magnitude of the shifts in price and quantity required for market clearing are far from marginal. As a result, the use of traditional neoclassical analysis, relying as it does upon assumptions of instantaneous adjustment to incremental changes in the conditions of supply and demand, is not entirely appropriate for Mexico. Nor is it meaningful to analyze this disequilibrium system in terms of Keynesian assumptions about general underemployment which, for example, might be associated with an overall excess demand for liquidity. Though there are almost always a number of markets in excess demand (such as the market for investable funds due to credit rationing in recent years), others are experiencing considerable excess capacity. Thus given changes in public expenditure tend to produce an unsymmetrical and somewhat unpredictable effect on output and final demand. The immediate impact of public policy on employment, resource allocation, and growth is difficult if not impossible to determine with precision. In view of these problems the following pages confine themselves to measurement of injections and leakages in the economy through the public sector, using the best indicators available, as a precondition for further analysis of the functional role of fiscal policy.

THE HISTORICAL TREND IN MEXICAN PUBLIC EXPENDITURE

The most direct influence of the public sector on the national economy is in terms of its demand for goods and services as shown by the level and distribution of public expenditure. In this section government expenditures are divided into two major categories, those which place demands upon the productive capacity of the economy (*exhaustive expenditures*) and those which redistribute purchasing power

Development; Campos Andapia, "Teoría de la intermediación financiera y las sociedades financieras privadas Mexicanas" (thesis), part of which appeared as *Obstáculos al desarrollo económico,* CEMLA, Mexico; Bennett, *Financial Sector and Economic Development;* David H. Shelton, "The Banking System," pp. 111–90; Goldsmith, *Financial Development of Mexico.*

Table 7.1
Economic Classification of Total Federal, State,
and Local Government Budgeted Expenditures, 1935–62
(millions of current pesos)

| | *Exhaustive Expenditures* | | | | | |
| | *1* | *2* | *3* | *4* | *5* | *6* |
Year	*Consumption*	*Investment*	*Total Exhaustive (3) = (1) + (2)*	*Non-exhaustive Expenditures*	*Total Federal, State, and Local Expenditures (5) = (3) + (4)*	*Gross Domestic Product*
1935	345	72	418	26	444	
1936	442	89	531	34	565	
1937	511	87	598	46	644	
1938	498	144	642	53	695	
1939	513	159	672	53	725	6,559
1940	538	189	767	64	791	7,108
1941	485	262	747	62	809	8,413
1942	604	275	879	100	979	10,332
1943	787	322	1,109	110	1,219	12,989
1944	801	487	1,288	194	1,483	16,895
1945	1,073	561	1,634	190	1,824	19,666
1946	1,136	569	1,705	170	1,875	25,329
1947	1,265	820	2,085	176	2,261	27,798
1948	1,647	1,050	2,696	250	2,947	29,997
1949	2,517	1,141	3,658	255	3,913	33,482
1950	1,722	1,392	3,114	262	3,376	41,060
1951	1,842	1,561	3,403	374	3,777	53,026
1952	2,169	1,870	4,040	517	4,556	59,384
1953	2,340	1,642	3,982	1,548	5,530	58,926
1954	2,782	2,156	4,937	1,850	6,787	72,205
1955	3,431	2,189	5,620	2,619	8,238	88,218
1956	3,955	2,344	6,299	3,447	9,746	100,600
1957	4,668	2,946	7,613	3,676	11,289	115,542
1958	5,506	2,933	8,439	4,139	12,578	128,570
1959	5,924	3,207	9,130	4,414	13,544	137,676
1960	7,085	3,175	10,260	4,591	14,851	155,867
1961	7,591	3,178	10,769	6,079	16,848	165,672
1962	8,358	3,496	11,854	7,193	19,047	179,874

Note: Rows may not sum to totals due to rounding.
Source: Muro González, "Estructura y Evolución del Gasto Público en México"
(typescript).

within the private sector (*nonexhaustive expenditures*).[3] Government exhaustive expenditures are those which can best be associated with other value-added components of gross national product. They include government purchases of goods and services on current and capital account. Government consumption is confined for the most part to administrative expenditures essential to its day-to-day operations. Government investment, on the other hand, represents the increase in the stock of physical capital brought about directly through public expenditures.

Government nonexhaustive expenditures represent transfer payments on both current and capital account. Since the eventual disposition of these payments in terms of consumption or investment is under the control of private decision makers, nonexhaustive expenditures are separated from direct government purchases of goods and services for analytical purposes. The assumption is made in such a separation that even though the social welfare function underlying public expenditure may be identical to that for private expenditure, the former represents collective purchases of public goods and services which would not be demanded in the same proportion if left to individuals, owing to externalities both in production and consumption. In the case of government expenditure on social and economic infrastructure such as health, education, and welfare, as well as roads, dams, and irrigation systems, society has benefited collectively from these public goods though it is sometimes difficult to equate cost with benefit. Furthermore, the expenditure decisions were usually made by government officials acting on behalf of society but relying on their own judgment for a sense of priorities. While in some cases transfer payments such as investment subsidies serve a similar purpose by allocating resources toward the creation of public goods, they are generally placed in households and are used for individual consumption purposes.

A classification of total government spending in Mexico from 1935 to 1962 in terms of exhaustive and nonexhaustive expenditures is presented in Table 7.1. The percentage relationships, including the share of public expenditure in GDP, are found in Table 7.2. The

3. The methodology employed in this section, including the distinction between "exhaustive" and "nonexhaustive" expenditures, is described in Francis M. Bator, *The Question of Government Spending*. Calculations for Mexico were prepared with the assistance of Bosco A. Muro Gonzalez at El Colegio de México, 1964, and were presented in Muro, "Estructura y evolución del gasto público en México" (typescript). Detailed information as to the basis for these calculations is available on request.

Table 7.2
The Composition of Public Expenditure and Its Share of Gross Domestic Product
(percentages)

| | Share of Government Exhaustive Expenditure | | Share of Total Government Expenditure | | Share of Gross Domestic Product | | |
| | Government Consumption | Government Investment | Exhaustive Expenditure | Nonexhaustive Expenditure | Government Exhaustive Expenditure | Total Gov't. Exhaustive Expenditure plus Investment of Gov't. Enterprises | Total Gov't. Exhaustive & Nonexhaustive Expenditure (not including Investment of Gov't. Enterprises) |
Year	(1)	(2)	(3)	(4)	(5)	(6)	(7)
1935	83	17	94	6	—[a]	—	—
1936	83	17	94	6	—	—	—
1937	86	15	93	7	—	—	—
1938	78	22	92	8	—	—	—
1939	76	24	93	7	10.2	11.9	11.0
1940	74	26	92	8	10.2	12.3	11.1
1935–40	80	20	93	7	—	—	—
1941	65	35	92	8	8.9	10.3	9.6
1942	69	31	90	10	8.5	10.6	9.5
1943	71	29	91	9	8.5	11.7	9.4
1944	62	38	87	13	7.6	9.0	8.8
1945	66	34	90	10	8.3	10.3	9.3
1941–45	66	34	90	10	8.4	10.4	9.3
1946	67	33	91	9	6.7	8.9	7.4
1947	61	39	92	8	7.5	9.7	8.1
1948	61	39	92	8	9.0	11.0	9.8
1949	69	31	94	6	10.9	13.4	11.7
1950	55	45	92	8	7.6	10.8	8.2
1946–50	62	38	92	8	8.3	10.8	9.0

Table 7.2—Continued

	Share of Government Exhaustive Expenditure		Share of Total Government Expenditure		Share of Gross Domestic Product		
Year	Government Consumption	Government Investment	Exhaustive Expenditure	Nonexhaustive Expenditure	Government Exhaustive Expenditure	Total Gov't. Exhaustive Expenditure plus Investment of Gov't. Enterprises	Total Gov't. Exhaustive & Nonexhaustive Expenditure (not including Investment of Gov't. Enterprises)
	(1)	(2)	(3)	(4)	(5)	(6)	(7)
1951	54	46	90	10	6.4	9.2	7.1
1952	54	46	89	11	6.8	9.5	7.7
1953	59	41	72	28	6.8	9.5	9.4
1954	56	44	73	27	6.8	9.9	9.4
1955	61	39	68	32	6.4	9.1	9.3
1951–55	57	43	78	22	6.6	9.4	8.6
1956	63	37	65	35	6.3	8.8	9.7
1957	61	39	67	33	6.6	9.1	9.8
1958	65	35	67	33	6.6	9.4	9.8
1959	65	35	67	33	6.6	9.3	9.8
1960	69	31	69	31	6.6	10.2	9.5
1956–60	65	35	67	33	6.5	9.4	9.7
1961	70	30	64	36	6.5	10.6	10.2
1962	70	30	62	38	6.6	10.5	10.6
1961–62	70	30	63	37	6.5	10.5	10.4

ᵃ Data not available.
Sources: Columns 1 through 5 and 7: Table 7.1.
Column 6: Table 7.5.

figures in Table 7.2 reveal that the proportion of federal, state, and local government expenditure in gross domestic product has not increased since the late 1930s.[4] Meanwhile, exhaustive expenditures as a share of total government expenditures have declined from an average of 93 percent in the 1930s to 67 percent in the last half of the 1950s. The government's command over resources in the economy has lagged accordingly during the most rapid period of Mexican growth, the very period when the economy was developing its strongest central controls and declaring itself "socialist within the Constitution."

Concurrent with this downtrend in the share of government purchases of goods and services, a rising share of public revenues was being disbursed in the form of transfer payments to the private sector. The share of exhaustive expenditures in GDP has fallen steadily from 10.2 percent in the last half of the 1930s to 6.5 percent from 1956–62 (Table 7.2). Although most developing countries experience a secular rise in the share of total government expenditures in GDP, this has not been true for Mexico since the 1930s. Normally, that proportion of government expenditures devoted to transfer payments to households (included in our figures under nonexhaustive expenditures) rises steadily as a share of GDP while other expenditures remain fairly proportional.[5] In Mexico, however, a comparison of the columns in Table 7.2 shows that while nonexhaustive expenditures have risen from less than 1 percent of GDP to almost 4 percent over the period 1935–62, exhaustive expenditures have fallen by the same proportion, so that total government expenditures have failed to in-

4. The share of total government spending in GDP in 1900 was between 5 and 6 percent, compared to 11 percent in 1939. (The earlier calculation is based on government expenditure data from El Colegio de México, *Fuerza de trabajo*, and GDP estimates for 1900 as described in Chapter 1.)

5. For a similar analytical perspective see Richard S. Thorn, "The Evolution of Public Finances during Economic Development," Table 1, p. 21 and context.

Briefly the hypothesis that is set forth . . . is that the social and political tendencies that are inherent in the process of economic development result in a rate of growth of public social expenditures substantially in excess of the rate of growth of national product while other public expenditures taken together tend to grow at a substantially lesser rate than social expenditures but not at a low enough rate to offset the growth in social expenditures so that the ratio of total public expenditures to GNP tends to rise historically. [pp. 22 ff.]

The author supports this hypothesis with cross-sectional data for 36 countries for the period 1950–59.

crease their share of gross domestic product. We shall see later that this is partly due to fiscal constraints arising from the desire for price stability and a low capacity to tax, and partly because investments of private and mixed enterprise were sufficient to sustain a high rate of economic growth. Most of the increase in the share of government transfer payments occurred *after* 1950, particularly during the administrations of Ruíz Cortines (1952–58) and López Mateos (1958–64). Before 1952, government exhaustive expenditure including investment in economic and social infrastructure maintained an important share of both total government expenditure and GDP (Table 7.2, columns 3 and 5).

Among the three branches of government, the federal share of exhaustive expenditures has not changed significantly since 1940. It was 67 percent in that year, 71 percent in 1950, and 67 percent in 1960.[6] This reflects the concentration of political power in the hands of the federal government. The regional allocation of public expenditure is subject to a high degree of control by the president and his ministers. There is evidence that considerable regional reallocation of resources through the maintenance of net surpluses or deficits on public account by the federal government has taken place since 1940. For example, a large share of public investment in rural infrastructure was concentrated in the north and northwest during the 1940s.[7] In recent years a greater balance of regional investment has been maintained. Meanwhile the share of the Federal District [8] has risen sharply from 6.8 percent in 1940 to 10.5 percent in 1950, and 11.3 percent of exhaustive expenditures in 1960. Since the Federal District does not customarily run a deficit, the relative increase in spending reflects the agglomeration of industry and population in the capital city. It is probable that total taxes exceeded expenditures in the Federal District. If so, then a net outflow of public expenditure to the rest of Mexico may have partly compensated for government subsidies to industry and labor, which in the past have contributed to what many observers regard as overconcentration of manufacturing and commerce in the center of the country.

Although exhaustive expenditures have declined as a share of total

6. These figures are taken from Muro, "Estructura y evolución," Tables 1 and 6.

7. For a regional breakdown of state revenues and expenditures for the years 1910, 1920, 1930, 1940, and 1960, see Appendix Tables E.14 and E.15.

8. The government of the Federal District has pursued its tax and expenditure policy independently of the federal government.

government outlays since the late 1930s, this is by no means true of public investment expenditures. From 1940 to 1960 there was a sharp rise in the share of direct investment expenditures in both exhaustive and total government expenditures. Government direct investment increased steadily, particularly during the last years of the Alemán administration. Alemán's public works projects involved large-scale construction of roads, dams, and irrigation systems. These expenditures were widely criticized at the time as being grandiose, extravagant, and inflationary, but subsequent analysis has revealed their true importance. By uniting both domestic and foreign markets and permitting the opening of new land for cultivation, they facilitated economies of scale and a more efficient allocation of resources, as preceding chapters have shown.

Tax revenues were insufficient to cover the cost of this upswing in government investment between 1947 and 1952. Because it was impossible before the mid-1950s to attract a large amount of private savings to sustain the desired level of government investment, government deficits progressively increased. These deficits were offset by unsupported credits from the Central Bank, resulting in a severe postwar inflation. Two major devaluations were necessary (1948 and 1954) before it became possible for the government to utilize increased private savings to finance public investment. The relative price stability presently enjoyed by Mexico was possible only after more than a decade of rapid growth with inflation during which the rate of savings virtually doubled due to a rise in the profit share of GDP as prices rose faster than wages. Time has tended to erase the memory of Mexico's postwar inflation; yet the problems of those years were cited at the time as a prime example of the difficulty of sustaining high rates of savings and investment without large and inflationary government deficits and aggregate excess demand.

Commentators are mixed in their interpretation of the necessity and wisdom of inflationary fiscal policy during the 1940s and early 1950s. Barry Siegel, in *Inflación y desarrollo; las experiencias de México* (CEMLA, 1960), used Mexico's performance from 1939 to 1955 to argue hypothetically that, although developing countries are extremely susceptible to inflation in times of rapid growth, growth and inflation might not have to coexist in Latin America. His contention was that, if the public sector had pursued a balanced budget policy by increasing the rate of taxation, factor mobility and profit rates in Mexico would have been even higher. Inflationary financing of government expenditures was not dictated by necessity, he held, but by unwise government policies that forced savings from the masses indirectly through lagging real wages rather than by channeling savings from industry and commerce directly into public investment through a high effective rate of taxation.[9] Siegel's argument was based on the assumption that higher tax rates could have been absorbed by the economy without substantially lowering the rate of private savings and investment. Most Mexican officials of the period were convinced, on the other hand, that sharp tax increases would have so reduced private investment that these declines would have offset any gains from increased government investment.

An analysis that illustrates the official position was presented in a 1949 Harvard doctoral dissertation by Alfredo Navarrete, "Exchange Stability, Business Cycles, and Economic Development: An Inquiry into Mexico's Balance of Payments Problems, 1929–46." [10] Navarrete noted the existence of supply inelasticities in the domestic economy necessitating a high degree of protection and internal price rises to stimulate private investment in manufacturing. Wartime and postwar inflation were regarded as essential to permit rising rates of return on capital in the private sector. He predicted that, although excess demand and balance of payments disequilibria were certain to result in the short run, in the long run the investments would bear fruit in expanded production, eventually eliminating excess demand. Rapid inflation would be overcome by the process of development itself. This prophecy was fulfilled in the 1950s, as we have seen.

The debate over the necessity for inflation in the early stage of Mexican growth remains open. Its resolution depends to a large extent on the scholar's interpretation of two imponderables: (1) the ability of the government to have increased and/or shifted substantially the incidence of taxation during those early years of rapid growth without causing political instability or offsetting reductions in private investment expenditure, and (2) the effectiveness with which public investment might have been substituted for the high and sustained rate of private investment that actually took place. In fairness to those who took a position similar to that of Siegel, the earlier statistical evidence he relied upon eventually was superseded by data

9. Siegel, *Inflación y Desarrolla,* pp. 179–87.
10. Later published as *Estabilidad de cambios, el ciclo, y el desarrollo económico. Una investigación sobre los problemas de la balanza de pagos de México, 1929–1946,* Mexico, D.F., 1951.

that indicated a far greater rate of increase, both in private investment and GDP, than had been known at the time. In retrospect it is likely that political, administrative, and institutional constraints during the years before 1954 placed serious limits on the rate of growth of public investment. Attempts to apply major tax increases probably would have considerably retarded the growth of the private sector of the economy. The government's strategy did in fact work to bring about rapid and sustained growth, with eventual price stability and a high rate of public investment. As a result, one is inclined to accept this as *ex post facto* evidence favoring the Navarrete position, though the pattern of output that resulted may reflect a loss of efficiency through the protection of local manufacturing at relatively high prices. A more detailed examination of the nature of fiscal constraints of the period is presented below. The entire episode illustrates the high degree of uncertainty and risk under which public policies are pursued during times of rapid growth. As a qualification to those who would have urged even more government investment in earlier years, it is important to emphasize that the actual rate of growth of GDP as well as the level and rate of private investment were unknown to policy-makers until long after the fact. Hence effective global planning would have been extremely difficult and government investors would have had to follow incremental decision rules similar to those of private firms.

Recent trends in public expenditure suggest that the market mechanism and private decision-making are more important than ever in the allocation of goods and services in Mexico. Not only has the share of total expenditure in gross domestic product remained at approximately the same level since the late 1930s, but that of direct consumption expenditures has fallen sharply. Only government investment expenditures have increased their share of gross domestic product, with the greatest rise occurring in the early 1950s.

AN INTERNATIONAL COMPARISON
OF PUBLIC EXPENDITURE AS A SHARE OF GNP

The share of direct government expenditure in gross domestic product in Mexico is much below that of other countries for which comparable figures are available. Among countries of a similar level of per capita income, Mexico's share of both exhaustive and total government expenditure in GDP is only slightly more than half of the average (see Table 7.3). Current exhaustive expenditures of government in a representative country with per capita income between 200 and 500 dollars average 10.6 percent of GNP, but in Mexico the figure was only 5.3 percent of GDP in the 1940s. Furthermore, although cross-sectional data suggest that this percentage rises with the level of per capita output, the Mexican share declined from 5.3 percent in the 1940s to 4.0 percent in the 1950s. Total Mexican current expenditures as a share of GDP fell from 6.1 percent to 5.3 percent over the two decades, although the corresponding world average was well over twice that figure, or 14.8 percent for countries in the same income class as Mexico. Furthermore, cross-sectional evidence suggests a *rise* in the share of current expenditures in GNP, though the Mexican share *declined* during its period of rapid growth. It should be noted that this decline is due completely to a fall in the share of current exhaustive expenditures in GDP. Current transfer payments actually rose as a share of GDP from 0.8 percent to 1.3 percent (compare rows 4 and 5 with 7 and 8 in Table 7.3). Total government expenditures in Mexico were only 9.2 percent of GDP in each decade, while in the rest of the world similar countries showed an average of 17.8 percent for total government consumption plus savings. Note that the discrepancy between the Mexican performance and that of the average underdeveloped country included in the sample would be still greater had total government investment and consumption expenditures been taken into consideration in the sample for the rest of the world. Estimates of government exhaustive expenditures similar to those employed here are available for more developed countries during the 1950s. For example, government exhaustive expenditures as a share of GNP were 16.8 percent in Belgium (1952), 18.4 percent in Sweden (1952), 22.9 percent in the United Kingdom (1953), and 18.2 percent in the United States (1957).[11] The similar figure for Mexico averaged only 8.3 percent in the 1940s and 6.5 percent in the 1950s (Table 7.2).

A comparison of Mexican budgeted expenditures as a share of GNP with comparable figures for other Latin American countries shows Mexico to be among the lowest in the hemisphere, as of 1966 (see Table 7.4). Furthermore, Mexico is the only country that has shown a decline in the share of budgeted expenditures in GNP between 1950 and 1966, with the possible exception of Argentina.

11. Bator, *The Question of Government Spending,* p. 158.

Table 7.3
Government Expenditures as Share of Gross
National Product: Mexico and Rest of World
(percentages)

	Per Capita Product ($U.S.)			
	I	*II*	*III*	*IV*
	under 200	*201–500*	*501–1200*	*over 1200*
A. Rest of world (1950–59)				
1. Current exhaustive expenditures ÷ GNP	10.9	10.6	12.7	14.1
2. Total current expenditures ÷ GNP	12.7	14.8	24.0	24.3
3. Total current expenditures & gov't. saving ÷ GNP	15.9	17.8	29.0	27.3
B. Mexico (1941–50)				
4. Current exhaustive expenditures ÷ GDP		5.3		
5. Total current expenditures ÷ GDP		6.1		
6. Total government expenditures ÷ GDP		9.2		
C. Mexico (1951–60)				
7. Current exhaustive expenditures ÷ GDP		4.0		
8. Total current expenditures ÷ GDP		5.3		
9. Total government expenditures ÷ GDP		9.2		

Sources: Rows 1–3: Thorn, "The Evolution of Public Finances," Table 1, p. 21, based upon data for 36 countries.

Rows 4, 6, 7, and 9: From Tables 7.1 and 7.2 above, averaging the annual percentages by five-year intervals.

Rows 5 and 8: From Table 7.6 below, again averaging the percentages by five-year intervals.

Those countries, such as Bolivia, Chile, and Venezuela, which are export monocultures show high and rising shares of government expenditures, averaging over 20 percent of GNP. Argentina, Brazil, and Colombia, on the other hand, have a much lower government share, averaging under 12 percent. Only Colombia has maintained a comparably low share through the period 1950–66, and Colombia's share rose from 6.7 to 8 percent while that of Mexico declined. Since actual expenditures have tended to outstrip budgeted outlays in Mexico, the decline in its share is somewhat exaggerated. Neverthe-

Table 7.4
Government Expenditures as a Percentage
of Gross National Product, 1950, 1960, 1966
(percentages)

	1950	*1960*	*1966*
Mexico	9.1	9.0	7.2
Argentina	12.9	13.2	12.8
Bolivia	—ᵃ	39.8	43.0ᵇ
Brazil	9.4	11.0	14.0
Chile	15.5ᶜ	22.1	22.8
Colombia	6.7	8.4	8.0ᵈ
Ecuador	6.0	13.1	15.8
Peru	12.3	15.1	16.7ᵈ
Venezuela	20.1	25.9	21.4

ᵃ Data not available.
ᵇ 1963.
ᶜ 1953.
ᵈ 1965.
Sources: United Nations, *Statistical Yearbook 1967*, pp. 550–59, 631, 635–41.
United Nations, *Statistical Yearbook 1963*, pp. 577, 581–87. United Nations,
Statistical Yearbook 1952, pp. 447, 450–54.

less, the figures are sufficient to illustrate that Mexico has been able
to experience a rapid and sustained rate of growth with an absolute
minimum of public expenditure, even compared with the poorest
countries of Latin America.

INVESTMENT EXPENDITURES OF PUBLIC ENTERPRISE

In contrast to the low and falling share of direct government expenditures in GDP, those of public and mixed public-private enterprise have accounted for an increasing share of aggregate demand.
The investment expenditures of wholly and partially government-
owned enterprise have been added to total exhaustive expenditures
of government in Table 7.5. The figures show that in recent years investment of public enterprises has amounted to as much as one-third
to one-half of total exhaustive expenditures of government. Direct
government expenditure, including the investment of government enterprises, averaged 10.6 percent of GDP in the 1940s, fell to 9.4
percent in the 1950s, and rose to 10.5 percent in 1961–62 (Table
7.2).

Since the investment decisions of government-owned industry appear until recently to have been largely independent of the federal

Table 7.5
Total Direct Expenditures of Government and Government Enterprise
(millions of current pesos)

Year	1 *Total Exhaustive Expenditures of Government*	2 *Investment of Wholly or Partially-Owned Government Enterprise*	3 *Total Direct Government Expenditures* *(1) + (2) = (3)*
1935	418	41	459
1936	531	48	579
1937	598	56	654
1938	642	57	699
1939	672	106	778
1940	737	148	874
1941	747	121	869
1942	879	217	1,096
1943	1,325	200	1,525
1944	1,288	236	1,525
1945	1,634	388	2,023
1946	1,705	561	2,266
1947	2,085	609	2,694
1948	2,696	591	3,288
1949	3,658	823	4,481
1950	3,114	1,132	4,446
1951	3,403	1,466	5,869
1952	4,040	1,630	5,670
1953	3,982	1,627	5,608
1954	4,937	2,232	7,160
1955	5,620	2,488	8,008
1956	6,299	2,567	8,866
1957	7,613	3,043	10,556
1958	8,439	3,594	12,033
1959	9,130	3,673	12,803
1960	10,260	5,604	15,864
1961	10,769	6,715	17,484
1962	11,854	7,077	18,931

Sources: Column 1: Table 7.1, column 3.
Columns 2 and 3: These are from Muro G., "Estructura y Evolución del Gasto Público en México," Table 7.

budget, and since public corporations have drawn heavily upon retained earnings and nongovernmental sources of financing for new investment, one might expect their relationship to the level and rate of growth of output to be more analogous to that of private investment than to other forms of government investment. Nevertheless, the investment expenditures of public enterprises have proven to be negatively correlated with private investment outlays (see below), suggesting that the government does exercise some direct influence over its semiautonomous enterprises. This causes them to register investment expenditures that are more closely related to total government spending than to private investment (the latter being negatively correlated with direct government investment).

No matter how inclusive one makes the definition of direct government expenditures, the total has not risen as a share of gross domestic product in Mexico since 1940, as Table 7.2 shows. Yet one should not suppose that the relative influence of the public sector in the economy has declined proportionally. Actually the overall impact of public policy on resource allocation has steadily increased since 1940. For example, in oligopolistic industries such as steel, automobiles, and chemicals, the government has exercised an influence on output disproportionate to direct expenditures through the establishment of state corporations which engage in highly effective price leadership.[12] Commercial policy, tax concessions, and numerous other indirect controls have also been widely applied since World War II to alter the pattern of resource allocation, without the need for large increases in direct expenditure. The shortages of well-trained civil servants and the limited tax capacity of the system have made indirect controls more or less mandatory as instruments of indicative planning in the short run. These have been relatively successful, since the private sector has demonstrated great flexibility and responsiveness to changing profit expectations and credit availability, both of which have been influenced by public policy.

THE HISTORICAL TREND IN FEDERAL REVENUES

Because of the government's extensive reliance upon investment in the private sector, public expenditures have been kept relatively low, so that the Mexican federal budget has not gone severely out of balance by Latin American standards except during the immediate postwar period. More recently, public policy has been increasingly successful in permitting growth with price stability, largely because rural and urban infrastructure expenditures of earlier years are now

12. An analysis of the theoretical implications of the use of public enterprise as an instrument of antitrust policy and its illustration in the case of the Mexican steel industry is found in Norman Schneider, "Mixed Oligopoly" (Ph.D. dissertation).

beginning to demonstrate their productivity. The revealed preference of Mexican policy-makers for a maximum degree of price stability consistent with rapid growth means that the level of public expenditure may be regarded as a function of the country's joint capacities to (1) tax the private sector, (2) borrow abroad, and (3) channel private savings into public investment through the bank and nonbank financial intermediaries. The latter two methods of financing public deficits have become increasingly important since the mid-1950s. Before then, virtually the only source of financing government expenditure was through taxation or increased liquidity. The following section deals with the level and composition of federal revenues since 1940.[13]

The tax structure of a developing country has been shown to depend upon the level and distribution of economic activity and particularly upon the relative importance of foreign trade. Professor Harley Hinrichs has shown that the capacity to tax varies from sector to sector in a developing country, with exports and imports being the most easily taxed component of GNP. Accordingly, indirect taxes on foreign trade customarily provide the largest share of government revenue in the early stages of growth. Import substitution policies, as they reduce the traded share of output, tend to lower the government's capacity to tax. All of these observations hold true for Mexico since 1940.[14]

Meanwhile, as the internal market of the economy expands, along with the growth of commercial agriculture and industry, it is likely that direct taxation of income and property will increase in relative importance.[15] The Mexican case illustrates both of these trends, as shown in Table 7.6. Indirect taxes in Mexico have declined from 59

13. Two comprehensive surveys of Mexican tax legislation have appeared in recent years, Henry J. Gumpel and Hugo B. Margain, *Taxation in Mexico,* and Stanford G. Ross and John B. Christensen, *Tax Incentives for Industry in Mexico.* See also the more recent volume by Ifigenia M. de Navarrete, which provides insights into contemporary policies of the federal government, *Los incentivos fiscales y el desarrollo económico de México,* Instituto de Investigaciones Económicas, Universidad Nacional Autónoma de México, 1967.

14. For a detailed examination of his approach, involving cross-sectional analysis of a number of countries at various stages of growth, see Harley H. Hinrichs, *A General Theory of Tax Structure Change During Economic Development.*

15. A discussion of the composition of agricultural tax revenues and their share of total tax revenue (24 percent in 1943; 20 percent in 1948) is presented by Aron J. Aizenstat, "Structure and Taxation of Agriculture in Mexico," pp. 305–21.

Table 7.6
Level and Distribution of Total Federal Revenues, 1940–63
(millions of current pesos and percents)

Year	Total Federal Receipts (million current pesos)	(percent)	Direct Taxes				Indirect Taxes						Other Income (percent)
			Sum	Income Tax (percent)	Export Revenues (percent)	Other	Sum	Natural Resources	Production & Commerce (percent)	Mercantile Revenues (percent)	Import Duties	Other	
1940	510	100	21	11	9	1	59	8	24	6	18	3	20
1941	544	100	19	10	8	1	60	7	20	7	23	3	21
1942	631	100	25	12	12	*	55	8	22	7	15	3	21
1943	916	100	36	24	12	*	44	6	19	6	10	3	20
1944	1,082	100	38	28	10	*	47	7	21	6	11	3	16
1945	1,168	100	35	25	10	*	48	6	21	7	12	3	17
1946	1,600	100	31	23	7	*	50	5	18	11	13	3	19
1947	1,728	100	35	28	6	1	50	8	14	10	15	3	16
1948	1,932	100	29	23	5	1	50	9	13	9	17	2	21
1949	2,687	100	40	22	17	1	42	6	13	9	13	2	18
1950	3,057	100	41	25	15	1	42	3	12	11	14	2	17
1951	4,353	100	44	27	15	1	40	5	10	9	14	2	16
1952	4,842	100	45	30	14	1	39	5	11	9	13	2	17
1953	4,315	100	50	26	13	1	42	4	13	9	15	2	17
1954	5,161	100	43	24	18	1	40	3	11	10	15	2	16
1955	7,133	100	49	28	20	1	37	3	11	9	13	2	14
1956	7,981	100	47	31	16	1	36	2	11	9	12	2	16
1957	8,037	100	47	34	13	1	36	1	11	10	12	2	17
1958	8,610	100	44	32	11	1	39	2	11	10	15	2	17
1959	9,053	100	45	34	10	1	45	2	13	11	17	3	20
1960	10,967	100	43	33	9	1	43	2	12	10	16	3	15
1961	11,418	100	44	36	8	1	43	2	13	11	15	3	16
1962	12,829	100	44	37	7	1	43	2	14	11	15	2	13
1963	14,615	100	48	42	5	1	41	2	13	11	13	2	11

* Less than one percent.
Source: Appendix Table D.2.

percent of total federal income in 1940 to 41 percent in 1963. Import duties that were between 18 and 20 percent of government revenues before the war are now from 13 to 15 percent. Export duties (included by the government under "direct taxes") that rose from 9 percent in 1940 to as high as 20 percent in 1955, fell back to 5 percent in 1963. Indirect taxes on natural resources, reflecting the relative decline in mining production, have fallen from 7 percent of total revenues in the early 1940s to 2 percent by 1960. Income taxes, on the other hand, have risen from 11 percent in 1940 to 42 percent of federal revenues in 1963.

The changing structure of the Mexican economy has shifted the tax base away from foreign trade toward internal production. Import substitution has not only reduced the share of commodity exports in GDP, it has also shifted the composition of trade from highly dutiable imports such as luxury consumer goods toward intermediate goods, machinery, and equipment which tend to receive tax advantages because they are associated with the full employment of domestic resources. Moreover, mineral exports generally contain a larger component of economic rent in value added and can therefore sustain a higher incidence of taxation than manufacturing or commerce. The falling share of mineral exports in total Mexican trade has meant that the share of export duties has declined more than in proportion to the share of exports in total output. Thus the recent pattern of Mexican economic development has served to reduce the traditional source of revenues, in relative terms, and has helped to bring about the appearance of a regressive tax structure even though tax legislation itself has tended to be progressive.

The government, seeking to encourage private investment, has kept effective rates of taxation of industrial profits fairly low and has maintained only the most casual attitude about auditing of corporate accounts.[16] While this treatment has not always extended to foreign investors, and the latter cannot apply for tax exemption, tax neutrality is in principle applied to all firms. On the other hand, employees of large corporations and institutions that maintain regular payrolls (from which deductions may conveniently be made) have come to bear a disproportionate share of direct taxation. Since these income recipients constitute a significant portion of the urban middle class

16. See Enrique Helguera, "Mexican Tax Policy on Foreign Investments," Chapter 11, in Tax Institute of America, *Tax Policy on U.S. Investment in Latin America.*

who also receive a large share of the benefits of federal expenditure, the fact that tax incidence falls heavily upon them is somewhat less onerous than would otherwise be the case from a welfare viewpoint. But it is clear that the effective tax structure, which is very progressive through the middle income groups, becomes highly regressive beyond that point.[17]

The foregoing factors help to explain why, although direct taxes have risen sharply since 1940, they have no more than offset the falling share of indirect taxes in GDP. Accordingly, total revenue as a share of GDP did not rise notably in more than two decades. Tax collection is much more difficult in Latin America than, for example, in northern Europe or the United States where qualified administrative personnel are more readily available, higher salaries provide less incentive for graft, and society is conditioned to accept a higher incidence of taxation without protest. Still, there is reason to criticize the failure of Mexican tax policy to keep pace with the growing demands for public expenditures that one would expect to accompany the rapid pace of development, urbanization, and social change that Mexico has experienced since 1940. Mexico's fiscal performance has been far from adequate to support even the most modest revenue requirements as revealed by international comparison (Table 7.3). While legal rates of taxation in Mexico are relatively high by international standards, the law is not being strenuously enforced and tax incidence is extremely uneven among the various income groups. In the area of trade alone, millions of dollars a year are lost in contraband through willingness of the executive branch of the federal government to permit customs officials a high degree of discretion in the performance of their duties.

One foreign observer of Mexican fiscal policy has suggested that major revisions in the tax structure be instituted immediately so as to increase the rate of taxation by more than 50 percent in terms of its 1957 performance.[18] Although such extreme proposals cannot be

17. This point is supported statistically in terms of legal rates of taxation in Ifigenia M. de Navarrete, "The Tax Structure and the Economic Development of Mexico." It should be noted that this article maintains that taxes as a share of GNP have increased from 7 percent of GNP in 1940 to 11 percent in 1960 (p. 161). More recent estimates of GNP than those obtained by that author would suggest the share to be only 9.5 percent in 1960, using her figures for total taxes.

18. British economist Nicholas Kaldor, after a one-month visit to Mexico in 1960, prepared an indictment of the existing tax structure accompanied by sweeping proposals for tax reform. The personal and corporate income tax

taken seriously, they simply reflect the fact that tax policy in recent years has been grossly inadequate. Public revenues alone do not permit the government to cope with even the normal requirements for increased public expenditure in growth. Thus the burden shifts to savings captured from the financial sector and to a perilously high level of foreign borrowing. While a number of improvements in collection have been brought about in recent years, and some tax reforms have been instituted to make laws more equitable, the data in Table 7.6 reveal how much remains to be done. One of the results of the fiscal limitations on public expenditure is that Mexico still has one of the highest illiteracy rates and poorest systems of secondary education in Latin America. In lieu of an adequate fiscal system the Mexican government has increasingly resorted to the use of monetary policy to channel private savings into public investment. Mexican monetary policy, despite its remarkable success in recent years, is viewed by some officials as a second-best alternative to fiscal reform.

As a larger share of the economy has become monetized and as accounting and reporting procedures have improved in private enterprise, the effectiveness of tax collection has tended to increase as well, without major legislative reforms. This is reflected in the rise in income tax shares from 33 to 42 percent of federal revenue since 1960 (Table 7.6). However, it is unlikely that, without new legislation, the tax structure will become significantly progressive in the

---

rates revisions he proposed would have increased federal revenues from 8.1 to 12.6 million pesos (based on 1957 figures) or from 7 to 11 percent of GDP in that year. He argued in this (suppressed) report that federal revenues should ultimately be increased to from 15 to 16 billion pesos (based on 1957 levels) to permit double the share of federal expenditures in GDP. The report may be taken as an extreme position, as the following excerpt admits:

> I am under no illusion that in the political and social context of Mexico the implementation of these proposals will cause a change that is little short of a social revolution, comparable in nature to that caused by the land reform which followed the Revolution in 1910. [p. 6]

Nevertheless Kaldor's report contained much worthwhile analysis of the level, incidence, and implications of existing tax policies. Its call for reform echoed the sentiments of many Mexican economists of high repute. Unfortunately, the report made no proposals for the effective utilization of the increases in revenue which its policies would have provided. The assumption was always implicit that virtually no constraint existed in terms of government absorptive capacity so that as much as twice the current level of tax revenue might be readily utilized without any major loss in efficiency of public expenditure. Such an assumption can be seriously challenged in terms of the present limitations of the government's administrative apparatus. Nicholas Kaldor, "Report on Mexican Tax Reform" (unpublished).

near future. If and when the share of taxation in GDP begins to rise, attention may be expected to turn to fiscal efficiency. A much higher degree of coordination of public revenue and expenditure policy will be required than has existed in the past, since fiscal planning in Mexico is still in its infancy.[19] The problems of data alone have only begun to be surmounted. Communications among the many branches of government, federal, state, and local, remain weak, although greater liaison has been established in the context of budgetary planning. As communications within the public sector and between the public and private sectors improve, and as more information about the economy becomes available to policy-makers, the efficiency of Mexican planning will undoubtedly increase. One may look forward to effective budgetary planning of the public sector as a precondition for the efficient use of tax and expenditure policy for stabilization and growth. For the time being, indirect controls and monetary policy are being relied upon to regulate the level of aggregate demand.

THE COMPOSITION OF FEDERAL EXPENDITURES, 1940–63

The figures presented above indicate that public expenditures have maintained a relatively low and constant share of GDP. Tax constraints and the desire for monetary stability have been largely responsible for the conservative performance of the public sector. But within a relatively modest total, the composition of government expenditures has varied considerably. In Table 7.2 it was shown that the planned share of government transfer payments rose from an average of less than 10 percent before 1956 to between 20 and 30 percent between 1956 and 1962. In Table 7.7 ex post data indicate that actual transfers were even greater than planned. Transfer payments in this table have been divided between current and capital outlays. The former averaged 10 percent in the 1940s and 20 percent in the 1950s and the latter (representing the acquisition of real estate and the financing of other sectors in the economy) averaged 9 percent in the 1940s and 15 percent in the 1950s.[20] Meanwhile ad-

19. A number of studies have appeared on fiscal policy and planning, including: Miguel Wionczek, "Incomplete Formal Planning:Mexico"; Robert J. Shafer, *Mexico;* and Ifigenia M. de Navarrete, *Los incentivos fiscales.* See also United Nations, ECLA, "Planning in Latin America," and Comité de los Nueve, *Evaluación del Plan de Acción Inmediata de México.*

20. The estimates on which the federal exhaustive expenditure figures on current and capital account are based in Table 7.1 are for budgeted expenditures,

Table 7.7
Level and Distribution of Actual Federal Expenditures, 1940–63
(average percents)

| | Total Federal Expenditures | | Current Expenditures | | Transfers | | | Capital Expenditures | | | | Other |
| | (million current pesos) | (per-cent) | Sum | Adminis-trative Expenses | To Consumption & Investment | Interest on the Debt | Unclassi-fied | Sum | Direct Physical Investment | Acqui-sition of Real Estate | Financing of Other Sectors | Expenses |
Year												
1940	552	100	75	62	7	1	4	25	19	*	6	1
1941–45	942	100	68	54	5	3	6	32	25	*	6	1
1946–50	2,147	100	64	45	11	3	4	36	27	*	9	*
1951–55	5,176	100	54	34	14	4	2	46	28	1	17	1
1956–60	9,548	100	62	37	20	4	1	38	24	*	13	1
1961–63	8,992	100	73	39	28	5	1	27	20	*	7	1

The figures in this table do not correspond to the subtotals of exhaustive and nonexhaustive expenditures of the federal government used to arrive at total government expenditures in Table 7.1, since the figures above are for realized rather than budgetary expenditures of the federal government.

* Less than one percent.
Source: Appendix Table D.2.

ministrative expenditures of the federal government fell from 60 percent of federal outlays to under 40 percent between 1940 and 1963. On the other hand, the share of federal investment in total investment in Mexico has been high, as revealed by Table 7.7. Averaging around 30 percent at the beginning and the end of the period under consideration, the government investment share rose to as high as 40 percent between 1946 and 1955. During the immediate postwar period the government, by conserving on current outlays and especially on transfer payments to households, was able to devote 28 percent of its budget to capital formation. Between 1950 and 1955, capital transfers to private and mixed enterprise averaged an additional 18 percent. We shall see below how this investment was allocated among productive activities. As the more detailed analysis of the regional and sectoral pattern of Mexican development expenditures since 1940 (Chapters 3 to 5) indicates, the initial redirection of public expenditure away from current toward capital outlays in the 1940s and early 1950s was largely responsible for the subsequent high and sustained rate of private investment.

The functional distribution of federal expenditures since 1940 is presented in Table 7.11. It has been noted already that the 1940s and early 1950s were a time of major investment in rural economic infrastructure. This is brought out by the figures that show the share of expenditures in agriculture, transportation, and communications to be relatively high during the 1940s and early 1950s. Expenditures for the promotion of industry and commerce, on the other hand, expanded from 1946–55, while investment expenditures in education and cultural services have only recently begun to increase their relative importance. One factor that has enabled Mexico to get more development out of its tax dollar than most Latin American countries is the low and declining share of military expenditures in total government outlays. These have fallen from 20 percent of federal expenditure to 9 percent between 1940 and 1963. The general administrative budget has also maintained a low share of total expenditures.

The trend in the distribution of public expenditures has been moving toward health, education, and welfare and away from the promotion of agriculture, industry, and transportation and communications.

---

while those in Tables 7.7 and 7.8 are for actual expenditures. Hence the two tables are not strictly comparable. It is likely that the data underlying the estimate of exhaustive capital expenditures of the federal government after 1950 (Table 7.1) inadvertently include some capital transfers as well.

It is apparent that, unless the share of government revenues in GDP increases sharply, government investment in physical (as opposed to human) capital is likely to decline. The ever-increasing Mexican population, confronted with outstanding material progress for almost three decades, is now demanding broader participation in the spoils of growth. If these demands are to be met, expenditures on social infrastructure as well as transfer payments to households must rise as a share of the budget. The only way to which the government then will be able to maintain its extensive share of total domestic investment will be to increase the share of public expenditures in GNP. Otherwise, government physical investment expenditures will be eroded by social outlays, and growth will become increasingly dependent upon the private sector. There is little likelihood that increases in net foreign borrowing by the government can be sustained for very much longer or that the structure of financial intermediaries will accommodate a much larger net transfer of private savings into public investment than presently exists. On the other hand, there is reason to believe that the stage of major public investments in economic infrastructure is passing. Inducements for private investment are now far greater than they were twenty years ago. There is still considerable excess demand for private investment in Mexico. This suggests that, unless new political and social events seriously alter expectations, the private sector might be able to bear a larger share of total investment without serious difficulty.

PUBLIC EXPENDITURE AND ECONOMIC STABILITY

Although the share of public expenditure in aggregate demand has not changed importantly since 1940, year-to-year fluctuations have been considerable. Changes in the composition of public expenditure have probably had an additional disturbing impact on economic stability in Mexico owing to the differing influence of individual components of government spending on the private sector. The relationship between fiscal policy and full employment is too complex to be handled adequately in a volume concerned primarily with growth; instead some suggestions will be made as to relationships between the major components of government expenditure and aggregate demand since 1940 as a stimulus to further research. The previous chapter indicated that among the major exogenous disturbing influences in aggregate demand, exports have fallen as a share of GDP since 1940. Moreover, exports have become increasingly diversified and no longer represent a small number of mineral and agricultural commodities. Tourism and manufactured exports, both of which are far less sensitive to international trade cycles, have greatly increased their share in exports so that trade is less important as a destabilizing influence on GDP. At the same time, the investment share of GDP has risen sharply (from 10 to 20 percent) between 1940 and 1960 (Table 7.8).[21] Whatever investment indicator one uses, the share of total investment in GDP corrected for trend proves to be relatively stable on a year-to-year basis. Nevertheless this is *not* the case for the private and public components of gross investment, as shown in Table 7.9. These shares fluctuate around a downtrend in the relative importance of government investment in total capital formation in Mexico.

The fact that public and private investment move in offsetting directions was at one time taken to suggest that government investment was acting to stabilize the economy following exogenous changes in the level of private expenditure.[22] However, more recent research has produced evidence that reverses the direction of causality, suggesting that it is public expenditure rather than private investment which initially disturbs the level of aggregate demand and that the private sector is then called upon to offset the influence of wide swings in government spending. In response to these disturbances, private investment has been regulated by credit rationing policies of the Central Bank through its manipulation of the reserve requirements of financial intermediaries.[23]

21. Table 7.8 reflects the sensitivity of this crucial indicator to various estimating procedures, both in terms of its magnitude and rate of growth. The first column represents the most recent and reasonable estimates of total investment, using the best price reflator obtainable. It should be noted that the real rate of growth of columns 1 and 2 are the same, the differences arising from the conversion into current prices.

22. This point is made by Raymond Vernon in *The Dilemma of Mexico's Development,* Chapter 4. Vernon's analysis, based upon conventional trade cycle theory in which private investment plays the initiating role, points to the need for government expenditures to compensate for fluctuations in private demand. It suggests that the political constraints under which that country's major party operates prevent the government from having sufficient fiscal flexibility to permit the implementation of effective full employment policies in periods such as the late 1950s and early 1960s.

23. John E. Koehler, "Information and Policy Making: Mexico" (Ph.D. dissertation). Koehler's analysis reveals a significant negative correlation between the independent variable private investment (plus exports minus imports) and alternative independent variables (1) public investment plus government consumption, (2) government consumption, (3) government investment, (4) federal government investment, (5) investment of autonomous or-

Table 7.8
Alternative Measures of Gross Fixed Investment
as a Share of Gross Domestic Product

	Gross Fixed Investment in Mexico				Gross Investment as Share of Gross Domestic Product			
	1	*2*	*3*	*4*	*5*	*6*	*7*	*8*
	Est. A	*Est. B*	*Est. C*	*Est. D*				
	(Cossío)	*(Banco de*						
	(Reynolds)	*México)*	*(Grupo)*	*(Vernon)*	*Est. A*	*Est. B*	*Est. C*	*Est. D*
	1968	*1962*	*1964*	*1963*	*÷ GDP*	*÷ GDP*	*÷ GDP*	*÷ GDP*
Year	*(millions of current pesos)*				*(percentage)*			
1940	702	539	754	793	9.9	7.6	10.6	11.2
1945	1,660	1,486	2,257	2,301	8.4	7.6	11.5	11.7
1950	6,041	4,828	6,041	5,960	14.7	11.8	14.7	14.5
1955	16,674	12,617	11,943[a]	12,560	18.9	14.3	13.5	14.2
1960	33,132	23,226	21,192	21,168	21.3	14.9	13.6	13.6
1962	32,344	24,791	22,552	–[b]	18.0	13.8	12.5	–
1965	[40,843][c]				19.5[c]	–	–	–

[a] This figure includes government budgeted rather than realized investment.

[b] Data not available.

[c] The figure for gross investment and the corresponding GDP estimate are in 1960 pesos, from memo, Banco de México, Departamento de Estudios Económicos, February 1968.

Sources: Columns 1 and 2 are from Table 7.9. The figures in Estimate A represent the most recent unofficial estimates of the Depto. de Estudios Económicos of the Banco de México (Feb. 1968) using the best available reflators for the underlying indexes as explained in Table 7.9. For that reason, this series forms the basis for calculations of investment and the capital stock in the rest of this study. Estimate B is an earlier series of the Banco de México, using less accurate (and lower) reflators.

Column 3: Estimate C corresponds to Estimate II in Banco de México, Departamento de Estudios Económicos, "Alternativas de Estimación de la Inversión Bruta Fija en México, 1939–1962" (mimeographed), and is from Grupo Secretaría de Hacienda-Banco de México, "Manual," Table 3-1. The Grupo Secretaría de Hacienda-Banco de México prepared this series by summing two independently derived series on (1) public investment (from Secretaría de la Presidencia, Dirección de Inversiones Públicas, *México Inversión Pública Federal, 1925–1963;* Banco de México, *Informes Anuales,* etc.) and (2) private investment (from Ortiz Mena, *et al., El Desarrollo Económico de México,* Table 14 for years 1939 to 1950, and Nacional Financiera, Dirección de Investigaciones Económicas, for the years 1951–62). The private investment figures in Est. C since 1950 appear to have a strong and increasing negative bias, causing the total investment in Est. C for 1960 to be 9 percent below Est. B and 36 percent below Est. A.

Column 4: Est. D is the total investment figure from Vernon, *The Dilemma of Mexico's Development,* Table A-3, p. 199. This figure is arrived at like that of Est. C by summing public and private investment, the latter index taken from *Anuarios* of the Nacional Financiera. It also suffers from a negative bias in the private investment share and from independently derived and noncomparable components.

Several reasons may be suggested for the high degree of fluctuation in government investment expenditures: (1) the degree of decentralization and lack of coordination among the government's operating ministries; (2) the tendency of planned budgets to underestimate revenues, permitting considerable discretion in actual expenditure policies;[24] (3) the independent nature of the expenditure criteria of each successive six-year presidential administration; and (4) a major shift in the occupational structure of the government bureaucracy every six years resulting in a time lag between the execution of expenditure proposals and their implementation. Some have gone so far as to suggest that there is a predictable "six-year cycle" in public expenditures which has been described as follows:

In the first year of a six-year presidential term government activity coasts on its previous momentum. The administration takes office in December, but the budget for its first year has already been prepared in September. The outgoing president is reluctant to encumber his successor with large new programs, so this budget will likely be somewhat small. The new administration will be passing time getting organized and planning its particular "style" rather than spending money, so actual first-year expenditures will be low. By the second year, the government will have found its stride and be undertaking its new projects, so expenditures will rise with exceptional speed. For the third, fourth, and fifth years expenditure growth will taper off somewhat. The final year of the administration will be marked by a rush to complete as many of the projects as possible before the end of the term, in part to assure that one's monuments will in fact be finished, in part to give the next president a freer hand.[25]

---

ganisms and state enterprise, and (6) investment of the Federal District government. His data covers the period 1948–65.

24. A detailed analysis of federal budgets and the relationship between stated and actual expenditure policy by presidential administrations since the Revolution is presented in Wilkie, *The Mexican Revolution,* Part 1. Wilkie has disaggregated the accounts of the federal government in terms of projected and actual budgetary expenditure for economic, social, and administrative activities since 1921. The results are then compared with actual statements of policy by the respective presidents through 1963. The classifications used in his study are different from those above and do not break down expenditures into current and capital or exhaustive and nonexhaustive outlays. Nevertheless, they offer useful insights into the economic and social implications of very different presidential administrations.

25. Koehler, "Information and Policy Making," p. 17, cf. Wilkie, *The Mexican Revolution,* p. 107.

Table 7.9

Alternative Measures of Gross Fixed Investment and the Share of Direct Government Investment in Mexico: 1939–62

	1	2	3	4	5	6
	Total Gross Fixed Investment in Mexico		Government Exhaustive Investment Expenditures in Mexico	Government Exhaustive Investment plus Investment of Wholly or Partially-Owned Government Enterprises	Direct Government Investment as Share of Gross Investment	Investment of Government and Government Enterprise as Share of Gross Investment
Year	Estimate A	Estimate B			$(3) \div (1) = (5)$	$(4) \div (1) = (5)$
			(millions of current pesos)		(percent)	
1939	429	359	159	265	36.9	61.7
1940	702	539	189	336	26.9	47.9
1941	953	717	262	384	27.5	40.3
1942	857	680	275	493	32.1	57.5
1943	825	749	322	522	39.1	63.3
1944	1,183	979	487	724	41.2	61.2
1945	1,660	1,486	561	950	33.8	57.2
1946	2,965	2,442	569	1,130	19.2	38.1
1947	3,797	3,046	820	1,429	21.6	37.6
1948	4,087	3,358	1,050	1,641	25.7	40.2
1949	4,610	4,009	1,141	1,964	24.8	42.6
1950	6,041	4,828	1,392	2,524	23.0	41.8
1951	9,165	6,907	1,561	3,027	17.0	33.0
1952	10,721	8,188	1,870	3,501	17.4	32.7
1953	11,006	8,117	1,642	3,268	14.9	29.7
1954	12,676	10,076	2,156	4,388	16.7	34.1
1955	16,674	12,617	2,189	4,677	13.1	28.0
1956	22,235	16,803	2,344	4,910	10.5	22.1
1957	25,429	19,192	2,946	5,991	11.6	23.6

Table 7.9—Continued

	1	2	3	4	5	6
	Total Gross Fixed Investment in Mexico		Government Exhaustive Investment Expenditures in Mexico	Government Exhaustive Investment plus Investment of Wholly or Partially-Owned Government Enterprises	Direct Government Investment as Share of Gross Investment	Investment of Government and Government Enterprise as Share of Gross Investment
Year	Estimate A	Estimate B			$(3) \div (1) = (5)$	$(4) \div (1) = (5)$
			(millions of current pesos)		(percent)	
1958	25,122	18,926	2,933	6,527	11.7	26.0
1959	27,385	19,584	3,207	6,880	11.7	25.1
1960	33,132	23,226	3,175	8,779	9.6	26.5
1961	32,829	24,071	3,178	9,893	9.7	30.1
1962	32,344	24,791	3,496	10,573	10.8	32.7

Sources: Columns 1 and 2 correspond to Estimates III and I, respectively, of memo by Cossío, "Alternativas de Estimación de la Inversión Bruta Fija en México, 1939–1962," Table 17. Both estimates are based on a physical investment index composed of four components: construction and installations, capital goods imports, domestic production of machinery and equipment, and clearing of land. Estimate I, used in earlier published reports of the Banco de México, uses lower reflators than Estimate III for both capital goods imports and the current value of construction activity. Thus the rate of growth of Estimate III in current prices (our A) is considerably higher than that of Estimate I (our B), although the growth rates of the underlying real indexes are the same. The absolute level of investment in Estimate III is higher than I, since the latter excludes costs of repair, replacement, and reconstruction. It should be noted that still a third estimate of gross investment in current prices based upon the summation of independently derived indexes of private-public investment was used by Vernon in *The Dilemma of Mexico's Development*, Table A-3, p. 199, and Chart 3, p. 100. The private investment total in this estimate is from annual reports of the Nacional Financiera. The total thus derived appears to seriously understate the level of investment in 1960 compared with estimates I and III above. Since the figure for public investment is not different from those used in the present analysis, this would suggest that the Nacional Financiera figures severely underestimate the rate of growth of private investment since 1950. The level of investment in 1950 in the Vernon study (5,960) corresponds to that of Estimate A above (6,041), whereas Vernon's figure for 1960 is 21,168 compared to 33,132 above.

Column 3 above is from Table 7.1, column 2.

Column 4 is the sum of column 3 and Table 7.4, column 2.

The hypothesis that the rate of growth of public expenditures is "relatively high from the first to the second year, lower from the second to the fifth, and high again from the fifth to the sixth," [26] seems to be supported by actual expenditure data for the presidential administrations of Cárdenas (1935–40), Avila Camacho (1941–46), Alemán (1947–52), Ruíz Cortines (1953–58), and López Mateos (1959–64). As Koehler shows, years two and three of each term are above the trend line eleven out of twelve times, whereas years four and five are below the trend nine out of twelve times.[27] These results are sufficient to reject the null hypothesis that the two classifications of expenditures are independent and that their observations are distributed randomly in response to random movements in private autonomous expenditures.

Whether or not exogenous changes in public expenditure follow a predictable six-year pattern, one must still explain why private investment outlays appear to be stabilizing. The answer to this lies beyond the realm of fiscal policy. A full discussion of the stabilizing influence of monetary policy through its influence on the rationing of investable funds to the private sector cannot be included here and is now the subject of a growing literature.[28] We shall touch only briefly on the matter so as to set fiscal policy in proper historical perspective.

Since 1950, the Mexican Central Bank has stabilized the nominal rate of interest in the economy by fixing the discount rate at approximately 10 percent. As the rate of inflation has declined from well over 10 percent to only a few percentage points per annum, the real rate of interest (for those able to obtain investable funds at the official rate) has risen from zero in the early 1950s to 10 to 12 percent in recent years. Despite the rise in real borrowing rates, excess demand for investable funds continues to exist. Credit has therefore been allocated by financial intermediaries to those sectors favored for treatment by the federal government. By regressing the profit share of GDP on lagged investment in the economy as a whole, one author estimates the incremental gross rate of return on capital to be "at least 30 percentage points above the possible rate of interest." [29] In view of the fact that effective tax rates as a share of corporate profits are much less than the nominal rate of 40 percent and almost cer-

---

26. Koehler, p. 17.
27. Koehler, pp. 18–21.
28. Ref. Chapter 7, footnote 2.
29. Koehler, pp. 36 ff.

tainly well under 20 percent of gross profits, continuing excess investment demand in the private sector is understandable. Although the marginal rate of return on capital after taxes and risk discounts is undoubtedly well below the average rate, there is little question that the official interest rates have been kept at a below-equilibrium level throughout most of the period under discussion. By pegging the prime borrowing rate and thereby causing excess demand for investable funds, monetary authorities have been able to ration credit by varying the level of deposits that financial intermediaries must maintain in the Central Bank.[30] By adjusting these reserve requirements to changes in the total level of liquidity (bank deposits and foreign exchange reserves) and the price level (wholesale price and cost of living indexes), the Central Bank has been able to raise or lower the amount of private investment so as to counteract fluctuations in aggregate demand brought about by government spending and export sales.

The increased price stability, fixed exchange rate since 1954, and free convertibility enjoyed by the Mexican economy have tended to reduce exchange risk, permitting the interest on prime borrowing to rise above international rates of return. Foreign credit has accordingly increased rapidly since 1954. This has meant that internal controls on liquidity could potentially have been offset by fluctuations in both short- and long-term borrowing abroad. To counter this effect, an additional arm of stabilization policy has been government regulation of foreign direct investment, borrowing by government and mixed enterprises abroad, and a high reserve requirement for foreign exchange deposits. By regulating investment expenditure at home and borrowing from abroad, the government is now able to exercise a high degree of control over aggregate demand. This has provided a weapon to use whenever public expenditures destabilize the system. Internal stabilization policy has therefore relied for its effectiveness,

30. Koehler notes that the marginal reserve ratio rather than the average ratio is varied to prevent banks from having to recall loans.

The reserve regulations have been adjusted more than 30 times since 1950, on occasion to 100 per cent for certain liabilities and institutions. Furthermore, the information on which manipulation of the reserve ratio is based is timely and accurate; the two indicators, the supply of money and Banco de México holdings of gold and foreign exchange, are known precisely with negligible lags—28 days at the most in the case of the money supply, immediately in the case of foreign exchange. ["Information and Policy Making," p. 39]

not upon fluctuations in the rate of interest, but upon selective reserve requirements. In this case, as in the reliance on quotas as an instrument of commercial policy, the use of direct controls, while generally acknowledged by economists to be inconsistent with allocative efficiency, has served well in accomplishing the objective of price stability and balance of payments equilibrium. It is possible that the maintenance of a fixed exchange rate and a fixed rate of return on prime borrowing has improved the expectations of private investors, so that the loss of efficiency which these policies entailed has been more than offset by a higher internal rate of savings and domestic investment than might otherwise have occurred.

PUBLIC EXPENDITURES AND GROWTH

Although consistent data on government investment are available for the period since 1940, the same is not true for the private sector. As a result, several semiofficial indexes of total investment in the economy have been prepared (independently from those of public investment) which show rather wide deviations one from another, as Tables 7.8 and 7.9 reveal. Before Estimates A and B in Table 7.9 were available, economists concluded that the public share of total investment was rising steadily in the 1950s.[31] Now that these more reliable figures on gross investment exist, it is necessary to modify those conclusions. In Table 7.9 the share of direct government investment in gross investment based on Estimate A was 27 percent in 1940, 23 percent in 1950, and 10 percent in 1960. Furthermore, the investment of government and government enterprises as a share of gross investment was 48 percent in 1940, 42 percent in 1950, and 27 percent in 1960. If such calculations had relied only on the earlier figures for gross investment (Estimate D), the share of direct investment of

31. For example, Professor Vernon used Estimate D (Table 7.8) in his Chart 3, *Dilemma of Mexico's Development*, p. 100, to show the increase in importance of public over private investment during the late 1950s. He regarded this as an indication that private investment was not increasing sufficiently to permit sustained growth, and that as a result public investment would have to continue to expand its share of total capital formation if growth was to be maintained. He used this as partial evidence for the major conclusion of his book that Mexican policy-makers faced a dilemma as to financing and administration of "necessary" increases in the share of public investment. While there is some evidence from Table 7.9, column 6 that total public investment did increase its share of gross investment between 1956 and 1962, the earlier figure (22.1 percent) was far below that of 1940 (47.9 percent), 1950 (41.8 percent), or 1955 (28.0 percent).

government and government enterprises of 42 percent in 1940 would have remained at the same level in 1950 and 1960. It is obvious from the foregoing that an unambiguous evaluation of the overall impact of public investment on growth is impossible due to the complexity of interactions as well as the measurement problems involved. One may conclude, however, from Table 7.9, column 5, that direct government investment continues to play a significant though decreasing role in total capital formation. This is supported by the analysis of the preceding section, which suggests that considerable excess demand for investment still exists in the private sector. Meanwhile, investments of government enterprise have increased as a share of gross investment, offsetting the decline in direct government expenditure since 1950 and particularly from 1955 to 1962 (column 6).

Little more than this can be said about the government share of investment until considerably more basic research on Mexican capital formation is undertaken. An independent study should be made of the recent history of public and private savings to provide consistency checks on alternative investment series. Measures of the capital stock in Mexico, most of which have depended until now upon the application of hypothetical depreciation rates to alternative investment indexes, are also subject to the findings of such research. Attempts should be made to reconcile independent measures of capital formation by economic activity (such as those made in this study for agriculture and manufacturing) with series on total fixed reproducible assets. Until then, the importance of public investment in Mexican development will be difficult if not impossible to ascertain with any degree of precision. Because of these problems, the present study relies heavily upon sectoral disaggregation of the role of public expenditure, with particular emphasis on agriculture and manufacturing. In each instance government investment has played a crucial role in breaking bottlenecks and permitting social returns to be realized by providing external economies to private investors.

In addition to the expansion of physical capital, public expenditure on human capital continues to rise. The level of total government investment in education for selected years since 1925 is presented in Table 7.10. Federal investment in education tripled in the 1940s and increased by six times in the 1950s, illustrating a trend toward a much higher share of government expenditure on human capital in recent years. The regional pattern of investment in primary education has expanded in rather more balanced fashion than secondary, tech-

Table 7.10
Primary Students Registered in Public Schools and
Annual Federal Investment in Education, 1925–60

Year	Primary Students Registered in Public Schools (number)	(1925 = 100)	Annual Federal Investment in Education (thousands of 1950 pesos)
1925	1,034,353	100	4,000
1930	1,367,849	132	7,000
1935	1,817,498	176	8,000
1940	1,994,602	193	9,000
1945	2,705,725	262	14,000
1950	3,026,691	293	29,000
1955	3,936,028	381	48,000
1960	5,401,509	522	191,900[a]

[a] This figure is expressed in thousands of 1960 pesos.

Sources: Registered Students: *Anuarios Estadísticos* for selected years. The 1925 figure is for enrollment of all public schools in Mexico. For 1930 and 1935 the total includes enrollment in public kindergarten, primary, secondary and preparatory, normal, and technical public schools. For 1940 and 1945, total includes only kindergarten and primary school enrollment. For 1950, 1955, and 1960, the figures represent the population of primary school age receiving an education.

Investment in Education: Totals for the years 1925–50 are from Secretaría de la Presidencia, Dirección de Inversiones Públicas, *México Inversión Pública Federal, 1925–1963*, Table 6, pp. 47–52; the 1960 figure is from Table 12, p. 119.

nical, and higher education, for which there has been an increasing concentration of expenditures in the Federal District and Nuevo León. One observer has written:

> In 1960, the Federal District, with only 13.9 per cent of the national population, had 53 percent of all people with 12 years of education or more and 56.2 percent of all people with 16 years of education or more. Nuevo Leon and the District combined, with 17 percent of the national population, had 59.1 percent of the former group, and 62 percent of the latter. Moreover, it is certain that the concentration of educated people in the advanced areas, and particularly in the Federal District, has been a constant feature of the pattern of human resource development in Mexico.[32]

Table 7.11 shows that outlays on education and cultural services

32. Charles N. Myers, *Education and National Development in Mexico*, pp. 111–12.

Table 7.11
Functional Distribution of Federal Expenditures

Year	Total Federal Expenditures (million current pesos)	(per cent)	Transportation & Communications	Agriculture, Cattle & Forestry Development	Promotion of Industry & Commerce	Educational & Cultural Services	Hospitals & Health Services	Welfare & Social Security	Army, Navy, & Military Services	General Administration	Public Debt	Other Expenditures
							(percent)					
1940	551.9	100.0	16.6	12.9	4.4	13.5	7.1	3.0	20.7	16.1	5.7	—
1941	613.6	100.0	18.6	15.8	5.0	12.4	7.3	7.4	19.8	11.6	2.1	—
1942	761.2	100.0	26.5	16.6	5.0	11.1	7.3	2.4	18.9	9.5	2.7	—
1943	934.2	100.0	28.8	15.0	3.2	10.1	6.3	5.8	18.5	9.4	2.9	—
1944	1,079.5	100.0	24.5	17.4	4.8	12.1	6.3	2.7	17.9	9.5	4.8	—
1945	1,320.6	100.0	18.6	18.0	4.0	13.0	7.3	2.5	15.6	15.6	5.4	—
1946	1,463.3	100.0	19.9	15.4	7.4	13.6	4.1	8.6	13.2	11.4	6.4	—
1947	1,762.8	100.0	22.3	17.5	3.0	11.1	6.0	4.7	14.9	11.0	9.5	—
1948	2,178.3	100.0	25.8	13.4	11.8	10.6	5.1	2.6	12.4	13.8	4.5	—
1949	2,530.9	100.0	30.7	14.8	7.5	12.3	4.9	3.0	11.8	11.1	3.9	—
1950	2,795.9	100.0	25.7	12.5	18.0	11.1	4.6	3.8	10.9	9.1	4.3	—
1951	3,703.2	100.0	23.0	12.3	21.9	10.0	4.0	3.6	9.5	11.3	4.4	—
1952	5,069.8	100.0	25.4	16.6	14.2	9.8	3.6	3.9	8.7	13.7	4.1	—
1953	4,662.5	100.0	23.7	15.4	21.9	10.8	3.7	3.7	9.7	7.6	3.5	—
1954	5,854.2	100.0	22.4	17.1	16.2	12.2	3.9	4.3	9.1	11.5	3.3	—
1955	6,590.5	100.0	25.5	15.0	13.6	11.9	4.5	4.1	8.2	12.6	3.4	1.2
1956	7,752.1	100.0	19.7	12.8	18.0	12.2	4.7	4.0	8.3	16.1	4.0	0.2
1957	8,595.0	100.0	23.7	12.8	15.4	12.3	5.6	4.0	9.3	11.2	5.5	0.2
1958	9,485.4	100.0	25.8	12.1	11.4	13.7	5.6	4.6	9.2	13.2	4.3	0.1
1959	9,979.7	100.0	22.8	11.7	15.6	15.1	5.6	5.2	8.9	11.3	3.7	0.1
1960	11,927.8	100.0	21.0	10.8	13.3	16.5	5.3	6.2	9.3	12.6	4.9	0.1
1961	13,311.4	100.0	20.4	10.1	12.7	16.9	4.8	6.9	9.0	12.9	6.2	0.1
1962	14,839.5	100.0	18.1	12.8	12.7	17.2	4.7	8.1	8.9	11.7	5.7	0.1
1963	16,806.7	100.0	19.2	11.7	10.5	20.4	5.1	8.6	9.1	11.3	4.0	—

Source: Grupo Secretaría de Hacienda-Banco de México, "Manual," Table 6-8.

(of which investment in education is only a part) have risen from 14 percent of federal expenditures in 1940 to 20 percent in 1963. An independent estimate shows the share of total public and private educational expenditures in GNP for 1962 to have been 7 percent, suggesting that a much higher proportion of the cost of education is borne by students and their families in Mexico than in most developed countries.[33] Estimates of the return to total expenditure on education by year of schooling, by Martin Carnoy, indicate that the marginal rate rises to a peak at the sixth year, declines gradually to the thirteenth year, and then rises sharply again for years 14 to 16, particularly for those who have completed a university education. These findings differ from those of the United States, where the marginal rates of return on educational expenditure decline steadily from the eighth grade through the completion of university.[34] Carnoy has estimated both the social and private internal rate of return to expenditure on education for 1963 by year of schooling.[35] The social internal rate of return reaches a peak of 37.5 percent for grades five to six, falls steadily to 12.4 percent for years 12 to 13 and then rises to 29.5 percent for years 14 to 16. The private internal rate of return is, of course, significantly higher (since it excludes the costs of education borne by the state) rising to 48.6 percent for years five to six, falling to 15.8 percent for years 12 to 13, and rising again to 36.7 percent for years 14 to 16. The institutional investment per student year in pesos (1963) is shown to rise sharply in terms of the level of education, from 414 pesos for primary to 2,082 pesos for secondary and 3,720 pesos for university education.

These rates of return suggest that, in spite of the significant opportunity cost of schooling to Mexican youngsters and their families,[36]

33. Martin Carnoy, "The Cost and Return to Schooling in Mexico: A Case Study" (Ph.D. dissertation).

34. The U.S. comparison is from W. Lee Hansen, "Total and Private Rates of Return to Investment in Schooling," as cited in Carnoy, "Cost and Return to Schooling in Mexico," p. 5.

35. These calculations do not include any estimate of the consumption returns or external economies arising from education. The figures remain high even after adjustment for father's occupation (which is highly correlated with years of schooling). Hansen, p. 5.

36. This is reflected in the estimates, since the peak in return to education is two years earlier in Mexico than in the U.S. (five to six rather than seven to eight years of schooling). This is because half of the investment costs in Mexico at years seven to eight represent income foregone, whereas this factor in nil in the U.S. for the same number of years of schooling. The return in Mexico to seven to eight years of education is somewhat less than that of the

government expenditures in both primary and secondary education are extremely productive in terms of alternative rates of return on capital and could reasonably be much higher than at present if fiscal circumstances permitted. This conclusion is supported by UN data on educational attainment levels in Latin America as of 1960 (Table 7.12). In that year Mexico ranked among the poorest countries in the hemisphere in terms of the share of population having at least a minimum level of schooling. Seventy-three percent of males and 76 percent of females, over the age of twenty-five, had less than four years of education. While the recent record has been much better than these figures suggest, they illustrate the large backlog of investment in human resources yet to be made in Mexico. This is true not only for the share of the population in school, or for the average number of years of schooling per pupil, but more particularly for the *quality* of education. Standards in the past have been extremely low at all levels. Recent academic reforms, particularly under the past two presidential administrations, have met with considerable success despite some opposition from a minority of students and faculty who might be disadvantaged by higher standards. But much remains to be done.

The financing of education is most appropriately accomplished through taxation, since a large share of the benefits accrue to society at large. But the limitations of Mexico's fiscal system, as described above, have made it necessary to finance additional government investment outlays with loans from the private sector that require repayment out of profits. This has produced a financial constraint on government investment, tending to direct public expenditure toward those projects which are most likely to become self-supporting. This works against federal aid to education. Improvement in the effectiveness of taxation would do much to permit an even greater share of GDP to be devoted to public educational expenditures than is now the case. Mass education and improvements in the quality of education may be expected to bring about broader social participation in the benefits of economic growth. A broadening of the capital stock in Mexico to include a greater share of human resources at all levels will facilitate the redistribution of income by widening the distribution of labor skills. This may be expected also to increase the produc-

---

U.S. for the same period (23.4 percent social rate of return for Mexico, 29.2 percent for the U.S.). Carnoy, "Cost and Return to Schooling in Mexico," p. 81.

Table 7.12
Percentage Distribution of Male and Female Population 25 Years of Age and Over
by Educational Attainment in Selected Latin American Countries

Country & Year	Male					Female				
	Population 25 Years and Over (thousands)	Less than First Level[a]	Percentage First Level[b]	Second Level[c]	Third Level[d]	Population 25 Years and Over (thousands)	Less than First Level[a]	Percentage First Level[b]	Second Level[c]	Third Level[d]
Mexico 1960[e]	5,199	73	24	2.4	1.4	5,285	76	22	1.7	0.3
Argentina[f] 1947	4,884	37	58	3.6	1.4	4,556	40	55	4.8	0.2
Bolivia[g,h] 1950	1,110	81	15[i]	3.2[i]	1.0[i]	1,168	88	9.5[i]	2.2[i]	0.1[i]
Brazil[h] 1950	9,895	78	17[i]	3.2[i]	1.4[i]	9,861	81	15[i]	3.1[i]	0.1[i]
Chile 1952	1,246	21[j]	56[j]	19[j]	3.4[j]	1,333	26[j]	54[j]	19[j]	1.4[j]
1960	1,457	41	45	12	2.3	1,583	43	46	11	0.9
Colombia 1951	1,200	55	37	6.0	2.0	1,092	50	44	6.1	0.2
Ecuador 1950	602	68	27	3.1	1.1	635	76	23	1.5	0.1
1962[k,l]	1,667	64[m]	26[m]	8.1[m]	1.3[m]	—[r]	—	—	—	—
Paraguay[h] 1950	231	75	23	2.1	0.7	265	83	16	0.8	0.1
Peru[n] 1961	1,725	26[j]	56[j]	12[j]	3.9	1,835	56[j]	34[j]	7.9[j]	1.4[j]
Uruguay[o] 1963	711	61[p]	28[p]	9.0[p]	2.2[p]	739	56[p]	32[p]	9.1[p]	0.8[p]
Venezuela[h] 1950	988	72	24[q]	3.0[q]	1.8[q]	967	80	18[q]	1.7[q]	0.3[q]

Table 7.12—*Continued*

[a] In general, persons having completed less than 4 years at the first level of education, including illiterates and persons without formal schooling.

[b] In general, persons having completed 4 years or more at first level of education but less than 4 years at second level.

[c] In general, persons having completed 4 years or more at second level of education but less than 4 years at third.

[d] In general, persons having completed 4 years or more at third level of education.

[e] Thirty years and over.

[f] Twenty years and over.

[g] Five years and over.

[h] Excluding tribal or jungle Indian population.

[i] Including persons having completed an unstated number of years respectively in primary, secondary, and higher education.

[j] These figures refer to persons who possess respectively: no certificate; primary school certificate; secondary school cerificate; higher education degree or diploma.

[k] Excluding Indian jungle population, data are based on a 3 percent sample of census returns and refer to male and female population.

[l] Data by level of education refer to literate persons who are attending or have attended school; illiterate population is included with "Unknown."

[m] Data refer respectively to persons who have completed 4 years or more of primary education, 6 years or more of secondary education, 5 years or more of higher education.

[n] Based on approximately 15 percent sample of census returns. Excluding Indian jungle population estimated at 455,000 in 1960.

[o] Data are based on a 5 percent sample of census returns.

[p] Data refer respectively to persons with no schooling or having completed 0–5 years of primary education, 6 years of primary education and 1–3 years of secondary education, first cycle, 4 years of secondary education, first cycle, those who are attending or have attended secondary agricultural or trade school and those having completed 3 years of higher education including those who have completed secondary education second cycle (usually 2 years), 4 years or more of higher education. "Unknown" includes persons who have attended or are attending military school.

[q] Including persons having completed an unstated number of years respectively in primary, secondary, and higher education.

[r] Data not available.

Source: United Nations Statistical Office, *Compendium of Social Statistics: 1967*, Table 33, pp. 338, 341–42.

tivity of plant and equipment, much of which is being underutilized due to shortages of skilled labor. Such an investment policy will tend to unite the objectives of economic growth and social progress in a positive manner.

The pace of Mexican fiscal development has been relatively slow. Government spending as a share of gross domestic product has not risen significantly for thirty years, despite rapid growth of the rest of the economy. Moreover, the share of public demand for goods and services has declined as a share of GDP, while that of government transfer payments has increased significantly. Hence the characteristic pattern of relatively rapid growth of the public sector in Latin America has not been borne out by the Mexican case. This has been due in part to the failure of taxation to keep pace with structural change. Those sectors of economic activity that traditionally contribute the largest share of tax revenues have lagged, while tax incentives have been used to stimulate the growth of leading sectors. Slow growth within the public sector has also been due to the favorable growth of private investment, which has reduced the relative need for government outlays. Meanwhile, an ever-expanding share of public investment has been financed out of private savings rather than taxes.

Within the limits described above (and some might argue because of this fiscal restraint), Mexico's public expenditure policy has been successful in increasing the rates of capital formation and growth in both agriculture and industry. Public investment has maintained a high and sustained share of total government outlays since the late 1930s. Expenditures on public administration and defense have been kept within tight limits, as have transfer payments to households. Government investment in power, transportation, and communications provided external economies that stimulated private investment in manufacturing and commerce. In recent years the government has turned to public education, a hitherto neglected sector, to reduce skilled labor bottlenecks that are increasingly responsible for the underutilization of plant and equipment.

Resource allocation in Mexico, while strongly influenced by government spending, has been somewhat distorted in recent years. There is evidence that public expenditure policies have produced over-investment in physical infrastructure, plant, and equipment and under-investment in human resources. Because of its policies in the 1940s and early 1950s, Mexico continues to lag behind the rest of Latin America in terms of the quantity as well as quality of education of its population. The result is a higher physical capital/output ratio and a smaller participation of society in the benefits of growth than would have been true had educational needs been met earlier. The social and political legacies of this allocative shortcoming remain to be fully appreciated, although it is already clear that education has created a demand for wider participation in the political process.

The impact of government spending on economic stability has been negative in recent years. As traditional exports have decreased their share of GDP along with their disturbing influence on final demand, government investment has become the most important destabilizing element in the economy. Public expenditures have fluctuated according to a "presidential cycle" independent of the level of private demand; an unprogressive tax structure has failed to provide built-in stabilizers. Hence the burden of income stabilization policy has fallen on monetary authorities. In earlier years, monetary stabilization policy was not conspicuously successful and growth was accompanied by excess demand, with high rates of inflation and periodic balance of payments crises typical of most of the major Latin American countries. Since the mid-1950s, however, the Central Bank has been increasingly able to influence the level of private investment spending through manipulation of the reserve requirements of financial intermediaries. As a result, fluctuations in export earnings and government investment have continued with less inflation and fewer prolonged periods of unemployment. Despite the favorable response of monetary authorities to the challenges presented by fiscal limitations, there is reason to believe that much would be gained by bringing Mexican fiscal policy up to the level of efficiency of the economy as a whole.

Epilogue

As an example of rapid economic growth in a mixed enterprise system, the Mexican experience cannot be ignored, however much one may question facts and interpretation. Under post-Revolutionary governments, the advantages of private initiative have been combined with far-sighted public expenditure and indicative planning policies to steer the economy through three initial decades of political crisis, economic recession, and institutional reform into three subsequent decades of rapid growth. In the process, certain economic sectors and interest groups gained at the expense of others. Numerous restrictions were imposed on commerce and investment. Foreign capital was subjected to strict control and in some cases nationalized. Mining and the extractive industries in general were allowed to stagnate, while manufacturing was favored with public participation, protection from foreign competition, and low interest loans. Commercial agriculture received massive public investments—but only after the old latifundia system had been broken by one of the most sweeping agrarian reforms in history. These policies broadened participation of the population in the market economy, permitting gains in both productivity and social welfare. Yet the share of the public sector in GDP has remained relatively constant over the past thirty years while private enterprise has been permitted to prosper. Mexico therefore represents an economy that has combined the advantages of both worlds, individual economic freedom together with political regulation in the public interest.

In order to explain and evaluate the pattern of contemporary Mexico economic development, this study has relied on what might be termed an historical-inductive approach to development theorizing. Rather than testing a priori development hypotheses, it has taken as a point of departure an examination of the principal economic variables, placed in the framework of a relatively straightforward growth model. Output has been related to inputs of labor, capital, and natural resources, with regional as well as sectoral disaggregation providing supporting detail. Once these basic relationships have been examined and the share of growth explained by traditional inputs estimated, the unexplained residual has then been related to the specific historical-institutional framework within which growth occurred. An attempt has been made to determine (1) what additional inputs including economic factors and technological change as well as social, political, and psychological factors may account for the unexplained component of growth, and (2) what factors might have produced variations in the level of crucial parameters such as savings and investment propensities as well as shifts in these parameters over time.

The growth in Mexican per capita output since 1910 has been shown to have resulted primarily from increases in labor, capital, and natural resources employed in commercial agriculture and manufacturing, plus a shift of labor from lower to higher productivity occupations. This expansion in output took place together with an accelerated rate of population growth (except for setbacks during the Revolution), rapid urbanization, and increased absorption of labor in the service sector. Statistics on output per worker in tertiary activities since 1940 indicate that per capita income in this sector grew even more rapidly than that of agriculture or industry despite the major shift of labor into services in recent decades.

In agriculture, capital formation began with large public investments in roads, dams, and irrigation systems. Since the geographical distribution of these expenditures was quite unbalanced, the regional pattern of per capita output has remained skewed. Private investment in agriculture responded favorably to economic incentives created by public works, but both depended for their success upon technological innovations in earth-moving, construction, highway building, and improvements in farm machinery, pesticides, and crop dusting, as well as new seed varieties developed in recent years. Thus Mexico's agricultural revolution was due in part to twentieth-century improvements in production techniques developed abroad and applied to local land and water resources.

The impressive growth of agricultural production which has been observed since 1940 depended on a net flow of savings via the public sector into agriculture, at the beginning of the period. However, this flow appears now to have reversed as rental income and foreign exchange earnings from rural development are helping to support the expansion of industry and services. Yet almost as many persons are found in subsistence agriculture today as in 1910, living at a standard not significantly above that of their pre-Columbian or Colonial ancestors; projecting on the basis of past performance, the turning point in rural marginal productivity lies well in the future. In this respect, although the agrarian reform program did much to provide income security for thousands of landless peasants, it has yet to realize its ultimate objective of social welfare for all campesinos.

Capital formation in manufacturing since 1940 has benefited from improved technology introduced from the United States, England, Western Europe, and more recently Japan. There has been little subsequent adaptation of this technology to fit Mexican conditions, and most of the imported equipment is still far less productive than that of the home country, though some branches of Mexican industry seem to be on the verge of international competitiveness. High profits in manufacturing due to import protection have attracted both domestic and foreign investors to all levels of the production process from final products to intermediate and capital goods. Bottlenecks have been broken quickly by government and mixed enterprise, and entrepreneurship has not been lacking in Mexico since the Revolution.

With a few exceptions, including the state-run petroleum industry, the extractive industries have been allowed to stagnate. Much revenue that might have been obtained from the economic rents of subsoil resources was foregone through the neglect of this sector. In view of the history of foreign domination of the Mexican mining industry and the popular disfavor into which such arrangements fell at the time of the Revolution, the political justification for its neglect is understandable. The economic justification involved a desire to reduce the country's sensitivity to fluctuations in the world market and foreign control, to diversify the structure of production, and to widen the internal market through the encouragement of alternative activities that entailed a broader distribution of income. Because of the relatively small number of linkages that mining provides, it was felt that the loss to domestic growth would be minimal. Therefore the development of infrastructure after 1910 shifted away from public works to serve the mining industry toward dams and irrigation systems, highways, feeder roads, power and telecommunications networks all of which linked the internal market and opened up new regions to trade. While these expenditures tended to benefit the export of cash crops and tourism, they were also productive of increased gains from internal trade.

The service sector remains something of an enigma. Productivity gains in tertiary production have outstripped both agriculture and manufacturing since 1940, if the statistics are to be believed, and services have absorbed most of the labor released from the rural sector. So many levels of productivity are lumped together under services, and such different capital and labor requirements are implicit in each, that generalization about the development of this sector is impossible. Since it is not customary among Latin American countries for services as a whole to achieve major productivity gains, an in-depth analysis of this sector is a priority item for future scholars despite the scanty and somewhat tenuous nature of the data available on service output, employment, and investment. The analytical difficulties are further complicated by a paucity of economic theory that relates the growth of specific services to the expansion of other key sectors of the economy, including agriculture and manufacturing.

Almost certainly the Mexican experience reflects gains from increased internal trade and specialization as well as improved financial intermediation. This is reflected in the value added of domestic services, which has risen as a share of gross domestic product as internal trade has increased relative to trade in exports. Furthermore, the growth of Mexican tourism, which has responded to large government investments in recent years, has had a disproportionate influence on the growth of value added in this sector. In addition, a high-income elasticity of demand for services on the part of the middle class has permitted productivity gains in agriculture and manufacturing to be passed on to workers in tertiary employment through a multiplier effect that has increased with the pace of urbanization.

The composition of foreign trade is one of the best indicators of changes in a nation's structure of production relative to the pattern of final demand, since trade is a residual category in which commodities in excess supply at home are exported while those in excess demand are imported, subject to public policy. The changing pattern of Mexican trade clearly reflects the natural growth process of the country by which capital, skilled labor, and technology have increased relative to natural resources and unskilled labor. It also reflects the application of a succession of changing and occasionally inconsistent

public policies that have shaped the economy since 1910. Among
exports, the shares of minerals and traditional agricultural commodities have fallen sharply, while those of new cash crops, tourism,
and manufactures have risen. The import shares of foodstuffs and
consumer goods have fallen, while those of capital and intermediate
goods have increased over time. On capital account, the economy in
recent years has increasingly become a net borrower, reflecting a
relatively high domestic return on investment, entrepreneurship, and
skilled labor. As net capital inflows have offset the deficit on current
account in recent years, the balance of payments has on average enjoyed a surplus permitting substantial accumulation of foreign exchange reserves.

The current account deficit is widening each year, however, while
the service of foreign investment represents an increasingly burden-
some share of Mexico's capacity to import. The economy is accordingly reaching a point at which it will become necessary either to
force greater efficiency in domestic manufacturing so as to increase
exports of industrial goods or to expand mineral exports or both.
While such possibilities seem to be well within the productive potential of the economy, the former would require the dissolution of a
number of unprofitable enterprises that presently rely on a high level
of protection for their survival and exercise a significant political influence; the latter would call for a more positive approach to the use
of the "national patrimony" of mineral resources than has previously been possible. Either prospect calls for the acceptance of
increased Mexican exports by the U.S., Latin American, and European markets. As of 1970 Mexico does not suffer from a serious
foreign exchange bottleneck and no strong immediate pressure on
the balance of payments exists, although attempts to increase the
efficiency of manufacturing through reduced protection might require
a slight reduction in the exchange rate, which has remained un-
changed since 1954. On the other hand, if U.S. inflation continues
at the present rate, the Mexican peso may be able to withstand
pressures for devaluation indefinitely.

Much of the foregoing is descriptive rather than explanatory; it
remains necessary to show *why* Mexico was able to achieve so rapid
a rate of growth in recent years compared to the rest of Latin
America. The high rate of internal savings and investment that has
been sustained since the 1940s, along with the relatively large amount
of public and private investment in agriculture, represents a unique
phenomenon in the hemisphere. Government investment was due in

large part to the revolutionary mandate that broadly based agricultural development and rural welfare become a primary objective of public policy. Manufacturing investment was due to a nationalistic growth policy favoring import-competing industrial growth vis-à-vis the expansion of traditional exports. While other major Latin American countries began their industrialization push during the depression of the 1930s, this step was delayed somewhat in Mexico as a result of the political pressure for agrarian reform and public investment in the rural sector. As a result, once public policy shifted in favor of industrialization, agriculture had already received a major impetus from land redistribution and public investment. It was then possible for balanced growth to be maintained between the rural and urban sectors of the economy without producing serious distortion in internal prices or the balance of payments. For this reason, industrialization was able to proceed more effectively in Mexico without running into shortages in footstuffs or raw materials, and therefore with a minimum drain on foreign exchange reserves for agricultural imports.

The expansion of transport, commerce, and services reflected a postrevolutionary program of increased internal trade through unification of the national market and greater specialization in production and exchange. Such a policy was designed to shift the basis of growth from traditional exports toward the internal economy and, as a result, to distribute as broadly as possible the economic benefits of increases in income and product. The payoff to public investment in social and economic infrastructure that was designed to achieve this objective was slow in coming. Per capita product between 1925 and 1940 increased but little, owing to the opportunity cost of the reform programs as well as world depression. Growth did not really begin to take place until the export boom of the 1940s. At that time considerable excess capacity existed that could be drawn upon, to be combined with a backlog of new foreign technology once U.S. wartime restrictions permitted and the requisite funds could be obtained by Mexican investors. The rapid increase in wartime demand, combined with lagging real wages resulting from a relatively elastic supply of labor, permitted rising profits to be earned by those farms and businesses which had begun the decade with excess capacity. These profits were reinvested in expansion of plant and equipment once capital goods imports became available again in large quantities after the war.

Because both business and labor identified with the process of economic growth and nation-building and tended to believe in the "ethos of revolution," and because the growth rate was sufficiently rapid for relative shifts in income distribution to take place in favor of profits and rent without seriously affecting the welfare of the working class, it was possible to force savings through inflation and to stimulate a much larger share of investment than would have occurred otherwise. The process of inflation elsewhere in Latin America failed to bring about a major increase in the savings and investment rates owing to a clash among income recipients for relative shares—a clash that had important political overtones as business and labor pressured the government for cheap credit as well as price and wage increases. Labor unions in Mexico were subject to stricter control, while peasants were provided with land (at minimum cost to the government, through agrarian reform) that gave them a certain amount of income security, tended to place a floor on real wages, and reduced the pressure for wage increases and income subsidies in the cities.

By the 1950s, population growth in the rural sector had caught up with the earlier land redistribution program and rising numbers of unskilled workers flowed to the cities. However, sufficient capital formation had taken place in industry and commercial agriculture by this time to permit a major expansion in output that could be passed on in the form of rising employment in the service sector. Real wages increased for all but the lowest income groups. In other words, the timing of agrarian reform, which retarded the rate of urbanization during the crucial period of investment in infrastructure, agriculture, and manufacturing, plus large public investments in commercial agriculture early in the development process, combined to make urbanization in the 1950s a stimulus rather than a deterrent to continued growth. Not only did a high rate of domestic physical investment continue throughout the 1950s and 1960s, but the inflow of foreign investment increased as well, with the exception of a slight downturn between 1958 and 1961. Meanwhile inflation was gradually brought under control as supply increases outstripped demand. One of the most important elements in this inductive model of Mexican growth is the *sequence* of public policies as applied to agrarian reform and rural investment, followed by the expansion of internal transport, communication, and industrialization. Had this sequence been reversed, it is quite conceivable that excess urbanization, agricultural bottlenecks, and chronic inflation would have arisen, producing stagnation rather than sustained growth.

U.S. proximity has been cited frequently as a condition that makes Mexican development a special case. The preliminary estimates from this study indicate that since 1940 less than 4 percent of GDP and less than one-half of one percentage point of the annual rate of growth may be ascribed to the proximity factor alone. Indeed, Mexico has foregone large amounts of U.S. trade and investment in the past so as to follow a more independent set of domestic and foreign policies. Economic nationalism created a psychological framework in which local (and foreign) investors learned to rely upon the Mexican government's objective of stability and growth and its capacity to enforce economic policies. The stability of the Mexican government and the dependability of its programs have tended to bring risk discounts in Mexico well below those elsewhere in Latin America thereby creating conditions for a higher rate of internal saving and investment. This has accordingly permitted a more rapid rate of growth of the domestic economy and a greater export potential than would have existed otherwise, despite the numerous restrictions on traditional export activities.

Paradoxically, Mexico's policy of economic nationalism may be shown to have increased the amount of foreign trade and investment the country received, thereby reinforcing its "economic dependence." A different perspective might emphasize that import substitution was import-intensive and that policies restructuring the economy so as to reduce its dependence upon traditional exports relied heavily on foreign trade and investment. The evidence suggests that, despite radical social and political changes brought about by revolution, Mexico was unable to make many adjustments in the short run because of its straitjacket of dependence upon foreign trade. It also indicates that an economy that creates for itself the conditions of rapid growth, whether through revolution or evolution, might eventually obtain large amounts of private investment from the developed countries, once its internal political conditions as well as those of the major investing countries permit the survival of a mixed enterprise system. Clearly any conclusive test of the proximity effect of the United States on Mexican economic development requires a more extensive investigation than this book could provide. Hopefully, further studies of this nature will be made that include a comparison of Mexico with the cases of Canada, Puerto Rico, and Brazil, where large U.S. investments have also taken place since 1940 though under quite different political, economic, and locational circumstances.

FUTURE PERSPECTIVES

A number of problems appear when one looks into Mexico's economic future in the light of recent history. One of the most important has already been mentioned: the need to bring about increased industrial efficiency without relying upon costly trade cycles to weed out unproductive firms, and without removing the protection essential for infant industries. The use of direct controls on trade may facilitate selective reduction of effective protection, since individual import quotas may be adjusted by executive order without resorting to a general revision of tariff legislation. But the labor and management displaced by such policies must be helped to find alternative employment if political difficulties are to be avoided. The border industries that are now being successfully established to process labor-intensive manufactures for export might be permitted to compete with domestic manufactures to force increased efficiency for nonfrontier firms. Since there has been little research and development undertaken by Mexican manufacturing under private auspices, the government might be encouraged to subsidize such expenditures and perhaps to set up its own R&D facilities to assist in the development and application of modern technology to peculiarly Mexican conditions of supply and demand.

Agricultural development may be expected to become more labor-intensive in the future as the possibility of expansion of arable land diminishes. Livestock raising must receive far more attention from the government than it has in the past if the nation's animal protein needs are to be met and if beef exports are to continue as before. Rising wages in the United States plus the closing of the frontier to Mexican labor will tend to increase the market for Mexican agricultural products and make profitable large new investments in citrus and other tree crops, viticulture, and truck farming. It is to be expected that changes in crop production technology will tend to increase the productivity of existing land in commercial agriculture, while the subsistence sector will decline in both relative and absolute importance as the relative demand for traditional crops declines.

The problem of increasing labor productivity in the subsistence sector is a question of priority. In time, development itself will eliminate subsistence agriculture and bring about an increase in the marginal productivity of labor, but the rural population as well as those in low-skill urban employment cannot be expected to wait indefinitely. It may take at least two decades for a turning point to be reached through the natural evolution of the economy; such a rate of labor absorption may be too slow to satisfy the goals expressed by the government in its annual pronouncements. If so, it will be necessary to make increasing expenditures for rural education, income subsidies to the peasantry, and relocation of rural labor, as well as to increase the amount of land distribution, this time with better land, increased credit and extension facilities, and more efficient organizational forms so as to provide a better livelihood for the present generation of landless peasants. The curtailment of the bracero program with the United States has tended to intensify internal pressures for a solution to the problem of subsistence agriculture. Increased exports to the United States in labor-intensive goods and services may help to reduce wage inequalities between the two countries and between the subsistence and commercial sectors of the Mexican economy, though at best this would no more than partially compensate for more restrictive migration policies.

The need to take a new look at Mexico's mineral potential has already been discussed. Tax reductions in recent years have failed to provide much stimulus for new investment in mining and have been somewhat offset by recent problems in the sulfur industry. Nevertheless, preliminary findings of geological surveys have suggested the existence of substantial unexploited mineral reserves, particularly in the west and northwest. State-financed exploration and development plus public investment in infrastructure to serve these new mining regions might well be combined with Mexican or mixed Mexican-foreign enterprise to bring about a renaissance in Mexican mining unequaled since the Bourbon reforms or the boom of the late nineteenth century.

A potential new era of mineral production would be politically feasible provided it were subject to strong federal regulation and provided that Mexican citizens retained a majority interest in the new enterprises. Under such circumstances, the problems of the past could be avoided while the benefits of substantial economic rents from mineral resources could be made to accrue to nationals of the country. The present neglect of potentially productive subsoil resources tends to disregard the income from nature's bounty that might be used to improve the level of living of the masses who, rather than the minerals themselves, represent Mexico's true national patrimony. One essential precondition for a rational mineral investment program would be a detailed investigation into the past relationships between mineral development and growth of the domestic economy. There is yet no major study that combines the technical and economic aspects of Mexican mining during the period covered by this book.

A final note concerns the political framework within which sustained economic growth can take place. Until now the government has relied primarily upon indirect measures to affect the pattern of resource allocation, income distribution, and growth in Mexico. Tax revenues have maintained a small, relatively constant share of GDP over the past thirty years and, in the interest of stabilization, expenditure policies have been restricted as well. Hence, despite its declared policy of being "socialist within the constitution," and despite its "ethos of revolution," the Mexican government has relied more heavily on the private sector for growth than almost any major country in Latin America. While some would attribute the conspicuous success of post-1940 development to financial stability and fiscal restraint, others have been extremely critical of such policies, including the failure to introduce tax reforms and the undue emphasis placed upon monetary stabilization as well as the allegedly extravagant accumulation of foreign exchange reserves. Criticism has also been leveled at the extent of income inequality that prevails and the degree to which inequality has increased during the recent phase of rapid growth.

Such criticisms must be evaluated in terms of the range of feasible alternatives open to the government since 1940. In such a country, the formulation and implementation of development policy is heavily determined by, and to some extent constrained by, the pattern of economic activity itself. Interest groups have the potential to stimulate growth or to deter it, both individually and collectively. The working class may withdraw, reduce, or increase its services in response to changes in the psychological approach to material incentives, as well as changes in the incentives themselves. Periodic work stoppages in Mexico have involved significant losses in output (and growth) during the 1930s and 1940s. On the other hand, the "ethos of revolution" has tended to minimize opposition to government wage stabilization policies. Strong federal control of labor unions has been facilitated further by the ready availability of low-cost nonunion labor as well as the association of strike-breaking with the public interest.

Management and investors may aid or retard the effectiveness of development policies by increasing or withdrawing capital from the economy and by altering the intensity of use of existing capacity. In the 1920s and 1930s the private petroleum companies appear to have minimized the operation of their Mexican properties in an effort to bargain for more favorable treatment—a strategy that eventually failed; during World War II Mexican firms operated around the clock in response to patriotic as well as economic incentives; an appeal to the "ethos of revolution" motivated a number of public and private entrepreneurs to intensify their activity in the national interest. Society at large may work for or against particular government policies through political pressure groups, through creation of an atmosphere of pride or dissatisfaction with the government that affects responsiveness to its directives, and in extreme cases through armed insurrection. Foreign countries may also support or resist public policies through trade, investment, and ultimately military action.

Labor, capital, society-at-large, and foreign governments have both widened and narrowed the degrees of freedom open to the Mexican government in its efforts to formulate and implement an effective mixture of development policies. This has affected the feasibility of alternative development strategies and explains why major reform measures had to be taken in earlier years and why subsequent administrations have tended to minimize short-term reforms in order to pursue an incremental strategy of growth. The process of development since 1940 has depended upon a structure of production, distribution of wealth, and pattern of political power far different from that of 1910. The cost of this restructuring is shown to have been extremely high during the Revolution and not insignificant during the reform period.

Since 1940, however, the primary focus of public policy has been on growth-induced improvements in social welfare rather than on those which might have been accomplished by direct redistributive measures. What made this strategy viable was the broad popular support enjoyed by political leaders and the enormous flexibility of the private sector of the economy. Despite much grumbling and the opposition of certain intellectuals, labor leaders, peasants, and some members of the business and financial elite, there was a general willingness on the part of the public to accept the government's version of its revolutionary mandate as well as its unilateral, highly centralized, and occasionally repressive policy implementation.

Government by decree with a minimum of popular control has been accepted until recently as the price of revolution and rapid growth. As long as real incomes were rising for most Mexicans, the fact of increased inequality in income distribution was tolerated.

More recently, however, broadened social participation in the process of economic growth has produced a rising middle class which is better educated and better prepared to participate in the political process than ever before. Now the peasants, less willing to accept a growing gap in income and wealth between themselves and the urban elite, are pressuring for further land redistribution. At the same time those areas of the country that have lagged in the growth race are challenging the regional distribution of public expenditure, while other areas are attempting to better their already favorable position by calling for more decentralization of political control.

Given the high degree of uncertainty or even lack of information about the internal workings of the economy that has prevailed in the government until now, it is difficult to see how an alternative mixture of public policies could have increased the rate of growth or substantially improved the level of income of all sectors of the population since 1940, and it is easy to imagine how more extreme measures might have retarded the growth rate. Despite the severe limitations within which the government has been forced to move in terms of tax and expenditure policies, and despite its precarious position vis-à-vis the United States and its need to depend upon foreign borrowing to supplement internal savings, it has managed exceptionally well.

Nevertheless the dominant party (PRI) and its new leaders face mounting pressures for internal political reform in the direction of greater decentralization and popular control. Under these circumstances the president, cabinet ministers, governors of states, and other members of the PRI are finding unilateral action increasingly difficult. While the identification of public policy with the public interest has never been unquestioned in Mexico, recent economic success has created important new regional, occupational, and social interest groups, all of which demand a greater voice in the decision-making process. Channels must be opened in the political system through which such pressures can be relieved, or economic growth may well be curtailed through political discontent. Hence, although no major economic obstacles stand in the way of sustained growth, political pitfalls abound. It may become necessary for the government to turn from growth-promoting to political and economic redistribution programs in the near future in order to avoid a repetition of history. Just as social revolution once brought about changes in the structure of the economy that permitted increased social participation in the production process, so economic revolution in recent years has set the stage for broader social participation in the political process.

Appendix A

The Per Capita Income of New Spain Before Independence and After the Revolution

Despite the difficulties inherent in intertemporal comparisons of economic product, it is revealing to look at two independent measures of Mexican output during the last years of the Viceroyalty in the light of recent experience. The figures are taken from the writings of two contemporary observers of the economy during the decade 1800–10. The first of these was the renowned German scholar, Alexandre von Humboldt, who provides us with a detailed picture of the Mexican economy at the time of his visit in 1803. His statistics have recently been reworked by Henry Aubrey so as to provide an estimate of national income for the year 1803.[1] The second set of figures, which corresponds to the period 1800–10 (without specifying any particular year), are from a report by the Royal Secretary of the Consulate of Veracruz, Don José María Quiros. Fernando Rosenzweig has analyzed these statistics in detail and adjusted them to provide an estimate of the total value of Mexican production.[2]

From the original estimates, four alternative figures for the national income and product of New Spain around the year 1803 are presented in Appendix Table A.1. The range of these estimates varies from 90 to 190 million pesos which, assuming a population of slightly under 6 million in that year (Table 1.3), suggests a per capita income

1. Henry G. Aubrey, "The National Income of Mexico," *I.A.S.I. Estadística,* June 1950 (Journal of the Inter-American Statistical Institute). The author makes use of data presented in Humboldt's *Essai politique sur le royaume de la Nouvelle-Espagne,* Paris, F. Schoell, 1811, 5 vols.

2. Fernando Rosenzweig, "La economía Novo-Hispaña al comenzar el Siglo XIX," *Ciencias Políticas y Sociales,* U.N.A.M., vol. 9, no. 33, Julio-Septiembre, 1963. This article relies upon data from José María Quiros, *Memoria de estatuto; idea de la riqueza que daban la masa circulante de Nueva España sus naturales producciones en los años de tranquilidad, y su abatimiento en las presentes conmociones . . . ,* Veracruz, 1817.

of from 15 to 32 silver pesos per year. The most reasonable estimates
seem to be those of Aubrey and Rosenzweig which place per capita
income in the narrower range of from 20 to 32 pesos per year.

Our figures on per capita income of New Spain, as obtained from

Appendix Table A.1
National Income of New Spain around 1800
(thousands of silver pesos)

	Humboldt's Figures (1803)		Quiros's Figures (average 1800–10)	
	Original Figures (A)	Aubrey Adjustment of Humboldt's Data (B)	Original Figures Eliminating Double-Counting (C)	Rosenzweig Adjustment of Quiros's Data (D)
1. Agriculture	29,000		89,285	106,000
2. Mining	23,000		28,451	28,500
3. Manufacturing	8,000		72,386	55,500
Subtotal	60,000		190,122	190,000
4. Payments by the royal government in Mexico	8,800		–	–
5. Trade and domestic transport	21,500		–	–
6. Total	90,300	120,000 to 140,000	190,122	190,000

Note: A silver peso of 1803 (peso fuerte) equalled one ounce of silver, which was
equivalent to .0649 ounces of gold in that year. In 1934 the same amount of gold
equalled 7.25 Mexican pesos at the Banco de México's official purchase price.

Sources: Aubrey, "The National Income of Mexico," and Rosenzweig, "La
Economía Novo-Hispaña al Comenzar el Siglo XIX."

these early estimates, have been converted into contemporary value
equivalents in Table A.2, using Aubrey's conversion factor for the
comparison of 1803 income with that of the 1930s. This factor takes
account of the gold equivalent of the respective monetary units and
implicitly assumes that the real purchasing power of fine gold did not
vary over the 130-year period. (See Appendix Table A.1, Note.)
The lowest figure for total income in Table A.1, which is clearly an
underestimate, has been eliminated, leaving a range of from 600 to
slightly under 1,000 pesos of 1950 purchasing power during the last

Appendix Table A.2
Per Capita Income of New Spain Before Independence and After the Revolution

	(1934 pesos)	*(1950 pesos)*
Before Independence		
1. Per capita product in 1803		
(Humboldt/Aubrey)	145–170	613–719
2. Per capita income 1800–1810		
(Quiros/Rosenzweig)	232	981
After the Revolution		
3. Per capita product in 1930		903
4. Per capita product in 1935		990

Sources and Methods: 1. The estimate of per capita product is derived from the total product figures in Table A.1, column B in 1803 pesos divided by an estimated population of 6 million for that year (Table 1.3), and converted to 1934 pesos by a factor of 7.25 based on the gold equivalent of the respective monies (Table A.1,Note). The 1950 pesos equivalent of 1934 pesos is based on the wholesale price index for Mexico City (see Appendix C), which rose 4.23 times between the two years. (The exchange rate of pesos per dollar rose 2.40 times during the same period.)

2. The per capita income figure is from Table A.1, column D converted as described in 1. above.

3. & 4. These figures are from Table 1.1.

years of the Viceroyalty. When one compares these estimates with per capita income in the present century, the results are sobering.[3]

In Chapter 1 it was seen that between 1900 and 1930 per capita product rose from 628 to 903 pesos, or by 44 percent. Yet, when confronted with our estimates for 1803, one must conclude that if the earlier figures are correct, then either there was little or no increase in per capita income over the course of the nineteenth century, or per capita income actually declined over much of the nineteenth century despite the gains of the Porfiriato. In either case, the growth from 1900 to 1930 simply reflects a recovery of pre-Independence levels of productivity. One might argue that the conversion factor

3. An alternative calculation based on the data in this Appendix in 1803 silver pesos was made by converting the values to 1803 U.S. dollars assuming a 1/1 ratio of exchange. This dollar value for 1803 was then transformed to 1950 dollars using a composite index derived from the Warren and Pearson and Bureau of Labor Statistics wholesale price indexes. This method reduces the 1950 dollar equivalent of 1803 per capita product to $45 from our estimate of between $70 and $114. Ref. McGreevey, "Recent Research on the Economic History of Latin America," pp. 97–100. Even if this relatively low-income level were to have held on average in 1803, it would have meant a compound annual rate of growth of well under 1 percent during the nineteenth century.

for 1803 pesos overstates their 1934 purchasing power parity. This would be true if the real purchasing power of fine gold had actually increased significantly over the period. Nevertheless, the absolute level of per capita income in 1930 was extremely low, being the equivalent of only 59 U.S. dollars at the existing exchange rate.[4]

Obviously, any social welfare interpretation based upon these statistics alone could not be sustained. Output and the distribution of income in Mexico changed greatly between the pre-Independence and postrevolutionary periods. The population tripled in size, with undoubtedly significant effects on the structure of production, effectiveness of import substitution, degree of investor risk, and possibilities for economic innovation. Nevertheless, it appears more than likely that much of the improvement in material levels of living date back only a few decades and may well be attributable to changes associated with the Revolution and its aftermath.

4. This estimate is based upon the 1930 per capita production of 903 pesos (1950 purchasing power) deflated to 213 pesos (1934 purchasing power) using the Mexico City wholesale price index. The 1934 value is then converted to current dollars at the then-existing exchange rate of 3.599 pesos per dollar. If we use the 903 pesos figure and convert it at the 1950 exchange rate of 8.643 pesos per dollar, this gives us an estimate of US $105 (1950 value) per person. In each case the per capita income figure is so low that it is unlikely that the conversion factor for 1803 pesos could have been much less than Aubrey's 7.25, assuming constant terms of trade for gold.

Appendix B

The Opportunity Cost
of the Mexican Revolution[1]

This appendix provides a range of estimates of potential gross domestic product for the years 1925, 1930, and 1940 had the Mexican Revolution, postrevolutionary reforms, and associated economic disturbances not occurred. Estimates were made of value added in 1950 prices for individual production sectors under alternative assumptions about the growth of population and foreign trade. These results were then checked as to their consistency with domestic savings potentials and total foreign exchange earning possibilities implicit in the aggregate estimates. The values obtained should be regarded as mere approximations, but they represent reasonable orders of magnitude of sectoral and total output since they were constrained from outperforming similar sectors in other Latin American countries during the same period. The underlying assumption of the estimates was that economic conditions in Mexico would not have deviated sharply from those elsewhere in Latin America had the Revolution not occurred. Hence the impact of the world depression has been preserved in these results insofar as it affected similar economic activities throughout the hemisphere.

POPULATION

The Mexican population rose only slightly between 1910 and 1925 since, as a consequence of both war and epidemic, it had actually fallen between 1910 and 1921 (Appendix Table E.1). In order to allow for the growth in population that might have occurred during this fifteen-year period in the absence of Revolution, two estimates

1. This section was prepared with the assistance of Margery Coen, March 1968. An earlier version by Manuel Ramírez, summer 1967, provided a basis for some of the calculations.

were made, one using the Chilean rate of population growth[2] and the other the Brazilian rate.[3] The actual Mexican rate was used for the 1925–30 and 1930–40 periods.[4]

AGRICULTURE[5]

Agricultural output was divided into two components: (1) food and industrial crops for domestic consumption and (2) export crops. Estimates of the former were calculated on two different bases: (1) the observed trend in per capita agricultural output for domestic use, and (2) the assumption of constant per capita output in this sector. Each of the two approaches assumes that crop production in Mexico is in part determined by the number of workers employed in agriculture and that the marginal productivity of labor in this sector, while low and relatively constant, was not zero. These hypotheses provide four alternative estimates of the gross product in agriculture based on the high and low estimates of population growth applied to each estimate of the rate of growth of output.

For the export sector, the actual rates of growth of production of several crops were compared with the figures for the same commodities in other countries to determine whether or not production would have been greater in the absence of revolution. Mexico was the only producer of henequen, and its reduced production seems to have been primarily the result of growing competition from other fibers. Thus, the actual figures for henequen production were used in both sets of estimates.[6] The rate of increase in the production of sugar cane[6] was greater than that which occurred in Argentina[7] or Cuba,[8] so again the actual figures were used. Mexico's rate of increase in cot-

2. The population data for Chile were obtained from United Nations, ECLA, *Economic Survey of Latin America 1949,* Chapter 8.

3. The population data for Brazil were obtained from United Nations, ECLA, *Economic Survey of Latin America 1949,* Chapter 7.

4. The population data for Mexico are from Appendix Table E.1.

5. The agricultural data are from Appendix C. These were separated into domestic use and export components using, for 1925, 1930, and 1940 the percentage breakdown found in United Nations, ECLA, *Economic Survey of Latin America 1949,* pp. 430 and 439 and for 1910 figures from *Fuerza de Trabajo,* updated by the author.

6. United Nations, ECLA, *Economic Survey of Latin America 1949,* Chapter 9. Presidencia de la República, Secretaría Privada, and Nacional Financiera, S.A., *50 Años de Revolución Mexicana en Cifras,* Chapter 10.

7. United Nations, ECLA, *Economic Survey of Latin America 1949,* Chapter 6.

8. Cuba Económica y Financiera, *Anuario Azucarero de Cuba,* 1947.

ton[6] production was greater than Argentina's[9] and Brazil's[10] from 1910–25 and greater than Brazil's again from 1930–40. We therefore used the rate of increase of the joint Mexican, Brazilian, and Argentinian production. The rate of increase in the production of coffee[6] was greater during the entire period than the rate of increase of world production.[11] It was, however, smaller than the Brazilian rate of increase from 1925 to 1930.[12] The low estimate is based on the actual values. For the high estimate, actual values were used for the 1910–25 period, the Brazilian growth rate for 1925 to 1930, and the Mexican rate from 1930 to 1940.

LIVESTOCK[13]

Four alternatives were computed for this sector using the rates of growth of the four crop production estimates assuming that livestock production would have increased proportionately. Owing to the relative abundance of grazing land in the cattle-growing regions, Mexico's livestock and crop production activities appear to have been complementary rather than competing over the relevant period.

MINING[14]

The high estimate was derived by adding 15 percent to the actual figures for 1925 and 1940 to reflect likely increases in investment and output had taxes not risen as rapidly and as unpredictably after 1920. The same procedure was followed for the low estimate except that the actual figures for 1925 and 1940 were increased by only 10 percent.

PETROLEUM[15]

In this sector the actual figure was used for the low estimate. The high estimate was derived by adding 10 percent to the actual 1925

9. United Nations, ECLA, *Economic Survey of Latin America 1949*, Chapter 6.

10. Ibid., Chapter 7.

11. Contraloría General de la República de Colombia, *Anuario General de Estadística*, 1933 and 1943.

12. United Nations, ECLA, *Economic Survey of Latin America 1949*, Chapter 7.

13. Actual value estimates are from Appendix C.

14. Appendix C.

15. Ibid.

and 1940 figures and then computing the 1930 estimate on the basis of the rate of decline that would have prevailed. If the Mexican petroleum industry had kept drilling and producing at the pace of world production, its output in 1930 would have reached almost 1,200 million 1950 pesos and almost 1,500 million 1950 pesos in 1950. These figures are to be compared with our estimates of 552 and 1,109 million 1950 pesos for 1930 and 638 and 702 million 1950 pesos for 1940. The higher levels of production were reached by Mexico in the 1950s and 1960s[16] and were therefore feasible, given the country's petroleum reserves. It is probably unlikely, however, that the private petroleum industry would have increased output by this amount during the depressed 1930s.

MANUFACTURING[17]

The low estimate is based on the Chilean rate of increase from 1910 to 1925 [18] and an average of the Chilean and Argentine rates[19] for 1925 to 1940. For the high estimate it was assumed that the growth rate from 1910 to 1925 was equal to that which occurred from 1900 to 1910, the last years of the Porfiriato; the rates from 1925 to 1930, and 1930 to 1940 are those which actually took place.

TRANSPORTATION[20]

We assumed that the product of the transportation sector would depend upon the growth of the preceding sectors. According to the figures in Appendix C, the share of this sector as a proportion of the five others just discussed was 5.9 percent in 1910, 7.4 percent in 1925, 9.8 percent in 1930, and 9.1 percent in 1940. Using these percentages, we calculated the product of the transportation sector on the basis of the four estimates of the preceding five sectors.

16. Presidencia de la República, et al., *50 Años de Revolución Mexicana en Cifras.*

17. Actual value estimates are from Appendix C.

18. Marto A. Ballesteros and Tom E. Davis, "The Growth of Output and Employment in Basic Sectors of the Chilean Economy, 1908–1957," Part 1, p. 163.

19. Appendix C. and Carlos F. Díaz-Alejandro, "Essays on the Economic History of the Argentine Republic," Statistical Appendix, Tables 29 and 31, mimeograph, 1967.

20. Actual value estimates are from Appendix C.

OTHER SECTORS

At the time of preparation of this appendix there was no reliable basis for individual estimates of the other sectors—forestry, fishing, electricity, services, commerce, etc.—for the earlier periods. Therefore the product of these combined sectors was computed on the basis of its actual percentage of the total product of the sectors discussed above. Thus, in 1925, 102.1 percent, in 1930, 69.0 percent, and in 1940, 85.3 percent of the sum of output in each of the four estimates of those sectors was attributed to "other sectors."

The sectoral estimates and that of GDP are shown in Tables B.1 through B.9. Table B.10 gives estimates of per capita product. According to these estimates, GDP would have been between 12 and 61 percent higher in 1940 than it actually was. The per capita gross domestic product would, however, have been between 10 percent greater and 6 percent lower than the actual figure in 1925 and between 12 percent greater and 1 percent lower than the actual figure in 1930. By 1940 the hypothetical level of per capita product in-

Appendix Table B.1
Mexican Population
(thousands)

	1910	1925	1930	1940
Actual number	15,160	15,500	16,553	20,143
High estimate	15,160	21,482	22,941	27,916
Low estimate	15,160	17,783	18,991	23,110

Appendix Table B.2
Agriculture
(million 1950 pesos)

	1910	1925	1930	1940
Agriculture for domestic use				
Actual value	1,008	1,271	1,505	2,247
High population estimate (1)	1,008	1,762	2,086	3,114
High population estimate (2)	1,008	1,428	1,525	1,856
Low population estimate (1)	1,008	1,458	1,727	2,578
Low population estimate (2)	1,008	1,182	1,263	1,537
Agriculture for export				
Actual value	336	447	457	483
High estimate	336	782	974	1,576
Low estimate	336	782	828	1,382

Appendix Table B.3
Livestock
(millions of 1950 pesos)

	1910	1925	1930	1940
Actual value	1,510	1,620	1,591	2,247
High population estimate (1)	1,510	2,858	3,437	5,268
High population estimate (2)	1,510	2,483	2,808	3,856
Low population estimate (1)	1,510	2,517	2,871	4,450
Low population estimate (2)	1,510	2,060	2,193	3,061

Appendix Table B.4
Mining
(millions of 1950 pesos)

	1910	1925	1930	1940
Actual value	1,044	1,187	1,458	1,209
High estimate	1,044	1,365	1,371	1,390
Low estimate	1,044	1,306	1,313	1,330

Appendix Table B.5
Petroleum
(millions of 1950 pesos)

	1910	1925	1930	1940
Actual value	34	1,269	552	638
High estimate	34	1,396	1,109	702
Low estimate	34	1,269	552	638

Appendix Table B.6
Manufacturing
(millions of 1950 pesos)

	1910	1925	1930	1940
Actual value	1,620	2,076	2,489	3,889
High estimate	1,620	2,754	3,302	5,159
Low estimate	1,620	2,573	3,027	4,087

Appendix Table B.7
Transportation
(millions of 1950 pesos)

	1910	1925	1930	1940
Actual value	330	582	793	974
High population estimate (1)	330	808	1,203	1,566
High population estimate (2)	330	755	1,087	1,323
Low population estimate (1)	330	733	1,011	1,316
Low population estimate (2)	330	679	899	1,095

Appendix Table B.8
Other Sectors
(millions of 1950 pesos)

	1910	1925	1930	1940
Actual value	5,943	8,629	6,101	9,971
High population estimate (1)	5,943	11,971	9,303	16,015
High population estimate (2)	5,943	11,193	8,401	13,530
Low population estimate (1)	5,943	10,861	7,817	13,461
Low population estimate (2)	5,943	10,058	6,952	11,200

Appendix Table B.9
Gross Domestic Product
(millions of 1950 pesos)

	1910	1925	1930	1940
Actual value	11,825	17,081	14,946	21,658
High population estimate (1)	11,825	23,696	22,785	34,790
High population estimate (2)	11,825	22,156	20,577	29,392
Low population estimate (1)	11,825	21,499	19,146	29,242
Low population estimate (2)	11,825	19,909	17,027	24,330

Appendix Table B.10
Per Capita Product
(1950 pesos)

	1910	1925	1930	1940
Actual value	780	1,102	903	1,075
High population estimate (1)	780	1,103	993	1,246
High population estimate (2)	780	1,031	897	1,053
Low population estimate (1)	780	1,209	1,008	1,265
Low population estimate (2)	780	1,120	897	1,053

creases so that our estimates are between 18 percent greater and only 2 percent lower than the actual value. The lower per capita estimates are due to the much higher level of population in the years 1925–40 in the absence of revolution. The higher rates of growth of GDP in our estimates would not have been sufficient to absorb the larger labor force resulting from much higher rates of population growth before 1925. It is interesting to note that, as the effect of the actual retardation of population growth from 1910 to 1925 lessens, the estimated per capita product figures fall more in line with actual per capita product.

A further implication of the different rates of population growth is their effect on the labor force available. Under the assumption that the labor force would have been the same share of total population as actually prevailed, the economy would have had to find jobs for a work force of between 6.7 and 8.1 million persons in 1940 as compared with the actual 5.9 million workers. While the labor force actually grew at an annual rate of 0.3 percent, our population estimates indicate it would have risen by between 0.7 and 1.4 percent a year.

Tables B.11 through B.13 show the rates of increase of GDP, per

Appendix Table B.11
Compound Annual Rate of Growth of GDP

	1910/25	*1925/30*	*1930/40*
Actual value	2.5	−2.6	3.8
High population estimate (1)	4.8	−0.8	4.3
High population estimate (2)	4.3	−1.5	3.6
Low population estimate (1)	4.1	−2.3	4.3
Low population estimate (2)	3.5	−3.1	3.6

Appendix Table B.12
Compound Annual Rate of Growth of Per Capita GDP

	1910/25	*1925/30*	*1930/40*
Actual value	2.3	−3.9	1.8
High population estimate (1)	2.3	−2.0	2.3
High population estimate (2)	1.9	−2.7	1.6
Low population estimate (1)	3.0	−3.6	2.3
Low population estimate (2)	2.4	−4.3	1.6

Appendix Table B.13
Compound Annual Rate of Growth of Population

	1910/25	*1925/30*	*1930/40*
Actual value	0.1	1.3	2.0
High estimate	2.3	1.3	2.0
Low estimate	1.1	1.3	2.0

capita product, and population. The estimates for 1930–40 suggest that the reforms of this period did not seriously slow the growth of the economy during the 1930s. The same holds true for the rates of growth of per capita product from 1910 to 1925. The differences in the rates of growth of GDP in this period are primarily due to the differences in the rate of growth of population, suggesting that the major net disturbing effect of the Revolution on the economy before

1925 represented output losses due to a decrease in manpower rather than a decline in output per worker.

In order to determine whether the economy would have generated enough internal savings to permit the growth in capital stock needed to meet the hypothetical levels of production, estimates of the savings rate implied by those output estimates were made under the assumptions of capital-output ratios of 2.2 in 1910 and 3.3 in 1940 (see Table 1.7). After determining the accumulated net investment required in each case, we divided this figure by the accumulated gross domestic product for the period under each of the four estimates to determine the implicit net savings rate required to achieve each hypothetical level of GDP. The results indicated that savings rates from 11.4 to 13.0 percent would have been required for the high estimates and from 9.9 to 11.7 percent for the low estimates. These figures may be compared with the actual net investment rate in the 1950s of 7 to 9 percent and a somewhat lower rate in the early 1940s.

In order to determine whether the capital stock levels assumed for 1940 would have been sufficient to permit the hypothetical rates of growth of GDP after 1910, an implicit productivity residual was calculated based upon the difference between the growth of output and a weighted average of the growth rates of land, labor, and capital (see Chapter 1). The land under cultivation was presumed to increase at half the hypothetical rate of growth of agricultural production (which did occur in areas not favored by social overhead projects during the period). For the GDP estimates based on the high rate of population growth, the rates of growth of cultivated land area were 1.6 percent and 2.1 percent, and for the low estimates they were 1.3 percent and 1.9 percent, respectively. The rates of growth of capital, computed from the capital stock estimates described above, were 4.5 percent and 5.1 percent for the high estimates and 3.8 percent and 4.5 percent for the low. Weighting the growth of the factors of production by their share in GNP (.70 for labor, .25 for capital, and .05 for land), and assuming output to grow at the rate stated in our four hypothetical cases, we determined the rate of growth of productivity required for each GDP figure. Those rates, as shown in Table B.14, range from .43 to .90 and are close to the actual figure of .80 percent [21] achieved during the period 1925–40.

As the results in Table B.14 show, the Mexican economy would

21. See the methodology used to estimate the "unexplained" component of growth in Chapter 1.

Appendix Table B.14
Estimates of Capital Stock, Savings Rate, and Productivity Growth Rate

	1940 Capital Stock (millions 1950 pesos)	Net Investment 1910–40 (millions 1950 pesos)	Required Net Savings as Share of GDP (percents)	Compound Annual Rate of Growth of Productivity Consistent with Factor Inputs
High population estimate (1)	114,807	88,792	13.0	.85
High population estimate (2)	96,994	70,979	11.4	.43
Low population estimate (1)	96,499	70,484	11.7	.90
Low population estimate (2)	80,289	54,274	9.9	.41

probably not have been able to generate the total amount of net savings necessary to achieve our hypothetical growth rates over the period. Some net foreign borrowing would almost certainly have been required. If it were assumed that import-output and export-out-

Appendix Table B.15
Imports and Exports
(millions of 1950 pesos)

	1910		1925		1930		1940	
	Im-ports	Ex-ports	Im-ports	Ex-ports	Im-ports	Ex-ports	Im-ports	Ex-ports
Actual value	981	1,324	1,349	2,374	1,315	1,719	2,036	2,924
High population estimate (1)	981	1,324	1,872	3,294	2,005	2,620	3,270	4,697
High population estimate (2)	981	1,324	1,750	3,080	1,811	2,366	2,763	3,968
Low population estimate (1)	981	1,324	1,698	2,988	1,685	2,202	2,749	3,948
Low population estimate (2)	981	1,324	1,573	2,767	1,498	1,958	2,287	3,285

put ratios did not change,[22] Mexico would have maintained a surplus in the balance of payments on current account, as shown in Table B.15. This assumption needs some qualification, however, since in-

22. Import-output and export-output ratios for the period are taken from Table 6.2.

come inequality would have been more extreme in 1940, under any of the four hypothetical cases, because of inadequate labor absorption into the commercial sectors of the economy and lack of agrarian reform, which in fact broke up many estates into small subsistence plots and raised the income of the peasantry. The net effect of increased income inequality on import propensities is uncertain but there is some likelihood that imports would have risen as a share of GDP. The share of exports in GDP would almost certainly have increased, reflecting more favorable treatment of mining, petroleum, and commercial agriculture. On the other hand, net remittances of interest and principal on foreign investment would have been higher in 1940, tending to offset improvements in the balance of trade. Whether or not a foreign exchange gap would have existed for the years 1925 to 1940, the requirement of a net inflow of foreign capital to fill the savings gap suggested above would have been reflected in a rising share of imports relative to exports and a decline in the balance of payments surplus.

The opportunity cost of the Revolution and reform, expressed in purely economic terms—which ignore much of the agonizing social cost of anarchy, dislocation, disease, and death—was much less than one might suppose. This is particularly true in terms of per capita product, for which most of the actual shortfalls occurred before 1930 and are attributable to the unsettling effects of revolution and its immediate aftermath rather than the reform policies of the 1930s. On the other hand, the actual increase in per capita product before 1925 reflects the loss of population through war and pestilence. Since our hypothetical figures assume that no such decline in population occurred, only two of the estimates show per capita product to be rising more rapidly from 1910 to 1925. As was noted in Chapter 1, labor absorption by the growing sectors of the economy had already become a major problem in 1910. There is little reason to believe that in the absence of revolution this would have been resolved without a major structural transformation of the economy, including agrarian reform.

Had the economy been able to maintain some degree of political and economic stability in the absence of revolution and reform before 1940, GDP in that year might have exceeded the actual level by from 12 to 61 percent. But per capita product by the most favorable measure would have been only 18 percent above actual levels in 1940. In the case of per capita product, the hypothetical levels were in fact achieved by the mid-1940s. These measures suggest that the economic costs of a major restructuring of the Mexican economy between 1910 and 1940 were much less than might have been supposed. But any increment in the rate of growth after 1940 attributable to the institutional changes of the earlier period must be set against not only the economic opportunity costs of revolution and reform but also the appalling social costs. The latter cannot be measured. Numbers cannot be placed on human lives lost, families separated, and aspirations thwarted. These measures are only partial as they touch upon the narrowly material dimensions of social history. Yet rapid economic growth since 1940, much of which was due to the reforms of earlier years, has provided the Mexican population with longer life expectancy, improved levels of living, and a greater chance for inclusion in the benefits of progress for each citizen. In the minds of many observers these favorable consequences of the Revolution offset the enormous social costs and modest economic costs of the preceding decades.

Appendix C

A Brief History of National Income Estimation in Mexico

The present study was initiated as part of the country analysis program of the Economic Growth Center at Yale University. This program involves the collection and analysis of data on the contemporary process of economic growth and structural change in selected developing countries. Several volumes have already appeared in the series, and at least seven will eventually become available on Latin America alone.[1] One of the principal objectives of the program is to provide a set of internationally comparable data on the development process which will facilitate the generation and testing of hypotheses of growth and structural change. To assist in the assembling of basic economic statistics on each country, a system of national economic accounts and historical data was devised; it is this framework which provides the basis for the presentation of data in Appendix D.[2]

The program also called for a critical evaluation of the validity and reliability of existing data as well as its reclassification and extension in terms of the common system of national economic accounts wherever feasible. This material was to be supplemented by time series and benchmark data to provide historical information for periods prior to World War II; most of the material in Appendix E constitutes a judicious selection of historical material bearing most directly on the analysis in this volume. It therefore includes detailed annual

1. Baer, *Industrialization and Economic Development in Brazil.* Forthcoming volumes on Latin America include Argentina (Carlos Díaz-Alejandro), Chile (Markos Mamalakis), Colombia (R. Albert Berry), Peru (Shane Hunt), and Venezuela (James Hanson). For a discussion of the Country Analysis Program, see Economic Growth Center, Yale University, *Report 1961–1964,* and *Report 1964–1967.*

2. Economic Growth Center at Yale University, *A System of National Economic Accounts and Historical Data,* New Haven, n.d.

figures on the volume and value of production of nineteen major crops between 1925 and 1962. An annual index of manufacturing production between 1900 and 1965 also appears, as well as detailed production figures for selected manufacturing industries between 1950 and 1964. The material in Chapters 1–7 and Appendixes D and E includes numerous commentaries on the quality of Mexican economic statistics; and the present Appendix is designed to set the problem in historical perspective, to point out gaps in the data, and to suggest some priorities for future statistical collection and analysis.

A general rule has been followed throughout this volume: data should be generated as a basis for analysis rather than for its own sake; basic series should be estimated, not by use of hypothesized functional relationships or accounting identities, but in terms of independent evidence wherever possible. When two independent estimates exist, as in the case of agricultural production, they should be broken into their components to permit selection of the best figures from each series, which may then be recombined in a new superior indicator. For example, in the case of the production of certain crops such as oranges, henequen, and maize, data from the agricultural censuses have been supplemented by independent figures from the Ministry of Agriculture. Cross-sectional information from the decennial agricultural censuses are tied to time series data on annual production prepared by the Banco de México on the basis of annual samples made by the Ministry of Agriculture. This offers the advantage of combining more complete regional coverage of the censuses with more consistent measures of secular trends in production from annual data.

In some cases where existing indexes show widely divergent or doubtful trends, such as those used by the Banco de México for agricultural production from 1900 to 1930, I have constructed my own time series, based upon a broader sample of more recently available data. In the case of indexes using alternative deflators, I have selected those with the largest number of components, as in the case of gross domestic investment. For manufacturing, capital stock estimates derived by the commodity flow method have been prepared as an alternative to the use of capital-output ratios drawn from the industrial censuses. In general this study has ruled out guesswork in the estimation of components of GDP in those cases where reliable national accounting data were unavailable. This decision is justified by the appearance of a number of new series since the completion of the manuscript, some of which are cited below, including a set of integrated national accounts for the years 1950–67. Owing to the quality of the Mexican data, it was determined to minimize the filling of statistical empty boxes through the use of analytical ingenuity or accounting identities, since such estimates would simply multiply the influence of already large margins of error in the underlying data. The effect would be to weaken any cross-sectional analysis which relied on such figures, offsetting the advantages of increased generality.

For example, studies attempting to use data based on Mexico's figures for private consumption, as presented in the national accounts, would be of minimal value. Consumption is at present taken as a residual after deducting gross investment, government consumption, and foreign trade from gross domestic product. The gross investment series itself is subject to a wide margin of error, there is no cross-check on personal consumption, and consumption includes net inventory change. Similarly, capital stock estimates are highly sensitive to assumed depreciation rates since they are prepared by the commodity flow method which is applied to an independent estimate of fixed reproducible assets for 1950. In some cases where data on national income are readily available in published form elsewhere, and where proper use would require a detailed knowledge of the assumptions and methods underlying their compilation and presentation, the reader is referred to the original source. This procedure is followed, rather than to simply reproduce the figures here, in order to avoid errors in analysis that might arise from the uncritical application of estimates, such as in the case of the two unofficial sets of integrated national accounts prepared for the years 1950 [3] and 1954.[4]

RECENT PROGRESS IN NATIONAL ACCOUNT ESTIMATION

The methods of estimation of national accounts in Mexico and the statistical basis on which they depend have both improved considerably since the 1950s. Although the economic statistics of the Por-

3. Martin H. Ekker, "Algunas experiencias en la utilización de la técnica Insumo-Producto en los pronósticos económicos"; much of this information is reproduced in "Las cuentas nacionales de México," Banco de México, *Seminario de las Naciones Unidas sobre cuentas nacionales para América Latina.* The reader should be cautioned that these estimates are no longer considered reliable with respect to the functional or personal distribution of income.
4. C. A. Oomens, "Cuentas nacionales y las estadísticas económicas en México," p. 13 ff. (unpublished).

firiato were relatively advanced for the day, the changes wrought by revolution and reform plunged the country into a statistical dark age from which it has yet to fully emerge. Although Mexico has been fortunate to count upon an increasing number of well-trained economists and statisticians in recent years, the continued shortage of qualified personnel has greatly hampered the collection and presentation of data in such a way as to provide an adequate quantitative basis for development planning. As a result national income statistics until well into the 1950s were used primarily to reflect the successes or failures of political administrations rather than as an a priori basis for policy formulation.

One reason for the tendency of policy-makers in the early years to disregard aggregate economic indicators was the wide variation in data available on such crucial magnitudes as the level and rate of growth of agricultural and industrial production and the current value of national income and product. Table C.1 provides a list of selective approximations of national income and product made over the period between 1938 and 1969. It should be obvious from these figures that until well into the 1950s the range of variation of the estimates made them of little more than decorative value. It is not surprising, therefore, that an elaborate system of integrated national accounts has yet to appear for Mexico. The best that could be obtained as late as the mid-sixties was a reasonably accurate set of estimates of GDP and GNP by sector of industrial origin and by functional distribution.

The preparation of input-output tables for 1950 and 1960 has made possible a series of successive revisions of the national accounts by the Department of Economic Studies of the Bank of Mexico. Recently the Department, under the direction of Leopoldo Solís, has produced a new set of tentative annual estimates of national income and product by principal activity as well as factor shares for the years 1950–67.[5] The advantages of these new economic statistics for the evaluation and planning of contemporary economic performance should be evident. Recent expansion in the quality and quantity of staff in the principal data-gathering agency, the Dirección General de Estadística and the economic research divisions of the Secretaría de

5. Banco de México, S.A., Departamento de Estudios Económicos. "Cuentas nacionales y acervos de capital, consolidades y por tipo de actividad económica, 1950–67."

Industria y Comercio and the Banco de México bodes well for continued progress in this area.

Pioneering work on national income estimation from Mexico was begun in the late thirties. The first published estimate of national in-

Appendix Table C.1
Successive Approximations of Mexican National Income, 1929/1939/1942/1950
(million current pesos)

Author	*Date*	*Concept Used*	*1929-30*	*1939*	*1942*	*1950*
					Estimate	
Alanís Patiño	1938	National Income	$2,042_{1929}$			
Alanís Patiño	1943	National Income		3,070		
[Saenz]	1942	National Income	$2,044_{1929}$		$6,916_{1941}$	
Saenz	1943	National Income			6,918	
Saenz	1945	Net Domestic Output	$2,835_{1929}$	6,139	8,928	
World Bank Study	1951–52	National Product (at factor cost)		5,737	9,255	37,816
ECLA	1957	Gross Domestic Product				43,299
Bank of Mexico	1959	National Income		5,900	9,500	37,500
Bank of Mexico	1962	National Income				36,630
Bank of Mexico (Appendix D.1A)	1964	GNP		6,460	10,172	40,577
Bank of Mexico (Appendix D.1A)	1964	GDP		6,559	10,332	41,060
Pérez López[a]	1960	GNP	$4,111_{1930}$			
Reynolds[b]	1968	GDP	$3,954_{1930}$			
Gutierrez[c]	1969	GDP	$4,111_{1930}$			
Solís—Bank of Mexico	1969	GDP				44,016

[a] Based on the GDP estimate of 15,538 million 1950 pesos converted to current values using the wholesale price index for Mexico, D.F. (1930 = 100; 1950 = 378).

[b] Based on a GDP estimate of 14,946 million 1950 pesos converted to current values as in [a].

[c] Based on a GDP estimate of 15,540 million 1950 pesos converted as in [a].

[d] Banco de México, Depto. de Estudios Económicos. "Cuentas nacionales y acervos de capital, consolidados y por tipo de actividad económica, 1950–67."

Sources: See notes in text.

come by Emilio Alanís Patiño appeared in 1938 and was prepared on the basis of his own estimates of the national wealth for 1929 to which an arbitrary coefficient of .20 was applied to provide a national income estimate of 2,042 million pesos.[6] This figure may be compared with Alanís' estimate for GDP in 1930 of 14,946 million 1950 pesos. (If deflated by the wholesale price index for Mexico City, the figure becomes 3,954 million 1930 pesos.) [7] Later the same author provided an estimate of national income for 1939 of 3,070 million pesos based on the earlier study. This figure has subsequently been shown to have represented less than half of the national income of that year (see Table C.1).[8]

In 1942, ex-president Abelardo L. Rodriguez released statistics on national income in 1929 and 1941 that appear to have been developed on the basis of Alanís Patiño's earlier estimates.[9] Shortly thereafter, Josué Saenz published an estimate of national income for 1942 of 6,918 million pesos—a figure close to Rodriguez's 1941 figure. Since Saenz was at that time Director of the General Bureau of Statistics, his department may well have been the source of both estimates.[10] One additional estimate of Mexican national income for 1940 was prepared by Loreto M. Dominguez based on an estimate of the gross value of production of agriculture, mining, and manufacturing to which arbitrary value added coefficients were applied and which were then supplemented by a factor for service income applied to each sector based upon the relationship of services to producing industries in other countries. The estimate for 1940 was 3,142 million pesos, not far from the Alanís Patiño estimate of 3,070 for 1939 (Table C.1), though subsequent official estimates have more than doubled that figure.[11]

6. Secretaría de la Economía Nacional, Dirección General de Estadística, *México en cifras, 1938*. This and other references to historical estimates of national income prepared before 1950 are taken from Henry G. Aubrey, "The National Income of Mexico." A more recent survey of income estimates, which draws somewhat on the former article, was prepared by Eliel Vargas Torres, "Las estimaciones del ingreso nacional en México."

7. Alanís's assumption of a 5/1 capital-output ratio for 1929 is probably exaggerated, regardless of the validity of the capital stock estimate to which it is applied. The capital-output ratio derived by application of the commodity flow method to net investment series for the period 1925 to 1940 is 4.2 (Table 1.7, n. 3).

8. Emilio Alanís Patiño, "La riqueza de México." *Estadística*, Vol. 1, No. 1, March 1943, pp. 33–53.

9. "Sacrificios de la población rural," *El Universal*, December 28, 1942, pp. 1–13, as cited in Aubrey, "The National Income of Mexico," p. 190.

10. Josué Saenz, "El control de precios en una economía de guerra."

11. Loreto M. Dominguez, *National Income Estimates of Latin American Countries*, National Bureau of Economic Research, Studies in Income and Wealth, vol. 10, New York, 1947, p. 227, as cited in Aubrey, "The National Income of Mexico."

After Alanís Patiño, the major pioneer in Mexican national accounting was Josué Saenz. This prominent economist was largely responsible for the first consistent time series of national income estimates covering the period 1929 to 1945, a series which was subsequently expanded to include later years. Aubrey reproduces and slightly adjusts the series for 1929 to 1946 [12] from which the figures for 1929, 1939, and 1942 are presented in Table C.1.[13] This series represents an estimate of "net domestic output of goods and services" as prepared by the General Bureau of Statistics under the direction of Saenz, in which gross production of the various groups was adjusted wherever possible for payments to other industries for raw materials, fuel and power, depreciation, cost of transport, and indirect taxes.

It is clear from Table C.1 that the Saenz 1945 estimates for the years 1939 and 1942 are not far removed from more recent official estimates of the Bank of Mexico, although his earlier figures (for example, 1929) indicate considerable undercounting in terms of the best figures now available. Aubrey suggests that his figures on trade and finance (25 percent of the total in the 1940s) may be too low, especially considering wartime profit margins, that professional services based on tax returns are underestimated, and that livestock output as reported by the slaughterhouse industry undercounts total slaughtering; but for the most part "the estimates can certainly be accepted as the best available" as of 1950. Nevertheless, his conversion of the Saenz estimates into constant (1934) prices shows a net decline in per capita income between 1934 and 1946 from 177 pesos to 148 pesos, although per capita income is shown to have reached a height of 236 pesos in 1941 and 1942.[14]

12. Aubrey, "The National Income of Mexico," Table 6, p. 193.
13. The figures first appeared in an article by Saenz, "El ingreso nacional neto de México, 1929–1945," *Revista de Economía,* February 28, 1946. A subsequent updated series appeared in Secretaría de la Economía Nacional, Dirección General de Estadística, *Compendio Estadístico 1947,* Mexico, D.F., January 1947, p. 534.
14. There is evidence that Aubrey's price deflators exaggerated price increases (with 1934 = 100, his wholesale food price index for 1946 was 385, his mining and metallurgy price index was 217, and his cost of living index was 416). The wholesale price index of *El Trimestre de Barómetros Económicos,* vol. 1, no. 2, September 1946, "Indices de precios al mayoreo en la Cuidad de México y en Estados Unidos," gives a figure of 1929 = 100, 1934 = 89.9, and 1945 = 243.9. On the basis of this index, per capita income in 1946 would be slightly above that of 1934 based upon the Saenz figures, showing that they are still far too low to reflect the real rate of growth of the 1940s.

Despite the significant contribution made by the General Bureau of Statistics, Vargas, in a report to the Bank of Mexico in 1946, called attention to the wide discrepancies in existing estimates of net national product for 1942, ranging from a figure by Alanís of 4,079 million pesos, Saenz's second estimate of 8,928 million pesos (net domestic output), and a second estimate of the Bank of Mexico of 11,972 million pesos—all of which led him to exclaim: "One can consider that the diverse figures obtained are not worthy of confidence." [15] He pointed out that the basis for these conflicting estimates were censuses and time series which had yet to be subjected to critical evaluation to assess their reliability. He noted that a number of the series were prepared hastily with very few components—one might add that in 1946 the Bank of Mexico was attempting to estimate GNP not only by output but by distributive shares, a task that until recently has been given low priority compared with attempts to improve the quality of value added estimates of the principal production sectors.

As of 1947, the Bank itself embarked upon a major effort to prepare more reliable benchmark estimates of national income for the years 1939 to 1945, partly at the request of the IBRD. The resulting estimates were used as a basis for interpolation of intervening years, utilizing indexes of the volume of production of goods and services reflated by a combination of wholesale and retail price indexes. The resulting revised estimate of national income for 1945 was 16,000 million pesos (compared to Saenz's figure of 11,988 million pesos).[16] A continued stimulus for improved national income estimates was provided by the IBRD as a basis for evaluation of the performance of the Mexican economy and subsequent loan policy. In 1951, a joint working party comprised of Mexican and World Bank economists prepared a GNP series based upon four benchmark years (1939, 1944, 1946, and 1949) in which income was classified by principal production sector, by distributive shares, and on a functional basis, with annual statistics interpolated for the entire period 1939–49 and an estimate for 1950.[17]

The World Bank study, despite its numerous weaknesses, represented a milestone in Mexican economic statistical research. It would

15. Vargas Torres, "Estimaciones del Ingreso Nacional de México," p. 462.
16. Banco de México, *Informe Anual*, 1950.
17. Ortiz Mena et al., *El desarrollo económico de México y su capacidad para absorber capital del exterior.*

not have been possible, however, had there not been a decade of ex-
perimentation with national accounting methods and the preparation
of improved statistical indexes, many of which were first published in
an extremely useful though short-lived journal, *El Trimestre de Barómetros Económicos,* which appeared immediately after World War
II. Successive improvements in the quality and coverage of the postwar data eventually revealed a much more rapid rate of growth of real
output than earlier series had indicated. Indeed, it is almost axiomatic
that successive revisions of national income estimates as well as of
individual time series on agricultural and industrial production and
gross investment have tended to shift revealed growth rates upward.
This partially accounts for the misplaced pessimism of numerous
observers of the Mexican economy in earlier years who tended to
place too much confidence in the existing data and too little emphasis
on disaggregative analysis plus informed intuition.

In 1955 the Bank of Mexico drew upon the results of the 1950
population and agricultural censuses to revise its national income and
product series for the years 1939 to 1949, figures that have been revised, as shown in the Annual Reports of the Bank for each year
since 1954. The GNP figures for the years since 1950 reflect increases in physical production indexes adjusted by wholesale and retail price indexes to arrive at current values. The 1955 revision resulted in estimates for total GNP that exceeded those of the World
Bank study by 4 to 5 percent and changed relative shares to increase
that of agriculture as well as wages and salaries, especially for those
years in which income had been estimated by interpolation in the
earlier study. Meanwhile, in 1952 the Nacional Financiera began
estimating total supply and demand in the economy, based upon the
Bank of Mexico's gross product estimates plus its own series on
trade, public and private investment, public consumption, and net
inventory change. While some of these estimates are published in its
annual report, others are not generally available to the public.

A third source of national income figures for Mexico is the Economic Commission for Latin America, which has been estimating
"producto bruto real" (real gross product) in constant prices since
1950, using its characteristic method of weighting physical production indexes by base year (initially 1950) value relatives.[18] In addition to these estimates, ECLA in 1957 sponsored a study of the

18. See United Nations, ECLA, *Estudio Económico de América Latina,*
selected years since 1950.

actual and projected trade conditions of Mexico based upon a relatively detailed set of estimates of the principal components of Mexican national income and product for the period 1945 to 1955 with projections to 1965, all expressed in 1950 pesos. This study used as a basis the 1950 estimate of gross product published in the World Bank study mentioned above. Private consumption plus change in stocks was calculated as a simple residual after deducting public consumption, gross fixed investment, and the balance of payments on current account (net exports of goods and services). This study also provided the first estimate of domestic reproducible wealth in Mexico as of 1950, and served to revise upward previous estimates of gross product, especially for the years 1953 to 1955, by 6.6 percent, 7.5 percent, and 5.6 percent, respectively.[19] ECLA figures for the years 1953–58 exceeded the then current estimates of the Bank of Mexico by an average of 10 percent, while the Bank of Mexico national income figures exceeded those of the World Bank study by an average of 4 to 5 percent.

By the mid-1950s the picture of national income estimation was still very cloudy. It was at this point that enough influential policymakers began to appreciate the fundamental importance of accurate national income statistics to justify a renewed effort at overhauling the accounts. This was in part due to the arrival of a number of professionally trained economists in high office, individuals who found to their dismay that a reliable quantitative basis for consistent global policy formation did not exist. Nor could they fall back on the argument that, although absolute levels of estimates might be off, rates of change were subject to serial correlation of the error term and were therefore relatively reliable. Unfortunately, the differing composition of data from estimate to estimate, as well as the varying rates of growth of alternative component series, meant that both the distribution of income and rate of growth varied widely, depending upon the indicator used. It is not surprising, therefore, that until then most policy-making relied upon simple barometers of economic change such as the level of foreign exchange reserves held by financial intermediaries and the Central Bank, behavior of the price level, expectations of the business and financial community passed on to public policy-makers, and enlightened guesses in high places. Far from criticizing such an approach, it was probably the only salvation for

19. United Nations, ECLA, *External Disequilibrium in the Economic Development of Latin America,* vols. 1 and 2 (mimeograph).

the system during periods of extreme statistical uncertainty, since strict attention to any one of the arbitrary indicators might well have led to policies that would have worsened the very conditions they were supposed to relieve.[20]

Recognizing the need for improved national income estimates, the Mexican government and the Central Bank drew upon the services of Martin Ekker and Cornelius Oomens, Dutch experts in economic planning and national accounting, to review the statistics and provide recommendations for improvements. At the end of a six-month residence in the country, Oomens prepared a detailed survey of national accounts and economic statistics in Mexico. In the process of making the survey, it quickly became clear to him that "little or no relationship had existed between the statisticians of the Bank and those of the Dirección General de Estadística." [21] In order to overcome the lack of contact, he conducted his research in such a manner that the economists of the Bank were able to receive practical training in the preparation of improved statistical indicators by working with their counterparts in the General Bureau of Statistics. It was at this time that it was determined, in large part through the influence of Ekker and Oomens, to prepare an input-output table for 1950 as the basis for subsequent planning models as well as improvements in national accounts. Since much of the 1950 census data was yet unavailable, this first input-output table was not completed until 1958 and has subsequently been revised.[22]

20. It should be noted that in some countries statistical ignorance provides a convenient refuge for those whose policy preferences are either inconsistent with the public interest, or biased in favor of the advantages of laissez faire. In the Mexican case, however, the problem appears to have been one of scarce resources, including the shortage of adequate personnel and funds to collect reliable statistics and transform them into economic indicators. Statistical reform is a long and demanding process, especially when large quantities of data of dubious quality are already being generated by important bureaucratic entities that must undergo major transformation in staff and supervision before the requisite improvements are possible. The circumstances facing Mexico in the 1940s and 1950s were far from exceptional in Latin America and prevail in most of the countries even today. What is remarkable is that Mexican national accounting statistics have been so improved since 1955, not that they were of dubious quality before then.

21. Oomens, "Cuentas nacionales y las estadísticas económicas en México."

22. The original 1950 input-output table appears in condensed form in the article by Ekker in Kuznets et al., *Ingreso y riqueza*. See also Banco de México, Departamento des Estudios Económicos, *Estructura y proyecciones de la economía de México, 1950, 1960, and 1965,* Mexico, 1958, as cited in Vargas, "Las estimaciones del ingreso nacional."

The level of income and product in 1950 obtained from the regional input-output table was approximately 9 percent below that of the World Bank study for the same year. The low estimate in the table has subsequently been attributed to underestimation of the value-added component for wholesale and retail trade, for which data were scanty at the time of its preparation and which has subsequently been revised upwards by 34 percent. All subsequent Bank of Mexico official estimates of GDP and GNP through the end of 1968 relied upon the adjusted 1950 input-output table for the distribution of output and expenditure.

In 1969 figures on the structural composition of gross domestic product were again updated, based upon 1960 census data. The Bank of Mexico, with U.N. assistance, contracted with Professor Oomens to prepare a second input-output table for 1960 as a basis for a new revision of the Bank's national income and product estimates for both the 1950s and 1960s. The 1960 input-output table was used in the elaboration of a set of integrated national accounts for the years 1950–67 including the first detailed set of accounts for the public sector as well as the first official estimate of national income by distributive shares that has appeared since the early fifties.[23]

One disguised advantage of the national income statistical development dilemma is that historical analysis of the Mexican economy must rely heavily upon disaggregated regional and sectoral information if it is to be credible. Indeed such disaggregation may profitably be employed by the Bank to evaluate its aggregate estimates. For example, the pattern of regional income distribution within agriculture, as well as the distribution of income between rural and urban sectors as detailed in Chapters 2 and 3, provide a consistency check on conflicting aggregate measures of functional income distribution for the 1940s and 1950s. Similarly, our estimates of trends in real output in agriculture both regionally and nationally between 1900 and 1929 call for major adjustments in the Bank's series on gross domestic product for the same period. One lesson from this is that much is to be gained by additional quantitative research on individual regions and activities such as transport, commerce, services, mining, and livestock, as well as on such factors as personal and corporate

23. Banco de México, S.A., "Cuadro de insumo producto de México, 1960." See also Banco de México, Depto. de Estudios Económicos. "Cuentas nacionales y acervos de capital, consolidados y por tipo de actividad económica, 1950–67."

savings and investment and family consumption. Such research would provide the requisite underlying statistical information to those engaged in the improvement of national income estimates without which it will remain difficult to mount a comprehensive development plan for either the private or public sector.

In recent years growing attention has been directed to quantitative indicators of Mexican economic history. A number of gaps in the data for the Porfiriato have already been filled by scholars such as those at El Colegio de México under the direction of Daniel Cosío Villegas. Work is also beginning on the intervening years (1910–40), for which considerable original source material exists that has yet to be carefully researched. The first detailed estimate of gross national product on an annual basis from 1895 to 1959 was prepared by Miguel Flores Márquez for Enrique Pérez López and is based upon a combination of value added and gross production indexes for six principal sectors of production (agriculture, livestock, mining, petroleum, manufactures, and transport) plus a category of "other activities" that was assumed to have the same rate of growth over time. Beginning in 1939, the additional categories of construction and electricity were added to the series, although from that year forward the Flores Márquez estimates approximated the then official series of the Bank of Mexico (see Table C.2).[24]

The Flores Márquez–Pérez López estimates, covering as they do only about half of gross national product before 1939, pose a challenge to development historians. In addition to their incomplete coverage, some of the component indexes, and principally the one for agricultural output, suffer from a very narrow statistical base and therefore provide rather misleading information as to magnitude and trend of the economy during the period from 1895 to 1939. In an effort to improve the agricultural component of these figures, this author has recalculated production indexes for the period 1900 to 1907 and 1907 to 1929 (as described in Chapter 2). These adjustments were then used to prepare an independent estimate of gross domestic product for the years 1900, 1910, 1925, 1930, and 1940, as

24. The Flores Márquez estimates appear in an article by Enrique Pérez López, "El producto nacional," in López Mateos, *México: 50 años de revolución,* vol. 1 ("La economía"), pp. 587–89. A revision of the text of this essay appears in an article by the same author, "The National Product of Mexico: 1895 to 1964," along with revised figures for the years since 1939 and an important methodological note on the estimates for the entire period in Pérez López et al., *Mexico's Recent Economic Growth,* pp. 23–44.

Appendix Table C.2
Structure of Gross Domestic Product: Selected Years, 1900–50
(million 1950 pesos)

	1900			1910			1925		
	Reynolds	Pérez-López '67	Guitierrez '69	Reynolds	Pérez-López '67	Guitierrez '69	Reynolds	Pérez-López '67	Guitierrez '69
Agriculture	–	–	–	–	–	–	–	–	4,007
Crop Production	1,218	1,991	1,632	1,344	2,692	2,609	1,718	2,575	2,421
Livestock	1,335	907	1,335	1,510	1,020	1,501	1,620	1,101	1,521
Forestry	–	–	23	–	–	43	–	–	48
Fishing	–	–	–	–	–	–	–	–	17
Manufacturing	1,131	1,232	1,360	1,620	1,663	1,836	2,076	1,889	2,085
Mining	547	541	550	1,044	1,022	1,039	1,187	1,168	1,087
Electrical Energy	–	–	5	–	–	26	–	–	85
Petroleum	–	–	–	34	19	33	1,269	737	1,268
Construction	–	–	54	–	–	102	–	–	257
Transportation	264	237	265	330	295	329	582	521	581
Commerce	–	–	1,697	–	–	2,377	–	–	3,008
Government	–	–	194	–	–	220	641	–	374
Unclassified activities	4,045	4,983	1,135	5,943	6,813	1,535	7,988	8,111	2,063
Gross domestic product	8,540	9,891	8,250	11,825	13,524	11,650	17,081	16,102	14,816

Sources: See text.

Appendix Table C.2—*Continued*

	1930			1940			1950		
	Reynolds	*Pérez-López '67*	*Gutierrez '69*	*Reynolds*	*Pérez-López '67*	*Gutierrez '69*	*Reynolds*	*Pérez-López '67*	*Gutierrez '69*
Agriculture	–	–	3,773	5,266	–	5,171	9,242	–	9,242
Crop Production	1,962	1,975	2,283	2,730	2,739	2,898	5,999	5,912	5,999
Livestock	1,591	1,081	1,434	2,247	1,526	2,070	2,903	1,972	2,903
Forestry	–	–	42	265	–	180	263	–	263
Fishing	–	–	14	24	–	23	77	–	77
Manufacturing	2,489	2,189	2,416	3,889	3,629	4,264	8,437	7,643	8,437
Mining	1,458	1,435	1,458	1,209	1,190	1,241	1,243	1,223	1,243
Electrical energy	–	–	122	211	112	212	370	197	370
Petroleum	552	321	552	638	371	574	1,129	656	1,129
Construction	–	–	301	784	460	497	1,287	756	1,287
Transportation	793	710	793	974	871	865	1,988	1,780	1,988
Commerce	2,365	–	3,585	5,203	–	5,919	10,750	–	10,750
Government	543	–	368	668	–	898	1,294	–	1,294
Unclassified activities	3,193	7,827	2,172	2,816	9,833	3,248	5,320	21,361	5,320
Gross domestic product	14,946	15,538	15,540	21,658	20,721	22,889	41,060	41,500	41,060

presented in Chapters 1 and 2 and Table C.2. For the most part, changes in the values of the other sectors of the economy reflect the application of 1940 rather than 1950 weights to production indexes not very different from those of Pérez López.

A more recent revision of the Flores Márquez–Pérez López series for the period 1895 to 1939, including an updating of the data from 1939 to 1967 in 1950 pesos, was prepared by Mario Gutierrez Requenes under the direction of Leopoldo Solís, Chief of Economic Studies, Department of Economic Studies of the Bank of Mexico. The Gutierrez estimates include, in addition to the six sectors of the Pérez López index, data on forestry, fishing, construction, electric energy, government, and commerce. In this new series the data on agricultural output are revised downward considerably for earlier years (although not nearly as much as in the present author's adjustment, since the revised figures show agricultural production at 1,632 million 1950 pesos in 1900, 2,609 in 1910, 2,421 in 1925, and 2,283 in 1930).[25] Until the basis for these more complete estimates becomes available, it will not be possible to assess their reliability, although the very fact of greater detail in the calculation of GDP suggests that as indicators of secular trend they are an improvement over the present figures. There is little likelihood that long-term trends will be seriously affected by these estimates, however, since the Gutierrez GDP figures for selected years differ only slightly from my own estimates (Table C.2).

There is some question as to the short-run behavior of the new series, however, since the low estimate for 1925 (14,816 million 1950 pesos) suggests a net *increase* in GDP between that year and 1930, despite the impact of world depression and the unsettling conditions of the Cristero rebellion. It will be recalled that all previous series have suggested an increase in output through 1928 followed by a decline to 1930 that was considerably *below* 1925 levels. The growth rates implicit in the Gutierrez and Reynolds adjusted figures may be compared as follows: according to the Reynolds estimates, GDP grew at an annual rate of 2.5 percent from 1910 to 1925, then fell at a rate of −2.6 percent a year from 1925 to 1930. The Gutierrez figures show GDP rising at a yearly rate of 1.6 percent from 1910 to 1925 and then continuing to rise at 0.9 percent from 1925 to 1930.

25. Banco de México, S.A., Depto. de Estudios Económicos. "Producto bruto interno y series básicas 1895–1967." Prepared by Mario Gutierrez Requenes.

The greatest discrepancy between the two series is in the level of crop production in 1910, a year in which the Reynolds estimate is but one-half that of the Gutierrez figure. The former figure is based upon a backward extrapolation of data from 1929 relying upon my more comprehensive physical production index which indicates significant growth in total output for the period 1907 to 1929. The Gutierrez agricultural series, which appears to be taken largely from that of Pérez López, is heavily weighted toward a few staple crops and therefore shows a reduction rather than an increase in agricultural production between 1910 and 1930. This accounts for his higher figure for agricultural value added in the base year.

The following is a summary of some of the most significant problems that remain even in the most recent official estimates of income and product since 1940. The figures on level and rate of growth of value added in commerce are questionable, due to wide differences of opinion as to the share of this sector in GDP in 1950 and 1960 (the base years used for calculation of value added indexes) as well as to coverage and deflator. A strong possibility exists of an upward bias in the rate of growth of this sector, a problem that may account for the strange behavior of labor productivity growth in the combined service sector that appears to have outstripped the productivity performance of all other sectors in recent years (Chapter 2). Since tertiary activities have constituted a leading sector in GDP during the past three decades, the possibility of upward bias in the growth of value added in this sector could have a significant effect on the rate of growth of GDP, which is no more than a weighted average of the component series.

The valuation and growth of subsistence agricultural production also creates a problem—especially for those years for which data has been interpolated—since the decennial agricultural census, which is relatively broad in coverage but still far from complete, is used as a base for the application of indexes derived from annual samples by the Ministry of Agriculture that focus primarily on commercial crop production. The fact that subsistence agriculture has almost certainly lagged in recent years in terms of both income and product suggests an upward bias in the growth of value added in agriculture as reported in the national accounts as well as the possibility of a downward bias in the relative share of agriculture in the base period because of undercounting of subsistence production. This has implications for my own estimates of regional agricultural income distribution, since they may bias downward the share of poorer regions as a result of the inferior quality of census-taking in the subsistence sector and the use in this study of regional census value weights by decade. It should also be noted that the data on vegetable crops are incomplete, although figures on corn and bean production have been adjusted upwards on the basis of consumption estimates; furthermore, the data on corn production refer only to dry grain and not that which is transformed into tortillas and other food products. There is little or no data on wild greens and root crops, which are important in the diet of the rural inhabitants. The cattle census information is extremely incomplete and unreliable, the 1960 cattle census actually showing a decline in the stock of some animals over 1950 levels, although stocks almost certainly increased during the 1950s.

Nevertheless as we have seen considerable effort is now being made to improve the coverage and reliability of the underlying statistics and, ultimately, to prepare estimates of national income and product on a more inclusive basis than presently exists. Meanwhile the increased accommodation by officials of the Bank of Mexico, Finance Ministry, and General Bureau of Statistics of professional economists and statisticians interested in the constructive use and improvement of national accounting data bodes well for the future availability of a wide range of improved economic indicators. Clearly the public interest calls for considerably more expenditure on data collection and the preparation of regional and national income estimates than now exists, as well as greater economic analytical use of the quantitative measures which are now available, if rational decision making is to be assured.[26]

26. The economic payoff to efforts at extension and improvement of national income statistics is likely to be extremely high. The advice that Kenneth Arrow gave to Greek planners in 1965 applies as well to Mexico today:

In brief, then, I am arguing that increased knowledge of economic facts is likely to be as productive an investment as any economy is likely to have available. I would hold that this proposition is true even for the United States, which already has a rich and highly sophisticated and reliable statistical system. The proposition is *a fortiori* true for developing countries; on the one hand, their economies are undergoing radical structural alterations and therefore require for their understanding more thorough observation; on the other hand, such countries are very apt to be underdeveloped statistically as well.

Kenneth J. Arrow, *Statistical Requirements for Greek Economic Planning,* Center of Planning and Economic Research, Lecture Series 18, Athens, 1965, p. 14.

Appendix D

Mexican National Economic Accounts

Appendix Table D.1A

Expenditure on the Gross National Product, 1939–65

(million current pesos)

	1939	1940	1941	1942	1943	1944	1945	1946	1947
A. Private consumption expenditure[a]									
Estimate (1)	5,335	5,608	6,950	8,603	11,346	15,219	18,074	21,804	23,805
Estimate (2)	5,405	5,771	7,186	8,780	11,422	15,423	18,248	22,327	24,556
B. Government current expenditures									
Estimate (1)	513	538	485	604	787	801	1,073	1,136	1,265
Estimate (2)	–	–	–	–	–	–	–	–	–
C. Gross fixed capital formation									
Estimate (1)	429	702	953	857	825	1,183	1,660	2,965	3,797
Estimate (2)	359	539	717	680	749	979	1,486	2,442	3,046
D. Change in stocks[b]	–	–	–	–	–	–	–	–	–
E. Exports of goods and services	1,122	1,156	1,179	1,315	1,803	1,840	2,147	2,581	2,299
F. Less: Imports of goods and services	840	896	1,154	1,047	1,772	2,148	3,288	3,157	3,368
G. Gross Domestic Product	6,559	7,108	8,413	10,332	12,989	16,895	19,666	25,329	27,798
H. Plus: Net factor income from abroad	–99	–113	–149	–160	–50	56	7	–138	–241
I. Gross National Product[c]	6,460	6,995	8,264	10,172	12,959	16,951	19,673	25,191	27,557

Appendix Table D.1A—*Continued*

	1948	1949	1950	1951	1952	1953	1954	1955	1956
A. Private consumption expenditure[a]									
Estimate (1)	25,304	25,579	32,376	42,815	46,204	45,561	56,067	70,358	73,931
Estimate (2)	26,033	26,180	33,589	45,073	48,737	48,450	58,667	70,415	79,363
B. Government current expenditures									
Estimate (1)	1,647	2,517	1,722	1,842	2,169	2,340	2,782	3,431	3,955
Estimate (2)	–	–	1,769	2,167	2,534	2,602	3,148	3,783	4,420
C. Gross fixed capital formation									
Estimate (1)	4,087	4,610	6,041	9,165	10,721	11,006	12,676	16,674	22,235
Estimate (2)	3,358	4,009	4,828	6,907	8,188	8,117	10,076	12,617	16,803
D. Change in stocks[b]	–	–	–	–	–	–	–	–	–
E. Exports of goods and services	3,958	5,448	6,439	7,106	7,675	7,462	10,412	13,508	14,688
F. Less: Imports of goods and services	4,999	4,672	5,565	8,227	7,750	7,705	10,098	12,105	14,674
G. Gross Domestic Product	29,997	33,482	41,060	53,026	59,384	58,926	72,205	88,218	100,600
H. Plus: Net factor income from abroad	-303	-397	-483	-715	-741	-526	-665	-869	-1,277
I. Gross National Product[e]	29,694	33,085	40,577	52,311	58,643	58,400	71,540	87,349	99,323

Appendix Table D.1A—*Continued*

	1957	1958	1959	1960	1961	1962	1963	1964	1965
A. Private consumption expenditure[a]									
Estimate (1)	87,036	99,138	104,128	116,393	124,403	136,617	–	–	–
Estimate (2)	93,273	105,334	111,929	126,299	133,161	144,170	155,595	180,711	194,600
B. Government current expenditures									
Estimate (1)	4,668	5,506	5,924	7,085	7,591	8,358	–	–	–
Estimate (2)	5,203	5,937	6,196	7,993	8,600	9,557	11,200	12,500	13,800
C. Gross fixed capital formation									
Estimate (1)	25,429	25,122	27,385	33,132	32,829	32,344	–	–	–
Estimate (2)	19,192	18,926	19,584	23,226	24,071	24,791	28,000	36,600	38,700
D. Change in stocks[b]	–	–	–	–	–	–	–	–	–
E. Exports of goods and services	13,734	13,816	14,203	14,853	15,896	17,510	20,900	22,500	24,700
F. Less: Imports of goods and services	15,860	15,443	14,236	16,504	16,056	16,154	20,900	24,300	25,600
G. GROSS DOMESTIC PRODUCT	115,542	128,570	137,676	155,867	165,672	179,874	194,845	228,011	246,200
H. Plus: Net factor income from abroad	–1,317	–1,423	–1,465	–1,752	–1,914	–2,341	–2,600	–3,400	–3,500
I. GROSS NATIONAL PRODUCT[c]	114,225	127,147	136,211	154,115	163,758	177,533	192,245	224,611	242,700

Appendix Table D.1A—*Continued*

a Residual, including changes in stocks. The two alternatives are computed as follows:

1939–49	1950–65
A(1) = I − [B(1) + C(1) + E − F + H]	A(1) = I − [B(2) + C(1) + E − F + H]
A(2) = I − [B(1) + C(2) + E − F + H]	A(2) = I − [B(2) + C(2) + E − F + H]

b Data not available; changes in stocks are therefore included in the residual (line A).

c Line G + line H.

Sources: Data from, or based on, the following sources:

Banco '63–data received direct from the Banco de México, December 27, 1963.

Grupo–Grupo Secretaría de Hacienda-Banco de México, Estudios sobre Proyecciones, "Manual" and Annex (mimeograph).

Muro–Bosco A. Muro, "Estructura y evolución del gasto público en México" (typescript); "exhaustive consumption expenditures" discussed in Chapter 6 below.

Cossío–Banco de México, Departamento de Estudios Económicos, "Alternativas de Estimación de la Inversión Bruta Fija en México, 1939–1962" (prepared by Luis Cossío; mimeograph).

OECD–OECD Development Centre, *National Accounts of Less Developed Countries* (preliminary, February 1967), pp. 56–58.

Detailed table numbers and some descriptions are shown below by short titles:

	Table D.1A (current pesos)	Table D.1B (1950 pesos)	Remarks
B. Government current expenditure			
B(1) General government, "exhaustive" 1939–62	Muro	Based on D.1A	(1)
B(2) General government			
1950–62	Banco '63	Banco '63	
1963–65	OECD 17	—	
C. Gross fixed capital formation			
C(1) Cossío III 1939–62	Cossío B 17	Cossío B 18	
C(2) Cossío I 1939–62	Cossío B 17	Cossío B 18	
C(2) 1963–65	OECD 17	—	1950–62 check Cossío I

Appendix Table D.1A—*Continued*

	Table D.1A (current pesos)	Table D.1B (1950 pesos)	Remarks
E. Exports of goods and services			
1939–49	Grupo VII-12	Based on Grupo VII-13	(2)
1950–62	Banco '63	Banco '63	
1963–65	OECD 17	—	
F. Imports of goods and services			
1939–49	Grupo VII-14	Based on Grupo VII-15	(2)
1950–62	Banco '63	Banco '63	
1963–65	OECD 17	—	
G. Gross Domestic Product			
1939–49	Grupo II-1	Grupo II-3 ⎫	
1950–62	Banco '63	Banco '63 ⎬	All agree
1950–65	OECD 17	OECD 18 ⎭	
H. Net factor income from abroad			
1939–49	Grupo VII-12 and VII-14	Based on Grupo VII-13, VII-15	(3)
1950–62	Banco '63	Banco '63	
1963–65	OECD 17	OECD 18	

1. Deflated using the index for "federal" government current expenditures 1960 = 100, from Grupo VI-9, rebased to 1950 = 100.
2. Data in 1950 pesos approximated by linking data in 1960 pesos from Grupo VII-13 for exports and Grupo VII-15 for imports to corresponding Banco '63 figures, at the year 1950.
3. Data in 1950 pesos approximated by linking net data in 1960 pesos from Grupo VII-13 and VII-15 to corresponding Banco '63 net figures, at the year 1950.

Appendix Table D.1B
Expenditure on the Gross National Product, 1939–65
(*million 1950 pesos*)

	1939	1940	1941	1942	1943	1944	1945	1946	1947
A. Private consumption expenditure[a]									
Estimate (1)	16,517	16,236	18,473	20,037	21,657	24,481	24,885	26,326	26,330
Estimate (2)	16,832	16,842	19,252	20,708	21,888	24,930	55,542	27,343	27,617
B. Government current expenditures									
Estimate (1)	1,565	1,592	1,373	1,891	1,763	1,490	1,856	1,647	1,733
Estimate (2)	–	–	–	–	–	–	–	–	–
C. Gross fixed capital formation									
Estimate (1)	1,482	2,206	2,785	2,399	2,161	2,655	3,848	5,408	6,321
Estimate (2)	1,169	1,600	2,006	1,728	1,730	2,206	3,191	4,391	5,034
D. Change in stocks[b]	–	–	–	–	–	–	–	–	–
E. Exports of goods and services	4,085	3,887	4,445	4,598	4,948	4,480	4,587	4,542	4,931
F. Less: Imports of goods and services	2,195	2,263	3,037	2,476	2,852	3,818	4,656	6,008	6,308
G. GROSS DOMESTIC PRODUCT	21,456	21,658	24,039	26,449	27,477	29,288	30,520	31,915	33,007
H. Plus: Net factor income from abroad	–294	–312	–389	–370	15	222	136	–62	–179
GROSS NATIONAL PRODUCT[c]	21,162	21,346	23,650	26,079	27,492	29,510	30,656	31,853	32,828

Appendix Table D.1B—*Continued*

	1948	1949	1950	1951	1952	1953	1954	1955	1956
A. Private consumption expenditure[a]									
Estimate (1)	27,243	27,624	32,376	36,271	35,876	36,631	40,984	43,595	45,896
Estimate (2)	28,255	28,746	33,589	37,813	37,606	38,089	42,420	45,199	48,128
B. Government current expenditures									
Estimate (1)	1,992	2,693	1,722	1,562	1,668	1,757	1,916	2,059	2,219
Estimate (2)	–	–	1,769	1,930	2,078	1,990	2,056	2,166	2,376
C. Gross fixed capital formation									
Estimate (1)	5,733	5,362	6,041	7,784	8,213	7,701	7,945	8,889	10,837
Estimate (2)	4,712	4,240	4,828	6,242	6,483	6,243	6,509	7,288	8,605
D. Change in stocks[b]	–	–	–	–	–	–	–	–	–
E. Exports of goods and services	4,935	5,845	6,439	5,892	6,798	6,681	6,814	8,098	8,500
F. Less: Imports of goods and services	5,448	4,673	5,565	7,660	7,026	7,004	6,940	7,436	8,647
G. GROSS DOMESTIC PRODUCT	34,446	36,851	41,060	44,217	45,939	45,999	50,859	55,312	58,962
H. Plus: Net factor income from abroad	–280	–379	–483	–596	–573	–411	–468	–545	–748
I. GROSS NATIONAL PRODUCT[c]	34,166	36,472	40,577	43,621	45,366	45,588	50,391	54,767	58,214

Appendix Table D.1B—*Continued*

	1957	1958	1959	1960	1961	1962	1963	1964	1965
A. Private consumption expenditure[a]									
Estimate (1)	50,568	53,740	53,864	58,912	60,026	63,188	—	—	—
Estimate (2)	52,786	55,735	56,553	61,291	62,576	65,503	—	—	—
B. Government current expenditures									
Estimate (1)	2,441	2,747	2,908	3,252	3,484	3,744	—	—	—
Estimate (2)	2,648	2,714	2,514	3,031	3,170	3,400	—	—	—
C. Gross fixed capital formation									
Estimate (1)	11,334	10,647	11,388	12,387	12,690	12,359	—	—	—
Estimate (2)	9,116	8,652	8,699	10,008	10,141	10,044	10,900	13,200	—
D. Change in stocks[b]	—	—	—	—	—	—	—	—	—
E. Exports of goods and services	7,852	8,430	8,978	9,090	9,867	10,638	—	—	—
F. Less: Imports of goods and services	8,971	8,613	7,892	9,103	8,826	8,842	—	—	—
G. Gross Domestic Product	63,431	66,918	68,852	74,317	76,927	80,742	85,865	94,615	99,700
H. Plus: Net factor income from abroad	−723	−741	−733	−835	−889	−1,051	−1,200	−1,400	−1,500
I. Gross National Product[c]	62,708	66,177	68,119	73,482	76,038	79,692	84,665	93,215	98,200

Notes and sources: See Appendix Table D.1A.

Appendix Table D.2
Federal Government Revenue and Expenditure, 1939–65
(million current pesos)

A: FEDERAL GOVERNMENT RECEIPTS

	1939	1940	1941	1942	1943	1944	1945	1946	1947
Direct taxes									
Income tax	–	56.6	55.1	77.7	218.2	301.8	295.6	371.4	479.3
Export revenue	–	46.5	43.9	75.0	111.8	105.6	110.7	112.8	104.0
Other	–	2.7	3.0	2.4	2.0	1.8	2.1	2.8	13.2
Total	–	105.8	102.0	155.1	332.0	409.2	408.4	487.0	596.5
Indirect taxes									
Natural resources	–	39.4	40.5	48.7	53.7	69.9	66.6	88.5	137.8
Production and commerce	–	124.5	108.7	138.2	173.8	222.1	245.1	286.2	238.5
Mercantile revenues	–	31.9	37.5	45.2	56.8	63.6	77.6	167.9	173.0
Import duties	–	90.6	123.9	93.0	89.5	117.9	135.3	207.6	252.4
Other	–	15.2	17.0	19.8	26.2	29.7	34.3	52.3	53.9
Total	–	301.6	327.6	344.9	400.0	503.2	558.9	802.5	855.6
Other income	–	103.0	114.5	131.1	184.1	169.4	201.0	310.0	276.2
Grand total receipts	–	510.4	544.1	631.1	916.1	1,081.8	1,168.3	1,599.5	1,728.3

Appendix Table D.2—*Continued*

B: FEDERAL GOVERNMENT EXPENDITURES

	1939	1940	1941	1942	1943	1944	1945	1946	1947
Current expenditures									
Administrative	—	343.9	376.3	423.9	476.1	556.3	636.7	705.7	818.8
Transfers									
To consumption and investment	—	39.7	18.6	37.4	60.3	58.8	79.2	88.8	150.6
Interest on the debt	—	6.3	5.5	19.3	43.4	39.4	50.1	51.8	51.3
Unclassified	—	22.7	48.3	22.7	52.8	61.7	84.3	70.4	73.0
Total	—	412.6	448.7	503.3	632.6	716.2	850.3	916.7	1,093.7
Capital expenditures									
Direct physical investment	—	102.6	129.3	195.7	237.9	285.1	360.2	453.8	468.3
Acquisition of real estate	—	0.3	0.3	0.7	1.8	2.7	4.3	3.1	0.4
Financing of other sectors	—	33.3	23.7	54.1	56.1	71.8	101.6	86.3	193.8
Other expenses	—	3.1	11.6	7.4	5.8	3.7	4.2	3.4	6.6
Total	—	139.3	164.9	257.9	301.6	363.3	470.3	546.6	669.1
Grand total expenditures	—	551.9	613.6	761.2	934.2	1,079.5	1,320.6	1,463.3	1,762.8

Appendix Table D.2—*Continued*

A: FEDERAL GOVERNMENT RECEIPTS

	1948	1949	1950	1951	1952	1953	1954	1955	1956
Direct taxes									
Income tax	451.2	586.0	766.2	1,195.6	1,441.0	1,137.4	1,261.7	1,984.9	2,432.4
Export revenue	98.1	458.6	470.3	672.7	677.9	558.9	911.9	1,431.2	1,261.0
Other	18.7	19.2	28.4	37.1	43.0	50.8	58.2	72.1	87.2
Total	568.0	1,063.8	1,264.9	1,905.4	2,161.9	1,747.1	2,231.8	3,488.2	3,780.6
Indirect taxes									
Natural resources	162.8	151.0	87.3	230.7	254.7	182.2	135.5	220.1	145.1
Production and commerce	251.6	348.5	364.6	420.8	525.3	540.2	587.3	771.3	905.8
Mercantile revenues	180.1	247.9	320.8	394.4	420.1	404.1	494.4	641.6	727.5
Import duties	323.4	345.2	432.3	622.3	608.6	634.1	782.0	894.7	980.9
Other	42.0	46.0	61.2	74.5	72.3	70.9	84.4	124.5	148.5
Total	959.9	1,138.6	1,266.2	1,742.7	1,881.0	1,831.5	2,083.6	2,652.2	2,907.8
Other income	404.4	484.6	525.6	704.7	799.5	736.2	845.3	993.0	1,292.7
Grand total receipts	1,931.9	2,687.0	3,056.7	4,352.8	4,842.4	4,314.8	5,160.7	7,133.4	7,981.1

Appendix Table D.2—*Continued*

B: FEDERAL GOVERNMENT EXPENDITURES

	1948	1949	1950	1951	1952	1953	1954	1955	1956
Current expenditures									
Administrative	928.2	1,099.5	1,267.0	1,290.2	1,515.0	1,586.5	2,021.9	2,355.4	2,602.9
Transfers									
To consumption and investment	287.3	387.7	335.2	475.4	687.8	617.7	903.3	952.0	1,451.1
Interest on the debt	85.6	87.2	85.5	142.5	184.7	152.7	219.6	254.5	291.5
Unclassified	137.2	118.9	42.9	99.6	251.3	59.9	46.1	94.2	91.1
Total	1,438.3	1,693.3	1,730.6	2,007.7	2,638.8	2,416.8	3,190.9	3,656.1	4,436.6
Capital expenditures									
Direct physical investment	595.5	649.1	655.2	933.4	1,401.3	1,377.9	1,772.9	1,890.6	1,999.4
Acquisition of real estate	1.3	0.6	6.2	6.5	35.6	9.3	84.9	22.2	44.7
Financing of other sectors	136.3	185.4	398.7	720.5	985.7	823.2	795.1	985.0	1,221.8
Other expenses	6.9	2.5	5.2	35.1	8.4	35.3	10.4	36.6	49.6
Total	740.0	837.6	1,065.3	1,695.5	2,431.0	2,245.7	2,663.3	2,934.4	3,315.3
Grand total expenditures	2,178.3	2,530.9	2,795.9	3,703.2	5,069.8	4,662.5	5,854.2	6,590.5	7,752.1

Appendix Table D.2—*Continued*

A: FEDERAL GOVERNMENT RECEIPTS

	1957	1958	1959	1960	1961	1962	1963	1964	1965
Direct taxes									
Income tax	2,700.1	2,729.9	3,056.2	3,628.1	4,070.9	4,723.9	6,164.7	–	–
Export revenue	1,003.6	940.8	926.7	932.0	913.5	863.0	777.0	–	–
Other	95.2	114.8	98.0	111.1	87.5	96.9	126.0	–	–
Total	3,798.9	3,785.5	4,080.9	4,671.2	5,071.9	5,683.8	7,067.7	–	–
Indirect taxes									
Natural resources	70.0	129.7	135.6	260.7	252.0	239.4	259.6	–	–
Production and commerce	882.0	936.6	1,158.4	1,314.2	1,465.8	1,802.4	1,903.8	–	–
Mercantile revenues	774.9	878.6	952.3	1,102.0	1,269.1	1,449.1	1,545.0	–	–
Import duties	986.1	1,262.8	1,552.8	1,752.6	1,677.7	1,687.7	1,885.2	–	–
Other	161.6	176.1	241.1	269.8	280.0	300.7	336.0	–	–
Total	2,874.6	3,383.8	4,040.2	4,699.3	4,944.6	5,479.3	5,929.7	–	–
Other income	1,363.1	1,440.9	932.3	1,596.0	1,401.3	1,666.1	1,617.7	–	–
Grand total receipts	8,036.6	8,610.2	9,053.4	10,966.5	11,417.8	12,829.2	14,615.0	–	–

Appendix Table D.2—*Continued*

	1957	1958	1959	1960	1961	1962	1963	1964	1965
	B: FEDERAL GOVERNMENT EXPENDITURES								
Current expenditures									
Administrative	2,852.5	3,462.3	3,939.2	4,806.1	5,197.2	5,705.8	6,436.2	–	–
Transfers									
To consumption and investment	1,808.8	1,641.1	2,310.4	2,468.3	3,471.0	4,450.0	4,840.3	–	–
Interest on the debt	308.1	329.3	379.5	513.3	902.8	709.2	685.9	–	–
Unclassified	134.7	135.9	113.5	96.2	104.3	132.6	176.5	–	–
Total	5,104.1	5,568.6	6,742.6	7,883.9	9,675.3	10,997.6	12,138.9	–	–
Capital expenditures									
Direct physical investment	2,085.7	2,596.3	1,826.9	2,795.9	2,734.8	2,954.1	3,099.1	–	–
Acquisition of real estate	29.5	33.2	63.9	40.2	20.1	43.9	31.2	–	–
Financing of other sectors	1,313.5	1,223.4	1,307.8	1,082.5	773.4	770.5	1,457.4	–	–
Other expenses	62.2	63.9	38.5	125.3	107.8	73.4	80.1	–	–
Total	3,490.9	3,916.8	3,237.1	4,043.9	3,636.1	3,841.9	4,667.8	–	–
Grand total expenditures	8,595.0	9,485.4	9,979.7	11,927.8	13,311.4	14,839.5	16,806.7	–	–

Source: Data on the Secretaría de Hacienda y Credito Público, Dirección de Estudios Hacendarios, based on *Cuenta de la Hacienda Pública Federal*, taken from *Grupo*, Tables 6-3 for "effective" receipts, and Tables 6-5 for expenditures. See text tables 7.6 and 7.7 for components as percent of total.

Appendix Table D.3
External Transactions, 1939–65
(*million current pesos*)

A: Receipts from Abroad

	1939	1940	1941	1942	1943	1944	1945	1946	1947
Exports of goods and services									
Merchandise									
Excluding gold and silver	527	510	566	701	1,114	1,127	1,317	1,545	2,056
Production of gold and silver[a]	321	353	290	305	300	250	239	242	287
Total	848	863	856	1,006	1,414	1,377	1,556	1,787	2,343
Tourism									
Internal	97	94	128	80	133	156	223	415	394
Frontier[b]	156	178	176	208	221	261	314	320	320
Total	253	272	304	288	354	417	537	735	714
Other services	21	21	19	21	35	46	54	59	242
Total goods and services	1,122	1,156	1,179	1,315	1,803	1,840	2,147	2,581	3,299
Factor income from abroad									
Bracero income	–	–	–	–	176	244	267	165	142
Other	–	–	–	7	10	13	15	19	21
Total	–	–	–	7	186	257	282	184	163
Grand total receipts	1,122	1,156	1,179	1,322	1,989	2,097	2,429	2,765	3,462

Appendix Table D.3—*Continued*

	1939	1940	1941	1942	1943	1944	1945	1946	1947
				B: Payments to Abroad					
Imports of goods and services									
Merchandise									
Ordinary[c]	665	715	967	835	1,029	1,508	1,807	2,913	3,494
Frontier imports[d]	93	108	123	145	154	182	241	244	244
Total	758	823	1,090	979	1,183	1,690	2,048	3,157	3,737
Tourism	47	43	29	29	29	29	49	70	71
Other services	35	30	34	39	44	53	50	61	60
Total goods and services	840	896	1,154	1,047	1,256	1,772	2,148	3,288	3,868
Factor income paid abroad									
Service of foreign direct investment	99	113	149	152	195	168	241	283	365
Other	–	–	–	15	40	33	34	39	39
Total	99	113	149	167	236	201	275	322	404
Grand total payments	939	1,009	1,302	1,214	1,491	1,973	2,422	3,610	4,273
			C: Net Receipts (+) or Net Payments (−)						
Balance	+183	+147	−123	+108	+498	+124	+7	−845	−811

Appendix Table D.3—*Continued*

A: Receipts from Abroad

	1948	1949	1950	1951	1952	1953	1954	1955	1956
Exports of goods and services									
Merchandise									
Excluding gold and silver	2,404	3,256	4,268	5,117	5,409	4,836	6,984	9,233	10,090
Production of gold and silver[a]	311	396	437	95	255	449	513	594	534
Total	2,715	3,652	4,705	5,212	5,664	5,285	7,497	9,827	10,624
Tourism									
Internal	503	804	959	959	994	941	972	1,476	1,670
Frontier[b]	614	689	1,054	1,283	1,411	1,746	2,798	3,271	3,474
Total	1,117	1,493	2,013	2,242	2,405	2,687	3,770	4,747	5,144
Other services	126	303	234	176	120	143	223	249	252
Total goods and services	3,958	5,448	6,952	7,630	8,189	8,115	11,490	14,823	16,020
Factor income from abroad									
Bracero income	124	141	168	255	250	291	316	310	473
Other	25	27	30	25	48	43	47	51	55
Total	149	168	198	280	298	334	363	361	528
Grand total receipts	4,107	5,616	7,150	7,910	8,487	8,449	11,853	15,184	16,548

Appendix Table D.3—*Continued*

B: PAYMENTS TO ABROAD

	1948	1949	1950	1951	1952	1953	1954	1955	1956
Imports of goods and services									
Merchandise									
Ordinary[e]	3,395	4,120	5,161	7,688	7,169	6,985	8,944	11,046	13,395
Frontier imports[d]	450	391	662	765	879	1,109	1,839	1,890	2,148
Total	3,846	4,511	5,823	8,453	8,048	8,094	10,784	12,936	15,543
Tourism	72	46	60	90	99	104	123	149	195
Other services	82	115	125	158	129	158	292	264	261
Total goods and services	3,999	4,672	6,008	8,701	8,275	8,356	11,198	13,349	15,999
Factor income paid abroad									
Service of foreign direct investment	386	433	571	879	931	717	854	995	1,501
Other	66	132	169	157	147	182	216	296	349
Total	452	565	740	1,037	1,078	899	1,070	1,291	1,850
Grand total payments	4,451	5,237	6,748	9,737	9,353	9,255	12,268	14,640	17,849

C: NET RECEIPTS (+) OR NET PAYMENTS (—)

	1948	1949	1950	1951	1952	1953	1954	1955	1956
Balance	−344	+379	+402	−1,827	−866	−806	−415	+544	−1,301

Appendix Table D.3—*Continued*

A: Receipts from Abroad

	1957	1958	1959	1960	1961	1962	1963	1964	1965
Exports of goods and services									
Merchandise									
Excluding gold and silver	8,826	8,864	9,038	9,234	10,044	11,244	11,699	12,794	13,924
Production of gold and silver[a]	650	640	414	596	510	556	641	569	554
Total	9,476	9,504	9,452	9,830	10,554	11,800	12,340	13,363	14,478
Tourism									
Internal	1,610	1,677	1,772	1,903	2,050	2,232	2,633	3,008	3,470
Frontier[b]	3,916	3,945	4,425	4,575	4,909	5,084	5,574	5,791	6,307
Total	5,526	5,622	6,197	6,478	6,959	7,316	8,207	8,799	9,777
Other services	237	229	222	291	297	271	385	376	554[c]
Total goods and services	15,239	15,355	15,871	16,599	17,810	19,387	20,931	22,538	24,809
Factor income from abroad									
Bracero income	415	446	472	451	426	399	385	361	152
Other	59	65	108	60	55	50	50	59	—[e]
Total	474	511	580	511	481	449	435	420	152
Grand total receipts	15,713	15,866	16,451	17,110	18,291	19,836	21,366	22,958	24,961

Appendix Table D.3—*Continued*

B: PAYMENTS TO ABROAD

	1957	1958	1959	1960	1961	1962	1963	1964	1965
Imports of goods and services									
Merchandise									
Ordinary[c]	14,440	14,107	12,583	14,830	14,232	14,287	15,496	18,663	19,495
Frontier imports[d]	2,407	2,360	2,756	2,764	3,025	3,058	3,315	3,458	3,679
Total	16,848	16,468	15,339	17,594	17,257	17,345	18,811	22,120	23,174
Tourism	249	243	306	356	384	433	1,104	1,253	1,491
Other services	209	234	260	375	488	468	916	908	1,158[f]
Total goods and services	17,305	16,944	15,905	18,325	18,129	18,246	20,831	24,280	25,823[f]
Factor income paid abroad									
Service of foreign direct investment	1,465	1,532	1,608	1,770	1,851	1,991	2,320	3,028	2,952
Other	365	439	461	494	554	769	791	804	777[g]
Total	1,830	1,972	2,069	2,263	2,405	2,760	3,111	3,831	3,729[g]
Grand total payments	19,135	18,915	17,974	20,589	20,534	21,006	23,942	28,111	29,552

C: NET RECEIPTS (+) OR NET PAYMENTS (−)

	1957	1958	1959	1960	1961	1962	1963	1964	1965
Balance	−3,422	−3,049	−1,523	−3,479	−2,243	−1,170	−2,576	−5,153	−4,591

Note: This table differs from the Yale Economic Growth Center Standard External Transactions Account (Economic Growth Center Yale, *A System of National Economic Accounts and Historical Data*, Table 4, 1964) because international "transfer payments" to and from individuals and government are not available for Mexico. Some transactions that are more usually considered as transfer payments, such as emigrant remittances, may be included in the factor payments shown above. The Net Receipts or Payments shown here differ from the "surplus of the nation on external account" in the standard table by the net remaining uncounted transfer payments which appear as part of the errors and omissions of the balance of payments.

Appendix Table D.3—*Continued*

Total exports and total imports of goods and services, and the net of the factor payments shown here for 1939–49 appear also in Appendix Table D.1; different series for merchandise appear in Appendix Table D.6 and D.7. Net Receipts or Payments appear, in million dollars, as one of the items in the Balance of Payments Table in Appendix E.

ᵃ Exported share of gold and silver production.

ᵇ Including other border transactions. This accounting device reflects the fact that the U.S. data used by Mexico on U.S. tourist expenditures make a disaggregation of commodity and service exports difficult.

ᶜ Including imports to free zones.

ᵈ Not classified by commodity, largely associated with tourism. There appears to be a higher commodity component of Mexican border expenditures relative to those of the U.S., partly because of the large flow of contraband from the free zones along the border into the rest of Mexico. These commodities are contained in the data on border trade and are difficult to separate from simple border transactions such as tourism.

ᵉ Other factor income included with other services.

ᶠ Too high for comparison with earlier years since some factor payments are included.

ᵍ Too low for comparison with earlier years by at least 100 million pesos, since the "other" shown here is interest on the official debt only.

Sources: *Grupo*, Tables 7-12 and 7-14, which credit the Banco de México; and for 1965 México, Secretaría de Indústria y Comercio, Dirección General de Estadística, *Anuario estadístico del comercio exterior de los Estados Unidos Mexicanos, 1966*, p. 659.

Appendix Table D.3A
Balance of Payments, 1939–65
(*million current dollars*)

Year	Balance on current account			Net capital account			Net errors and omissions	Change in reserves[a]
	Receipts	Pay-ments	Net	Total	Long term	Short term		
1939	216.1	181.0	35.1	20.7	20.5	0.2	−55.8	–
1940	214.0	186.9	27.1	17.5	7.0	10.5	−22.5	22.1
1941	243.1	268.5	−25.4	31.2	17.3	13.9	−7.0	−1.2
1942	272.6	250.5	22.1	24.8	26.8	−2.0	−3.0	43.9
1943	410.1	307.5	102.6	−8.6	2.4	−11.0	40.2	134.2
1944	432.4	406.8	25.6	12.0	35.6	−23.6	−0.5	37.1
1945	500.8	499.4	1.4	11.5	48.8	−37.3	72.6	85.5
1946	570.2	744.3	−174.1	−7.6	22.2	−29.8	75.2	−106.5
1947	713.9	881.0	−167.1	61.5	65.0	−3.5	−20.0	−125.6
1948	715.5	775.4	−59.9	44.3	31.8	12.5	−39.0	−54.6
1949	701.1	651.8	49.3	10.8	30.4	−19.6	−20.5	39.6
1950	826.6	780.1	46.5	109.7	66.0	43.7	−24.7	131.5
1951	914.4	1,125.7	−211.3	105.8	75.5	30.3	93.8	−11.7
1952	981.2	1,081.3	−100.1	73.0	82.1	−9.1	8.2	−18.9
1953	976.8	1,069.9	−93.1	87.0	85.8	1.2	−19.9	−26.0
1954	1,045.2	1,081.8	−36.6	81.1	126.5	−45.4	−79.6	−35.1
1955	1,214.7	1,171.2	43.5	227.0	135.8	91.2	−70.4	200.1
1956	1,323.8	1,427.9	−104.1	210.0	153.1	56.9	−45.4	60.5
1957	1,257.0	1,530.8	−273.8	192.3	191.7	0.6	68.0	−13.5
1958	1,269.3	1,513.2	−243.9	90.4	181.6	−91.2	76.3	−77.2
1959	1,316.1	1,437.9	−121.8	150.0	140.8	9.2	27.8	56.0
1960	1,368.8	1,647.1	−278.3	191.3	122.0	69.3	78.4	−8.6
1961	1,463.3	1,642.7	−179.4	288.0	285.5	2.5	−130.1	−21.5
1962	1,586.8	1,680.5	−93.7	174.4	260.9	−86.5	−63.8	16.9
1963	1,709.2	1,915.3	−206.1	243.7	301.4	−57.7	72.1	109.7
1964	1,836.6	2,248.8	−412.2	557.1	503.6	53.6	−113.3	31.6
1965	1,996.9	2,364.1	−368.2	138.8	172.3	−33.5	208.4	−21.0

[a] Change in reserves of the Banco de México .

Source: *Grupo*, August 1965, Table 7-1; and for 1965 México, Secretaría de Indústria y Comercio, Dirección General de Estadística, *Anuario estadístico del comercio exterior de los Estados Unidos Mexicanos, 1966*, p. 659.

Appendix Table D.4
Gross Fixed Capital Formation, 1939–62

Year	Total	Construction and installation	Imports of capital goods	Domestic production of machinery and equipment	Land clearing
		A: MILLION CURRENT PESOS			
1939	429	214	181	21	13
1940	702	312	194	168	28
1941	953	355	276	287	35
1942	857	421	177	194	65
1943	825	514	195	39	77
1944	1,183	742	313	48	80
1945	1,660	1,045	502	80	33
1946	2,965	1,619	898	359	89
1947	3,797	1,712	1,199	746	140
1948	4,087	1,861	1,255	866	105
1949	4,610	2,128	1,237	1,148	97
1950	6,041	3,000	1,699	1,288	54
1951	9,165	3,942	2,792	2,385	46
1952	10,721	5,237	2,498	2,902	84
1953	11,006	5,669	2,645	2,622	70
1954	12,876	6,082	3,585	3,096	113
1955	16,674	7,950	4,604	4,022	98
1956	22,235	10,024	5,603	6,456	152
1957	25,429	12,596	6,250	6,506	77
1958	25,122	12,579	6,275	6,205	63
1959	27,385	13,615	5,810	7,923	37
1960	33,132	17,974	7,097	8,033	28
1961	32,829	17,223	6,813	8,752	41
1962	32,344	17,364	6,714	8,239	27
		B: MILLION 1950 PESOS			
1939	1,482	954	441	69	18
1940	2,206	1,158	491	520	37
1941	2,785	1,197	729	814	45
1942	2,399	1,275	530	511	83
1943	2,161	1,356	624	89	92
1944	2,655	1,641	816	107	91
1945	3,848	2,134	1,352	326	36
1946	5,408	2,546	1,894	870	98
1947	6,321	2,598	2,160	1,410	153
1948	5,733	2,516	1,839	1,308	110
1949	5,362	2,546	1,471	1,244	101
1950	6,041	3,000	1,699	1,288	54
1951	7,784	3,284	2,287	2,167	46
1952	8,213	3,699	2,048	2,382	84
1953	7,701	3,413	2,083	2,137	68
1954	7,945	3,675	2,070	2,095	105
1955	8,889	4,095	2,278	2,432	84
1956	10,837	4,728	2,687	3,300	122
1957	11,334	5,349	2,788	3,140	57
1958	10,647	5,166	2,601	2,835	45
1959	11,388	5,280	2,559	3,525	24
1960	12,387	6,048	2,696	3,625	18
1961	12,690	6,108	2,654	3,903	25
1962	12,359	6,175	2,526	3,642	16

Source: Banco de México, Departamento de Estudios Económicos, "Alternativos de estimación de la inversión bruta fija en México, 1939–1962" (mimeograph), Estimate III, Appendix B, Tables 1 and 2. The total appears above in Appendix Table D.1A as C(1), and is discussed in Chapter 7, Tables 7.8 and 7.9, nn.

Appendix Table D.5A
Industrial Origin of Gross National Product, 1939–65
(million current pesos)

	1939	1940	1941	1942	1943	1944	1945	1946	1947
Agriculture, total	1,428	1,557	1,846	2,300	2,940	3,804	4,192	5,075	5,672
Crop production	782	857	1,019	1,273	1,658	2,131	2,317	2,777	3,213
Livestock	550	598	709	884	1,108	1,452	1,617	1,968	2,136
Forestry	88	93	106	128	155	195	227	290	275
Fishing	8	9	12	15	19	26	31	40	48
Manufacturing	1,106	1,245	1,523	1,957	2,535	3,414	4,163	5,578	5,946
Mining	311	304	321	351	378	413	438	504	664
Electric energy	84	84	92	105	119	140	160	202	246
Petroleum	197	203	227	257	323	382	459	606	722
Construction	187	211	258	334	433	586	705	933	995
Transportation	416	443	513	625	766	978	1,104	1,364	1,437
Commerce	1,488	1,650	2,018	2,463	3,150	4,230	5,016	6,684	7,318
Government	290	292	319	363	413	483	521	610	736
Other activities[a]	1,052	1,119	1,296	1,577	1,932	2,465	2,908	3,773	4,062
Gross Domestic Product	6,559	7,108	8,413	10,332	12,989	16,895	19,666	25,329	27,798
Plus: Net factor income from abroad	−99	−113	−149	−160	−50	56	7	−138	−241
Gross National Product	6,460	6,995	8,264	10,172	12,959	16,951	19,673	25,191	27,557

Appendix Table D.5A—*Continued*

	1948	1949	1950	1951	1952	1953	1954	1955	1956
Agriculture, total	6,262	7,479	9,242	11,190	11,671	11,785	14,932	17,757	19,042
Crop production	3,662	4,719	5,999	6,802	6,537	6,795	9,269	10,657	11,150
Livestock	2,292	2,473	2,903	4,003	4,754	4,627	5,253	6,531	7,261
Forestry	252	224	263	313	262	294	332	468	515
Fishing	56	63	77	72	58	69	78	101	116
Manufacturing	6,263	6,632	8,437	11,228	12,437	12,220	14,636	17,851	21,295
Mining	844	1,055	1,243	1,506	1,676	1,438	1,663	2,413	2,615
Electric energy	296	355	370	419	426	511	597	743	807
Petroleum	847	993	1,129	1,277	1,369	1,429	1,672	2,124	2,256
Construction	1,049	1,111	1,287	1,691	2,247	2,433	2,610	3,411	4,300
Transportation	1,496	1,564	1,988	2,393	2,635	3,163	3,418	3,781	4,234
Commerce	7,687	8,537	10,750	13,895	15,067	15,472	18,189	21,893	24,915
Government	872	1,032	1,294	1,457	1,728	1,980	2,509	2,968	3,349
Other activities[a]	4,381	4,724	5,320	7,970	10,128	8,495	11,979	14,408	17,787
GROSS DOMESTIC PRODUCT	29,997	33,482	41,060	53,026	59,384	58,926	72,205	88,218	100,600
Plus: Net factor income from abroad	−303	−397	−542	−757	−780	−565	−707	−930	−1,322
GROSS NATIONAL PRODUCT	29,694	33,085	40,518	52,269	58,604	58,361	71,498	87,288	99,278

Appendix Table D.5A—*Continued*

	1957	1958	1959	1960	1961	1962	1963	1964	1965
Agriculture, total	21,804	23,202	24,004	25,919	–	–	–	–	–
Crop production	13,357	14,432	13,995	14,841	–	–	–	–	–
Livestock	7,825	8,136	9,205	10,241	–	–	–	–	–
Forestry	516	501	584	569	–	–	–	–	–
Fishing	106	133	220	268	–	–	–	–	–
Manufacturing	23,799	26,277	29,891	33,284	–	–	–	–	–
Mining	2,599	2,338	2,465	2,666	–	–	–	–	–
Electric energy	993	1,120	1,238	1,315	–	–	–	–	–
Petroleum	2,493	2,790	3,646	3,941	–	–	–	–	–
Construction	5,405	5,396	5,840	7,712	–	–	–	–	–
Transportation	4,374	4,545	5,488	6,193	–	–	–	–	–
Commerce	28,234	30,583	32,750	36,947	–	–	–	–	–
Government	3,844	4,484	5,226	6,189	–	–	–	–	–
Other activities[a]	21,997	27,839	27,128	31,701	–	–	–	–	–
GROSS DOMESTIC PRODUCT	115,542	128,574	137,676	155,867	165,672	179,874	194,845	228,011	246,200
Plus: Net factor income from abroad	−1,356	−1,461	−1,489	−1,752	−1,924	−2,311	−2,676	−3,411	−3,500
GROSS NATIONAL PRODUCT	114,186	127,109	136,187	154,115	163,748	177,563	196,646	224,600	212,700

[a] Includes the statistical discrepancy resulting from reflation of sector data—originally in 1950 prices—by sector price indexes, and the total GDP in current pesos as estimated by the Banco de México.
Source: *Grupo*, Table 2-1; and Appendix Table D.1A above for net factor income from abroad and GNP.

Appendix Table D.5B
Industrial Origin of Gross National Product, 1939–65
(*million 1950 pesos*)

	1939	1940	1941	1942	1943	1944	1945	1946	1947
Agriculture, total	5,357	5,266	5,826	6,361	6,222	6,372	6,029	6,388	6,953
Crop production	2,958	2,730	3,215	3,689	3,497	3,755	3,575	3,671	4,025
Livestock	2,110	2,247	2,319	2,433	2,412	2,354	2,200	2,412	2,619
Forestry	265	265	265	210	279	221	199	247	251
Fishing	24	24	27	29	34	42	55	58	58
Manufacturing	3,695	3,889	4,480	5,113	5,391	5,805	6,328	6,454	6,277
Mining	1,270	1,209	1,231	1,465	1,411	1,258	1,279	965	1,258
Electric energy	206	211	211	219	229	230	256	278	301
Petroleum	659	638	684	606	625	674	752	844	947
Construction	831	784	871	1,012	1,144	1,295	1,440	1,467	1,510
Transportation	964	974	1,002	1,127	1,306	1,404	1,390	1,527	1,539
Commerce	5,068	5,203	6,024	6,526	6,773	7,399	7,879	8,401	8,519
Government	699	668	718	785	854	1,000	1,004	985	1,013
Other activities	2,707	2,816	2,992	3,235	3,522	3,851	4,163	4,606	4,690
GROSS DOMESTIC PRODUCT	21,456	21,658	24,039	26,449	27,477	29,288	30,520	31,915	33,007
Plus: Net factor income from abroad	-331	-351	-438	-416	22	255	158	-67	-199
GROSS NATIONAL PRODUCT	21,125	21,307	23,871	26,033	27,499	29,543	30,678	31,848	32,808

Appendix Table D.5B—*Continued*

	1948	1949	1950	1951	1952	1953	1954	1955	1956
Agriculture, total	7,434	8,299	9,242	9,748	9,509	9,495	11,182	12,219	11,891
Crop production	4,499	5,303	5,999	6,299	6,017	6,053	7,571	8,417	7,931
Livestock	2,627	2,659	2,903	3,109	3,222	3,164	3,315	3,460	3,603
Forestry	236	263	263	267	209	208	226	256	255
Fishing	72	74	77	73	61	70	70	86	102
Manufacturing	6,775	7,374	8,437	9,332	9,744	9,632	10,575	11,605	12,915
Mining	1,145	1,136	1,243	1,198	1,330	1,316	1,240	1,437	1,452
Electric energy	332	362	370	411	447	447	526	586	655
Petroleum	974	1,053	1,129	1,242	1,310	1,330	1,432	1,545	1,648
Construction	1,418	1,329	1,287	1,409	1,587	1,465	1,577	1,757	2,028
Transportation	1,501	1,738	1,988	2,179	2,403	2,479	2,658	2,851	3,159
Commerce	8,857	9,443	10,750	11,793	12,147	12,427	13,169	14,233	15,157
Government	1,178	1,141	1,294	1,378	1,466	1,492	1,563	1,599	1,694
Other activities	4,832	4,976	5,320	5,527	5,996	5,916	6,937	7,480	8,363
Gross Domestic Product	34,446	36,851	41,060	44,217	45,939	45,999	50,859	55,312	58,962
Plus: Net factor income from abroad	−313	−426	−542	−625	−593	−429	−517	−615	−796
Gross National Product	34,133	36,425	40,518	43,592	45,346	45,570	50,342	54,697	58,166

Appendix Table D.5B—*Continued*

	1957	1958	1959	1960	1961	1962	1963	1964	1965
Agriculture, total	12,899	13,839	13,320	14,018	14,416	15,175	15,498	16,512	17,300
Crop production	8,669	9,430	8,711	9,178	9,417	10,013	10,163	10,986	11,600
Livestock	3,893	4,076	4,233	4,450	4,624	4,779	4,922	5,094	5,300
Forestry	243	225	254	254	228	236	258	277	300
Fishing	94	108	122	136	147	147	155	155	100
Manufacturing	13,763	14,500	15,800	17,116	17,726	18,862	20,597	23,522	25,200
Mining	1,547	1,539	1,587	1,648	1,579	1,599	1,655	1,670	1,700
Electric energy	707	761	818	898	983	1,047	1,147	1,318	1,400
Petroleum	1,756	1,962	2,224	2,346	2,613	2,662	2,827	3,084	3,200
Construction	2,295	2,216	2,265	2,595	2,620	2,649	3,065	3,568	3,500
Transportation	3,298	3,403	3,507	3,638	3,664	3,671	3,830	4,067	4,300
Commerce	16,318	17,157	17,608	19,167	19,780	20,769	22,077	24,461	—[a]
Government	1,815	1,837	1,892	1,985	2,129	2,264	2,382	2,620	2,700
Other activities	9,033	9,704	9,831	10,906	11,417	12,044	12,787	13,793	40,300[a]
GROSS DOMESTIC PRODUCT	63,431	66,918	68,852	74,317	76,927	80,742	85,865	94,615	99,700
Plus: Net factor income from abroad	−757	−771	−761	−851	−910	−1,055	−1,204	−1,444	−1,500
GROSS NATIONAL PRODUCT	62,674	66,147	68,091	73,466	76,017	79,687	84,661	93,171	98,200

[a] Commerce included with other activities.

Source: *Grupo*, Table 2-3; and Appendix Table D.1B above for net factor income from abroad and GNP. Data for 1965 are from OECD Development Centre, *National Accounts of Less Developed Countries* (preliminary, February 1967), p. 57, and from the Banco de México work sheets (for agriculture).

Appendix Table D.6
Merchandise Exports by Commodity Groups, 1939–65

	1939	1940	1941	1942	1943	1944	1945	1946	1947
			A: Million Current Pesos						
Agricultural and forest products	177	152	206	240	422	478	480	629	919
Livestock and fishery products	32	30	34	53	82	58	75	93	77
Fuels and lubricants	83	89	70	35	38	33	41	56	43
Minerals	486	483	343	392	346	312	349	416	709
Manufactures and other products	11	20	53	116	288	278	412	474	398
Total[a]	789	774	706	836	1,174	1,158	1,357	1,668	2,146
			B: Million 1960 Pesos						
Agricultural and forest products	1,566	1,196	1,473	1,570	2,005	1,844	1,579	1,959	2,247
Livestock and fishery products	936	704	776	776	769	556	670	761	263
Fuels and lubricants	422	447	353	139	136	129	175	195	107
Minerals	2,280	2,116	2,134	2,477	1,772	1,721	1,920	1,662	2,008
Manufactures and other products	84	110	249	488	988	784	904	815	724
Total	5,289	4,573	4,985	5,450	5,670	5,034	5,247	5,391	5,349

Appendix Table D.6—*Continued*

A: MILLION CURRENT PESOS

	1948	1949	1950	1951	1952	1953	1954	1955	1956
Agricultural and forest products	948	1,410	2,354	2,677	2,871	2,767	4,105	5,547	5,561
Livestock and fishery products	203	310	236	301	373	276	263	534	468
Fuels and lubricants	164	83	217	291	263	220	430	616	635
Minerals	936	1,266	1,376	1,628	1,727	1,504	1,968	2,399	2,786
Manufactures and other products	238	190	306	591	443	280	372	697	565
Total[a]	2,488	3,259	4,488	5,488	5,677	5,047	7,138	9,793	10,014

B: MILLION 1960 PESOS

	1948	1949	1950	1951	1952	1953	1954	1955	1956
Agricultural and forest products	1,882	2,362	2,680	3,501	3,019	3,362	3,474	4,323	4,457
Livestock and fishery products	445	588	410	514	585	503	365	654	774
Fuels and lubricants	288	142	340	358	349	323	456	515	472
Minerals	1,939	2,223	2,282	1,750	2,032	2,195	2,203	2,176	2,284
Manufactures and other products	489	374	522	728	704	500	492	798	664
Total	5,043	5,689	6,234	6,851	6,689	6,882	6,990	8,466	8,452

Appendix Table D.6—*Continued*

	1957	1958	1959	1960	1961	1962	1963	1964	1965
A: Million Current Pesos									
Agricultural and forest products	4,615	4,869	4,837	5,251	5,292	5,942	—	—	—
Livestock and fishery products	640	1,750	1,187	1,109	1,416	1,686	—	—	—
Fuels and lubricants	475	361	364	244	428	480	—	—	—
Minerals	2,701	2,013	2,150	2,172	2,247	2,514	—	—	—
Manufactures and other products	648	762	855	758	938	995	—	—	—
Total[a]	9,080	9,155	9,394	9,533	10,321	11,617	12,240	13,386	—
B: Million 1960 Pesos									
Agricultural and forest products	3,911	4,601	4,988	5,251	5,209	6,036	—	—	—
Livestock and fishery products	804	1,128	1,109	1,109	1,269	1,751	—	—	—
Fuels and lubricants	305	286	349	244	408	480	—	—	—
Minerals	2,418	1,075	1,172	2,172	2,276	2,676	—	—	—
Manufactures and other products	733	859	993	758	946	892	—	—	—
Total	8,171	7,949	8,611	9,533	10,109	11,835	11,822	12,048	—

[a] These totals do not check with the merchandise component of exports of goods and services shown in Appendix Table D.3, which was taken from another table in the source cited. The discrepancies are due to different handling of some gold and silver products, and possibly also to different adjustments for undervaluation. Totals, made from unrounded data, are not necessarily exact sums of the items shown.

Source: *Grupo*, Table 10-1 for current pesos credited to the United Nations, ECLA, and Table 10-2 for 1960 pesos calculated by the Grupo on the basis of 10-1.

Appendix Table D.7A
Merchandise Imports by Commodity Groups, 1939–65
(million current pesos)

Commodity Class	1939	1940	1941	1942	1943	1944	1945	1946	1947
Consumer goods									
Nondurable	96	100	143	143	178	253	301	450	438
Durable	89	98	144	88	72	113	167	335	413
Total	185	198	287	231	250	366	468	785	852
Fuels and lubricants	19	22	22	25	29	40	50	73	94
Primary materials									
Metals	54	64	79	44	64	103	123	258	385
Nonmetals	221	230	303	311	365	576	543	750	868
Total	275	294	382	354	429	679	666	1,008	1,253
Capital goods									
Construction equipment	35	41	48	45	49	71	84	154	199
Agricultural equipment	15	15	23	15	15	26	39	73	80
Industrial and mining equipment	82	90	126	86	118	183	293	454	623
Transport equipmen	48	50	72	41	24	41	70	192	256
Total	180	196	270	186	205	322	486	872	1,158
Grand total[a]	664	715	767	803	922	1,416	1,681	2,743	3,363

Appendix Table D.7A—*Continued*

Commodity Class	1948	1949[b]	1950	1951	1952	1953	1954	1955	1956
Consumer goods									
Nondurable	346	–	462	563	736	776	768	770	915
Durable	238	–	386	546	560	582	730	932	972
Total	573	–	848	1,109	1,296	1,358	1,498	1,702	1,887
Fuels and lubricants	135	–	213	226	310	413	684	873	1,019
Primary materials									
Metals	327	–	568	872	987	792	918	1,150	1,799
Nonmetals	803	–	1,440	2,073	1,852	1,863	2,450	2,963	3,356
Total	1,129	–	2,008	2,945	2,838	2,656	3,368	4,113	5,156
Capital goods									
Construction equipment	217	–	351	539	518	419	488	655	832
Agricultural equipment	129	–	211	314	223	214	326	553	514
Industrial and mining equipment	795	–	1,011	1,542	1,455	1,481	2,085	2,507	3,296
Transport equipment	80	–	138	378	320	421	457	625	672
Total	1,221	–	1,710	2,772	2,516	2,535	3,356	4,339	5,314
Grand total[a]	3,123	3,808	4,807	7,112	6,984	6,985	8,926	11,046	13,395

Appendix Table D.7A—*Continued*

Commodity Class	1957	1958	1959	1960	1961	1962	1963[c]	1964	1965
Consumer goods									
Nondurable	825	910	856	932	892	968	1,156	–	–
Durable	970	920	622	759	860	776	995	–	–
Total	1,794	1,830	1,479	1,691	1,752	1,744	2,151	–	–
Fuels and lubricants	1,111	774	593	625	425	362	446	–	–
Primary materials									
Metals	1,735	1,612	1,692	1,619	1,795	1,815	1,808	–	–
Nonmetals	3,875	3,957	3,785	4,424	3,526	3,708	4,035	–	–
Total	5,611	5,569	5,478	6,042	5,321	5,522	5,842	–	–
Capital goods									
Construction equipment	905	892	339	746	560	688	566	–	–
Agricultural equipment	454	470	519	538	472	358	364	–	–
Industrial and mining equipment	3,828	3,594	3,294	3,672	4,046	3,918	4,238	–	–
Transport equipment	782	958	836	1,468	932	1,096	852	–	–
Total	5,906	5,914	4,988	6,424	6,011	6,059	6,020	–	–
Grand total[a]	14,440	14,108	12,582	14,831	14,232	14,288	15,504	18,662	–

[a] For most years prior to 1955 these totals, which exclude unclassified frontier imports by tourists, do not check with the corresponding figures shown in Appendix Table D.3, which was taken from another table in the source cited. The reasons for these discrepancies are not clear, but may be related to the different sources used by the Grupo in their preparation. The sums of components are slightly below the totals (less than 1 percent below) because the Grupo was unable to distribute ECLA's group X (others) according to the above classification. Subtotals do not always check due to rounding.

[b] ECLA did not make estimates by groups for 1949.

[c] Preliminary.

Source: *Grupo*, Table 9-1 credited to Economic Commission for Latin America (ECLA).

Appendix Table D.7B

Merchandise Imports by Commodity Groups, 1939–65

(million 1960 pesos)

Commodity Class	1939	1940	1941	1942	1943	1944	1945	1946	1947
Consumer goods									
Nondurable	442	515	637	570	585	787	871	1,107	1,039
Durable	334	372	617	362	297	502	779	1,104	1,188
Total	776	887	1,254	932	882	1,289	1,650	2,212	2,226
Fuels and lubricants	89	107	130	122	148	184	222	295	352
Primary materials									
Metals	441	453	368	188	442	753	759	924	1,025
Nonmetals	1,215	1,070	1,718	1,481	1,555	2,253	2,078	2,522	2,342
Total	1,655	1,524	2,086	1,669	1,998	3,006	2,836	3,445	3,367
Capital goods									
Construction equipment	288	287	346	278	315	486	529	837	1,148
Agricultural equipment	149	154	225	117	109	192	318	538	530
Industrial and mining equipment	490	562	813	688	972	1,190	1,970	2,413	2,783
Transport equipment	338	368	592	333	141	250	417	1,063	1,298
Total	1,264	1,371	1,976	1,416	1,537	2,118	3,234	4,850	5,759
Grand total[a]	3,810	3,920	5,488	4,172	4,608	6,645	7,997	10,825	11,704

Appendix Table D.7B—*Continued*

Commodity Class	1948	1949[b]	1950	1951	1952	1953	1954	1955	1956
Consumer goods									
Nondurable	846	—	771	866	1,130	1,178	934	848	1,011
Durable	594	—	687	921	900	956	1,028	1,013	1,167
Total	1,441	—	1,458	1,787	2,031	2,134	1,963	1,861	2,179
Fuels and lubricants	359	—	418	406	534	633	909	1,044	1,140
Primary materials									
Metals	903	—	986	1,601	1,674	1,374	1,236	1,281	1,858
Nonmetals	1,962	—	2,565	3,033	2,909	2,870	2,965	3,109	3,459
Total	2,866	—	3,551	4,634	4,583	4,244	4,201	4,390	5,317
Capital goods									
Construction equipment	883	—	878	1,260	1,171	802	715	875	1,048
Agricultural equipment	531	—	520	681	503	493	530	732	702
Industrial and mining equipment	2,692	—	2,331	3,150	2,962	2,985	2,923	3,000	3,764
Transport equipment	376	—	584	795	637	729	736	955	986
Total	4,482	—	4,313	5,886	5,273	5,009	4,904	5,561	6,500
Grand total[a]	9,343	8,334	9,797	12,820	12,461	12,061	12,006	12,877	15,159

Appendix Table D.7B—Continued

Commodity Class	1957	1958	1959	1960	1961	1962	1963[c]	1964	1965
Consumer goods									
Nondurable	961	1,077	1,095	932	875	930	1,111	—	—
Durable	1,078	1,025	950	759	843	746	956	—	—
Total	2,039	2,102	2,046	1,691	1,718	1,676	2,068	—	—
Fuels and lubricants	1,226	836	665	625	417	348	429	—	—
Primary materials									
Metals	1,636	1,583	1,760	1,619	1,760	1,744	1,737	—	—
Nonmetals	4,134	4,177	3,583	4,424	3,457	3,564	3,878	—	—
Total	5,770	5,760	5,343	6,043	5,217	5,308	5,616	—	—
Capital goods									
Construction equipment	1,082	987	638	746	549	661	544	—	—
Agricultural equipment	545	591	620	538	463	344	350	—	—
Industrial and mining equipment	4,138	3,623	3,601	3,672	3,967	3,765	4,073	—	—
Transport equipment	932	1,147	994	1,468	914	1,054	819	—	—
Total	6,696	6,348	5,852	6,424	5,893	5,832	5,786	—	—
Grand total[a]	15,751	15,070	13,957	14,831	13,953	13,733	14,902	16,938	—

[a] For most years prior to 1965 these totals, which exclude unclassified frontier imports by tourists, do not check with the corresponding figures shown in Appendix Table D.3, which was taken from another table in the source cited. The reasons for these discrepancies are not clear, but may be related to the different sources used by the Grupo in their preparation. The sums of components are slightly below the totals (less than 1 percent below) because the Grupo was unable to distribute ECLA's group X (others) according to the above classification.

[b] ECLA did not make estimates by groups for 1949.

[c] Preliminary.

Source: Grupo (ref. Table D.1A) Table 9-2, calculated by the Grupo based on its 9-1 for current pesos.

Appendix Table D.8
National Balance Sheet, 1960
(billion current pesos)

I. TANGIBLE ASSETS	592		IV. FOREIGN LIABILITIES	40
1. Structures and equipment	350		V. DOMESTIC LIABILITIES	245
2. Livestock	21		VI. NATIONAL NET WORTH	552
3. Inventories	40		VII. NATIONAL LIABILITIES AND	
4. Consumer durables	25		NET WORTH	837
5. Gold and for. exch.	6			
6. Land	150			
II. FINANCIAL ASSETS	245			
1. Assets of fin. inst.	65			
2. Claims against fin. institutions	50			
3. Claims among nonfinancial units	65			
a) Bonds	10			
b) Mortgages	10			
c) Trade and consumer credit	40			
d) Miscellaneous	10			
4. Corporate stock	60			
III. NATIONAL ASSETS	837			

Description:

I.1. Obtained by adding to the ECLA estimate for 1950 of 92 bill. pesos (see Goldsmith, *Table 6*) an estimate for net capital formation for the years 1951–60 put at 65% of the period's gross fixed capital expenditures given in Goldsmith, *Table 8*, and reflating the sum so obtained on the basis of the implicit deflator of Goldsmith, *Table 12* column 6. (The resulting figure is about twice as high as an unpublished estimate by Oomens which, however, was based on the old capital expenditure figures and apparently did not include government capital formation).

I.2. Preliminary figure from Census.

I.3. Estimated on basis of 1950 relationship between structures and equipment and inventories (CEPAL, *El Caso de México*, 1957, p. 137). The (supposedly incomplete) figure in 1960 Census is 33 bill. pesos.

I.4. Rough estimate based on expenditures in 1963 (unpublished household sample enquiry).

I.5. *International Financial Statistics, 1963/64 Supplement*, p. 150. Includes only holdings of banking system.

I.6. Very rough estimate.

II.1. From Goldsmith, *Table 35*.

II.2. Estimated at 75% of II.1 to take account of interfinancial assets, and of financial institutions' equity.

II.3*a*. Banco de México, *Informe Anual*, 1962.

II.3*b*. and *d*. Very rough estimates.

II.3*c*. Estimated as equal to inventories.

II.4. Very rough estimate based partly on paid-in capital of corporations (value of stocks listed on Mexico City Stock Exchange about $10 billion).

IV. Rough estimate of total foreign investments in Mexico.

V. Equal to II.

VI. Residual (VII − IV − V).

Source: Raymond W. Goldsmith, *The Financial Development of Mexico*, p. 79.

Appendix E

Mexican Economic Historical Data

Appendix Table E.1
Total Population of Mexico, Specified Dates, 1803–1963
(thousand people)

	Selected years			Annual estimates	
Author	Date	Population		Year	Population
Humboldt	1803	5,837		1940	20,143
García Cubas	1856	8,283		1941	20,698
Official Estimate	1877	9,384		1942	21,268
Census	1895	12,632		1943	21,854
Census	Oct. 28, 1900	13,607		1944	22,456
–	– 1907	14,750[a]		1945	23,075
Census	Oct. 27, 1910	15,160		1946	23,710
				1947	24,364
Census	Nov. 30, 1921	14,335		1948	25,035
Loyo	Nov. 30, 1921	14,800		1949	25,724
				1950	26,433
–	– 1925	15,500[a]		1951	27,263
Census	May 15, 1930	16,553		1952	28,118
–	– 1935	18,000[a]		1953	29,000
				1954	29,911
Census	Mar. 6, 1940	19,654		1955	30,849
Adjusted	Mar. 6, 1940	20,143		1956	31,817
				1957	32,816
Census	June 6, 1950	25,791		1958	33,846
Adjusted	June 6, 1950	26,433		1959	34,908
				1960	36,003
Census	June 8, 1960	34,923		1961	37,272
Adjusted	June 8, 1960	36,003		1962	38,585
				1963	39,944

[a] Interpolations between censuses, used in various computations in the text.

Sources: Census data, and estimates for 1921 and earlier years credited to specific authors are taken from Dirección General de Estadística, *Anuario Estadístico de los Estados Unidos Mexicanos, 1960–1961*, p. 23, which further documents the early figures as follows:

1803–Humboldt, "Ensayo Político sobre la Nueva España"

1856–A. García Cubas, "Noticias Geográficas y Estadísticas de la República Mexicana" (México, 1857)

1877–Secretaría de Gobernación

1921–Gilberto Loyo, "La Emigración de Mexicanos a los Estados Unidos" (Rome, 1931)

Annual estimates for 1940 and later years, and the adjusted census figures for 1940–60 are taken from Grupo Secretaría de Hacienda-Banco de México, Estudios sobre Proyecciones, "Manual." This source uses the 1960 adjustment by Raúl Benítez Zenteno and Gustavo Cabrera, *Nuevo Cálculo de Población y Proyección*, Banco de México; it adjusts the 1940 and 1950 censuses in the same proportion and interpolates for intervening years.

Appendix Table E.2
Economically Active Population by Industry Group or Region, and Active
in Agriculture by Region, Census Years 1895–1960
(thousand people)

Industry group or region[a]	1895	1900	1910	1921[b]	1930	1940	1950	1960
TOTAL MEXICO BY INDUSTRY								
Total population	12,632	13,607	15,160	14,335	16,553	20,143[e]	26,433[e]	36,003[e]
Economically active[d]								
Total	4,762[e]	5,131[e]	5,338[e]	4,884	5,166	5,858[f]	8,272[e]	11,253[f]
Agriculture	2,976	3,178	3,584	3,488	3,626	3,831	4,824	6,086
Extractive industries	89	107	104	26	51	107	97	141
Other industries	604	696	699	535	692	640	1,222	2,000
Services and other activities	1,093	1,150	950	834	796	1,281	2,129	3,027
Unemployed	180[e]	229[e]	243[e]	–	–	59[f]	73[e]	30[f]
ECONOMICALLY ACTIVE BY REGION								
Mexico	4,762	5,131	5,338	4,884	5,166	5,858	8,268	11,332[g]
North	909	969	1,022	876	976	1,120	1,615	2,166
Gulf	491	518	640	593	648	710	970	1,299
North Pacific	268	284	297	278	316	363	546	829
South Pacific	636	653	725	724	721	769	1,069	1,444
Center	2,458	2,706	2,653	2,412	2,505	2,895	4,068	5,594
ACTIVE IN AGRICULTURE BY REGION[a]								
Mexico	2,976	3,178	3,584	3,488	3,626	3,829	4,824	6,145[g]
North	505	557	693	–	666	729	952	1,186
Gulf	363	388	462	–	480	507	643	832
North Pacific	151	170	201	–	219	239	330	471
South Pacific	438	490	562	–	613	653	836	1,159
Center	1,520	1,574	1,666	–	1,648	1,701	2,063	2,497

[a] Agriculture includes crop and livestock production, forestry, fishing and hunting; extractive industries includes mining, petroleum, etc.; other industries includes manufacturing, construction, electricity and gas, etc.; services and other activities in addition to trade, transportation and communication, etc. includes unspecified activities that amounted to more than 25 percent of this item in 1895 and 1900 but only 3 percent in 1960.

The states included in the specified regions are as follows:

North—Coahuila, Chihuahua, Durango, Nuevo León, San Luís Potosí, Tamaulipas, Zacatecas

Gulf—Campeche, Quintana Roo, Tabasco, Veracruz, Yucatán

North Pacific—Baja California Norte, Baja California Sur, Nayarit, Sinaloa, Sonora

South Pacific—Colima, Chiapas, Guerrero, Oaxaca

Appendix Table E.2—*Continued*

Center—Aguascalientes, Distrito Federal (Mexico City), Guanajuato, Hidalgo, Jalisco, Mexico, Michoacán, Morelos, Puebla, Querétaro, Tlaxcala

[b] As reported; see Appendix Table E.1 for total as adjusted upward by G. Loyo.

[c] As adjusted; see Appendix Table E.1, source note. Since the adjustments were all for population aged nine or under, the economically active population remains as reported.

[d] Economically active figures for 1940, 1950, and 1960, except by regions, are for ages 12 and over; earlier years may include ages 8–11.

[e] Total and industry groups exclude those unemployed; for 1950 specifically noted unemployed 13 weeks or more.

[f] Total and industry groups include those unemployed 13 weeks and more. For 1960, also exclude 79 thousand aged 8–11; of these, 59 were in agriculture, none in extractive industries, nine in other industries, and nine in services and other activities.

[g] Total and regions include ages 8–11.

Sources: Census data for all years except as noted ([c]). All data for 1895 to 1910 taken from El Colegio de México, *Fuerza de Trabajo*, pp. 25, 38–60; data for the whole country for 1921 and 1930 from Dirección General de Estadística, *Anuario Estadístico de los Estados Unidos Mexicanos, 1941*, pp. 65–66; data for the whole country 1940–60 from Grupo Secretaría de Hacienda-Banco de México, "Manual," Table 11-1 and 11-2; regional data for 1921–60 compiled from Dirección General de Estadística, *Censo General de Población* for the specified years.

Appendix Table E.3

Population by Regions, Urban and Rural, Census Years 1895–1960

(thousand people)

Region[a]	1895	1900	1910	1921[b]	1930	1940	1950	1960[b]
TOTAL POPULATION								
Mexico	12,632	13,607	15,160	14,335	16,553	19,654	25,791[c]	34,923
North	2,336	2,580	2,971	2,580	3,133	3,903	5,177	6,865
Gulf	1,388	1,537	1,756	1,816	2,083	2,432	3,069	4,057
North Pacific	641	716	812	843	975	1,204	1,724	2,613
South Pacific	1,681	1,854	2,151	2,056	2,318	2,684	3,360	4,289
Center	6,587	6,921	7,470	7,040	8,044	9,430	12,449	17,099
RURAL POPULATION[d]								
Mexico	–	9,758	10,812	9,869	11,012	12,757	14,808	17,218
North	–	1,868	2,140	1,744	2,061	2,518	2,988	3,341
Gulf	–	1,215	1,273	1,275	1,424	1,661	1,947	2,356
North Pacific	–	588	649	607	666	854	1,050	1,242
South Pacific	–	1,436	1,687	1,650	1,905	2,253	2,590	3,165
Center	–	4,651	5,063	4,594	4,956	5,471	6,233	7,114
URBAN POPULATION								
Mexico		3,849	4,348	4,466	5,541	6,897	10,983[c]	17,705
North	–	712	831	836	1,072	1,385	2,189	3,524
Gulf	–	322	483	541	659	771	1,122	1,701
North Pacific	–	128	163	236	309	350	674	1,371
South Pacific	–	418	464	406	413	431	770	1,124
Center	–	2,270	2,407	2,446	3,088	3,959	6,216	9,985

[a] See Appendix Table E.2, note a, for the states included in each region.

[b] As reported; see Appendix Table E.1 for adjusted totals.

[c] Includes 12 thousand not assigned to a region.

[d] Rural population is defined as those living in communities of 2,500 or less.

Sources: Census data for all years; for 1895–1910 taken from El Colegio de México, *Fuerza de Trabajo*, pp. 26–29; for 1921–60 compiled from Dirección General de Estadística, *Censo General de Población*, for the specified years.

Appendix Table E.4
Population by Size of Locality, 1900 and 1960

Size of locality	Thousand people		Percent of total	
	1900	*1960*[a]	*1900*	*1960*[a]
Total	13,607	34,923	100.0	100.0
Under 2,500	9,758	17,218	71.7	49.3
2,501– 5,000	1,284	2,959	9.4	8.5
5,001– 10,000	844	2,366	6.2	6.8
10,001– 20,000	459	2,027	3.4	5.8
20,001– 50,000	536	2,109	3.9	6.0
50,001–100,000	280	1,731	2.1	5.0
Over 100,000	445	6,512	3.3	18.6

[a] As reported: See Appendix Table E.1 for adjusted total.
Sources: Data for 1900 from El Colegio de México; *Fuerza de Trabajo*, pp. 27, 29; for 1960 from Dirección General de Estadística, *VIII Censo General de Población, 1960, Resúmen General*, p. 59.

Appendix Table E.5
Characteristics of Mexican Farmland[a]
(thousand hectares)

	Number of Farms in Census				Total Land Area in Census				Arable Land[b]			
	1930	1940	1950	1960	1930	1940	1950	1960	1930	1940	1950	1960
North												
ejidos	977	3,790	4,353	4,574	3,657	13,048	16,421	18,566	482	1,683	2,105	2,485
non-ejidos	109,921	173,027	192,938	184,970	67,267	54,233	54,019	61,587	2,503	1,876	2,562	3,447
total	110,898	176,817	197,291	189,544	70,923	67,280	70,440	80,153	2,985	3,560	4,667	5,933
Gulf												
ejidos	668	2,314	2,817	3,050	1,453	3,985	5,933	7,375	393	1,342	1,488	1,812
non-ejidos	105,075	123,576	141,282	177,233	13,911	13,544	14,395	17,739	2,497	1,222	1,925	2,444
total	105,743	125,890	144,099	180,283	15,364	17,528	20,328	25,114	2,890	2,565	3,413	4,256
North Pacific												
ejidos	110	1,004	1,163	1,265	458	2,773	4,065	4,465	71	596	799	1,095
non-ejidos	34,861	34,808	38,024	44,208	12,949	10,971	14,603	18,170	851	551	1,277	1,394
total	34,971	35,812	39,187	45,473	13,407	13,744	18,668	22,635	922	1,147	2,076	2,489
South Pacific												
ejidos	432	1,510	2,138	2,522	590	2,346	4,028	5,299	161	739	1,175	1,622
non-ejidos	139,303	158,665	215,656	224,799	12,388	10,876	13,130	15,936	2,311	1,433	2,146	2,968
total	139,735	160,175	217,794	227,321	12,978	13,222	17,157	21,235	2,472	2,173	3,592	4,590
Center												
ejidos	2,002	6,062	7,108	7,288	2,187	6,772	8,447	8,792	834	2,743	3,224	3,314
non-ejidos	464,860	728,853	777,733	715,232	16,735	10,203	10,477	11,155	4,515	2,684	2,957	3,234
total	466,862	734,915	784,841	722,520	18,922	16,975	18,924	19,947	5,349	5,427	6,181	6,549
Mexico												
ejidos	4,189	14,680	17,579	18,699	8,345	28,923	38,894	44,497	1,941	7,045	8,791	10,329
non-ejidos	854,020	1,218,929	1,365,633	1,346,442	123,250	99,826	106,623	124,587	12,677	7,826	11,137	13,478
total	858,209	1,233,609	1,383,212	1,365,141	131,595	128,749	145,517	169,084	14,618	14,871	19,928	23,817

Appendix Table E.5—*Continued*

	Pasture Land				Forest Land				Economically Productive But Uncultivated Land				Agriculturally Unproductive Land			
	1930	1940	1950	1960	1930	1940	1950	1960	1930	1940	1950	1960	1930	1940	1950	1960
North																
ejidos	2,118	6,107	8,433	10,545	410	3,168	3,271	2,532	103	1,077	1,206	1,987	544	1,013	1,406	1,016
non-ejidos	42,445	30,373	30,987	35,522	10,147	15,522	13,503	14,484	2,851	2,940	3,631	4,257	9,322	3,521	3,335	3,877
total	44,563	36,480	39,420	46,067	10,556	18,690	16,774	17,016	2,953	4,017	4,837	6,245	9,866	4,534	4,741	4,894
Gulf																
ejidos	97	382	1,055	1,248	131	1,155	2,746	2,880	7	441	238	926	824	664	406	510
non-ejidos	2,318	1,997	2,686	3,313	6,234	5,464	6,002	8,413	338	3,685	1,877	2,058	2,524	1,176	1,905	1,511
total	2,415	2,379	3,742	4,562	6,365	6,618	8,748	11,292	345	4,126	2,115	2,984	3,349	1,840	2,311	2,020
North Pacific																
ejidos	238	1,032	1,778	2,003	60	866	870	615	4	35	153	286	85	244	467	466
non-ejidos	7,478	6,842	9,533	12,142	2,047	2,139	2,487	3,562	170	110	200	246	2,403	1,328	1,105	826
total	7,716	7,874	11,311	14,146	2,107	3,006	3,357	4,176	175	145	353	532	2,487	1,572	1,572	1,292
South Pacific																
ejidos	228	684	1,603	2,094	101	633	836	947	8	39	47	402	94	251	366	233
non-ejidos	3,684	2,413	3,634	4,024	4,038	5,728	5,679	7,008	202	180	250	485	2,153	1,122	1,151	1,453
total	3,911	3,096	5,237	6,118	4,138	6,361	6,515	7,955	210	220	297	887	2,247	1,373	1,517	1,685
Center																
ejidos	877	2,455	3,662	3,723	219	1,051	1,078	1,057	25	109	74	346	233	473	409	352
non-ejidos	7,011	3,889	4,008	4,478	2,470	2,390	2,364	2,183	227	165	100	199	2,512	1,017	1,047	1,061
total	7,888	6,343	7,670	8,201	2,689	3,441	3,442	3,240	252	274	174	545	2,745	1,490	1,457	1,412
Mexico																
ejidos	3,557	10,659	16,530	19,614	920	6,872	8,801	8,030	147	1,700	1,718	3,947	1,779	2,646	3,055	2,577
non-ejidos	62,936	45,513	50,849	59,478	24,935	31,243	30,035	35,649	3,788	7,081	6,060	7,245	18,914	8,164	8,542	8,727
total	66,493	56,172	67,379	79,092	25,856	38,115	38,836	43,679	3,935	8,781	7,777	11,193	20,694	10,810	11,597	11,304

[a] Columns may not sum to totals due to rounding.

Appendix Table E.5—*Continued*

ᵇ Arable land is defined in the census as that land whose natural conditions make it usable for the sowing, cultivation, and harvest of vegetable products by means of available agricultural technology. This might be subject to any water supply conditions, including the need for irrigation. The definition does not include land planted in orchards or cactus.

Sources: 1930 and 1950: *1950 Agricultural Census,* Table 1, pp. 7–12. The data on non-ejidos were broken down into farms of more than five hectares and farms of five hectares or less. The section covering 1930 contains no figures for farms of five hectares or less for the categories "Pasture land," "Forest land," "Economically productive but uncultivated land," and "Agriculturally unproductive land." The section covering 1950 contains no figures for farms of five hectares or less for these same categories with the exception of "Pasture land."

1940: *1940 Agricultural Census,* Table 1, pp. 11–22.
1960: *1960 Agricultural Census,* Table 1, pp. 1–3.

Appendix Table E.6
Index of Crop Production by Region, 1929–59
(1929 = 100)

Region	1929	1939	1949	1959
North	100	206	373	433
Gulf	100	121	174	376
North Pacific	100	104	184	537
South Pacific	100	138	304	529
Center	100	137	185	283
Mexico	100	139	231	379

Sources and Methods: These national and regional indexes were computed by the author on the basis of quantity statistics for 21 crops (four classifications of corn [maize], sugarcane, alfalfa, beans, barley, peanuts, wheat, sesame, tomatoes, cotton, henequen, tobacco, coffee, rice, bananas, garbanzo beans, oranges, and cocoa) from the decennial agricultural censuses. The regional data were adjusted to conform to national figures by crop from Rosenzweig, "Indices de los Rendimientos Agrícolas," based upon estimates of the Secretaría de Agricultura y Ganadería. The national index used here is derived from Rosenzweig, to ensure comparability; my regional indexes of production (using base year weights) were reconciled with the national index of physical output in agriculture prepared by Rosenzweig, by adjusting them by the percentage difference between my national index and the index based on Rosenzweig's paper. Implicit in this was a decision to rank the accuracy of the data of the Oficina de Estudios sobre Proyecciones Agrícolas (Rosenzweig) above that of the Dirección General de Estadística (which publishes the agricultural census), since wide discrepancies exist among the sources for some crops.

Appendix Table E.7
Volume of Production of Major Crops
(thousand tons)

	1925	1926	1927	1928	1929	1929 *Census*	1930	1931	1932	1933	1934	1935	1936	1937
Alfalfa	1,621	1,769	1,703	1,769	1,875	1,222	1,668	1,637	1,649	1,528	1,694	1,568	1,438	1,488
Bananas	—a	—	199	217	228	218	244	226	205	262	339	441	499	525
Barley	83	94	98	86	55	83	59	69	66	69	69	76	74	71
Chick-peas	62	82	81	64	69	67	49	84	44	48	53	68	43	27
Cocoa	2	1	1	1	1	2	1	1	1	1	1	1	1	1
Coffee	42	50	52	53	53	49	49	47	41	55	46	52	64	60
Corn (maize)	1,968	2,135	2,059	2,173	1,991	2,253	1,866	2,139	2,574	2,612	2,429	2,446	2,414	2,552
Cotton	44	78	39	60	53	60	39	46	22	57	48	68	86	74
Henequen	137	117	148	139	122	135	119	95	109	113	104	81	115	101
Kidney beans	188	200	190	176	87	97	80	140	142	209	144	146	132	132
Oranges	—	—	100	101	101	61	111	125	113	92	113	113	146	147
Peanuts	6	7	7	8	6	6	5	5	5	5	7	8	9	11
Potatoes	38	43	53	54	39	22	46	50	52	52	59	60	76	69
Rice, unhusked	86	91	83	83	67	75	75	72	72	67	69	71	86	75
Sesame	10	11	12	15	11	8	8	15	16	13	15	19	25	27
Sugarcane	2,873	3,158	2,997	2,947	3,029	4,001	3,293	3,694	3,405	2,778	2,774	3,573	4,341	4,057
Tobacco	9	9	10	13	13	12	11	11	11	10	12	14	13	20
Tomatoes (jitomate)	60	68	84	89	95	64	81	78	86	66	51	53	69	76
Wheat	298	334	385	357	367	307	370	525	313	392	354	347	440	342

Appendix Table E.7—*Continued*

	1938	1939	1939 Census	1940	1941	1942	1943	1944	1945	1946	1947	1948	1949	1949 Census
Alfalfa	1,540	1,737	1,067	1,719	1,806	1,786	1,964	2,037	2,100	2,126	2,122	2,248	2,291	2,280
Bananas	519	507	290	270	238	272	310	296	299	302	298	300	308	305
Barley	70	90	117	103	93	91	78	80	85	84	88	149	160	131
Chick-peas	56	56	54	66	72	83	76	90	100	106	111	111	97	95
Cocoa	2	1	3	1	2	2	2	2	3	5	6	7	7	9
Coffee	57	55	83	52	52	52	52	60	55	57	55	53	59	295
Corn (maize)	2,731	2,989	3,296	2,494	3,249	3,633	2,793	3,392	3,404	3,723	3,947	4,454	4,529	4,936
Cotton	67	68	179	66	81	103	116	106	98	91	96	120	208	486
Henequen	80	86	106	96	102	113	132	130	106	108	117	123	104	104[b]
Kidney beans	148	197	217	128	212	243	209	242	214	184	263	277	372	422
Oranges	167	183	116	208	230	240	264	284	295	342	345	400	411	450
Peanuts	12	15	14	17	29	39	46	39	30	33	33	35	38	39
Potatoes	71	71	42	71	92	118	124	125	127	124	129	128	131	103
Rice, unhusked	80	103	132	108	109	108	115	104	121	140	138	163	185	187
Sesame	26	33	30	27	60	63	55	66	58	62	84	73	70	96
Sugarcane	4,132	4,556	5,157	4,973	5,677	6,800	6,858	6,754	6,742	7,197	8,412	9,559	10,432	11,734
Tobacco	19	21	19	24	20	24	21	32	34	36	40	36	34	29
Tomatoes (jitomate)	65	80	38	80	126	157	173	209	234	225	241	286	335	180
Wheat	386	429	468	464	434	489	364	374	347	340	422	477	503	572[c]

Appendix Table E.7—Continued

	1950	1951	1952	1953	1954	1955	1956	1957	1958	1959	1959 Census	1960	1961	1962
Alfalfa	2,304	2,399	2,432	2,323	2,366	2,456	3,282	4,067	4,278	4,362	3,171	4,240	4,456	4,465
Bananas	257	187	204	203	205	207	246	270	274	285	343	317	341	293
Barley	162	164	165	165	167	192	197	174	178	179	178	180	185	190
Chick-peas	84	83	84	87	92	94	103	106	108	114	85	115	118	119
Cocoa	9	9	9	8	13	14	14	15	17	22	14	24	26	27
Coffee	66	68	71	88	85	93	88	97	122	98	570	124	122	144
Corn (maize)	4,696	4,935	4,441	4,983	5,819	5,653	5,369	5,378	6,161	6,357	5,706	6,073	6,152	6,516
Cotton	260	288	265	274	391	509	426	478	526	380	1,038	470	450	458
Henequen	101	95	97	91	105	110	111	119	123	149	149[b]	156	156	158
Kidney beans	312	285	279	328	425	449	432	410	510	581	663	528	617	680
Oranges	555	502	534	557	598	595	625	656	662	674	369	767	687	691
Peanuts	64	68	70	73	78	81	84	81	82	90	42	89	90	90
Potatoes	135	138	139	150	150	167	180	197	224	250	157	294	307	325
Rice, unhusked	187	180	151	152	170	210	235	240	253	261	205	326	333	452
Sesame	80	87	91	88	91	91	100	113	117	125	142	129	138	146
Sugarcane	9,419	9,830	10,730	11,682	13,013	14,002	10,679	14,597	16,252	17,765	12,852	19,542	19,732	19,880
Tobacco	35	36	36	37	38	53	54	70	71	72	37	72	74	75
Tomatoes (jitomate)	355	359	350	370	375	369	372	341	355	373	235	389	390	406
Wheat	587	590	512	671	840	850	1,243	1,376	1,337	1,266	1,135	1,190	1,373	1,415

a Data not available.

b Calculation is misleading in the census, since it goes by the number of leaves cut rather than by kilos or tons. Instead of the 1950 and 1960 census figures therefore, the figures on total output from *Consumos Aparentes* are used. In computing my own indexes of the volume of agricultural production, I assumed that tons were proportional to the number of leaves cut, by region, and distributed the volume regionally, using the census regional proportions for weights.

c "Trigo de temporal" added to 1949 data for comparability with the 1959 figure.

Sources: *Consumos Aparentes 1925–1962*. Agricultural Censuses of 1930, 1940, 1950, and 1960.

Appendix Table E.8
Value of Production of Major Crops
(thousands of current pesos)

	1925	1926	1927	1928	1929	1929 Census	1930	1931	1932	1933	1934
Alfalfa	22,936	27,510	26,350	25,091	29,419	17,034	23,320	18,869	18,624	15,060	17,204
Bananas	—[a]	—	7,640	8,113	7,145	6,036	8,537	8,186	7,547	10,567	12,488
Barley	4,356	5,689	5,831	4,425	3,358	4,257	3,641	3,185	3,003	3,065	3,454
Chick-peas	8,897	9,293	9,088	7,019	8,917	8,395	6,169	6,818	3,396	5,336	6,642
Cocoa	2,514	2,448	2,301	2,170	2,119	2,054	1,113	1,097	1,088	870	1,299
Coffee	37,525	38,858	37,510	36,959	34,408	21,705	26,161	19,749	17,765	20,942	23,021
Corn[b] (maize)	148,397	149,285	143,652	148,283	149,515	150,157	144,804	102,443	136,445	128,750	126,554
Cotton	44,279	61,045	40,838	61,430	41,701	44,343	23,250	21,848	13,807	45,269	44,806
Henequen	39,603	32,713	36,771	31,983	32,726	31,603	18,940	10,521	12,068	20,339	16,971
Kidney beans[b]	34,398	20,771	19,229	17,359	11,723	12,720	15,408	17,618	14,953	12,853	9,973
Oranges	—	—	6,825	7,620	7,784	3,869	7,935	6,909	5,449	5,031	6,561
Peanuts	727	746	881	1,003	739	707	587	570	628	671	844
Potatoes	4,539	4,040	4,687	3,855	3,386	1,719	4,433	3,448	3,891	4,038	5,388
Rice, unhusked	12,743	10,484	9,171	10,248	9,544	7,028	8,331	7,450	5,731	5,757	6,373
Sesame	1,324	1,425	1,625	2,027	1,337	760	935	1,611	1,915	1,915	2,260
Sugarcane	23,215	25,458	25,654	24,533	26,944	31,685	27,530	27,559	25,904	25,534	25,651
Tobacco	4,147	4,462	4,635	5,356	4,819	3,700	4,360	3,563	3,485	3,345	3,787
Tomatoes (jitomate)	6,060	7,274	8,424	11,118	9,861	6,857	7,025	10,468	5,278	4,255	5,560
Wheat	36,888	37,111	40,080	38,469	41,808	31,424	39,472	36,327	27,855	47,093	47,151

Appendix Table E.8—*Continued*

	1935	1936	1937	1938	1939	1939 Census	1940	1941	1942	1943	1944
Alfalfa	17,856	16,063	20,027	22,644	22,037	18,559	25,353	27,260	28,884	45,338	53,226
Bananas	17,428	23,293	19,996	22,017	20,944	14,618	11,951	12,764	22,250	37,403	40,980
Barley	4,498	4,524	5,721	6,216	6,853	6,466	7,595	7,788	9,009	10,394	17,554
Chick-peas	8,984	4,624	3,838	9,763	11,025	6,657	12,641	15,630	14,654	20,264	26,801
Cocoa	1,523	1,570	2,032	3,280	2,350	5,270	2,918	3,873	4,644	5,848	4,908
Coffee	23,838	26,785	30,569	31,661	30,640	31,504	30,962	39,664	46,089	47,748	60,017
Corn[b] (maize)	151,158	200,083	299,873	296,620	312,056	277,464	238,205	332,356	410,870	487,120	851,767
Cotton	55,339	80,629	70,397	65,874	70,860	67,010	64,693	95,486	165,017	216,220	202,526
Henequen	17,736	27,674	23,100	16,307	24,726	15,436	25,839	30,596	42,256	64,394	72,515
Kidney beans[b]	14,216	18,471	26,558	37,563	46,380	36,409	27,215	43,645	48,941	48,126	71,442
Oranges	7,507	10,176	11,725	12,219	14,693	6,384	16,427	17,227	21,485	29,077	42,727
Peanuts	997	1,229	1,890	2,207	3,377	2,103	3,462	6,716	10,121	15,137	14,345
Potatoes	6,129	7,999	8,794	8,284	9,106	3,815	8,031	11,427	17,628	23,175	30,233
Rice, unhusked	7,262	9,177	8,147	10,672	14,908	16,009	16,333	18,249	23,102	27,918	30,026
Sesame	2,965	5,046	6,887	5,650	9,977	8,033	7,972	20,081	25,165	30,812	43,095
Sugarcane	32,546	43,677	41,333	43,197	48,802	49,523	51,558	56,331	75,001	102,040	113,366
Tobacco	4,684	4,281	8,867	9,522	10,522	8,068	11,772	10,976	15,932	15,658	31,114
Tomatoes (jitomate)	9,665	10,920	10,378	13,008	13,663	3,508	24,680	32,616	46,804	61,657	78,904
Wheat	39,959	54,626	63,601	72,866	77,885	74,153	84,905	80,270	92,346	89,687	107,978

Appendix Table E.8—*Continued*

	1945	1946	1947	1948	1949	1949 Census	1950	1951	1952	1953
Alfalfa	76,666	84,803	87,511	96,083	100,133	91,994	104,640	109,940	114,113	110,802
Bananas	59,264	74,241	75,712	81,197	92,512	85,571	65,370	47,487	52,630	54,467
Barley	17,839	20,204	23,748	38,684	39,843	31,509	44,536	45,119	45,748	48,898
Chick-peas	32,889	40,430	44,393	46,676	48,848	43,280	43,687	43,987	44,953	47,350
Cocoa	8,547	18,000	19,185	26,000	27,990	33,295	36,252	36,830	39,177	36,610
Coffee	67,211	78,392	92,084	114,052	152,922	378,166	244,351	264,951	283,007	537,880
Corn[b] (maize)	932,665	1,062,610	1,233,990	1,344,692	1,331,434	1,160,931	1,818,413	2,465,603	2,220,237	2,485,449
Cotton	189,995	227,506	258,459	387,482	824,589	806,027	1,565,029	1,500,576	1,386,585	1,424,646
Henequen	64,311	90,453	120,828	135,544	118,206	32,609	122,493	117,329	128,020	122,932
Kidney beans[b]	79,769	125,046	215,057	190,701	255,870	255,169	225,547	201,050	206,096	253,359
Oranges	51,650	71,421	73,570	83,021	91,075	84,761	141,180	131,123	142,029	166,554
Peanuts	13,261	17,357	16,539	19,869	23,601	21,638	40,081	43,336	46,254	49,362
Potatoes	36,617	37,530	37,527	43,877	48,070	34,399	56,383	59,196	62,278	69,859
Rice, unhusked	41,700	59,068	63,104	71,136	77,371	69,740	80,591	78,341	66,947	69,645
Sesame	48,194	58,668	75,370	74,048	64,402	80,886	76,123	82,820	88,639	90,671
Sugarcane	133,693	159,520	201,811	254,739	289,300	163,996	252,000	288,608	316,498	366,681
Tobacco	42,223	56,128	61,577	60,645	62,504	59,001	66,815	69,939	70,239	75,136
Tomatoes (jitomate)	78,348	82,504	127,148	165,549	180,562	79,799	184,002	179,266	179,266	192,064
Wheat	106,376	139,305	185,052	219,056	237,318	206,773	322,185	442,452	375,626	506,244

Appendix Table E.8—*Continued*

	1954	1955	1956	1957	1958	1959	1959 Census	1960	1961	1962
Alfalfa	120,035	144,648	229,696	300,946	341,690	360,512	244,868	387,597	374,270	379,525
Bananas	58,589	62,002	71,962	126,118	134,284	151,609	151,485	184,969	194,299	170,085
Barley	59,350	73,969	92,282	115,845	122,418	125,702	122,476	128,803	134,757	142,643
Chick-peas	51,228	69,887	91,075	94,679	97,111	107,423	70,913	112,202	116,405	118,560
Cocoa	61,239	88,856	67,896	76,284	87,401	125,504	83,445	126,502	153,327	159,120
Coffee	553,575	644,498	636,642	1,137,920	1,088,400	773,982	1,017,503	945,894	982,905	1,166,400
Corn[b] (maize)	2,994,777	2,976,228	3,414,155	3,762,069	4,370,506	4,545,527	4,049,436	4,426,575	4,552,749	4,886,647
Cotton	2,589,743	3,287,982	2,718,607	3,035,621	3,183,228	2,281,421	1,889,413	2,848,306	2,934,488	3,001,295
Henequen	157,569	182,575	192,964	209,713	211,567	261,015	415,677	274,141	278,937	283,500
Kidney beans[b]	378,244	461,792	481,615	511,448	651,274	766,806	857,553	708,969	832,495	924,800
Oranges	193,331	218,573	255,682	334,922	366,923	391,021	208,246	481,886	429,098	442,256
Peanuts	55,318	88,444	89,304	73,017	77,529	89,994	41,686	94,108	102,107	106,200
Potatoes	81,305	101,576	99,692	112,354	136,763	156,235	94,075	166,972	208,692	227,500
Rice, unhusked	87,922	111,122	186,888	203,298	216,832	227,909	178,970	291,850	308,990	417,638
Sesame	101,695	107,903	157,036	200,779	213,669	233,918	261,656	247,499	276,576	296,156
Sugarcane	426,807	502,448	405,224	687,894	758,715	850,944	621,866	962,813	986,580	1,013,880
Tobacco	78,918	113,490	141,695	161,859	207,427	224,400	118,403	250,964	236,720	245,916
Tomatoes (jitomate)	200,341	238,260	271,882	340,806	311,837	300,325	198,877	293,694	331,840	353,525
Wheat	655,545	676,410	1,025,486	1,116,714	1,152,804	1,110,429	1,012,910	1,033,213	1,235,293	1,280,187

[a] Data not available.

[b] There were no value figures for the revised corn and kidney bean data (see Table E.7). These figures were derived by multiplying the revised volume data times the prices in the unrevised data.

Sources: *Consumos Aparentes 1925–1962.* Agricultural Censuses of 1930, 1940, and 1950.

Appendix Table E.9
Estimates of Land Area Cultivated from the Agricultural Census
and Secretaría de Agricultura: 1930–60
(thousand hectares)

Region	1930	1940	1950	1960
Census				
North	1,664	2,081	2,946	3,711
Gulf	821	694	1,239	1,833
North Pacific	521	581	988	1,582
South Pacific	761	807	1,477	2,067
Center	3,398	3,376	4,214	4,590
Mexico	7,165	7,539	10,863	13,783
Secretaría de Agricultura y Ganadería				
Mexico	6,240	7,420	9,726	13,550

Sources: *Census:* Decennial agricultural censuses—hectares "cultivadas," not all of which were harvested. A hectare is two and a half acres. The percentage of cultivated land actually harvested was 81 percent in 1930, 84 percent in 1940 (est.), 79 percent in 1950, and 78 percent in 1960, reflecting the increasing use of marginal land, as plantings have virtually doubled since 1930. The 1940 figure is equivalent in the aggregate to that presented in Rosenzweig, "Indices de los Rendimientos Agrícolas," with regional shares proportional to the hectares harvested ("cosechadas") for that year, since the 1940 census did not provide data on hectares cultivated. For slightly different figures for 1930 and 1940 (crop years 1929/30 and 1939/40), see Table 4.1.

Secretaría: Rosenzweig, "Indices de los Rendimientos Agrícolas." The figures represent the land area planted in 65 crops and are available annually though not regionally since 1925, along with quantity of output (in 1958–60 prices) for six categories of food crops, four categories of industrial crops, and forage crops.

Appendix Table E.10
Fixed Reproducible Assets in Agriculture, 1930–60
(million 1950 pesos)

Region	1930	1940	1950	1960
North:				
Private	371	493	989	1,410
Public	38	463	1,272	2,245
Total	409	956	2,261	3,655
Gulf:				
Private	174	141	183	273
Public	–	–	18	211
Total	174	141	201	484
North Pacific:				
Private	324	187	442	804
Public	–	171	1,407	3,374
Total	324	358	1,849	4,178
South Pacific:				
Private	66	88	125	206
Public	–	–	73[a]	98[a]
Total	66	88	198	304
Center:				
Private	502	532	611	1,047
Public	278	584	865	1,604
Total	780	1,116	1,476	2,651
Mexico:				
Private	1,437	1,441	2,350	3,740
Public	316	1,218	3,635	7,532
Total	1,753	2,659	5,985	11,272

[a] For reasons explained in the source note, public investment in irrigation in the South Pacific in the 1950s has probably been understated. Thus the growth of inputs has a downward bias for this region between 1950 and 1960.

Sources: The value of private capital stock in agriculture, which includes buildings, hydraulic works (private), machinery and implements, tools and fixtures, private roads and railroads, is available by region in current prices in the decennial agricultural censuses. The 1930 figures were converted into 1950 peso values, using the wholesale price index (Mexico City). The 1940 and 1960 figures were converted into 1950 peso values by using the implicit deflator in Cossío's estimate of the Mexican capital stock in current and constant pesos in Banco de México, Departamento de Estudios Económicos, "Alternativas de Estimación de la Inversión Bruta Fija en México, 1939–1962."

The value of the publicly produced capital stock in 1950 pesos was accumulated from figures on annual gross federal investment in agriculture since 1925 (disregarding depreciation, since most of these expenditures were on dams and irrigation systems which have lives in excess of thirty years) as presented in Secretaría de la Presidencia, Dirección de Inversiones Públicas, *México Inversión Pública Federal, 1925–1963*. The regional shares for each year were based upon the percentage of total hectares benefited by public irrigation projects in each state, as obtained from Orive Alba, *La Política de Irrigación en México*, Anexo 6 (see Table E.11). Since these data were available by Comisiones (irrigation districts) they sometimes fail to fall within regional boundaries. In such cases the hectares of land ("nuevos" and "mejorados") benefited by irrigation were placed within the regions receiving the primary benefit from the district. Examples of such cases are the Tepalcatepec (Center), Papaloapan and Grijalva (Gulf), Fuerte, Region Indígena del Yaqui (North Pacific). Both the Papaloapan and Grijalva projects also benefit portions of the South Pacific, although no land was receiving water from the Grijalva project as late as 1958, which is the terminal year for the regional breakdown. It should also be noted that "pequeña irrigación" was not included in the regional data.

Appendix Table E.11
Total Value Added in Manufacturing

Year	*Amount* (*million 1950 pesos*)	*Index* (*1950 = 100*)
1900	1,131	13.4
1910	1,620	19.2
1920	1,249	14.8
1925	2,076	24.6
1926	2,345	27.8
1927	2,118	25.1
1928	2,227	26.4
1929	2,345	27.8
1930	2,489	29.5
1931	2,489	29.5
1932	2,151	25.5
1933	1,966	23.3
1934	2,945	34.9
1935	2,869	34.0
1936	3,324	39.4
1937	3,476	41.2
1938	3,552	42.1
1939	3,780	44.8
1940	3,889	46.1
1941	4,480	53.1
1942	5,113	60.6
1943	5,391	63.9
1944	5,805	68.8
1945	6,328	75.0
1946	6,454	76.5
1947	6,277	74.4
1948	6,775	80.3
1949	7,374	87.4
1950	8,437	100.0
1951	9,331	110.6
1952	9,745	115.5
1953	9,635	114.2
1954	10,572	125.3
1955	11,601	137.5
1956	12,917	153.1
1957	13,761	163.1
1958	14,503	171.9
1959	15,803	187.3
1960	17,116	202.9

Appendix Table E.11—*Continued*

Year	Amount (million 1950 pesos)	Index (1950 = 100)
1961	17,726	210.1
1962	18,862	223.6
1963	20,597	244.1
1964	23,522	278.8
1965	25,200	298.7

Sources: The figures for 1940 to 1962 are from the Banco de México official statistics. Estimates for the years 1910 to 1940 are based on an index of output in manufacturing appearing in *Trimestre de Barómetros Económicos*, No. 8, March 1948 (which includes construction). These figures differ slightly from those prepared by Flores Márquez, which appear in Pérez López, "El Producto Nacional," *México: 50 Años de Revolución*, Vol. I ("Economía"), pp. 587–89. The corresponding figures for Flores Márquez are: 1900: 1,232; 1910: 1,663; 1925: 1,889; 1940: 3,629. Data for the years 1900 and 1910 are based on estimates of manufacturing output for 1877/1910 from El Colegio de México, *Fuerza de Trabajo*, p. 106. Figures for 1963 and 1964 are from Grupo Secretaría de Hacienda-Banco de México, "Manual," Table 2-3. Figures for 1965 are from OECD Development Centre, *National Accounts of Less Developed Countries* (preliminary, February 1967), p. 57.

Appendix Table E.12
Principal Characteristics of the Industrial Sector, 1930, 1950, and 1960

| | Manufacturing[a] | | | | Mining and Manufacturing | | | |
| | 1930 | | 1950 | | 1950 | | 1960[b] | |
	Amount	Percent	Amount	Percent	Amount	Percent	Amount	Percent
North								
number of establishments	7,509	15.5	13,873	18.8	14,204	19.1	17,598	17.4
number of employees	59,659	19.1	204,124	26.2	225,124	27.8	194,720	20.0
value of production (thous. pesos)	205,719	23.2	2,317,779	13.5	6,368,779	28.1	12,227,411	22.9
total capital (thous. pesos)	216,933	22.7	5,599,088	30.5	5,988,088	31.6	12,170,772	24.5
Gulf								
number of establishments	6,292	13.0	8,641	11.7	8,655	11.7	10,010	9.9
number of employees	44,581	14.2	81,705	10.5	81,705	10.1	82,268	8.5
value of production (thous. pesos)	119,543	13.5	3,400,640	19.8	3,400,640	15.0	3,944,065	7.4
total capital (thous. pesos)	127,800	13.4	1,590,109	8.7	1,590,109	8.4	4,305,904	8.7
North Pacific								
number of establishments	1,891	3.9	3,710	5.0	3,741	5.0	5,548	5.5
number of employees	15,930	5.1	36,437	4.7	37,437	4.6	54,907	5.7
value of production (thous. pesos)	68,205	7.7	1,571,376	9.1	1,704,376	7.5	3,427,755	6.4
total capital (thous. pesos)	78,056	8.2	1,577,517	8.6	1,624,517	8.6	3,701,987	7.5
South Pacific								
number of establishments	9,236	19.0	5,581	7.6	5,599	7.5	6,235	6.2
number of employees	28,115	9.0	22,292	2.9	23,292	2.9	25,761	2.7
value of production (thous. pesos)	24,111	2.7	431,018	2.5	431,018	1.9	675,517	1.3
total capital (thous. pesos)	20,958	2.2	239,825	1.3	277,825	1.5	545,311	1.1
Center (excluding Federal District)								
number of establishments	20,169	41.5	25,435	34.5	25,633	34.5	30,683	30.3
number of employees	103,867	33.2	189,705	24.3	196,703	24.3	269,748	27.8
value of production (thous. pesos)	223,310	25.2	3,004,662	17.5	4,217,662	18.6	13,056,467	24.5
total capital (thous. pesos)	330,069	34.5	5,164,872	28.1	5,260,872	27.8	7,181,472	28.8

Appendix Table E.12—*Continued*

| | Manufacturing[a] | | | | Mining and Manufacturing | | | |
| | 1930 | | 1950 | | 1950 | | 1960[b] | |
	Amount	Percent	Amount	Percent	Amount	Percent	Amount	Percent
Federal District								
number of establishments	3,476	7.2	16,420	22.3	16,420	22.1	31,137	30.8
number of employees	61,001	19.5	244,994	31.4	244,994	30.3	344,205	35.4
value of production (thous. pesos)	245,860	27.7	6,475,122	37.6[c]	6,475,122	28.6	19,976,837	37.5
total capital (thous. pesos)	182,323	19.1	4,194,166	22.8	4,194,166	22.1	15,375,183	14.5
Mexico								
number of establishments	48,573	100.0	73,660	100.0	74,252	100.0	101,212	100.0
number of employees	313,153	100.0	779,257	100.0	809,257	100.0	971,609	100.0
value of production (thous. pesos)	886,748	100.0	17,200,597	100.0	22,677,597	100.0	53,308,052	100.0
total capital (thous. pesos)	956,139	100.0	18,365,577	100.0	18,935,577	100.0	49,607,709	100.0

[a] These data exclude extractive industry except for petroleum and salt manufacturing.
[b] Data only for manufacturing and extractive firms in the private sector.
[c] The shares of the Federal District in manufacturing in 1940 and 1955, based on the industrial censuses for those years, were 37 percent and 48 percent respectively, according to Yates, *El Desarrollo Regional de México*, p. 49.

Sources and Methods: These data were taken from industrial censuses of 1930, 1950, and 1960. The 1930 census of manufacturing failed to include extractive industries in the sample but did provide independent estimates of these activities in the resumé, though they were far from complete. The results were so incomplete for this category that I elected to compare the 1930 regional disaggregation with that of the 1950 census after removing extractive industry from the regional totals for the later year.

An earlier critical comparison of the two censuses that does not exclude extractive industries from 1950 totals notes that the share of the Federal District in the value of mining and manufacturing rose only slightly between 1929 and 1950, although there was a considerable increase in its share of the number of firms and labor force employed in industry. This is explained in that study by the proliferation of labor-intensive industry in Mexico City, including auto mechanics, machinery and appliance repair shops, soldering, welding, electric installations, plumbing, etc. (The coverage of these activities was much more complete in 1950, the first year in which the U.N. standard industrial classification was used.) Ref. Bonilla G., "El Información Censal y su Aplicación al Análisis de los Cambios Estructurales de la Industria en México," (thesis); also, unpublished Chapter III, "Síntesis Históricas de los Censos Industriales Mexicanos," in which a critical comparison of the censuses of 1929, 1951, and 1956 appears.

The relative growth of industry in Mexico City is best seen by comparing the manufacturing columns, since the failure to include more than a sample share of extractive industries in 1930, and the concentration of these industries in the North, biases upward the D.F. share in 1930, cf. 1950 under mining and manufacturing.

Appendix Table E.13
Production of Selected Manufactures, 1950-64

	Units	1950	1951	1952	1953	1954	1955	1956	1957
Petroleum									
Crude oil refined	thous. barr.	55,825	62,713	64,801	71,048	76,735	80,506	82,061	86,373
Electric energy generated	millions kwh	4,423	4,908	5,337	6,703	6,282	7,002	7,827	8,451
Sugar	thous. tons	618	645	721	776	836	886	762	1,078
Beer	thous. liters	500,608	579,200	583,798	572,240	653,168	678,327	750,925	745,460
Cotton cloth	tons	65,649	66,852	70,720	61,490	70,800	72,017	74,429	81,973
Artificial fibers	tons	8,106	10,583	12,725	10,068	13,732	16,746	20,279	17,421
Iron and steel	thous. tons								
Primary materials[a]		922	1,678[d]	1,246	1,208	1,376	1,647	2,053	2,716
of which: steel ingots		618	1,320	837	765	852	1,041	1,240	1,461
Elaborated products[b]		390	467	533	523	600	713	832	1,029
		126	145	156	198	237	296	404	486
Products for final consumption[e]		178	212	254	245	286	310	410	769
Sulfuric acid	tons	43,374	56,667	92,208	102,503	109,962	124,887	156,915	186,203
Caustic soda	tons	8,440	6,140	9,140	13,050	17,575	22,909	25,589	33,952
Derivatives of coal	tons								
Pitch		10,417	11,048	12,495	17,754	15,206	15,820	20,008	20,410
Naphthalene		4,500	2,850	3,775	7,570	5,605	6,195	8,433	4,387
Creosote		–	–	–	–	–	82	243	397
Benzene products		3,306	5,584	5,673	6,940	6,726	5,898	6,922	8,913
		2,611	3,047	3,047	3,244	2,875	3,645	4,410	6,713
Fertilizers	tons								
Ammonium sulfate		2,642	33,753	64,466	66,210	63,242	70,232	87,790	99,287
Ammonium nitrate		–	–	–	–	–	–	–	–
Simple superphosphate		15,462	19,154	56,000	62,977	61,132	74,919	77,137	84,587
Triple superphosphate		–	–	–	–	–	–	–	–
Anhydrous ammonia		–	–	–	–	–	–	–	–
Compound chemical fertilizers		17,980	8,381	15,720	15,852	15,662	17,481	20,219	21,060
Organic fertilizers		3,648	29,833	37,380	33,283	41,992	47,725	54,632	73,534
Other		–	2,594	1,741	2,650	2,404	2,277	3,166	2,362
		–	–	–	–	–	–	11,094	11,409
Motor vehicles, assembled	number	21,575	46,081	47,987	35,709	33,380	32,275	39,387	41,106
Cars		10,384	21,833	20,867	18,791	13,325	12,405	13,134	18,297
Trucks		11,191	24,248	27,300	21,918	20,055	19,870	26,253	22,809

Appendix Table E.13—Continued

	Units	1958	1959	1960	1961	1962	1963	1964
Petroleum								
Crude oil refined	thous. barr.	95,311	104,928	107,279	118,961	118,452	119,611	126,976
Electric energy generated	millions kwh	9,098	9,774	10,636	11,747	12,507	13,707	15,748
Sugar	thous. tons	1,097	1,325	1,426	1,404	1,441	1,638	1,789
Beer	thous. liters	732,796	800,843	852,499	840,331	858,588	849,581	965,702
Cotton cloth	tons	92,862	99,984	101,575	102,447	109,926	115,422	120,386
Artificial fibers	tons	19,953	22,592	23,261	23,614	25,225	29,694	33,009
Iron and steel	thous. tons	2,635	3,124	3,599	3,980	3,982	4,673	5,375
Primary materials[a]		1,589	1,977	2,292	2,651	2,703	3,045	3,498
of which: steel ingots		1,083	1,328	1,492	1,693	1,711	2,017	2,326
Elaborated products[b]		466	545	645	656	619	842	1,012
Products for final consumption[c]		580	602	662	673	660	785	864
Sulfuric acid	tons	200,000	242,927	248,828	275,984	338,891	387,370	439,728
Caustic soda	tons	39,461	51,975	65,888	71,338	83,425	90,565	94,886
Derivatives of coal	tons	20,353	21,173	26,247	26,580	29,468	33,760	35,659
Pitch		3,913	6,122	9,741	9,788	12,952	15,908	17,628
Naphthalene		660	707	751	823	1,114	1,481	1,690
Creosote		9,143	9,774	10,611	10,814	9,753	10,049	9,770
Benzene products		6,637	4,570	5,144	5,155	5,649	6,322	6,571
Fertilizers	tons							
Ammonium sulfate		113,576	143,941	147,186	152,519	157,260	159,604	166,954
Ammonium nitrate		—	10,210	54,337	70,969	123,947	124,737	126,416
Simple superphosphate		78,081	95,410	93,232	104,031	109,400	117,025	122,613
Triple superphosphate		—	—	—	—	23,862	44,669	41,442
Anhydrous ammonia		21,428	21,594	19,676	38,344	100,012	151,236	175,950
Compound chemical fertilizers		70,436	94,314	74,211	76,194	83,443	145,595	176,948
Organic fertilizers		2,865	2,294	1,383	991	1,806	671	1,055
Other		14,985	13,713	13,017	10,292	11,744	18,563	17,083
Motor vehicles, assembled	number	38,955	51,118	49,807	62,563	66,637	75,349	59,079
Cars		20,373	27,159	28,121	39,524	40,801	49,458	62,757
Trucks		18,582	23,959	21,686	23,039	25,836	25,891	32,322

Appendix Table E.13—*Continued*

	Units	1950	1951	1952	1953	1954	1955	1956	1957
Railroad cars	number	—	—	—	—	—	858	1,134	1,507
Freight cars		—	—	—	—	—	858	1,134	1,507
Cabooses		—	—	—	—	—	—	—	—
Cattle cars		—	—	—	—	—	—	—	—
Express cars		—	—	—	—	—	—	—	—
Hoppers		—	—	—	—	—	—	—	—
Gondolas		—	—	—	—	—	—	—	—
Pulp	tons	60,323	66,020	59,459	87,820	62,506	80,000	120,000	170,000
Chemical pulp		—	—	—	—	—	—	—	—
a. for paper		—	—	—	—	—	—	—	—
b. for dissolving		—	—	—	—	—	—	—	—
Mechanical pulp		—	—	—	—	—	—	—	—
Paper	tons	157,803	193,438	182,379	187,362	197,537	254,000	294,500	299,611
Cement	thous. tons	1,388	1,535	1,640	1,672	1,764	2,086	2,277	2,518
Glass									
Bottles	number	313,088	375,705	299,437	419,511	451,394	480,283	641,501	588,051
Glassware	number	64,745	82,938	58,388	51,031	71,902	85,851	73,660	51,562
Light bulbs	number	175,960	241,945	201,258	256,655	260,505	302,967	335,384	367,245
Sheet glass	thous. M^2	5,055	6,546	6,350	5,956	7,546	7,787	7,989	7,645
Tires for cars and trucks	thous.	635	807	748	794	823	893	931	930
Inner tubes for cars and trucks	thous.	380	457	542	548	572	510	584	616

Appendix Table E.13—Continued

	Units	1958	1959	1960	1961	1962	1963	1964
Railroad cars	number	1,791	1,761	1,686	2,274	787	679	1,076
Freight cars		1,791	1,755	1,513	1,710	83	432	263
Cabooses		–	6	173	46	–	–	–
Cattle cars		–	–	–	518	–	–	–
Express cars		–	–	–	–	88	48	14
Hoppers		–	–	–	–	315	–	49
Gondolas		–	–	–	–	301	199	750
Pulp	tons	182,939	203,739	245,700	265,390	285,434	458,820	506,405
Chemical pulp		146,739	157,239	186,700	202,890	220,832	234,271	258,505
a. for paper		139,239	148,679	180,000	193,169	208,610	224,549	247,900
b. for dissolving		7,500	8,560	6,700	9,721	12,222	9,722	10,605
Mechanical pulp		36,200	46,500	59,000	62,500	64,602	69,251	69,726
Paper	tons	324,820	352,743	413,346	451,110	459,121	504,976	557,664
Cement	thous. tons	2,496	2,638	3,086	2,984	3,266	3,680	4,339
Glass								
Bottles	number	584,523	767,479	687,661	584,380	740,528	778,070	881,413
Glassware	number	58,884	85,558	195,500	175,065	184,753	–	–
Light bulbs	number	341,171	300,913	319,870	467,867	150,368	187,625	186,105
Sheet glass	thous. M²	5,313	6,886	7,276	8,502	9,513	8,329	11,462
Tires for cars and trucks	thous.	1,088	1,173	1,242	1,240	1,372	1,530	1,797
Inner tubes for cars and trucks	thous.	684	771	795	864	910	978	1,130

a Includes *fierro de primera fusión, ferroesponja, ferroaleaciones,* and steel ingots.

b Includes *plancha, lámina hojalata,* skelp *(cinta para tubo),* and *alambrón.*

c Includes seamed tubes, seamless tubes, *tubos fundidos, perfiles estructurales, perfiles comerciales, varilla corrugada,* and *material fijo para vía.*

d The component of iron and steel primary materials called "iron of first fusion" is peculiarly high in 1951, which is the reason this component is so high in that year.

Source: United Nations, ECLA, "El Desarrollo Industrial de Mexico," Tables 21–27 29–32 34–39, pp. 43, 46, 49, 51, 53, 54, 57, 60, 61, 63, 65, 68, 70, 72, 74, 76, and 77.

Appendix Table E.14
State Revenues by Type of Tax
(thousands of pesos)

Region	1910		1920		1930		1940		1960	
	Amount	% of Total	Amount	% of Total	Amount	% of Total	Amount	% of Total	Amount	% of Total
North Pacific										
Direct Taxes	968	41	4,398	53	3,959	31	3,057	15	97,667	28
Indirect Taxes	626	27	2,024	25	7,286	58	14,470	73	183,261	52
Income Taxes	742	32	1,835	22	1,360	11	2,265	11	70,074	20
North										
Direct Taxes	3,130	41	3,733	46	4,446	34	7,816	25	124,863	23
Indirect Taxes	2,425	32	2,952	36	7,984	62	19,115	62	312,587	59
Income Taxes	2,065	27	1,436	18	480	4	3,916	13	95,958	18
Center (less Federal District)										
Direct Taxes	6,153	50	8,791	52	6,817	33	13,089	36	133,604	25
Indirect Taxes	3,829	31	4,419	26	12,663	60	19,310	54	315,232	59
Income Taxes	2,454	20	3,578	21	1,468	7	3,618	10	81,609	15
Gulf										
Direct Taxes	2,811	53	5,269	52	2,939	25	3,133	16	44,602	16
Indirect Taxes	1,649	31	2,900	28	6,978	60	15,179	75	192,648	70
Income Taxes	870	16	2,056	20	1,818	16	1,940	10	37,998	14
South Pacific										
Direct Taxes	1,191	38	1,430	50	1,379	32	2,342	27	25,598	16
Indirect Taxes	899	29	812	29	2,867	65	5,157	60	120,365	74
Income Taxes	1,037	33	603	21	121	3	1,049	12	17,347	11
Total										
Direct Taxes	14,253	46	23,621	51	19,540	31	29,437	26	426,334	23
Indirect Taxes	9,428	31	13,107	28	37,778	60	73,231	63	1,124,093	61
Income Taxes	7,168	23	9,508	21	5,247	8	12,788	11	302,986	16

Source: Prepared from *Boletín Oficial* of the states, with the assistance of Jorge Herrera Castañeda.

Appendix Table E.15
State Expenditures by Economic Classification
(thousands of current pesos)

Region	1910		1920		1930		1940		1960	
	Amount	% of Total	Amount	% of Total	Amount	% of Total	Amount	% of Total	Amount	% of Total
North Pacific										
Current Expenditures	2,592	84.9	7,550	90.0	9,421	79.9	11,201	61.7	273,807	74.1
Investment Expenditures	200	6.6	631	7.5	1,671	15.0	2,585	14.2	64,613	17.5
Transfer Payments	261	8.5	209	2.5	703	6.0	4,374	24.1	31,261	8.5
North										
Current Expenditures	6,404	88.3	6,325	85.8	10,523	78.2	18,865	64.1	392,600	77.0
Investment Expenditures	528	7.3	547	7.4	2,257	16.8	5,124	17.4	79,327	15.6
Transfer Payments	324	4.5	499	6.8	672	5.0	5,445	18.5	37,933	7.4
Center										
Current Expenditures	11,518	88.3	14,812	89.2	16,379	79.7	22,466	63.7	387,801	72.9
Investment Expenditures	1,279	9.8	1,214	7.3	2,962	14.4	6,993	19.8	89,405	16.8
Transfer Payments	254	1.9	578	3.5	1,198	5.8	5,793	16.4	54,890	10.3
Gulf										
Current Expenditures	4,794	88.2	9,233	89.5	9,800	80.4	14,155	70.2	191,689	69.9
Investment Expenditures	577	10.6	740	7.2	1,582	13.0	2,618	13.0	37,612	13.7
Transfer Payments	62	1.1	348	3.4	814	6.7	3,398	16.8	44,939	16.4
South Pacific										
Current Expenditures	2,795	90.4	2,370	88.0	3,449	79.6	4,741	55.1	109,420	74.7
Investment Expenditures	256	8.3	207	7.7	665	15.3	1,047	12.2	32,081	21.9
Transfer Payments	40	1.3	117	4.3	221	5.1	2,818	32.7	4,940	3.4
Total										
Current Expenditures	28,103	88.1	40,290	88.8	49,572	79.5	71,428	64.0	1,355,317	74.0
Investment Expenditures	2,840	8.9	3,339	7.4	9,137	14.7	18,367	16.5	303,038	16.5
Transfer Payments	941	3.0	1,751	3.9	3,608	5.8	21,828	20.0	173,963	9.5

Source: Same as Appendix Table E.14.

Bibliography

The following is a selective compilation of sources used in the preparation of this volume as well as incidental publications on related topics of interest to the Mexican development historian. No attempt at full inclusiveness has been made, nor have the numerous interviews given the author been cited here, despite their relative importance in the shaping of the study. This should rather be regarded as a critical compendium of items which shed considerable light on the quantitative and institutional economic history of the period. Only a few references for the Porfiriato have been listed, owing to the excellent list by Enrique Florescano, "Bibliografía de la historia económica de México (Epoca prehispánica—1910)," El Colegio de México, 1969, mimeo, esp. pp. 58–72. See also the bibliography and comments by Enrique Florescano and Alejandra Moreno Toscano, "Historia económica y social," *Historia Méxicana,* 58–59, vol. XV, Oct. 1965–Mar. 1966, nums. 2–3, esp. pp. 322–27 and 366–78, "VI. México contemporáneo." The principal archives utilized for the present selection were those of the New York Public Library, Banco de México, Economic Growth Center and Sterling Library of Yale University, Bancroft Library of the University of California, and the collections of El Colegio de México and Stanford University. Those items available primarily at the New York Public Library are coded NYPL, while those principally at the library of the Banco de México are coded BML.

BOOKS

Adams, Robert McCormick. *The Evolution of Urban Society: Early Mesopotamia and Prehistoric Mexico.* Chicago: Aldine Publishing Company, 1966.

Ashby, Joe C. *Organized Labor and the Mexican Revolution under Lázaro Cárdenas.* Chapel Hill: University of North Carolina Press, 1967.

Attolini, José. *Economía de la cuenca del Papaloapan; bosques, fauna, pesca, gandería e indústria.* Mexico, D.F.: Instituto de Investigaciones Económicas, 1950.

Aubey, Robert T. *Nacional Financiera and Mexican Industry.* Los Angeles: Latin American Center, University of California, 1966.

Baer, Werner. *Industrialization and Economic Development in Brazil.* Homewood, Ill.: R. D. Irwin, Inc., 1965.

Bancroft, Hubert Howe. *Resources and Development of Mexico.* San Francisco: Bancroft Company, 1893.

Barajas Manzano, Javier. *Aspectos de la industria textil del algodón en México.* Mexico: Instituto Mexicano de Investigaciones Económicas, 1959.

Bases para la planeación económica y social de México. Seminario, Escuela Nacional de Economía, Universidad Nacional Autónoma de México, April 1965. Mexico: Siglo XXI Editores, S.A., 1966.

Bator, Francis M. *The Question of Government Spending; Public Needs and Private Wants.* New York: Harper & Brothers, 1960.

Bazant, Jan. *Historia de la deuda exterior de México (1823–1946),* El Colegio de México, México D.F., 1968.

Bell, Purl L., and Mackenzie, H. Bentley. *Mexican West Coast and Lower California: A Commercial and Industrial Survey.* Washington, D.C.: U.S. Government Printing Office, 1923. (Department of Commerce, Bureau of Foreign and Domestic, Special Agents Series No. 220).

Belshaw, Michael. *A Village Economy: Land and People of Huecorio.* New York and London: Columbia University Press, 1967.

Benítez Zenteno, Raúl, and Cabrera Acevedo, Gustavo. *Proyecciones de la población de México 1960–1980.* Mexico: Banco de México, Departamento de Investigaciones Industriales (Oficina de Recursos Humanos, Estudios de los Recursos Humanos de México), 1966.

Bennett, Robert L. *The Financial Sector and Economic Development: The Mexican Case.* Baltimore: The Johns Hopkins Press, 1965.

Bermúdez, Antonio J. *The Mexican National Petroleum Industry.* Special Issue, *Hispanic American Report,* Stanford University, 1963.

Bernstein, Marvin D. *The Mexican Mining Industry, 1890–1950; A Study of the Interaction of Politics, Economics, and Technology.* Albany, 1965.

Bett, Virgil M. *Central Banking in Mexico: Monetary Policies and Financial Crises, 1864–1940.* Ann Arbor: Bureau of Business Research, School of Business Administration, University of Michigan, 1957.

Bonaparte, Roland (Mm le Prince), et al. *Le Mezique au début du XXᵉ siècle.* 2 vols. Paris: C. Delagrave, 1904. (BML)

Brandenburg, Frank R. *The Making of Modern Mexico.* Englewood Cliffs, N.J.: Prentice-Hall, 1964.

Brothers, Dwight S., and Solís M., Leopoldo. *Mexican Financial Development.* Austin: University of Texas Press, 1966.

Busto, Emiliano. *Estadística de la República Mexicana. Estado que guardan la agricultura, industria, minería y comercio. Resúmen y análisis de los informes rendidos á la Secretaría de Hacienda por los agricultores, mineros, industriales y comerciantes de la República y los agentes de México en el exterior, en respuesta á las circulares de 1º de Agosto de 1877.* 3 vols. Mexico: Impr. de I. Cumplido, 1880. (BML)

Calderón, Francisco R. "El Porfiriato: la vida económica." Vol. II of *Historia moderna de México.* Edited by Daniel Cosío Villegas. 7 vols. Mexico: Editorial Hermes, 1955–65.

Callegari, Guido Volerio. *Messico, condizioni naturali ed economiche.* Rome: Fratelli Terves, 1926 (NYPL).

Campos Andapia, Antonio. *Obstáculos al desarrollo económico.* Mexico: Centro de Estudios Monetarios Latinoamericanos.

Cancian, Frank. *Economics and Prestige in a Maya Community.* Stanford University, 1965.

Carreño, Alberto María. *La evolución económica de México en los últimos cincuenta años.* Mexico: Academia Nacional de Ciencias "Antonio Alzate," 1937.

Carrillo, Alejandro. *La revolución industrial de México.* Mexico: Universidad Obrera, 1945.

Caves, Richard E., and Holton, Richard H. *The Canadian Economy.* Cambridge: Harvard University Press, 1961.

Ceceña Gamez, Jose Luis. *El capitalismo monopolista y la economía Mexicana.* Mexico: Cuadernos Americanos, 1963.

Cleland, R. G., ed. *The Mexican Year Book; The Standard Authority on Mexico, 1920/21–1922/24.* 2 vols. Los Angeles, Calif.: Mexican Year Book Publishing Company, 1922–24.

Cline, Howard F. *Mexico: Revolution to Evolution, 1940–1960.* London: Oxford University Press, 1962.

———. *The United States and Mexico.* Cambridge, Mass.: Harvard University Press, 1953; rev. ed., New York: Atheneum, 1963.

Cole, William E. *Steel and Economic Growth in Mexico.* Austin: University of Texas Press, 1967.

Collver, O. Andrew. *Birth Rates in Latin America: New Estimates of Historical Trends and Fluctuations.* Research Series, No. 7. Berkeley: Institute of International Studies, University of California, 1965.

Cosío Villegas, Daniel, ed. *Historia moderna de México.* 7 vols. Mexico: Editorial Hermes, 1955–65.

Cue Cánovas, Augustín. *La industria en México (1521–1845).* Mexico: Eds. Centenario, 1959.

Cumberland, Charles C. *Mexican Revolution, Genesis Under Madero.* Austin: University of Texas Press, 1952.

Davis, Tom E., ed. *Mexico's Recent Economic Growth; The Mexican View.* Austin: University of Texas, 1967.

De la Peña, Moises T. *El pueblo y su tierra; mito y realidad de la reforma agraria en México.* Mexico: Cuadernos Americanos, 1964.

De la Peña, Sergio. *Introducción a la planeación regional.* Mexico: Banco de México, S.A., Departamento de Investigaciones Industriales, 1959.

Denison, Edward F. *The Sources of Economic Growth in the United States and the Alternatives Before Us.* New York: Committee for Economic Development, Supplementary Paper No. 13, 1962.

———. *Why Growth Rates Differ; Postwar Experience in Nine Western Countries.* (Assisted by Jean-Pierre Poullier). Washington, D.C.: The Brookings Institution, 1967.

D'Olwer, Luis Nicolau; Calderón, Francisco R.; et al. "El Porfiriato: la vida económica." Vol. VII, Tomo I and II of *Historia moderna de México.* Edited by Daniel Cosío Villegas. 7 vols. Mexico: Editorial Hermes, 1955–65.

Ducoff, Louis Joseph. *Los recursos humanos de Centroamérica, Panamá y México en 1950–1980 y sus relaciones con algunos aspectos del desarrollo económico.* Mexico: Naciones Unidas,

1960. (See United Nations, Economic Commission for Latin America.)

Durán, Marco Antonio. *La redistribución de la tierra y la explotación agrícola ejidal.* Mexico: Liga de Agrónomos Socialistas, Publs. Núm. 4, 1937.

Eckstein, Solomón. *El ejido colectivo en México:* Fondo de Cultura Económica, 1966.

————. "El marco macroeconómico del problema agrario Mexicano," *Trabajos de investigacion sobre tenencia de la tierra y reforma agraria,* Trabajo no. 11, Washington: CIDA, January, 1969 (versión preliminar).

Economic Growth Center, Yale University. *Report 1961–1964.* New Haven, Conn., April 1965.

————, Yale University. *Report 1964–1967.* New Haven, Conn., December 1967.

————, Yale University. *A System of National Economic Accounts and Historical Data.* New Haven, Conn., n.d.

Ellsworth, Paul T. *Chile, An Economy in Transition.* New York: The Macmillan Company, 1945.

Enríquez Filio, Antonio. . . . *Nueva economía social (Plan Sexenal Mejicano 1935–40).* Mexico: Talleres Linotipográficos Mejicanos, 1935.

Esquivel Obregón, Toribio. . . . *Influencia de España y los Estados Unidos sobre México (ensayos de sociología Hispano-Americana).* Madrid: Casa Editorial Calleja, 1918. (BML)

Fabila, Alfonso. *México (ensayo socioeconómico del estado).* 2 vols. Mexico, 1951. (NYPL)

Fei, John C. H., and Ranis, Gustav. *Development of the Labor Surplus Economy: Theory and Policy.* Homewood, Ill.: R. D. Irwin, 1964.

Fernández Bravo, Vicente. *México y su desarrollo económico; panorama económico del ingreso nacional, intervencionismo del estado.* Mexico: Costa-Amic, 1963.

Fernández y Fernández, Ramón. *Propiedad privada versus ejidos.* Mexico: Ediciones conmemorativas del centenario de la Escuela Nacional de Agricultura, 1954

Flores, Edmundo. *Tratado de economía agrícola.* Mexico: Fondo de Cultura Económica, 1961.

Freithaler, William O. *Mexico's Foreign Trade and Economic Development.* New York: Praeger, 1968.

García Treviño, Rodrigo. *Precios, salarios y mordidas.* Mexico: Editorial America, 1953. (BML)

Germán Parra, Manuel. *La industrialización de México.* Mexico: Imprenta Universitaria, 1954.

Gibson, Charles. *The Aztecs Under Spanish Rule.* Stanford, Calif.: Stanford University Press, 1964.

Glade, William P., Jr., and Anderson, Charles W. *The Political Economy of Mexico.* Madison: The University of Wisconsin Press, 1963.

Goldsmith, Raymond W. *The Financial Development of Mexico.* Paris: Organization for Economic Cooperation and Development, Development Centre Studies, 1966.

Gómez de Cervantes, Gonzalo. *La vida económica y social de Nueva España al finalizar el siglo XVI.* Mexico: Antigua Librería Robredo, de J. Porrua e hijos, 1944. (BML)

González Navarro, Moisés. *La colonización en México, 1877–1910.* Mexico, 1960.

―――. "El Porfiriato: la vida social." Vol. III of *Historia moderna de México.* Edited by Daniel Cosío Villegas. 7 vols. Mexico: Editorial Hermes, 1955–65.

Gregg, Josiah. *Commerce of the Prairies.* 2 vols. New York: Henry G. Langley, 1844; Ann Arbor, Mich.: University Microfilms, 1966. (BML)

Gruening, Ernest. *Mexico and Its Heritage.* New York: Appleton-Century-Crofts, Inc., 1928.

Gumpel, Henry J., and Margáin, Hugo B. *Taxation in Mexico.* Harvard Law School International Program in Taxation. New York: Little Brown, 1957.

Haberler, Gottfried. *A Survey of International Trade Theory.* (Special Papers in International Economics No. 1). Princeton, N.J.: International Finance Section, Department of Economics and Sociology, Princeton University, 1961.

Herring, Hubert Clinton, and Weinstock, Herbert. *Renascent Mexico.* New York: Covici, Friede, 1935.

Hinrichs, Harley H. *A General Theory of Tax Structure Change During Economic Development.* Cambridge, Mass.: Law School of Harvard University International Tax Program, 1966.

Hirschman, A. O. *The Strategy of Economic Development.* New Haven, Conn.: Yale University Press, 1958.

Horowitz, Morris A.; Zymelman, Manuel; and Herrnstadt, Irwin L.

Manpower Requirements for Planning: An International Comparison Approach. 2 vols. Boston, Mass.: Department of Economics, Northeastern University, 1966.

Humboldt, Alexandre von. . . . *Ensayo político sobre el Reino de la Nueva España.* 6th ed. Mexico, D.F.: Editorial Pedro Robredo, 1941 (5 vols.). Also in French and English: *Essai politique sur le Royaume de la Nouvelle-Espagne.* Paris: F. Schoell, 1811 (5 vols.); also translated from the original French by John Black. New York: I. Riley, 1811 (2 vols.).

Illinois Institute of Technology, Armour Research Foundation, *Technological Audit of Selected Mexican Industries with Industrial Research Recommendations.* Chicago: Armour Research Foundation of Illinois Institute of Technology, 1946.

International Bank for Reconstruction and Development, Combined Mexican Working Party. *The Economic Development of Mexico.* Baltimore: Johns Hopkins Press, 1953. (See Raúl Ortiz Mena et al.)

International Bureau of American Republics. *Mexico, A Geographical Sketch, With Special Reference to Economic Conditions and Prospects of Future Development.* Washington, D.C.: Government Printing Office, 1900. (BML)

Jaffe, Abram J. *People, Jobs and Economic Development; A Case History of Puerto Rico Supplemented by Recent Mexican Experiences.* Glencoe, Ill.: Free Press, 1959.

Johnson, Harry G., ed. *Economic Nationalism in Old and New States.* Chicago: University of Chicago Press, 1967.

Jones, Chester Lloyd. *Mexico and Its Reconstruction.* New York and London: D. Appleton & Co., 1921.

Kemmerer, Edwin W. *Inflation and Revolution; Mexico's Experience of 1912–1917.* Princeton, N.J.: Princeton University Press, 1940.

Ker, Annita Melville. . . . *Mexican Government Publications. A Guide to the More Important Publications of the National Government of Mexico, 1821–1936.* Washington, D.C.: U.S. Government Printing Office, 1940.

Kuznets, Simon. *Capital in the American Economy, Its Formation and Financing.* Princeton, N.J.: Princeton University Press, 1961.

———. *Economic Growth and Structure.* New York: W. W. Norton & Co., Inc., 1965.

————, et al. *El ingreso y la riqueza.* Papers presented at the Conference of the International Association for Research on Income and Wealth, Rio de Janeiro, June 1959. Mexico: Fondo de Cultura Económica, 1963.

Leibenstein, H. *Economic Backwardness and Economic Growth.* New York: John Wiley & Sons, Inc., 1957.

Levin, Jonathan V. *The Export Economies.* Cambridge, Mass.: Harvard University Press, 1960.

Lewis, Oscar. *Pedro Martínez; A Mexican Peasant and His Family.* New York: Random House, 1964.

López Mateos, Adolfo. *The Economic Development of Mexico During a Quarter of a Century (1934–1959).* Mexico, D.F.: Nacional Financiera, 1959.

López Romero, Adolfo. *Plan México; sugerencias para una política económica del próximo gobierno.* 2nd ed. Mexico: Libro Mex., 1958.

López Rosado, Diego. *Ensayos sobre historia económica de México.* Mexico: Impr. Universitaria, 1957. (BML)

————, ed. *Problemas económicas de México.* Mexico: Universidad Nacional Autónoma de México, Instituto de Investigaciones Económicas, 1954; 2nd ed., 1966. (BML)

McBride, George McCutchen. *The Land Systems of Mexico.* New York: American Geographical Society, 1923.

McClelland, David C. *The Achieving Society.* Princeton, N.J.: Van Nostrand Co., 1961.

Maddison, Angus. *Foreign Skills and Technical Assistance in Economic Development.* Paris: Organization for Economic Cooperation and Development, Development Centre Studies, 1965.

Mendieta y Núñez, Lucio. *El problema agrario de México.* Mexico: Editorial Porrúa, 1954; 7th ed., 1959.

México: cincuenta años de revolución. 4 vols. Mexico: Fondo de Cultura Económica, 1960–62.

Middleton, Philip Harvey. *Industrial Mexico; 1919 Facts and Figures.* New York: Dodd, Mead & Co., 1919. (BML)

Moreno, Daniel A. *Los factores demográficos en la planeación económica.* Mexico, D.F.: Cámara Nacional de la Industria de la Transformación, 1958. (See Cámara Nacional de la Industria de Transformación.) (BML)

Moses, Bernard. *The Railway Revolution in Mexico.* San Francisco: The Berkeley Press, 1895. (BML)

Mosher, Arthur T. *Technical Co-operation in Latin-American Agriculture*. Chicago: University of Chicago Press, 1957.

Mosk, Sanford Alexander. *Industrial Revolution in Mexico*. Berkeley: University of California Press, 1950.

Myers, Charles N. *Education and National Development in Mexico*. Princeton, N.J.: Industrial Relations Section, Department of Economics, Princeton University, Research Project Series, no. 106, 1965.

Nash, June. *In the Eyes of the Ancestors*. New Haven: Yale University Press, 1970.

Navarrete, Alfredo, Jr. *Estabilidad de cambios, el ciclo, y el desarrollo económico. Una investigación sobre los problemas de la balanza de pagos de México, 1929–1946*. Mexico, D.F., 1951. (BML)

Navarrete, Ifigenia M. de. *La distribución del ingreso y el desarrollo económico de México*. Mexico: Instituto de Investigaciones Económicas, Escuela Nacional de Economía, Universidad Nacional Autónoma de México, 1960.

————. *Los incentivos fiscales y el desarrollo económico de México*. Mexico: Universidad Nacional Autónoma de México, Instituto de Investigaciones Económicas, 1967.

Organization for Economic Cooperation and Development. *National Accounts of Less Developed Countries*. Paris: Organization for Economic Cooperation and Development, February 1967. (Preliminary)

Oldman, Oliver Sanford, et al. *Financing Urban Development in Mexico City; A Case Study of Property Tax, Land Use, Housing, and Urban Planning*. Cambridge, Mass.: Harvard University Press, 1967.

Olizar, Marynka, comp. *A Guide to the Mexican Markets; A 1961 Statistical Study of the Mexican Economy*. Mexico, 1960–61.

Orive Alba, Adolfo. *La política de irrigación en México*. Mexico: Fondo de Cultura Económica, 1960.

Ortiz Mena, Raúl. *La moneda Mexicana; análisis histórico de sus fluctuaciones, las depreciaciones y sus causas*. Mexico: Editorial América, 1942.

————, Urquidi, Víctor L.; Waterston, Albert; et al. *El desarrollo económico de México y su capacidad para absorber capital del exterior*. Mexico: Nacional Financiera, S.A., 1953. (See IBRD, Combined Mexican Working Party.)

Parkes, Henry Bamford. *A History of Mexico.* Boston, Mass.: Houghton Mifflin, revised 1950; 3rd ed., rev. 1966. (BML)

Paris, France (city) Université, Institut des Hautes Études de l'Amérique Latine. *L'économie du Mexique d'aujord'hui.* Conferences faites par d'éminents économistes Mexicains. Paris, 1957. (BML)

Pérez López, Enrique, et al. *Mexico's Recent Economic Growth, The Mexican View.* Introduction by Tom Davis. Translated by Marjory Urquidi. Austin & London: University of Texas Press, 1967.

Poleman, Thomas T. *The Papaloapan Project: Agricultural Development in the Mexican Tropics.* Stanford, Calif.: Stanford University Press, 1964.

Powell, Jack R. *The Mexican Petroleum Industry, 1938–1950.* Berkeley: University of California Press, 1956.

Quirk, Robert E. *The Mexican Revolution 1914–1915.* Bloomington: Indiana University Press, 1960. Paperback: New York: Citadel Press, 1963.

Quiros, José Maria. *Memoria de estatuto; idea de la riqueza que daban a la masa circulante de Nueva España sus naturales producciones en los años de tranquilidad, y su abatimiento en las presentes conmociones . . .* Veracruz, 1817.

Ramírez Gomez, Ramón. *La posible revalorización del oro y sus efectos en la economía de México.* Conference held December 7, 1960 at the Instituto de Estudios Latinoamericanos, Mexico City. Introduction by Alonso Aguilar M. Mexico: Escuela Nacional de Economía, 1961. (BML)

———. *Tendencias de la economía Mexicana.* Mexico: Universidad Nacional Autónoma de Mexico, Escuela Nacional de Economía, Instituto de Investigaciones Economicos, 1962.

Regler, Gustav. *A Land Bewitched: Mexico in the Shadow of the Centuries.* Translated by Constantine Fitzgibbon. London: Putnam, 1955. (BML)

Reina Celaya, Alfonso. *La industria de la carne en México.* Mexico: Author's Edition, 1948.

Ross, Stanford G., and Christensen, John B. *Tax Incentives for Industry in Mexico.* Cambridge, Mass.: Law School of Harvard University, 1959.

Ross, Stanley R., ed. *Is the Mexican Revolution Dead?* New York: Alfred A. Knopf, 1966.

Rudenko, Boris T. *México en vísperas de la revolución democrático burguesa de 1910–1917.* Translated from Russian by A. Martinez Verdugo and A. Mendez. Mexico: Ediciones Arguial, 1958.

Sanchez Cuen, Manuel. *El crédito a largo plazo en México: reseña histórica.* El Banco Nacional Hipotecario Urbano y de Obras Publicas, S.A., 24 Años de Vida. Mexico: Gráfica Panamericana, 1958.

Santillán López, Roberto, and Rosas Figueroa, Aniceto. *Teoría general de las finanzas públicas y el caso de México.* Mexico: Universidad Nacional Autónoma le México, Escuela Nacional de Economía, 1962.

Schnitzler, Hermann, comp. and ed. *The Republic of Mexico, Its Agriculture, Commerce and Industries.* New York: Nicholas L. Brown, 1924. (NYPL)

Schultz, Theodore W. *Transforming Traditional Agriculture.* New Haven and London: Yale University Press, 1964.

Schumpeter, Joseph A. *The Theory of Economic Development.* Translated from German by Redvers Opie. Cambridge, Mass.: Harvard University Press, 1934; 5th printing, 1955.

Scott, Robert E. *Mexican Government in Transition.* Urbana: University of Illinois Press, 1959; rev. 1964.

Senior, Clarence O. *Land Reform and Democracy.* Gainesville: University of Florida Press, 1958.

———. *Mexico in Transition.* New York: League for Industrial Democracy, 1939. (NYPL)

Shafer, Robert J. *Mexico: Mutual Adjustment Planning.* Syracuse, N.Y.: Syracuse University Press, 1966.

Sherwell, G. Butler. *Mexico's Capacity to Pay, A General Analysis of the Present International Economic Position of Mexico.* Washington, D.C., 1929 (typescript); in print: copyright 1929 by the author, New York.

Siegel, Barry N. *Inflación y desarrollo; las experiencias de México.* Mexico: Centro de Estudios Monetarios Latinoamericanos, 1960.

Silva Herzog, Jesús. *Conferencias; apuntes sobre evolución económica de México.* Mexico: Sociedad Mexicana de Estudios Económicos, 1937.

Simpson, Eyler Newton. *The Ejido; Mexico's Way Out.* Chapel Hill: University of North Carolina Press, 1937.

Simpson, Lesley Byrd. *Many Mexicos.* Berkeley and Los Angeles: University of California Press, 1966.

Stakman, E. C.; Bradfield, Richard; and Mangelsdorf, Paul C. *Campaigns Against Hunger*. Cambridge, Mass.: Belknap Press, 1967.

Sterrett, Joseph Edmund, and Davis, Joseph Stancliffe. *The Fiscal and Economic Condition of Mexico*. Report submitted to the International Committee of Bankers on Mexico, New York, May 25, 1928.

Stetzmann, Alexander. *Mexico: Kultur und Wirtschaftkundliches*. Hamburg, 1930 (?). (NYPL)

Stewart, George Rippey. *N.A.1: The North-South Continental Highway*. 2 vols. Boston, Mass.: Houghton Mifflin, 1957.

Strassmann, W. P. *Technical Change and Economic Development, The Manufacturing Experience of Mexico and Puerto Rico*. New York: Cornell University Press, 1968.

Studenski, Paul. *The Income of Nations: Theory, Measurement and Analysis: Past and Present*. New York: New York University Press, 1958.

Tannenbaum, Frank. *Mexico, The Struggle for Peace and Bread*. New York: Knopf, 1950; 2nd ed., 1962.

Teichert, Pedro C. M. *Economic Policy Revolution and Industrialization in Latin America*. University, Miss.: Bureau of Business Research, University of Mississippi, 1959.

Tischendorf, Alfred P. *Great Britain and Mexico in the Era of Porfirio Diaz*. Durham, N.C.: Duke University Press, 1961.

Tucker, William P. *The Mexican Government Today*. Minneapolis: University of Minnesota Press, 1957.

Venezian, Eduardo, and Gamble, William. *The Agricultural Development of Mexico*. New York: Praeger, 1969.

Vernon, Raymond. *The Dilemma of Mexico's Development*. Cambridge, Mass.: Harvard University Press, 1963.

————, ed. *Public Policy and Private Enterprise in Mexico*. Cambridge, Mass.: Harvard University Press, 1964.

Villafuerte, Carlos. *Ferrocarriles*. Mexico: Fondo de Cultura Económica, 1959.

Villaseñor Angeles, Eduardo. *Ensayos interamericanos; reflexiones de un economista*. Mexico: Cuadernos Americanos, 1944. (BML)

Walling, William English. *The Mexican Question; Mexico and American-Mexican Relations under Calles and Obregon*. New York: Robins Press, 1927. (BML)

Weyl, Nathaniel. *The Reconquest of Mexico; The Years of Lázaro Cárdenas.* London, New York, etc.: Oxford University Press, 1939. (BML)

Whetten, Nathan L. *Rural Mexico.* Chicago: University of Chicago Press, 1948.

Wilkie, James W. *The Mexican Revolution: Federal Expenditure and Social Change Since 1910.* Berkeley: University of California Press, 1967.

————, and Wilkie, Edna Monzón de, *México visto en el siglo XX. Entrevistas de historia oral.* Mexico: Instituto de Investigaciones Económicas, 1969.

Wionczek, Miguel S. *El nacionalismo Mexicano y la inversión extranjera.* Mexico: Siglo XXI Editores, S.A., 1967.

Wood, Richardson, and Keyser, Virginia. *Sears, Roebuck de México, S.A.* Washington, D.C.: National Planning Association, 1953.

Yáñez-Pérez, Luis. *Mecanización de la agricultura Mexicana.* Mexico: Instituto Mexicano de Investigaciones Económicas, 1957.

Yates, Paul Lamartine. *El desarrollo regional de México.* Mexico: Talleres Gráficos Victoria, S.A., 1961.

Zamora, Fernando. *Diagnóstico económico regional, 1958.* Mexico: Secretaría de Economía y Instituto Mexicano de Investigaciones Económicas, 1959.

ARTICLES AND JOURNALS

"Achievement in Mexico." *The Economist* 178 (Jan. 7, 1956): p. 26.

Aizenstat, Aron J. "Structure and Taxation of Agriculture in Mexico." *Papers and Proceedings of the Conference on Agricultural Taxation and Economic Development.* Ed. H. P. Wald. Cambridge, Mass.: International Tax Program, Law School of Harvard University, 1954.

Alanís Patiño, Emilio. "La riqueza de México." *El Trimestre Económico* 10 (April-June 1943): 97–134.

————, and Vargas Torres, Eliel. "Observaciones sobre algunas estadísticas agrícolas." *El Trimestre Económico* 12 (Jan.-Mar. 1946): 589–625.

Alarcón M., Adolfo. "Las estadísticas Mexicanas sobre salarios y tiempo trabajado." *El Trimestre Económico* 6 (April-June 1939): 34–57.

Alba, Victor. "The Mexican Economy: Industrialization." *World Today,* 15 (Nov. 1959): 456–59.

———, "The Mexican Economy: State Action and Private Initiative." *World Today* 15 (Nov. 1959): 451–62.

Andic, Faut M. "El desarrollo económico y la desigualdad en el ingreso: el caso de México." *El Trimestre Económico* 30 (July-Sept. 1963): 375–81.

Angulo, Humberto G. "Indice de la producción agrícola." *Revista de Economía* 9 (Jan. 15, 1946).

Aubrey, Henry G. "Deliberate Industrialization." *Social Research* 16 (June 1949): 158–82.

———. "Mexico: Rapid Growth." *Economic Development: Principles and Patterns.* Ed. Harold F. Williamson and John A. Buttrick. New York: Prentice-Hall, Inc., 1954.

———. "The National Income of Mexico." I.A.S.I. *Estadística* (June 1950), pp. 185–98.

———. "Structure and Balance in Rapid Economic Growth: The Example of Mexico." *Political Science Quarterly* 69 (Dec. 1954): 517–40.

Bacha, Edmar L. "Comparación entre la productividad industrial de México y los Estados Unidos." *El Trimestre Económico* 33 (Oct.-Dec. 1966): 657–73.

Bach, Federico. "Un estudio del costo de la vida." *El Trimestre Económico* 2 (1935): 12–49.

———, and Reyna, Margarita. "El nuevo indice de precios al mayoreo en la Ciudad de México de la Secretaría de la Economía Nacional." *El Trimestre Económico* 10 (April-June 1943): 1–63.

Baklanoff, Eric N. "Argentina, Chile, and Mexico: Contrasts in Economic Policy and Performance." *Journal of Inter-American Studies* 3 (Oct. 1961): 497–503.

Balassa, Bela. "Tariff Protection in Industrial Countries: An Evaluation." *Journal of Political Economy* 73 (Dec. 1965): 573–94.

Ballesteros, Marto A., and Davis, Tom E. "The Growth of Output and Employment in Basic Sectors of the Chilean Economy, 1908–1957." *Economic Development and Cultural Change* 11 (Jan. 1963): 152–76.

Barry, John F. "Mexico, the Land of Business Opportunity." Editorial, *New York Commercial,* Nov. 17, 1920.

Bazant, Jan. "Feudalismo y capitalismo en la historia económica de

México." *El Trimestre Económico* 17 (Jan.-Mar. 1950): 81–98.

Belshaw, Michael. "Aspects of Community Development in Rural Mexico." *Inter-American Economic Affairs* 15 (Spring 1962).

Bernal Molina, Julián. "El mercado de valores en México." *El Trimestre Económico* 14 (July-Sept. 1947): 167–92.

Berumen L., Federico. "Algunas consideraciones ejidales." *El Trimestre Económico* 2 (1935): 288.

Borah, Woodrow Wilson. "New Spain's Century of Depression." *Ibero-Americana:* 35. Berkeley: University of California Press, 1951.

Bosch García, Carlos. "Discusiones previas al primer tratado de comercio entre México y Estados Unidos: 1822–1838." *El Trimestre Económico* 13 (July-Sept. 1946): 329–45.

———. "Preliminares políticos al primer tratado de comercio entre México y España." *El Trimestre Económico* 13 (Jan.-Mar. 1947): 712–54.

———. "Las primeras negociaciones comerciales entre México y Francia." *El Trimestre Económico* 12 (Jan.-Mar. 1946): 696–716.

———. "El primer tratado comercial Anglomexicano: intereses económicos y políticos." *El Trimestre Económico* 13 (Oct.-Dec. 1946): 495–532.

Brandenburg, Frank R. "Organized Business in Mexico." *Inter-American Economic Affairs* 12 (Winter 1958): 26–50.

Brothers, Dwight S. "El financiamiento de la formación de capitales en México, 1950–1961." Supl. al *Boletín Quincenal,* Centro de Estudios Monetarios Latinoamericanos, no. 9 (Sept. 1963).

———. "Nexos entre la estabilidad monetaria y el desarrollo económico en América Latina: un escrito doctrinal y de política." *El Trimestre Económico* 29 (Oct.-Dec. 1962): 587–98.

Bruton, Henry J. "Productivity Growth in Latin Amercia." *American Economic Review* 57 (Dec. 1967): 1099–116.

Bueno U., Aurelio. "El comercio exterior de México." *El Trimestre Económico* 1 (1934): 270.

Carrillo Flores, Antonio. "Mexico Forges Ahead." *Foreign Affairs* 36 (April 1958): 491–503.

Caves, Richard E. " 'Vent for Surplus' Models of Trade and Growth," in R. E. Baldwin et al., *Trade, Growth and the Balance of Payments: Essays in Honor of Gottfried Haberler.* Chicago and Amsterdam: Rand McNally and North Holland, Publ. Co., 1965. Pp. 95–115.

Chenery, Hollis B. "Patterns of Industrial Growth." *American Economic Review* 50 (Sept. 1960): 624–54.

Cook, Shelburne F., and Simpson, Lesley Byrd. "The Population of Central Mexico in the Sixteenth Century." *Ibero-Americana:* 31. Berkeley: University of California Press, 1948.

Cosío Villegas, Daniel. "La importancia de nuestra agricultura." *El Trimestre Económico* 1 (1934): 112.

―――. "La riqueza legendaria de México." *El Trimestre Económico* 6 (April-June 1939): 58–83.

Cossío, Luis, and Izquierdo, Rafael. "Estimación de la relación producto-capital de México, 1940–1960." *El Trimestre Económico* 29 (Oct.-Dec. 1962): 634–44.

Davis, Horace B. "Labor and the State in a Semi-Colonial Country: Mexico." *Weltwirtschaftliches Archiv* 74, no. 2 (1955), pp. 283–306.

―――. "Numerical Strength of Mexican Unions." *The Southwestern Social Science Quarterly* 35 (June 1954): 48–55.

De la Peña, Moisés T. "El crédito agrícola en la economía Mexicana." *El Trimestre Económico* 7 (April-June 1940): 96–115.

―――. "Crítica de las tarifas ferrocarrileras." *El Trimestre Económico* 4 (1937): 3–24.

―――. "La expropriación de los ferrocarriles nacionales de México." *El Trimestre Económico* 4 (1937): 195–226.

―――. "La industrialización de México y la política arancelaria." *El Trimestre Económico* 12 (July-Sept. 1945): 187–218.

―――. "El maíz—su influencia nacional." *El Trimestre Económico,* 3, no. 10 (1936): 186–220.

―――. "Los salarios en la industria textil." *El Trimestre Económico,* 1, no 2: (1934): 155 ff.

―――, and Navarrete, Alfredo. "Reorganización de los ferrocarriles nacionales." *El Trimestre Económico* 7 (Jan.-Mar. 1941): 616–34.

Del Pinal, Jorge. "Los trabajadores Mexicanos en los Estados Unidos." *El Trimestre Económico* 12 (April-June 1945): 1–45.

Denison, Edward F. "How To Raise the High-Employment Growth Rate by One Percentage Point." *American Economic Association Papers and Proceedings* 52 (May 1962): 67–75.

Díaz-Alejandro, Carlos F. "An Interpretation of Argentine Economic

Growth Since 1930, Parts I & II." *Journal of Development Studies,* Pt. I (Oct. 1966): Pt. II (Jan. 1967).

Durán Ochoa, Julio. "El crecimiento de la población Mexicana." *El Trimestre Económico* 22 (July-Sept. 1955): 331–49.

Ekker, Martin H. "Algunas experiencias en la utilización de la técnica insumo-producto en los pronósticos económicos." Chapter 12 in Kuznets et al., *El ingreso y la riqueza.* Papers presented at the Conference of the International Association for Research on Income and Wealth, Rio de Janeiro, June 1959. Mexico: Fondo de Cultura Económica, 1963, pp. 374–400.

Emery, Robert F. "Mexican Monetary Policy Since the 1954 Devaluation." *Inter-American Economic Affairs* 12 (Spring 1959): 72–85.

Fabila, Alfonso. "Exploración económico-social del Estado de Yucatán." *El Trimestre Económico* 8 (Oct.-Dec. 1941): 398–465.

Fernandez, Rene. "Cuánto deja a México la minería." *El Trimestre Económico* 3 (1936): 275–85.

Fernández y Fernández, Ramón. "La administración de crédito agrícola." *El Trimestre Económico* 30 (April-June 1963): 242–55.

———. "Aspectos económicos de la producción del frijol." *El Trimestre Económico* 3 (1936): 47–90.

———. "La clientela del crédito ejidal." *El Trimestre Económico* 26 (Jan.-Mar. 1959): 31–48.

———. "El crédito ejidal. Préstamos, recuperaciones y cartera." *El Trimestre Económico* 25 (April-June 1958): 157–88.

———. "Una doctrina sobre reforma agraria." *El Trimestre Económico* 29 (Jan.-Mar. 1962): 69–94.

———. "¿Existe un peligro de insuficiencia de tierras?" *El Trimestre Económico* 6 (July-Sept. 1939): 222–38.

———. "Historia del trigo en México." *El Trimestre Económico* 1 (1934): 429.

———. "Un indice del bienestar público." *El Trimestre Económico* 16 (Oct.-Dec. 1949): 531–59.

———. "Logros positivos de la reforma agraria Mexicana." *El Trimestre Económico* 13 (July-Sept. 1946): 221–48.

———. "Notas sobre el problema agrario Mexicano actual." *El Trimestre Económico* 27 (April-June 1960): 203–08.

———. "Problemas creados por la reforma agraria de México." *El Trimestre Económico* 13 (Oct.-Dec. 1946): 463–94.

————. "La reforma agraria Mexicana: logros y problemas deriva-
dos." *El Trimestre Económico* 24 (April-June 1957): 143–59.

————. "La regulación de precios de los productos agrícolas." *El
Trimestre Económico* 22 (July-Sept. 1955): 297–330.

————. "El salario mínimo en el sector agrícola." *El Trimestre
Económico* 2 (1935): 50–61.

Fernandez Hurtado, Ernesto. "La iniciativa privada y el estado como
promotores del desarrollo." *México: cincuenta años de revolución,* vol. 1 ("La economía"), Pt. 19, pp. 595–619. Mexico:
Fondo de Cultura Económica, 1960.

Flores, Edmundo. "Los braceros Mexicanos en Wisconsin." *El Trimestre Económico* 17 (Jan.-Mar. 1950): 23–80.

————. "El desarrollo agrícola y la 'revolución industrial' del Prof.
Mosk." *El Trimestre Económico* 18 (July-Sept. 1951): 549–
56.

————. "La estrategia del desarrollo económico de México." *Investigación Económica* 20 (1960): 105–16.

————. "Respuesta al Profesor Tannenbaum." *El Trimestre Económico* 17 (July-Sept. 1950): 482–83.

————. "The Significance of Land-Use Changes in the Economic
Development of Mexico." *Land Economics* 35 (May 1959):
115–24.

————. "La significación de los cambios del uso de la tierra en el
desarrollo económico de México." *El Trimestre Económico* 27
(Jan.-Mar. 1960): 1–14.

Forbes, Malcolm S. "Report from Mexico." *Forbes* 81 (Jan. 15,
1958): 11–12.

Foreman, W. James, "Changing Land Tenure Patterns in Mexico."
Land Economics 26 (Feb. 1950): 65–77.

Foster, George M. "The Folk Economy of Rural Mexico with Special
Reference to Marketing." *Journal of Marketing* 13 (Oct.
1948): 153–62.

Freebairn, Donald K. "Relative Production Efficiency Between Tenure Classes in the Yaqui Valley, Sonora, Mexico." *Journal of
Farm Economics* 45 (Dec. 1963): 1150–60.

Gamio, Manuel. "Los varios mercados Mexicanos." *El Trimestre
Económico* 2 (1935): 3–11.

Gall, Norman. "Uncle Sam's Other Neighbor: How Mexico Tackled
Foreign Ownership and the Price It Paid." *The Toronto Star,*
April 24 and 27, 1967.

Ganz, Alexander. "Problems and Uses of National Wealth Estimates in Latin America." *The Measurement of National Wealth.* Ed. Raymond Goldsmith and Christopher Saunders. International Association for Research in Income and Wealth, Series 8. Chicago: Quadrangle Books, 1959.

García Cruz, Miguel. "Economía de la región indígena Mixteca." *El Trimestre Económico* 7 (July-Sept. 1940): 231–70.

Gardiner, Clinton H. "Las patentes en México de 1867 a 1876." *El Trimestre Económico* 16 (Oct.-Dec. 1949): 576–99.

Glick, Edward B. "Tehuantepec Railroad: Mexico's White Elephant." *Pacific Historical Review* 22 (Nov. 1953): 373–82.

Gómez Palacio, R. Davila. "Concentración financiera privada de México." *Investigación Económica* 15 (April-June 1955): 249–62.

González Gallardo, Alfonso. "Investigación y experimentación de la caña de azúcar en México." *El Trimestre Económico* 16 (April-June 1949): 169–222.

————. "La orientación de la agricultura Mexicana." *El Trimestre Económico* 9 (Jan.-Mar. 1943): 506–35.

Griliches, Zvi. "Research Costs and Social Returns: Hybrid Corn and Related Innovations." *Journal of Political Economy* 66 (Oct. 1958): 419–31

Hansen, W. Lee. "Total and Private Rates of Return to Investment in Schooling." *Journal of Political Economy* 71 (April 1963): 128–40.

Harberger, Arnold C. "Using the Resources at Hand More Effectively." *American Economic Association Papers and Proceedings* 49 (May 1959): 134–46.

Hardin, Einar, and Strassmann, W. Paul. "La productividad industrial y la intensidad de capital de México y los Estados Unidos." *El Trimestre Económico* 35 (Jan.-Mar. 1968): 51–62.

Helguera, Enrique. "Mexican Tax Policy on Foreign Investments." Chapter 11 in Tax Institute of America, *Tax Policy on United States Investment in Latin America.* Princeton, N.J.: Tax Institute of America, 1963.

Hoselitz, Bert F. "Mexican Social Structure and Economic Development, A Review." *Economic Development and Cultural Change* 1 (Oct. 1952): 236–40.

Ibarra, Roberto. "Estudio sobre el ixtle." *El Trimestre Económico* 5, (Jan.-Mar. 1938): 193 ff.

"Indices de precios al mayoreo en la ciudad de México y en Estados Unidos." *Trimestre de Barómetros Económicos* 1 (Sept. 1946).

Investigación Económica, selected readings. Journal of the Escuela Nacional de Economía, Universidad Nacional Autónoma de México.

Izquierdo, Rafael. "Protectionism in Mexico." *Public Policy and Private Enterprise in Mexico.* Ed. Raymond Vernon. Cambridge, Mass.: Harvard University Press, 1964.

Johnston, Bruce F. "Agriculture and Economic Development: The Relevance of the Japanese Experience." *Food Research Institute Studies* 6, no. 3 (1966): 251–312.

————, and Mellor, John W. "The Role of Agriculture in Economic Development." *The American Economic Review* 51 (Sept. 1961): 566–93.

Keesing, Donald B. "Labor Skills and Comparative Advantage." *American Economic Review: Papers and Proceedings* (May 1966), pp. 249–58.

————, "Structural Change Early in Development: Mexico's Changing Industrial and Occupational Structure from 1895 to 1950," *Journal of Economic History,* Dec. 1969.

Kubler, George. "Population Movements in Mexico 1520–1600." *The Hispanic American Historical Review* 22 (Nov. 1942): 606–43.

Kühne, Rodolfo. "¿Cuánto le queda la pequeño productor de café del estado de Veracruz?" *El Trimestre Económico* 3, no. 12 (1936): 413–54.

Kunkel, J. H. "Economic Autonomy and Social Change in Mexican Villages." *Economic Development and Cultural Change* 10 (Oct. 1961): 51–63.

Kuznets, Simon. "Economic Growth and Income Inequality." *The American Economic Review* 45 (March 1955): 1–28. Reprinted in *Economic Growth and Structure.*

Lagunilla Iñárritu, Alfredo. "El ahorro y la banca central." *El Trimestre Económico* 19 (April-June 1952): 237–49.

————. "El crédito selectivo y la banca central." *El Trimestre Económico* 20 (Jan.-Mar. 1953): 141–49.

————. "La tasa del dinero en México." *El Trimestre Económico* 13 (Jan.-Mar. 1947): 662–79.

————. "La tasa natural en el mercado de capitales de México." *El Trimestre Económico* 15 (July-Sept. 1948): 229–42.

Lara Beautell, Cristóbal. "La productividad en la industria Mexicana." *El Trimestre Económico* 18 (Jan.-Mar. 1951): 56–75.

Lazcano Romero, Jose. "Aspectos económicos de la producción de arroz en Mexico." *El Trimestre Económico* 2, no. 7 (1935): 247 ff.

Lewis, Oscar. "Mexico Since Cárdenas." *Social Change in Latin America Today, Its Implications for United States Policy.* Richard N. Adams et al. New York: Harper & Brothers for the Council on Foreign Relations, 1960.

Lewis, William Arthur. "Economic Development with Unlimited Supplies of Labour." *The Manchester School of Economics and Social Studies* 22 (May 1954): 139–91.

Lobato López, Ernesto. "Contradicción interna del sistema bancario Porfirista." *El Trimestre Económico* 11 (Oct.-Dec. 1944): 439–70.

López Romero, Adolfo. "Desarrollo económico de México (1934–1959)." *El Trimestre Económico* 29 (Jan.-Mar. 1962): 30–68.

López Rosado, Diego G., and Noyola Vázquez, Juan F. "Los salarios reales en México, 1939–1950." *El Trimestre Económico* 18 (April-June 1951): 201–09.

Loredo Goytortúa, Joaquín. "Producción y productividad agrícolas." *México: cincuenta años de revolución* vol. 1, "La economía." Mexico: Fondo de Cultura Económica, 1960.

Loyo, Gilberto. "La población de México–estado actual y tendencias 1950–1980." *Investigación Económica* 20, 1st quarter (1960): 3–104.

Luna Olmedo, Agustín "Algunos aspectos de la balanza Mexicana de pagos." *El Trimestre Económico* 9 (April-June 1942): 14–51.

———. "Factores que influyen en la balanza de pagos de México." *El Trimestre Económico* 12 (Oct.-Dec. 1945): 371–403.

MacNeish, Richard S. "The Origins of New World Civilization." *Scientific American* 211 (Nov. 1964): 29–37.

McGreevey, William P. (assisted by Tyer, Robson B.). "Recent Research on the Economic History of Latin America." *Latin American Research Review* 3 (Spring 1968): 89–117.

Maddox, James G. "Economic Growth and Revolution in Mexico." *Land Economics* 36 (Aug. 1960): 266–78.

————. "Mexican Land Reform, A Report." (Pamphlet.) New York: American Universities Field Staff, 1957.

Manne, Alan S. "Key Sectors of the Mexican Economy, 1962–72." *The Theory and Design of Economic Development.* Ed. Irma Adelman and Erik Thorbecke. Baltimore: Johns Hopkins Press in cooperation with the Center for Agricultural and Economic Development of Iowa State University, 1966.

Manterola, Miguel. "El petróleo de México." *El Trimestre Económico* 5 (Oct.-Dec. 1938): 343–67.

Marino Flores, Anselmo. "Los problemas sociales de México en 1900 y 1950." *Journal of Inter-American Studies* 4 (April 1962): 157–84.

Martinez de Alva, E. "Las etapas ideológicas del ejido." *El Trimestre Económico* 2, no. 6 (1935): 180–88.

Martínez Ostos, Raúl. "Algunos aspectos de la política monetaria del Banco de México." *El Trimestre Económico* 11 (July-Sept. 1944): 209–29.

Medina, Manuel. "La carta geográfica de México." *El Trimestre Económico* 13 (Jan.-Mar.1947): 593–600.

"Mexican Opportunities–I." *The Economist* 187 (June 28, 1958): 1200.

"Mexican Opportunities–II." *The Economist* 188 (July 5, 1958): 44–45.

Milovanovic, Milorad. "La nacionalización del seguro en México." *El Trimestre Económico* 6 (Jan.-Mar. 1940): 537–97.

Moore, Clarence A. "Agricultural Development in Mexico." *Journal of Farm Economics* 37 (Feb. 1955): 72–80.

Mosk, Sanford Alexander. "Mexico." *Towards World Prosperity, Through Industrial and Agricultural Development and Expansion.* Ed. Mordecai Ezekiel. New York and London: Harper & Brothers, 1947.

Moyo Porras, Edmundo. "La importancia de la industria siderúrgica en México." *Investigación Económica* 19, no. 74 (1959): 337–64.

Nash, Manning. "Economic Nationalism in Mexico." *Economic Nationalism in Old and New States.* Ed. Harry G. Johnson. Chicago: University of Chicago Press, 1967.

————. "The Multiple Society in Economic Development: Mexico and Guatemala." *American Anthropologist* 59 (Oct. 1957): 825–33.

Navarrete, Alfredo, Jr. "El crecimiento económico de México: perspectivas y problemas." *El Trimestre Económico* 25 (April-June 1958): 189–205.

———. "El crecimiento económico de México y las inversiones extranjeras." *El Trimestre Económico* 25 (Oct.-Dec. 1958): 556–69.

———. "El desarrollo industrial de México: situación y perspectivas." *El Trimestre Económico* 30 (Oct.-Dec. 1963): 574–87.

———. "Una hipótesis sobre el sistema económico de México." *El Trimestre Económico* 18 (Jan.-Mar. 1951): 21–55.

———. "Productividad, ocupación y desocupación en México: 1940–1965." *El Trimestre Económico* 23 (Oct.-Dec. 1956): 415–23.

———. "Las relaciones financieras internacionales de México." *Investigación Económica* 15 (April-June 1955): 179–89.

Navarrete, Ifigenia M. de. "El financiamiento de la educación pública en México." *Suplementos del seminario de problemas científicos y filosóficos,* No. 15, Series 2a (1959). Mexico: Universidad Nacional de Mexico, 1959.

———. "El impuesto a las ganancias de capital en la teoría y en la práctica fiscal." *El Trimestre Económico* 30 (April-June 1963): 201–41.

———. "The Tax Structure and the Economic Development of Mexico." *Finances Publiques,* vol. 19/19th yr., no. 2 (1964), pp. 158–83.

Newcomer, Hale A. "Barter in Mexican Cotton: A New Concept in International Trade?" *Journal of Marketing* 23 (Oct. 1958): 159–63.

Nicholson, Irene. "Problems and Prospects in Mexico." *Contemporary Review* 195 (Feb. 1959): 115–17.

Ortiz Mena, Raúl "La balanza de pagos y el ingreso nacional." *El Trimestre Económico* 13 (Oct.-Dec. 1946): 451–62.

———. "Monetary Problems in Mexico." *Journal of Business* 20 (Jan. 1947): 1–8.

Padilla A., Enrique. "La devaluación del peso Mexicano: Cuatro Conferencias." *El Trimestre Económico* 15 (Oct.-Dec. 1948): 396–412.

———. "La dinámica de la economía Mexicana y el equilibrio monetario." *El Trimestre Económico* 25 (July-Sept. 1958): 349–77.

Parks, Richard W. "The Role of Agriculture in Mexican Economic

Development." *Inter-American Economic Affairs* (Summer 1964), pp. 3–27.

Pazos, Felipe. "Veinte años de pensamiento económico en la América Latina." *XX Aniversario de "El Trimestre Económico". El Trimestre Económico* 20 (Oct.-Dec. 1953): 552–70.

Pérez López, Enrique. "El desarrollo económico de México y la estabilidad monetaria." *El Trimestre Económico* 25 (July-Sept. 1958): 378–86.

――――. "El producto nacional." *México: cincuenta años de revolución,* vol. 1, "La economía." Mexico: Fondo de Cultura Económica, 1960.

Pletcher, David M. "The Building of the Mexican Railway." *The Hispanic American Historical Review* 30 (Feb. 1960): 26–62.

――――. "The Fall of Silver in Mexico, 1870–1910, and Its Effect on American Investments." *Journal of Economic History* 18 (March 1958): 33–55.

Potash, Robert A. "El 'comercio exterior de México' de Miguel Lerdo de Tejada: un error estadístico." *El Trimestre Económico* 20 (July-Sept. 1953): 474–79.

Prado Vértiz, Antonio. "El problema económico de la alimentación infantil en México." *El Trimestre Económico* 18 (Oct.-Dec. 1951): 601–16.

Ranis, Gustav. "Economic Development: A Suggested Approach," *Kyklos,* vol. 12, fasc: 3 (1959), pp. 428–50.

Rawlings, E. H. "Mexico's New Revolution." *Contemporary Review* 186 (Dec. 1954): 361–65.

Revista de Economía, selected issues. Mexico, D.F.

Revista de Economía y Estadística. Mexico: Secretaría de la Economía Nacional, 1933–36.

Revista de Estadística. Mexico: Dirección General de Estadística. Supercedes *Revista de Economía y Estadística.*

Reynolds, Clark W. "Development Problems of an Export Economy." *Essays on the Chilean Economy.* Markos Mamalakis and C. W. Reynolds. Homewood, Ill.: R. D. Irwin, Inc., 1965.

Rippy, J. Fred. "English Investments in Mexico: A Story of Bonanzas and Heartbreaks." *Journal of Business* 25 (Oct. 1952): 242–48.

Rippy, Merrill. "Land Tenure and Land Reform in Modern Mexico." *Agricultural History* 27 (Jan. 1953): 55–61.

————. "The Nationalized Oil Industry of Mexico: 1938–55." *The Southwestern Social Science Quarterly* 38 (June 1957): 6–18.

Rivera Marín, Guadalupe. "Los conflictos de trabajo en México, 1937–1950." *El Trimestre Económico* 22 (April-June 1955): 181–208.

————. "La mano de obra, el nivel de vida y los salarios en la ciudad de Oaxaca." *El Trimestre Económico* 24 (Oct.-Dec. 1957): 363–98.

Robles, Gonzalo. "México y la cuestión de materias primas." *El Trimestre Económico* 5, no. 1 (1938): 22 ff.

————. "Noticia sobre la industrialización de México." *El Trimestre Económico* 11 (July-Sept. 1944): 256–83.

Romualdi, Serafino. "Hands Across the Border." *The American Federationist* 61 (June 1954): 19–20.

————. "United States and Mexico; Cooperation is Paying Dividends." *The American Federationist* 62 (Nov. 1955): 25–27.

Rosenzweig Hernández, Fernando. "Crédito agrícola en el Papaloapan." *El Trimestre Económico* 24 (April-June 1957): 160–76.

————. El desarrollo económico de México de 1877 a 1911." *El Trimestre Económico* 32 (July-Sept. 1965) 405–54.

————. "La economía Novo-Hispaña al comenzar el siglo XIX." *Ciencias Políticas y Sociales* (Universidad Nacional Autónoma de México) 9 (July-Sept. 1963): 455–94.

————. "Las exportaciones Mexicanas de 1877 a 1911." *El Trimestre Económico* 27 (Oct.-Dec. 1960): 537–51.

————. "La industria." *Historia Moderna de México,* vol. 7, "El Porfiriato: la vida económica," vol. 1. Ed. Daniel Cosío Villegas. Mexico: Editorial Hermes, 1965.

————. "El proceso político y el desarrollo económico de México." *El Trimestre Económico* 29 (Oct.-Dec. 1962): 513–30.

Saenz, Josué. "El control de precios en una economía de guerra." *Revista de Economía* (Feb. 28, 1943).

————. "El ingreso nacional neto de México, 1929–1945." *Revista de Economía* (Feb. 28, 1946).

Salinas Lozano, Raúl. "El mercado de la plata." *El Trimestre Económico* 9 (Jan.-Mar. 1943): 614–35.

Scott, Robert E. "Budget Making in Mexico." *Inter-American Economic Affairs* 9 (Autumn 1955): 3–20.

―――. "Mexico, The Established Revolution." *Political Culture and Political Development.* Ed. Lucian W. Pye and Sidney Verba. Princeton, N.J.: Princeton University Press, 1965.

Sedwitz, Walter J. "Mexico's 1954 Devaluation in Retrospect." *Inter-American Economic Affairs* 10 (Autumn 1956): 22–44.

Servín, Armando. "Cuál debe ser la política del Gobierno Mexicano en materia de comercio exterior." *El Trimestre Económico* 9 (July-Sept. 1942): 219–40.

Shelton, David H. "The Banking System: Money and the Goal of Growth." *Public Policy and Private Enterprise in Mexico.* Ed. Raymond Vernon. Cambridge, Mass.: Harvard University Press, 1964.

―――. "Mexico's Economic Growth: Success of Diversified Development." *The Southwestern Social Science Quarterly* 41 (Dec. 1960): 304–19.

Sherwood, W. T. "Tax Administration in Mexico." *National Tax Journal* 2 (March 1949): 63–70.

Silva, José. "Consideraciones de orden demográfico sobre el Distrito Federal y prevision para 1950." *El Trimestre Económico* 10 (Jan.-Mar. 1944): 766–78.

Silva Herzog, Jesús. "El capitalismo hasto fines del siglo XVIII." *El Trimestre Económico* 5 (July-Sept. 1938): 151–82.

―――. "La cuestion del petróleo en México." *El Trimestre Económico* 7 (April-June 1940): 1–74.

―――. "El desarrollo de la enseñanza de las ciencias económicas en México, 1925–1953." *El Trimestre Económico* 21 (Jan.-Mar. 1954): 1–5.

Simpson, Lesley Byrd. "Unplanned Effects of Mexico's Planned Economy." *Virginia Quarterly Review* 29 (Autumn 1953): 514–32.

Smith, Robert S. "José María Quirós: 'Balanza del comercio marítimo de Veracruz' e ideas económicas." *El Trimestre Económico* 13 (Jan.-Mar. 1947): 680–711.

Solís M. Leopoldo. "Hacia un análisis general a largo plazo del desarrollo económico de México." *Demografía y Economía,* vol. 1, no. 1 (1967).

―――, and Ghigliazza, Sergio. "Estabilidad económica y política monetaria." *El Trimestre Económico* 30 (April-June 1963): 256–65.

Soustelle, Jacques. "México actual y el problema indígena." *El Trimestre Económico* 7 (April-June 1940): 139–47.

Sterling, Henry Somers. "The Emergence of the Medium-Size Private Farm as the Most Successful Product of Mexico's Agrarian Reform." Abstract of paper presented at the 1948 Annual Meeting, Madison, Wisc. Dec. 27–30, 1948. *Annals of the Association of American Geographers* 39 (March 1949): 58–59.

Strassmann, W. Paul. "Economic Growth and Income Distribution." *Quarterly Journal of Economics* 70 (Aug. 1956): 425–40.

Sturmthal, Adolf. "Economic Development, Income Distribution, and Capital Formation in Mexico." *Journal of Political Economy* 63 (June 1955): 183–201.

———. "Some Reflections on Economic Development in Mexico and the Labor Movement." *Proceedings of the Seventh Annual Meeting.* Industrial Relations Research Association, Detroit, Mich. Dec. 28–30, 1954, pp. 60–68.

Sweeney, Timothy D. "The Mexican Balance of Payments, 1947–50." International Monetary Fund *Staff Papers:* 3 (April 1953): 132–54.

Tamayo, Jorge L. "La administración de los distritos de riego Mexicanos." *El Trimestre Económico* 13 (July-Sept. 1946): 249–70.

———. "Las aguas internacionales del norte de México y el tratado de 1944." *El Trimestre Económico* 12 (Oct.-Dec. 1945): 466–87.

———. "Influencia de las condiciones fisiográficas de México en su desarrollo económico." *Investigación Económica,* vol. 15 (3) (1955).

———. "La generación de energía eléctrica en México." *El Trimestre Económico* 9 (Oct.-Dec. 1942): 405–39.

Tannenbaum, Frank. "La organización económica de la hacienda." *El Trimestre Económico* 2, no. 6 (1935): 189–217.

Thorn, Richard S. "The Evolution of Public Finances during Economic Development." *The Manchester School of Economic and Social Studies,* 35 (Jan. 1967): 19–53.

Torón, Luis. "El uso racional de los combustibles Mexicanos." *El Trimestre Económico* 12 (Oct.-Dec. 1945): 454–65.

Trejo Reyes, Sául. "Los patrones de crecimiento industrial y la sustitución de importaciones en México," *El Trimestre Económico,* (July-Sept. 1969).

Trimestre de Barómetros Económicos, June 1946-September 1950. Mexico: Secretaría de Economía, Dirección General de Estudios Económicos. Publication suspended 1951.

Urquidi, Víctor L. "Dos años de Alianza para el Progreso." *El Trimestre Económico* 30 (Oct.-Dec. 1963): 561–73.

―――. "Ensayo sobre el comercio exterior de México." *El Trimestre Económico* 9 (April-June 1942): 52–85.

―――. "El impuesto sobre la renta en el desarrollo económico en México." *El Trimestre Económico* 23 (Oct.-Dec. 1956): 424–37.

―――. "La postguerra y las relaciones económicas internacionales de México." *El Trimestre Económico* 10 (July-Sept. 1943): 320–44.

―――. "Problemas fundamentales de la economía Mexicana." *Cuadernos Americanos,* año 20, vol. 114, no. 1 (Jan.-Feb. 1961), pp. 69–103.

―――. "El progreso económico de México: problemas y soluciones." *El Trimestre Económico* 13 (April-June 1946): 1–33.

Vargas Torres, Eliel. "Estimaciones del ingreso nacional de México." *Primera Reunión de Técnicos sobre el Banco Central.* Mexico, D.F.: Banco de México, 1946.

―――. "Las estimaciones del ingreso nacional en México." *El Trimestre Económico* 27 (Oct.-Dec. 1960): 564–605.

Villaseñor Angeles, Eduardo. "La estructura bancaria y el desarrollo económico de México." *El Trimestre Económico* 20 (April-June 1953): 199–230.

―――. "Problemas financieros y de comercio interamericano." *El Trimestre Económico* 8 (Oct.-Dec. 1941): 355–97.

Watkins, M. H. "A Staple Theory of Economic Growth." *Canadian Journal of Economics and Political Science* 29 (May, 1963).

Wild(e), Payson S., Jr. "El derecho internacional y el petróleo Mexicano." *El Trimestre Económico* 7 (July-Sept. 1940): 271–90.

Wionczek, Miguel. "Incomplete Formal Planning: Mexico." *Planning Economic Development, A Study.* Ed. Everett E. Hagen. Homewood, Ill.: R. D. Irwin, Inc., 1963.

Wolf, Eric R., and Mintz, Sidney W. "Haciendas and Plantations in Middle America and the Antilles." *Social and Economic Studies,* 6 (Sept. 1957): 380–412.

Wythe, George. "Agricultura vs. industria: tres libros recientes sobre

México." *El Trimestre Económico* 18 (Jan.-Mar. 1951): 142–52.

Zamora, Adolfo. "Inversión de disponibilidades en instituciones de seguros sociales." *El Trimestre Económico* 3, no. 11 (1936): 286–316.

———. 'Situación y estructura del Banco Nacional Hipotecario Urbano y de Obras Públicas." *El Trimestre Económico* 13 (July-Sept. 1946): 271–305.

Zavala, Silvio. "Orígenes coloniales del peonaje en México." *El Trimestre Económico* 10 (Jan.-Mar. 1944): 711–48.

Zimmerman, Robert W. "Doing Business in Mexico." *Harvard Business Review* 20, no. 4 (1942): 508–16.

Zubryn, Emil. "Problems and Prospects in Mexico." *Contemporary Review* 190 (Nov. 1956): 301–03.

OFFICIAL PUBLICATIONS

Banco de México, S.A. "Cuadro de insumo producto de México, 1960." Mexico, December 1966. Mimeographed. For the 1950 input-output table, see Kuznets et al., *El ingreso y la riqueza.*

———. *Informe Anual,* selected years. Mexico.

———. *Seminario de las Naciones Unidas sobre cuentas nacionales para America Latina,* Rio de Janeiro, June 11–26, 1959. New York: United Nations, 1960. ST/TAO/Ser. C144.

———, Departamento de Estudios Económicos. "Alternativas de estimación de la inversión bruta fija en México, 1939–1962." Prepared by Luis Cossío, May 8, 1965. Mimeographed.

———, Departmento de Estudios Económicos. "Cuentas nacionales y acervos de capital, consolidades y por tipo de actividad económica, 1950–67." June 1969.

———, Departamento de Estudios Económicos. "Distribución del ingreso familiar–México 1963," September 24, 1965. Mimeographed.

———, Departamento de Estudios Económicos. "Estimación de la inversión fiji bruta de México." Prepared by Luis Cossío, June 4, 1963. Mimeographed.

———, Departamento de Estudios Económicos. "Producto bruto interno y séries básicas, 1895–1967." Prepared by Mario Gutierrez Requenes. Jan. 1969.

———, Departamento de Investigaciones Industriales. *El empleo de personal técnico en la indústria de transformación.* Mexico, D.F., 1959.

————, Departamento de Investigaciones Industriales. "Tendencias de crecimiento de la indústria de transformación en México–1950–1958." Mexico: Oficina Editorial, April 1962.

————, Departamento de Investigaciones Industriales, Oficina de Planeación Industrial. "La estructura industrial de México en 1950." Mexico.

————, Estudios sobre sustitución de importaciones. *Investigaciones Industriales.* 3 vols. Mexico, D.F., 1965.

————, Grupo Secretaría de Hacienda, Estudios sobre Proyecciones. "Manual de estadísticas básicas para análisis y proyecciones del desarrollo económico de México" and Annex. July 1964, rev. December 1964. Mimeographed. (Referred to as Grupo in Appendixes D and E.)

————, Oficina de Estudios sobre Proyecciones Agrícolas. "Indice de precios agrícolas al nivel del productor y quantum de la producción agrícola, 1939–1960." Under the direction of Fernando Rosenzweig. Mexico, May 1964. Mimeographed.

————, Oficina de Estudios sobre Proyecciones Agrícolas. "Indices de los rendimientos agrícolas y de las superficies cosechadas, 1925–1962." Prepared by Fernando Rosenzweig and staff. Mexico, August 1964. Mimeographed.

————, Office for the Study of Agricultural Projections. "Projections of Supply of and Demand for Agricultural and Livestock Products in Mexico to 1970 and 1975." Under the direction of Fernando Rosenzweig. Mexico, September 1965. Mimeographed.

————, Secretaría de Agricultura y Ganaderia, Secretaría de Hacienda y Crédito Público. *Projections of Supply of and Demand for Agricultural Products in Mexico to 1965, 1970, and 1975.* (See United States, Department of Agriculture, Economic Research Service.)

Banco Nacional de Comercio Exterior, S.A. *Comercio exterior de México 1940–1948.* Mexico: Editorial Cultural 1949.

Bibliografía sobre salarios y costos de la vida. Mexico, 1937.

Cámara Nacional de la Industria de Transformación, Comisión de Planeación Económica. *Los factores demográficos en la planeación económica.* Investigador, Daniel Moreno. Mexico: Ediciones de la Cámara Nacional de la Industria de Transformación, 1958. (See Daniel Moreno.)

El Colegio de México. *Estadísticas económicas del Porfiriato; comercio exterior de México, 1877–1911.* Mexico: El Colegio de México, 1960.

——. *Estadísticas económicas del Porfiriato: fuerza de trabajo y actividad económica por sectores.* Mexico: Seminario de Historia Moderna de México, 1965.

Colombia, Contraloría General de la República de Colombia. *Anuario general de estadística,* 1933 and 1943.

Comisión de Papaloapan. *Economía del Papaloapan.* Vol. I, "Evaluación de las inversiones y sus efectos." Mexico: Secretaría de Recursos Hidráulicos, 1958.

Comité de los Nueve, Alianza para el Progreso. *Evaluación del Plan de Acción Inmediata de México.* Mexico, August 1964.

Cuba Económica y Financiera. *Anuario azucarero de Cuba. Censo de la industria azucarera de Cuba y manual estadístico internacional.* Compiled and edited by Cuba Económica y Financiera. Habana: Editora Mercantil Cubana, S.A., 1938.

Dirección General de Economía Agrícola, Departamento de Programa Agrícola, Ganadero y Forestal. "Consumos aparentes 1925–1962." Mexico, 1963. Mimeographed.

Dirección General de Estadítica (Secretaría de Indústria y Comercio). *Anuario estadístico del comercio exterior de los Estados Unidos Mexicanos 1966.* Mexico, 1966; and selected years.

—— (Secretaría de Indústria y Comercio). *Annuario estadístico de los Estados Unidos Mexicanos,* selected years. Published yearly or in alternate years with *Compendio estadístico.*

——. *Anuarios estadísticos de la Republica Mexicana,* for years 1900–07. Under the direction of Antonio Peñafiel. Mexico.

—— (Secretaría de Industria y Comercio). "Catálogo general de las estadísticas nacionales." Mexico: Estados Unidos Mexicanos, Secretaría de Industria y Comercio, 1960.

——, Comisión Nacional de Salarios Minimos. Work sheets assembled by Jose S. Alarcón from data of the Comisión. Mexico.

—— (Secretaría de la Economía Nacional). *Compendio Estadístico.* Mexico, D.F.: Secretaría de la Economía Nacional, selected years.

—— (*Secretaría de Industria y Comercio*). *Censos agropecuarios.* Mexico: Talleres Gráficos de la Nación, 1959.

————. *Primer censo agrícola ganadero 1930. Resumen general.* Mexico, 1930.

————. *Segundo censo agrícola ganadero 1940. Resumen general.* Mexico, 1951.

———— (Secretaría de Economía). *Tercer censo agrícola ganadero y ejidal 1950. Resumen general.* Mexico, 1956.

————. *Cuarto censos agrícola-ganadero y ejidal, 1960. Resumen general.* Mexico, 1965.

————. *Segundo censo comercial de los Estados Unidos Mexicanos, 1945. Resumen general.* Mexico, 1950.

————. *Tercer censo comercial de servicios, 1956. Información censal 1955. Resumen general.* Mexico, 1961.

————. *Primer censo industrial de 1930. Resúmenes generales por entidades.* 2 vols. Mexico, D.F., 1933.

————. *Censo industrial 1950.* Mexico.

————. *Censo industrial 1956 (información censal 1955). Resumen general.* Mexico: Talleres Gráficos de la Nación, 1959.

———— (Secretaría de Industria y Comercio). *VII censo industrial 1961. Resumen general (Datos de 1960).* Mexico, D.F., 1965.

————. *Quinto censo de población, 15 de Mayo 1930. Resumen general.* Mexico: Talleres Gráficos de la Nación, 1934.

————. *Sexto censo general de población de México. March 1940.* Mexico, 1942.

————. *Sexto censo general de población, 1940. Resumen general.* Mexico, 1943.

————. *Septimo censo general de población 6 de Junio de 1950. Parte especial.* Mexico, 1955.

————. *Septimo censo general de población 6 de Junio de 1950. Resumen general.* Mexico, 1953.

———— (Secretaría de Industria y Comercio), *VIII censo general de población, 1960. Resumen general, 8 de Junio de 1960.* Mexico, D.F.: Estados Unidos Mexicanos, 1962.

———— (Secretaría de Economía). *Estadísticas sociales del Porfiriato, 1877–1910.* Mexico: Talleres Gráficos de la Nación, 1956.

———— (Secretaría de la Economía Nacional). *México en cifras, 1938.* Mexico, D.F., 1939.

————. *El progreso de México: estudio económico estadístico.* Mexico: Impresa del Diario Oficial, 1924.

Ferrocarriles Nacionales de México, Oficina de Estudios Económicos.

"Un estudio del costo de la vida en México." Directed by Jesús Silva Herzog. Mexico, 1931. Mimeographed.

Instituto Mexicano de Recursos Naturales Renovables. *Mesas redondas sobre problemas de las zonas áridas de México.* Mexico: I.M.R.N.R., 1955.

————. *Mesas redondas sobre problemas del trópico Mexicano.* Mexico, 1955.

Mexico, Government of. *El desarrollo industrial de México.* Document prepared for Simposio Latinoamericano de Industrializacion, Santiago de Chile, March 14–25, 1966. United Nations, February 9, 1966. ST/ECLA/Conf.23/L.38. (See United Nations, Economic Commission for Latin America.)

Ministerio de Industria, Comercio y Trabajo. *La industria, comercio, y el trabajo en México durante la gestion administrativa del Sr. Calles, Secretaría, de Industria, Comercio y Trabajo, 1925–27.* Mexico, 1928.

Nacional Financiera. *Anuarios,* selected years.

Partido Revolucionario Institucional. *Segundo plan sexenal, 1941–1946.* Mexico: Edición de el Nacional, 1939. Also in English: *The Second Six Year Plan, 1941–1946.* Mexico, 1939.

Presidencia de la República, Secretaría Privada, and Nacional Financiera, S.A., Subgerencia de Investigaciones Económicas. *50 años de revolución Mexicana en cifras.* Mexico, D.F., March 1963.

Secretaría de Economía Nacional, Dirección de Estudios Económicos. *Desarrollo de la economía nacional 1939–1947.* Mexico: Talleres Gráficos de la Nación, 1947.

Secretaría de la Economía Nacional, Oficina de Barómetros Económicos. "El desarrollo de la economía nacional bajo la influencia de la guerra, 1939–1944." Mexico, 1944.

Secretaría de Hacienda y Crédito Público, Dirección de Estudios Hacendarios. *Cuenta de la hacienda pública federal,* selected years. Mexico.

Secretaría de Industria, Comercio y Trabajo. *México: sus recursos naturales, su situación actual.* Mexico: Editorial Cultural, 1922.

Secretaría del Patrimonio Nacional. *Memorias,* selected years. Mexico.

Secretaría de la Presidencia, Dirección de Inversiones Públicas. *México inversión pública federal, 1925–1963.* Mexico: Talleres Gráficos de la Nación, 1964.

Universidad Nacional, Escuela Nacional de Economía. "La interven-

ción del estado en la economía; cursos de invierno de 1955."
Mexico: Instituto de Investigaciones Económicas, 1955.

————, Escuela Nacional de Economía. *Niveles de vida y desarrollo
económico. Investigación Económica.* Mexico, 1953.

United Nations. *Demographic Yearbook.* 1948–   . Prepared by the
Statistical Office of the United Nations in collaboration with the
Department of Social Affairs.

————, Economic Commission for Latin America. *El desarrollo industrial de México.* Document prepared for Simposio Latinoamericano de Industrialización, Organizado conjuntamente por
la Comisión Económica para América Latina y el Centro de
Desarrollo Industrial de las Naciones Unidas, Santiago de Chile,
March 14–25, 1966. United Nations, February 9, 1966. ST/
ECLA/Conf.23/L.38. (See Mexico, Government of.)

————, Economic Commission for Latin America. *Economic Sur-
vey of Latin America 1949.* Prepared by the Secretariat of
ECLA. New York: United Nations, Department of Economic
Affairs, 1951. [UN] Doc. E/CN.12.

————, Economic Commission for Latin America. *Economic Survey of Latin America (Estudio económico de América Latina),*
selected years since 1949. New York: United Nations. Published in English and Spanish.

————, Economic Commission for Latin America. *External Dis-
equilibrium in the Economic Development of Latin America:
The Case of Mexico.* 2 vols., April 1, 1957. Presented to the
Seventh Session of the Economic Commission for Latin Amer-
ica, La Paz, Bolivia, May 15, 1957. [UN] Doc. E/CN. 12/428.
This document is obtainable in mimeograph form from the UN
Documents Division, New York.

————, Economic Commission for Latin America. *A Measurement
of Price Levels and the Purchasing Power of Currencies in Latin
America, 1960–1962.* New York, 1963. [UN] Doc. E/CN.
12/653.

————, Economic Commission for Latin America. "Planning in
Latin America." New York: United Nations, March 2, 1967.
E/CN.12/772. Mimeographed.

————, Economic Commission for Latin America. *Process of Industrialization in Latin America,* Statistical Annex. New York:
United Nations, January 19, 1966. [UN] ST/ECLA/Conf.
23/L.2E/CN.12/716/Add.2.

————, Economic Commission for Latin America. *Los recursos humanos de Centroamérica, Panamá y México en 1950–1980 y sus relaciones con algunos aspectos del desarrollo económico.* Prepared by Louis J. Ducoff. Mexico: United Nations, 1960. Also in English: New York: United Nations, 1960. [UN] Doc. ST/TAO/K/LAT/1,E/CN.12/548.

————, Statistical Office. *Compendium of Social Statistics: 1967.* Statistical Papers, Series K, No. 3. New York: United Nations, 1968.

————, Statistical Office. *Monthly Bulletin of Statistics,* various numbers. New York: United Nations.

————, Statistical Office, Department of Economic and Social Affairs. *Statistical Yearbook 1952.* New York: United Nations, 1952.

————, Statistical Office, Department of Economic and Social Affairs. *Statistical Yearbook 1961.* 13th edition. New York: United Nations, 1961.

————, Statistical Office, Department of Economic and Social Affairs. *Statistical Yearbook 1963.* New York: United Nations, 1964.

————, Statistical Office, Department of Economic and Social Affairs. *Statistical Yearbook 1967.* New York: United Nations, 1968.

United States, Department of Agriculture, Economic Research Service. *Projections of Supply of and Demand for Agricultural Products in Mexico to 1965, 1970, and 1975.* In collaboration with Secretaría de Agricultura y Ganadería, Secretaría de Hacienda y Crédito Público, and Banco de México, S.A. Directed by Emilio Alanís Patiño and Víctor L. Urquidi. Jerusalem: S. Monsoon, August 1966. (See Banco de México, S.A., Secretaría de Agricultura y Ganadería, Secretaría de Hacienda y Crédito Público.)

————, Department of Commerce, Bureau of the Census. *Long Term Economic Growth 1860–1965.* Washington: U.S. Government Printing Office, October 1966.

————, Department of Commerce, Business Economics Office. *U.S. Business Investments in Foreign Countries.* Supplement to *Survey of Current Business.* By Samuel Pizer and Frederick Cutler. Washington D.C.: U.S. Government Printing Office, 1960.

————, Tariff Commission. *Economic Controls and Commercial*

Policy in Mexico. Washington, D.C.: U.S. Government Printing Office, 1946.

UNPUBLISHED

Aspra Rodríguez, Luis Antonio. "La transmisión de las fluctuaciones cíclicas a la economía Mexicana." Thesis for Licenciatura en Economía, Escuela Nacional de Economía, Universidad Nacional Autónoma de México. Mexico, D.F., 1964.

Barkin, David P. "Economic Development in the Tepalcatepec River Basin: A Quantitative and Qualitative Evaluation of a Public Investment Program." Ph.D. dissertation, Yale University, 1967.

Blakeley, Sibyl Dickinson. "American Investment in Mexican Railroads, Mines and Petroleum." M.A. thesis, University of California, 1920.

Bonilla Garcia, Jesus Javier. "La información censal y su aplicación al análisis de los cambios estructurales de la indústria en México." Thesis for Licenciatura in Economics, Instituto Tecnológico de México. Mexico, D.F., 1962.

Brunstein, Frances Fay. "Petroleum Politics in Mexico, 1910–1938." M.A. thesis, University of California, 1939.

Bueno, Gerardo, "La estructura de la protección effectiva en México en 1960." Typescript, 1968.

Campos Andapia, Antonio. "Teoría de la intermediación financiera y las sociedades financieras privadas Mexicanas." Thesis for Licenciatura in Economics, Escuela Nacional de Economía, Universidad Nacional Autónoma de México. Mexico, D.F., 1962.

Carnoy, Martin. "The Cost and Return to Schooling in Mexico: A Case Study." Ph.D. dissertation, Department of Economics, University of Chicago, 1964.

Caves, Richard E. "The Export-led Growth Model as a Research Tool in Economic History." (Draft), pp. 59.

Chenery, Hollis B., and Taylor, Lance. "Development Patterns: Among Countries and Over Time." Economic Development Report No. 102, Project for Quantitative Research in Economic Development, Harvard University, June 1968.

Cline, William R. "Economically Optimal Land Reform for Brazil." Ph.D. dissertation, Yale University, 1968.

Díaz-Alejandro, Carlos F. "Essays on the Economic History of the

Argentine Republic." Monograph for the Country Analysis Project, Economic Growth Center, Yale University, 1967. Mimeographed.

Flores de la Peña, H. "Los obstáculos al desarrollo económico (el desequilibrio fundamental)." Dissertation, Escuela Nacional de Economía, Universidad Nacional Autónoma de México. Mexico, D.F., 1955.

Flores Márquez, Miguel. "La distribución del ingreso en México." Thesis for Licenciatura in Economics, Escuela Nacional de Economía, Universidad Nacional Autónoma de México. Mexico, D.F., 1958.

Hymer, Stephen, and Resnick, Stephen. "The Supply Response of Agrarian Economics and the Importance of Z Goods." Center Discussion Paper No. 25, Economic Growth Center, Yale University, April 29, 1967 (rev. October 1, 1967). Mimeographed.

Kaldor, Nicholas. "Report on Mexican Tax Reform." September 28, 1960. Typescript.

King, Richard T. "Rationale and Limitations of the Mexican Import Substitution Policies." OECD Development Centre, Paris, 1967. Draft.

————. "River Basin Projects and Regional Development." Department of Agricultural Economics, Cornell University, 1964. Mimeographed.

Koehler, John E. "Information and Policy Making: Mexico." Ph.D. dissertation, Yale University, 1968.

Loyo, Gilberto. "La revolución Mexicana no ha terminado su tarea." Conferencia dada en la Escuela Nacional de Economía, July 10, 1959. Mexico, 1960.

Maneschi, A., and Reynolds, C. W. "The Effect of Import Substitution on Foreign Exchange Needs, Savings Rates and Growth in Latin America." Center Discussion Paper No. 18, Economic Growth Center, Yale University, December 20, 1966. Mimeographed.

Miller, Robert R. "Mexico Under Avila Camacho: Major Aspects of the 1940–1946 Administration." M.A. thesis, University of California, 1951.

Mirin, Linda Sue. "Public Investment in Aguascalientes." Ph.D. dissertation, Departments of Economics and Government, Harvard University, 1964.

Mueller, Marnie W. "Structural Inflation and the Mexican Experience." Ph.D. dissertation, Yale University, 1964.

Muro González, Bosco A. "Estructura y evolución del gasto público en México." El Colegio de México, December 20, 1964. Typescript.

———. "Una función de producción para la indústria manufacturera Mexicana 1963," 1966. Manuscript.

Myers, Herman L. "The Country's Development" U.S. Embassy, Mexico D.F. (undated). Mimeographed.

———. "Current Country Situation." September 1959. Mimeographed.

———. "The I.C.A. Program—A Brief Description." August 1960. Mimeographed.

———. "The Inter-American Program for Social Progress and Related Changes in FY 62 Programming." June 1961. Mimeographed.

———. "Mexico: Current Country Situation." September 1960. Mimeographed.

Navarrete, Alfredo, Jr. "Exchange Stability, Business Cycles, and Economic Development: An Inquiry into Mexico's Balance of Payments Problems, 1929–1946." Ph.D. dissertation, Harvard University, 1949.

Norstrom, Kathryn M. "Corporate Financing in a Developing Economy: The Case of Mexico." Ph.D. dissertation in progress, Yale University.

Oomens, C. A. "Cuentas nacionales y las estadísticas económicas en México." Mexico, D. F., 1955 (preliminary draft).

Randall, Laura R. "The Process of Economic Development in Mexico from 1940 to 1959." Ph.D. dissertation, Columbia University, 1962.

Reynolds, Clark W. "La capacidad para financiar la formación de capital en Sonora." Paper presented to the Mesa Redonda sobre Desarrollo Económico de Sonora, September 11, 1964. Mimeographed.

———. "Changing Trade Patterns and Trade Policy in Mexico: Some Lessons for Developing Countries." Discussion Paper No. 67–4, Food Research Institute, Stanford University, October 1967. Mimeographed.

———. "Notes on an Agricultural Productivity Model to Explain the Rise and Fall of a Pre-Conquest Civilization." October 26, 1964. Mimeographed.

Rios Medrano, Jorge. "La carestía de la vida y el problema agrario de México." Professional Examination Thesis, Universidad Nacional Autónoma de México, 1952.

Roach, Bessie Mary. "The History of Mexican Land with Special Consideration of the Modern Agrarian Situation." M.A. thesis, University of California, 1923.

Romero Campa, Marlena Irma. "La saturación industrial." Thesis, Escuela Nacional de Economía, Universidad Nacional Autónoma de México, 1960.

Salinas Lozano, Raúl. "La intervención del estado y la cuestión de los precios." Thesis for Licenciatura in Economics, Mexico, 1944.

Sanders, William T. "The Cultural Ecology of the Teotihuacán Valley; A Preliminary Report of the Results of the Teotihuacán Valley Project." Department of Sociology and Anthropology, The Pennsylvania State University, September 1965. Mimeographed.

Schneider, Norman. "Mixed Oligopoly: A Study in the Control of Industry in a Developing Economy." Ph.D. dissertation, Department of Economics, University of California, 1966.

Sentíes G., Octavio. "Federalismo constitucional y centralismo económico." Thesis, Facultad de Derecho y Ciencias Sociales, Universidad Nacional Autónoma de México, 1942.

Simpson, John W. "The International Economic Position of Mexico, 1900 to 1949." Ph.D. dissertation, Ohio State University, 1949.

Solís M., Leopoldo. "Apuntes para el análisis de desarrollo Económico de México." El Colegio de México, Centro de Estudios Económicos y Demográficos, Seminario de Investigación Económica, 1967.

⸺. "Producto bruto interno, millones de pesos de 1950." February 1969. Working draft.

⸺. "A Projection of the Development of the Mexican Economy in the Coming Decade." Paper presented to the conference on "The Next Decade of Latin American Development," Cornell University, April 19–22, 1966. Mimeographed.

⸺. "Recent Changes in the Structure and Behavior of the Mexican Economy." Banco de México, Department of Economic Studies, 1967. Mimeographed.

Sosa Sanchez, Alejandro. "La intervención del estado como factor de desarrollo económico." Thesis, Universidad Nacional Autónoma de México, 1963.

Van Bruggen, Elaine Tanner. "United States Investment in Mexico: A Study of Recent Developments in Mexican-American Economic Relations." M.A. thesis, University of California, 1951.

Velasco, Alfonso Luis. "Geografía y estadística de la República Mexicana." Oficina de Secretaría de Fomento, Mexico, 1889–92.

Index

Accounts, national economic, 329–83
Administrative costs. *See* Government administration costs
Agrarian reform, xxi–xxii, 9, 31–32, 35, 53, 56, 89–134, 136–38, 140–43, 145*n*, 146, 149–54, 160, 298; anarchic phase, 138–40; announcement phase, 35, 138*n*, 140*n*; centralized institutional phase, 138–41, 146; decentralized institutional phase, 138–44; re income distribution, 74; re industrialization, 162, 196, 303; re opportunity cost, 325; re social welfare, 300; re total economy, 3, 54, 61; re trade, 198, 252; re urbanization, 136, 183, 304. *See also* Investments, in agriculture; Land, tenure reform
Agriculture: commercial, *see* Agriculture, subsistence/commercial; data, 4–5, 8, 330; employment, *see* Agriculture, labor in; exports, 177, 179, 203; exports, data, 374–76; exports, decline, 153–54, 212, 302; exports, diversification, 281; exports, retail margins, 148*n*; exports, vs. internal market, 92–93, 96–97, 142–43; exports, in the Porfiriato, 20*n*, 136–37; exports, in the reform period, 28, 199–201, 205; exports, in the development period, 107, 134, 142–43, 205, 252; exports, opportunity cost, 316; exports, regionalism in, 113; re food imports, 91–92; foreign investment in, 19, 29, 143; fruit farming, 306; re GDP, 59–61, 104, 132, 339–43, 368–73; government policy re, 30, 194, 199, 205, 208, 210*n*, 255–56; re income distribution, 78–80, 84, 312, 338; re intermediate imports, 226–27, 229–30; labor in, 23–25, 33, 106, 111, 136, 115–27, 140, 143, 154, 299, 306; labor, data, 18, 62–71, 92–93, 116, 386; labor, rural/urban shift, 33, 37, 65–70, 132, 143, 148–52, 160, 180, 190; machinery in, *see* Technology, in agriculture; re manufacturing, *see* Manufacturing, re agriculture; Ministry of, 117, 328, 343; output, *see* Agriculture, product; pre-Colombian, 1, 300; price supports, 83; product, estimates, 335; product, growth, xxi–xxii, 13, 178, 272; product, in Porfiriato, 21–24; product, in the reform period, 32–34; product, in the development period, 38, 40, 42, 45; product, re land use, 140; product, per capita, 38, 92–118, 316; product, per worker, 93, 98–100, 110–15, 119, 136, 143, 145, 148; product, rural/urban share, 72–73, 75, 98–114, 118–33, 393; product, re total economy, 104–06, 142–43, 153–54, 198–99, 213; public policy, *see* Agriculture, government policy re; public works, *see* Agriculture, foreign investment in; reform, *see* Agrarian reform; regionalism, 6, 94–96, 98–114, 120–32, 134, 135*n*, 142, 145–48, 151; returns, *see* Agriculture, product; Secretary of, 117, 328; statistics, *see* Agriculture, data; subsistence/commercial, xxi, 6, 78, 92, 162, 306–7; subsistence/commercial re agrarian reform, 97–101, 106–07, 131–32, 135–36, 143–44, 146, 160, 183; subsistence/commercial in the development period, 42, 300; subsistence, re

453

ECONOMIC GROWTH CENTER BOOK PUBLICATIONS

*Werner Baer, *Industrialization and Economic Development in Brazil* (1965).

Werner Baer and Isaac Kerstenetzky, eds., *Inflation and Growth in Latin America* (1964).

*Bela A. Balassa, *Trade Prospects for Developing Countries* (1964).

Carlos F. Díaz Alejandro, *Essays on the Economic History of the Argentine Republic* (1970).

*John C. H. Fei and Gustav Ranis, *Development of Labor Surplus Economy: Theory and Policy* (1964).

*Gerald K. Helleiner, *Peasant Agriculture, Government, and Economic Growth in Nigeria* (1966)

*Lawrence R. Klein and Kazushi Ohkawa, eds., *Economic Growth: The Japanese Experience Since the Meiji Era* (1968).

*A. Lamfalussy, *The United Kingdom and the Six* (1963).

*Markos J. Mamalakis and Clark W. Reynolds, *Essays on the Chilean Economy* (1965).

*Donald C. Mead, *Growth and Structural Change in the Egyptian Economy* (1967).

*Richard Moorsteen and Raymond P. Powell, *The Soviet Capital Stock* (1966).

*Frederic L. Pryor, *Public Expenditures in Communist and Capitalist Nations* (1968).

Clark W. Reynolds, *The Mexican Economy: Twentieth-Century Structure and Growth* (1970)

*Lloyd G. Reynolds and Peter Gregory, *Wages, Productivity, and Industrialization in Puerto Rico* (1965).

*Donald R. Snodgrass, *Ceylon: An Export Economy in Transition* (1966).

* Available from Richard D. Irwin, Inc., 1818 Ridge Rd., Homewood, Ill. 60430.